European Communities (Amendment) Act 1993 with the Treaty of Rome (as amended)

AUSTRALIA
The Law Book Company
Brisbane : Sydney : Melbourne : Perth

CANADA
Carswell
Ottawa : Toronto : Calgary : Montreal : Vancouver

Agents:
Steimatzky's Agency Ltd., Tel Aviv;
N. M. Tripathi (Private) Ltd., Bombay;
Eastern Law House (Private) Ltd., Calcutta;
M.P.P. House, Bangalore;
Universal Book Traders, Delhi;
Aditya Books, Delhi;
MacMillan Shuppan KK, Tokyo;
Pakistan Law House, Karachi

European Communities (Amendment) Act 1993 with the Treaty of Rome (as amended)

with annotations by

Paul Beaumont

Senior Lecturer and Head of Department of Public Law, University of Aberdeen

and

Gordon Moir

Research Assistant and Tutor, Department of Public Law, University of Aberdeen

LONDON
SWEET & MAXWELL
1994

Published in 1994 by
Sweet & Maxwell Limited of
South Quay Plaza,
183 Marsh Wall, London
Typeset by MFK Typesetting Ltd.,
Hitchin, Herts
Printed and bound in Great Britain by
Butler & Tanner Ltd., Frome and London

A CIP catalogue record for this book is available
from The British Library

ISBN 0 421 51100 1

CONTENTS

European Communities (Amendment) Act 1993 with the Treaty of Rome (as amended)

References are to page numbers

PREFACE

This book is a comprehensive guide to the provisions of the European Communities (Amendment) Act 1993 and to the amendments made to the European Community Treaty (formerly European Economic Community Treaty) by the Treaty on European Union. The latter Treaty was agreed at Maastricht in December 1991 by the Heads of Government of the 12 Member States of the European Communities. It came into force on November 1, 1993.

The amendments to the EC Treaty provide for economic and monetary union; citizenship of the European Union; increased powers of the European Parliament; subsidiarity; revamped provisions on free movement of capital; new Community competences in relation to education, culture, public health, consumer protection, trans-European networks, industry, and development cooperation; enhanced Community policies in the areas of economic and social cohesion and environmental policy; and powers for the European Court of Justice to fine States which persistently fail to fulfil their Community law obligations. In addition a large number of relatively small changes are made. All amendments, large and small, are noted and, where appropriate, analysed in this book.

Although the book does not attempt to annotate the provisions of the Treaty on European Union relating to the intergovernmental pillars of the Common Foreign and Security Policy (CFSP) and Justice and Home Affairs Cooperation (JHA), these pillars are discussed in general terms in the Introduction and General Note.

It has been possible to incorporate analysis of *R.* v. *Secretary of State for Foreign and Commonwealth Affairs*, ex p. *Lord Rees Mogg* [1993] 3 C.M.L.R. 101 into the book and to take account of the implications for the prospect of economic and monetary union of the collapse of the narrow 2.25 per cent. bands in the ERM during the Summer of 1993.

Gordon Moir worked long hours from July to October 1993 as a research assistant on this project. Paul Beaumont spent part of that time in the United States and many faxes passed between Aberdeen and Baltimore. The authors bear equal responsibility for the final text. We wish to thank the University of Aberdeen for funding Gordon's work as a research assistant and providing the necessary information technology, secretarial, and library facilities.

Paul Beaumont
Gordon Moir
Aberdeen
October 18, 1993

TABLE OF CASES

Table of Cases

TABLE OF INTERNATIONAL LEGISLATION

TABLE OF EUROPEAN LEGISLATION

TABLE OF NATIONAL LEGISLATION

EUROPEAN COMMUNITIES (AMENDMENT) ACT 1993*

(1993 c. 32)

An Act to make provision consequential on the Treaty on European Union
signed at Maastricht on 7th February 1992.   [20th July 1993]

PARLIAMENTARY DEBATES

Hansard, H.C. Vol. 208, cols. 261, 509; Vol. 213, cols. 283, 410; Vol. 215, cols. 147, 289; Vol. 216, cols. 928, 1087, 1096; Vol. 217, cols. 35, 149, 270, 382, 1044, 1163, 1261, 1372; Vol. 218, cols. 22, 499; Vol. 219, cols. 683, 1023, 1107; Vol. 220, cols. 402, 665, 1127; Vol. 221, cols. 927, 1029, 1269; Vol. 222, cols. 160, 267, 961; Vol. 223, cols. 39, 121, 382, 451, 529; Vol. 224, cols. 25, 123, 195; Vol. 225, col. 381; Vol. 229, cols. 521, 627 (Social Protocol); H.L. Vol. 546, cols. 544, 655, 710, 843; Vol. 547, cols. 234, 300, 347, 428, 526, 533, 591, 678, 717, 793, 808, 872; Vol. 548, cols. 12, 35, 74, 126, 203, 239, 797 (Social Protocol).

INTRODUCTION AND GENERAL NOTE

The purpose of this Act is to amend the European Communities Act 1972, to take account of the agreement reached among the 12 Member States of the European Community at Maastricht on December 9 and 10, 1991.

After finalising the text and translating it into the official languages of the Community, the Member States signed this agreement on February 7, 1992 in Maastricht. It then took its official title of the Treaty on European Union (TEU). The TEU amends the European Economic Community (E.E.C.) Treaty, or Treaty of Rome, of 1957 and renames it the European Community (E.C.) Treaty. This is the second major amendment to the Treaty of Rome, the first having taken place when the Single European Act (SEA) came into force in 1987. The TEU amends the other two constituent Treaties of the European Communities: those governing the European Coal and Steel Community (ECSC) and the European Atomic Energy Community (Euratom). These sectoral Communities are of much less significance than the broad ranging E.C. The TEU preserves in a modified form the three founding Treaties of the European Communities. In addition the TEU contains a number of free-standing provisions at the beginning and end of the Treaty (Arts. A–F and J–S). These establish two spheres of inter-governmental co-operation, a common foreign and security policy and co-operation in the fields of justice and home affairs. The European Union is often referred to as a temple made up of five pillars; the three existing Communities as amended and the two spheres of inter-governmental co-operation. From a practising lawyer's perspective the E.C. pillar is much more important than any of the other four pillars.

The Treaty on European Union only entered into force on November 1, 1993 after it had been ratified in all 12 Member States, in accordance with their respective constitutional requirements (Art. R(1) TEU). The target date set for the successful completion of the national ratification processes was January 1, 1993 (Art. R(2) TEU), to coincide with the completion of the Internal Market (Art. 8a E.E.C., as inserted by the Single European Act (SEA), Cmnd. 455).

However, numerous domestic difficulties meant that the target date was not met. The German Constitutional Court only made a determinative ruling on the challenges raised to ratification in that country on October 12, 1993 and thus Germany was the last of the signatory states to complete the ratification process, despite overwhelming parliamentary support for the Treaty. In Denmark, the second Maastricht referendum on May 18, 1993 returned a positive verdict, overturning the narrow "No" vote of June 1992 (the result in the second referendum: 56.8 per cent. for, 43.2 per cent. against: on the first referendum and its implications see (1992) 29 C.M.L.Rev., 855–859). Part of the reason for the success of the second referendum was the adoption of the Decision Concerning Denmark at the Edinburgh Summit of Heads of State and Government (the European Council) in December 1992. The Danish Government's aim, prior to this meeting, was that any solution to their problems be legally binding, without necessitating any further Treaty amendment, which led to the adoption of a somewhat ingenious solution. For the first time, the European Council announced the adoption of a legally binding decision. While the legal status of this decision is a matter of some debate, it does not attempt to alter the TEU in any way; it simply clarifies its meaning in four key areas: citizenship; economic and monetary union; defence policy; and justice and home affairs. This decision would, nevertheless, appear to have been sufficient to persuade the Danish voters (see Weatherill and Beaumont, *EC Law*, (1993), Penguin, pp. 774–779).

---

* Annotations by Paul Beaumont, Senior Lecturer and Head of Department of Public Law, University of Aberdeen and Gordon Moir, Research Assistant and Tutor in the Department of Public Law, University of Aberdeen.

Meanwhile in Britain, the Bill's tortuous path through the upper and lower houses ended with Royal Assent on July 20, 1993. However, the Act itself required both Houses to adopt a resolution on the Social Protocol, which contains the U.K.'s opt-out from the agreement of the other 11 Member States on modest further steps in the construction of a Community social policy (see s.7 of the 1993 Act). On July 22, 1993 the House of Lords approved such a resolution but the House of Commons failed to do so. The Prime Minister made the adoption of a resolution a confidence issue and on the next day, July 23, obtained a comfortable majority for the Government's policy (*Hansard*, H.C. Vol. 229, col. 725). The coming into force of the Act had no effect on the subsequent U.K. ratification of the TEU itself; the purpose of the Act is simply the amendment of the European Communities Act 1972 to give effect to the changes to domestic U.K. law made by the relevant provisions of the TEU. Nevertheless, the actual ratification process was held up by the action for judicial review initiated by Lord Rees-Mogg (*R.* v. *Secretary of State for Foreign and Commonwealth Affairs*, ex p. *Rees-Mogg* [1993] 3 C.M.L.R. 101, D.C.). This case will be dealt with in the General Note on the 1993 Act itself. After Lord Rees-Mogg decided not to appeal the case, the U.K. ratified the TEU on August 2, 1993.

The Treaty on European Union (TEU)

The TEU marks a further stage in the founding of the E.E.C. Treaty's (the Treaty of Rome's) expressed desire to see an "ever closer union among the peoples of Europe". The Treaty establishes an entirely new creature known as the European Union. This novel entity is to be founded on the European Communities, supplemented by the policies and forms of co-operation established by the new Treaty (Art. A TEU). The bulk of the Treaty, however, consists of amendments to the founding Treaties of the European Communities. The amendments to the Treaty of Rome, which established the European Economic Community (as amended by the SEA, Cmnd. 455), are of the greatest practical significance and will be individually annotated. The amendments to the 1951 Treaty of Paris establishing the European Coal and Steel Community (ECSC) (see Art. H TEU) and the 1957 Treaty establishing the European Atomic Energy Community (Euratom) (Art. I TEU), essentially parallel the main amendments to the Treaty of Rome and generally reflect the institutional and procedural changes made therein. For this reason, and due to their relative lack of practical importance, they are not dealt with by these annotations.

Background

The decision to convene an inter-governmental conference under Art. 236 of the E.E.C. Treaty which set in motion the Treaty amendment process, was initially taken at the Madrid European Council in June 1989. The European Council is a separate entity from the Council. The latter is sometimes referred to as the Council of Ministers and has enjoyed institutional status in the European Communities since their inception. It is the Council which is the principal lawmaking body in the European Communities. It is made up of a government minister from each of the Member States. The European Council, on the other hand, was not envisaged in the original treaties making up the European Communities but its gradual emergence in practice was given legal recognition in the SEA. It is composed of the heads of government of the Member States (the only Head of State present is the French President) and the President of the Commission. They are assisted by the Foreign Ministers of the Member States and one other member of the Commission. The European Council takes many of the major political decisions in the European Union but does not make law (see Art. D TEU). It did, however, adopt what purported to be a legally binding decision at the Edinburgh European Council in December 1992 (see above at the beginning of this Introduction and General Note). For further discussion of the Council and European Council see Weatherill and Beaumont, *EC Law* (1993), Penguin, pp. 59–78. The deliberations of the European Council at Madrid centred around proposals for economic and monetary union and followed the examination of the issue by a committee consisting mainly of central bank governors, chaired by the President of the Commission, Jacques Delors (Report of the Committee for the Study of Economic and Monetary Union in the European Community (Delors Report), Luxembourg, Office for Official Publications of the E.C., (1989)).

The movement towards economic and monetary union can be seen as part of the momentum created by the Single European Market. The Delors committee and others were very quick to point out that a single market ultimately requires a single currency if the full benefits of market integration are to be achieved. The Commission's estimates put the economic benefits from a single currency in the European Community at about 10 per cent. of the Community's real gross national product, half a per cent. of which is from reduced transaction costs and the remainder from greater monetary stability and the elimination of exchange risks (E.C. Commission, Emerson and Huhne (eds.), *The ECU Report*, (1991), Pan). Indeed, the SEA, effective from July 1,

1987, had been in force for less than six months when the Hanover European Council meeting of December 1987 entrusted the Delors committee with the task of investigating and putting forward proposals on economic and monetary union.

The Delors committee's recommendation of a three-stage process towards economic and monetary union was quickly taken on board by the Member States, who authorised the commencement of the first stage of the economic and monetary union process in July 1990. The first stage required no Treaty amendment, simply emphasising the underlying aims of the internal market programme for the achievement of full economic and monetary union, and encouraging the Member States to pursue the objectives laid down under the SEA as well as the pursuit of currency stability within the ambit of the existing Exchange Rate Mechanism (ERM) of the European Monetary System (EMS).

Because the implementation of these proposals required the amendment of the founding treaties, it was necessary to convene an inter-governmental conference to look at the matter. At the Strasbourg European Council of December 1989, it was decided to convene such a conference by the end of 1990 to map out the latter stages of economic and monetary union. The reason for the lengthy period between the decision to convene the inter-governmental conference and its start was, originally, to allow the first stage of economic and monetary union to get off the ground. In fact, this year and a half proved to be a window of opportunity for all parties who felt that the Treaty revision should go beyond economic and monetary union and address a far wider agenda of political reform. It must also be emphasised that the pursuit of economic and monetary convergence is not an apolitical goal; while the economic benefits are undeniable, the resurgence of the drive for economic and monetary union was based on a desire to underline moves towards further European political integration.

In the early months of 1990, concrete proposals for political reform started to come through. The first set came from the European Parliament (the so-called "Martin" reports, named after the head of the institutional affairs committee, David Martin; see [1990] O.J. C96/114, C231/97 and C324/219) and advocated the strengthening of Community competences in the social and environmental fields, the integration of European political co-operation (Art. 30 SEA) into the Community sphere and increased legislative powers for itself, including some form of co-decision with the Council, a limited right of legislative initiative and the extension of the assent procedure to all international agreements entered into by the Community, and also Treaty revisions such as the Maastricht inter-governmental conference. The main impetus, however, for the convening of a parallel conference on political union was the joint Kohl/Mitterand communiqué to the then President in office of the Council, the Irish Prime Minister, Charles Haughey. The desire of Chancellor Kohl and President Mitterand to extend the European agenda was debated seriously at the extraordinary Dublin summit of April 28, 1990, but a decision on a further inter-governmental conference was postponed due to the reluctance of certain Member States to move in the direction suggested.

It was at the Dublin European Council of June 25 and 26, 1990 that the decision to convene an inter-governmental conference on political union was taken. Nevertheless, the debate in Dublin revealed the existence of entirely opposing views among the Member States on virtually all aspects of further political development of the Communities. Such disagreements would mark all stages of the negotiations leading up to the final deliberations at Maastricht.

Prior to the opening of the inter-governmental conferences in Rome in December 1990, the Commission produced its own proposals for political reform (Inter-governmental Conferences: Contributions by the Commission, E.C. Bull. Supp. 2/91). Its contribution to the debate called for, *inter alia*, increased Community competences in such areas as social policy, the free movement of persons, health protection, an increase in the effectiveness of the Community's decision-making procedures through extended qualified majority voting in the Council of Ministers, and the revision of the Treaty to include a new title on a common foreign and security policy.

It was the issue of the common foreign and security policy that dominated the debate at following conference meetings (Laursen and Vanhoonacker (eds.), *The Inter-governmental Conference on Political Union*, Nijhoff, ch.1). States concerned at the lack of a coherent Community foreign policy, especially in the light of the Gulf war and the Yugoslav crisis, were supportive of the Commission's proposals to back up the Community's undoubted economic strength with an effective external Community influence in the political arena. However, the predominance of the debate on proposals for change to such, previously inter-governmental, areas left many other issues unclarified. Indeed, many of the main issues, such as the powers of the European Parliament, extension of qualified majority voting in the Council, and increased Community competences in a number of fields, were left to be hammered out at the two-day Maastricht summit itself. This was evidenced by the U.K.'s eleventh hour opt-out from the TEU's development of the Social Protocol (see Arts. 117–122 E.C. and notes thereon).

Structure of the new Union

Much of the debate prior to the Maastricht summit concerned the extent to which sensitive national competences should be transferred to the Community sphere. This was particularly true with regard to foreign and security policy, defence, and elements of judicial and interior ministry affairs, where the Member States and Community institutions were substantially divided over the extent to which such a transfer should take place. While there was agreement on the need for some degree of co-operation on these matters, the means by which such co-operation would be achieved was a divisive issue. The ceding of national sovereignty in such areas, through their transfer to the Communities or the introduction of majority voting in the Council, proved highly sensitive.

These disagreements were mirrored in the Luxembourg Presidency's draft Treaty drawn up to provide an initial basis for negotiation. The publication of the Luxembourg Presidency's draft Treaty on Political Union on April 12, 1991 confirmed the fact that at least some Member States would not accept major areas of policy-making, *e.g.* foreign and defence issues, being brought within the framework of the E.C. The draft proposed what became known as the temple structure, whereby the three European Communities each constitute a pillar of the new European Union, while separate pillars were created to encompass, firstly, a common foreign and security policy and secondly, co-operation in the fields of justice and home affairs. Although economic and monetary union is often cited as a separate pillar, given the uniqueness of its process, it is encompassed in the body of the E.C. Treaty, so will be dealt with as part of the enlarged E.C. pillar. To complete the temple analogy, sitting atop these five pillars is the inter-governmental European Council; its rôle being to provide the Union with the necessary impetus for development and the definition of the general political guidelines thereof (Art. D TEU).

Much to the surprise of the Member States, one of the first acts of the Dutch Presidency when it took over in the run-up to the Maastricht inter-governmental conference was to revise completely the basis for negotiations at a time when everyone considered the Luxembourg draft determinative (see Agence Europe, September 25, 1991). The Dutch draft was based upon an organic Community with common foreign and security policy and justice and home affairs incorporated into the body of the Community and the introduction of majority voting in the Council of Ministers in all legislative matters. The sovereignty implications of such an overtly federalist plan, christened the "tree" approach (the new competences branching out of the main Community "trunk"), proved too much for all Member States except for the Netherlands and Belgium (Buchan, Why the temple proved stronger than the tree, *Financial Times*, December 7, 1991 and Corbett, The Inter-governmental Conference on Political Union, *Journal of Common Market Studies*, (1992) Vol. XXX, pp. 271–298 at p. 280). Negotiations then continued on the basis of the Luxembourg draft but with a number of amendments to appease the more federalist Member States. These included the provision that the "Union shall be served by a single institutional framework" (Art. C, first indent TEU). This has been described as paying mere lip service to an ideal; the Community institutions are lent to the new pillars, but with duties far removed from their classic Treaty functions. The two pillars of common foreign and security policy and justice and home affairs co-operation are essentially inter-governmental. They give no rôle to the European Court, very little influence to the European Parliament, the Commission has only a shared right of initiative and the Council acts predominantly by unanimity (see Curtin, The Constitutional Structure of the Union: A Europe of Bits and Pieces (1993) 30 C.M.L.Rev. 17–69 at 28 and editorial comments, Post-Maastricht (1992) 29 C.M.L.Rev. 199–203). Other amendments made to the original Luxembourg draft, apart from amendments to the E.C. provisions themselves which will be dealt with later, were the inclusion of the reference to the development of the *acquis communautaire* (the corpus of existing Community law) as one of the goals of the new Union and an explicit reference to the convening of a new inter-governmental conference in 1996 to revise the Union structure (Art. N TEU). On the other hand, at the U.K.'s insistence, any reference to the word "federal" in the TEU was removed at Maastricht (see below under Amendments to the E.E.C. Treaty).

The pillars of a common foreign and security policy and co-operation in the fields of justice and home affairs

The pillar structure of the Union is not an entirely new development. Foreign policy co-operation between the Member States in the guise of European political co-operation was given Treaty status for the first time by Art. 30 of the SEA but remained outwith the scope of the Community Treaties (on European political co-operation, see: Lodge, *The European Community and the Challenge of the Future*, Pinter, ch.12). Meetings of the foreign ministers to discuss European political co-operation were artificially distinct from Council meetings which involved the same people in their guise within the three Communities. This artificiality has been somewhat reduced by the TEU. The meetings of the foreign ministers will now take place under the normal guise of the Council, and the European political co-operation secretariat has been merged into the larger Council. It remains to be seen whether or not this will mark anything more than a shift towards greater involvement of the Council and its staff in the workings of foreign policy. It is still the same people who are taking the decisions, this much will depend on how strong the political desire is to see the development of a common European foreign policy. The overall retention of the unanimity requirement would tend to suggest that agreements will be limited (see Stein, "Foreign Policy at Maastricht: *Non in commotione Dominus* (1992) 29 C.M.L.Rev. 663–668). On the process of common foreign and security policy, see Title V, Arts. J.1–J.11 TEU.

Inter-governmental co-operation in the amorphous justice and home affairs field has also gone on between the Member States for many years. National authorities have been forced to reassess their policies in such areas over the last decade or so. Just as the drive to secure a single voice in foreign affairs necessitated the development of an embryonic common foreign and security policy, so the creation of the Single Market without internal frontiers necessitated developments in the fields of immigration and asylum policy and judicial co-operation. The E.E.C. Treaty failed to give any clear authority to the Community instruments to deal with such matters and, as a result, co-operation at the inter-governmental level became prevalent (*cf.* opinion of the European Parliament, [1990] O.J. C96/274, a call for Commission to initiate legislation in the fields of immigration and asylum). The bodies currently involved in this area are diverse including, for example, the Trevi group of ministers of the interior, established as early as 1975 to deal with international terrorism, but with a scope today covering virtually all aspects of international crime and policing. Over the years, these bodies have been created as and when a need was perceived. The TEU seeks to put all these bodies under one inter-governmental heading. Once again, the requirement of unanimity for action will prove a stumbling block to effective and rapid decision making (see notes on Art. 100c E.C.). This rationalisation does not fundamentally alter the nature of the process; that of inter-governmental co-operation. The provisions on justice and home affairs are set out in Title VI of the TEU, Arts. K.2–K.9. This envisages certain specified areas which the Member States are to regard as matters of common interest (Art. K.1 TEU). The nine topics for co-operation listed under Art. K.1 are: asylum; rules regarding the crossing of external borders; immigration; drugs; international fraud; judicial co-operation in civil matters and similarly in criminal matters; co-operation between customs services; and, finally, police co-operation. Of these areas, the last three must be distinguished from the others in that they are left exclusively the subject of inter-governmental co-operation; they are excluded from the process of "*passarelle*" (Art. K.9 TEU), described below, and the Commission is precluded from initiating action in these fields.

The pillars of justice and home affairs and common foreign and security policy are not therefore new, but they are strengthened by their inclusion within the TEU. Moreover, they are not as neatly separated from the Communities themselves as would appear to be the case from the classification of a pillar structure; as Curtin puts it: "the popular analogy coined, of the construction of a temple, implies a degree of architectural stability and aesthetic finish which is both inaccurate and pretentious" (Curtin, The Constitutional Structure of the Union: A Europe of Bits and Pieces (1993) 30 C.M.L.Rev. 17–69, at p. 24). Administrative expenditure incurred by these pillars will be charged to the normal European Community budget. Operational expenditure, on the other hand, will only come under the Community budget if Member States vote unanimously for this to take place. Otherwise, it will be charged to the Member States in accordance with a scale to be decided (Arts. J.11.2 and K.8.2 TEU). Any action taken by the Union in the common foreign and security field requiring agreements with third states or international organisations must be carried out under the Community guise of Art. 228 E.C. or by agreement among all 12 Member States; the Union lacking the legal personality to conclude such agreements itself (see Steenbergen, Maastricht: de externe betrekkingen 1992 SEW 741).

Further complicating the unwieldy relationship between the existing Community and Union structures are the "*passarelle*" provisions, providing for the transfer of certain Union competences into the Community arena. Article K.9 allows the Council, acting unanimously, to select any of the six areas of justice and home affairs co-operation listed under Arts. K.1(1)–1(6) TEU for transfer and to have the provisions of Art. 100c E.C. apply to such transferees (co-operation in criminal matters (Arts. K1(7)–1(9) TEU) does not fall under this provision). Any such transfer does not necessitate a Treaty revision but must be adopted by the Member States in accordance with their respective constitutional requirements (see notes on Art. 100c E.C.).

The inclusion of visa policy within the Community sphere during the inter-governmental conference negotiations (Art. 100c E.C.) means that the procedure for dealing with persons from third countries entering the Community is to be a twin track approach. For visa policy, the Council will follow the E.C. Treaty procedure by deciding unanimously, on the basis of a Commission proposal, which third countries require a visa for their nationals to enter the E.C. Qualified majority voting will apply from January 1, 1996. Other matters, such as immigration policy, will be determined at the inter-governmental level. This does not deal with the need, often expressed by many of the mainland European states dealing with the influx of refugees from Eastern Europe and further afield, for an integrated Community immigration policy dealing with both visas and asylum (for an excellent summary of the current position see Tomuschat, A Right to Asylum in Europe, (1992), 13 *Human Rights Law Review*, 257–265).

Finally, the Union provisions rely greatly on the Community institutions for their effective implementation; the only truly Union entities being the European Council and the bodies of national civil servants set up to oversee the operation of the new pillars. While these new pillars borrow the Community institutions for certain purposes they make only minimal use of them. The inter-governmental institutions of the Council and the European Council are given the key powers. The European Parliament is to be kept regularly informed of the main aspects of the co-operation in these fields, but this does not require prior consultation nor is failure to consult enforceable before the European Court (Art. L TEU; *cf.* Case 139/79, *Roquette Freres S.A.* v. *E.C. Council* [1980] E.C.R. 3393). The Commission is to be "fully involved" in the work carried out in these fields but will find itself in direct competition with the bodies of national civil servants created under these provisions; the co-ordinating committee under Art. K.4 (justice and home affairs) and the analogous committee of political directors under Art. J.8(5) (common foreign and security policy). It will also be forced to surrender its monopoly of policy initiative; the Member States and co-ordinating committees of national civil servants are both empowered to initiate proposals in these fields. Its strength of influence in these fields will depend on the strength of the Commission itself. It will prove difficult to wholly delimit those areas falling under the justice and home affairs title from those falling under the Community sphere of action. This is especially true with regard to the implications of justice and home affairs policy on existing Member State governmental co-operation on the free movement of persons in the Community under Art. 8a E.C. (see Schutte, Schengen: Its Meaning for the Free Movement of Persons in Europe (1991) 28 C.M.L.Rev. 549–570 and O'Keeffe, The Free Movement of Persons and the Single Market, (1992) 17 E.L.Rev. 3). This ought to give the Commission some extra degree of influence in the justice and home affairs sphere.

By virtue of Art. L TEU, the areas of common foreign and security policy and justice and home affairs are expressly non-justiciable by the European Court of Justice (E.C.J.), except in the very specialised situation where the Member States make express provision for such jurisdiction in relation to the provisions of a convention negotiated under the justice and home affairs pillar (Art. K.3 TEU). The exclusion of the jurisdiction of the E.C.J. marks the inter-governmental nature of the processes under these pillars. In his second reading speech on the 1993 Act giving effect to the amendments to domestic law encompassed in the TEU, John Major was swift to point out that in the fields of justice and home affairs and common foreign and security policy: "any dispute would go to the International Court of Justice, not to the European Court" (*Hansard*, H.C. Vol. 208, col. 267). Legally, this assertion is questionable. John Major's statement appears more of an emphasis on the inter-governmental nature of the process than an indication of U.K. intention to utilise the International Court of Justice as a dispute settler. Any disputes in this field would no doubt be resolved in a political rather than a judicial context. Everling states, on the other hand, that the TEU belongs in the category of integration treaties and thus sanctions under international law are not to be contemplated in cases of infringement, notwithstanding the lack of jurisdiction of the E.C.J. None of this, however, denies the binding effect of the TEU as an instrument of international law under the basic rule, *pacta sunt servanda* (see Everling, "Reflections on the Structure of the European Union" (1992) 29 C.M.L.Rev. 1053–1077, 1064).

Article L of the TEU also expressly excludes European Court jurisdiction over the common provisions in Title I. One of the most obvious results of this exclusion is that the express reference to the European Convention on Human Rights (E.C.H.R.) in Art. F(2) TEU adds nothing to current practice with regard to the Community protection of human rights. Prior to the Maastricht inter-governmental conference, there had been many calls for the incorporation into Community law of the E.C.H.R. or the inclusion of a Community charter of fundamental rights (the Commission supports Community accession to E.C.H.R.; E.C. Bull. Supp. 2/79, repeated in E.C. Bull. 11–90 and supported by the European Parliament, [1991] O.J. C290). In the end, the only references to such protection were included in the non-justiciable Art. F(2) and in the preamble. Any protection of fundamental rights under the Community system will have to continue on an ad hoc basis as individual cases are decided by the E.C.J. (for development of Community human rights see Hartley, *The Foundations of European Community Law*, (2nd ed.), pp. 132–139; Dauses, "The Protection of Fundamental Rights in the Community Legal Order", (1985) 10 E.L.Rev. 398–419 and Coppel and O'Neill, The European Court of Justice: Taking Rights Seriously? (1992) 29 C.M.L.Rev. 669–692).

In common with all prior Treaty revisions, the actual negotiations were conducted in strict secrecy and no official *travaux preparatoires* (records of the intentions of the negotiators) are available on the conduct of the conferences (for commentary on the negotiations see; Laursen and Vanhoonacker (eds.), *The International Conference on Political Union*, Nijhoff, 1992; also Corbett, The International Conference on Political Union, *Journal of Common Market Studies*, (1992), *supra*).

The scope of the 1993 Act: the amendments to the founding treaties of the communities
   The set-up of the TEU reflects the structure of the Union itself, with seven separate titles, each one dealing with a different aspect of the Treaty's role. Title I (Arts. A–F) contains the common provisions: legal declarations of intent covering such issues as the role of the Union and of the European Council and the relationship between the Union and the Communities themselves. Title II (Art. G) contains the amendments to the E.E.C. Treaty, constituting, as mentioned previously, by far the largest part of the TEU. Technical amendments to the European Coal and Steel Community and Euratom Treaties are then contained within Titles III (Art. H) and IV (Art. I) respectively. The provisions on common foreign and security policy are to be found in Title V (Art. J.1–J.11) and on co-operation in the fields of justice and home affairs under Title VI (Arts. K.1–K.9). Title VII (Arts. L–S) contains the Treaty's final provisions.
   The 1993 Act gives the force of law within the U.K. to Titles II, III and IV exclusively. These titles, amending pre-existing treaties having the force of law within the U.K. by virtue of s.1(2) of the European Communities Act 1972, give rise to domestic rights and obligations and thus need to be incorporated into U.K. law. There is no such requirement in relation to the other provisions of the Treaty; their having no direct effect within the U.K. Nevertheless, Sir Russell Johnston, moving the first of more than 400 amendments considered in the Committee stage in front of the whole House, accused the government of "ratification à la carte" and argued for the right of the House to express its view on the whole of the Treaty and not just a part of it. The court hearing the application for judicial review initiated by Lord Rees-Mogg gave authority to the Government's decision not to put the other titles of the TEU before Parliament, stating, in the context of common foreign and security policy; "Title V is not, of course, included in s.1(1) of the 1993 Act, since it is an inter-governmental Agreement, which could have no impact on U.K. domestic law" ([1993] 3 C.M.L.R. 101, 114). The same can be said to be true as regards the remainder of the "excluded" parts of the TEU.
   In *R.* v. *Secretary of State for Foreign and Commonwealth Affairs*, ex p. *Rees-Mogg* [1993] 3 C.M.L.R. 101, D.C., counsel for Lord Rees-Mogg, David Pannick Q.C., argued that the Crown could not transfer its prerogative powers in the areas of foreign and defence policy without statutory enactment. He contended that the U.K. could not ratify Title V of the TEU concerning common foreign and security policy because the 1993 Act did not authorise the inevitable loss of sovereign power. For the purposes of the case the Queen's Bench Division assumed that the issues raised by Mr Pannick were justiciable and that it would be unlawful for the Crown to transfer any part of its prerogative powers without statutory enactment. The court decided that the ratification of Title V of the TEU would constitute an exercise of the U.K.'s prerogative powers in relation to foreign policy and not a transfer of these powers. It concluded that:
   "So far as we know, nobody has ever suggested that the Charter of the United Nations, for example, or of the North Atlantic Treaty Organisation, involves a transfer of prerogative power. Title V should be read in the same light. In the last resort, as was pointed out in argument, though not pursued, it would presumably be open to the government to denounce the Treaty, or at least to fail to comply with its international obligations under Title V" (at p.116).
   The court here is endorsing the view that when prerogative powers are exercised within an inter-governmental framework, they are not lost, but are merely being exercised in a different manner.

Amendments to the Treaty of Rome establishing the European Economic Community
   Article G of the TEU contains the amendments to the E.E.C. Treaty (the Treaty of Rome), which established the European Economic Community. It contains 86 paragraphs, which amend large parts of the E.E.C. Treaty. The very first paragraph of Art. G stipulates that the term "European Economic Community" shall be replaced by the term "European Community". Thus references to the E.E.C. Treaty infer the position prior to the Maastricht amendments and references to the E.C. Treaty are post-Maastricht.
   The conception of the Treaty as a rearguard action fought by the U.K. Government against its more integrationist Community partners and thus the least bad option is difficult to avoid. The Prime Minister, John Major, certainly adopted this attitude, stating at the second reading: "what we kept out of the Treaty is as important as what went into it . . . there is no social chapter, there is no power for the European Parliament to approve decisions rejected by the Council of Ministers, no weakening of our power of national decision taking in foreign policy, no word "federal" and no commitment to a federal—by which I mean centralising—Europe" (*Hansard*, H.C. Vol. 208, col. 265).

Much of the concern in the U.K. with the TEU and the European Communities themselves lies in the extent to which increased powers for the E.C. will remove sovereign rights from the U.K. One of the more bizarre manifestations of this concern was the U.K. Government's insistence that they were unable to ratify a Treaty incorporating the word "federal" into the text. The Luxembourg draft Treaty's reference to "a process leading gradually to a Union with a federal goal" (Art. A, Luxembourg draft) was removed at Maastricht after intense pressure from the U.K. negotiators (U.K. Wins Battle to Drop the Federal Goal, *Financial Times*, December 4, 1991).

The reliance on the reference to the word federal is simply a distraction. The real concern over the Treaty was the extent to which it was a "centralising force". Whether having a "federal" goal is synonomous with moving towards a more centralised Europe is highly debatable; many of today's federal states exhibit a much greater degree of decentralisation than the U.K. itself, with its highly centralised governmental machinery. In any case, Lord Mackenzie Stuart, formerly President of the European Court, has observed that the words "federal" and "federation" have no precise meaning and thus should not be used in legal texts (see a letter to *The Times*, June 22, 1991). While a definitive breakdown of the Treaty in this respect is impossible, the determination of the centralising nature of the Treaty, in the E.C. context, must centre firstly, on an assessment of the increased instances of qualified majority voting in the Council (Council of Ministers) and secondly, on any increase in the powers of the European Parliament at the expense of the Council. If one is to use these as indicators of the extent to which the TEU amendments to the E.E.C. Treaty signal a movement towards the centre, then the omens for John Major are good. The increase in the scope of qualified majority voting is negligible; there are only 11 new instances in the Treaty as amended (emergency visa requirements, Art. 100c(2); education (incentive measures and recommendations), Art. 126(4); vocational training measures (replacing simple majority voting), Art. 127(4); health (incentive measures and recommendations) Art. 129; consumer protection, Art. 129a(2); trans-European networks guidelines (inter-operability and finance), Art. 129d; research and technological development, Art. 130j–l; environment (except fiscal, land use, water and energy), Art. 130s; development policy, Art. 130w; approval of European Parliament regulations governing the ombudsman, Art. 138e; and certain aspects of social policy among the 11, Art. 2(2), Protocol No. 14). In the field of economic and monetary union, the majority process is more prevalent but the U.K. opt-out from the third stage of economic and monetary union ensures that the most wide-ranging applications of this procedure, such as the imposition of sanctions upon the Member States for non-compliance with economic guidelines, need not apply to the U.K. Unanimity is retained in the Treaty for the majority of politically sensitive matters such as the harmonisation of indirect taxes (Art. 99), approximation of laws falling within the common market but outside the internal market (Art. 100), granting of Community financial assistance to a Member State in difficulties (Art. 103a), and the general power to pass laws coming within the objectives of the Community (Art. 235). In the constitutional sphere, the vast majority of provisions continue to require the unanimous agreement of the Member States; these include decisions concerning the Community's own resources (Art. 201), the acceptance of a new Member State (Art. 237 E.E.C./ Art. O TEU), changes in the number of judges and advocates-general in the E.C.J. (Arts. 165 and 166) and the approval of a uniform procedure for the European Parliamentary elections (Art. 138(3)). All in all, the amended E.C. Treaty provides for 55 instances of unanimity voting in Council. The case that the Maastricht amendments to the E.E.C. Treaty constitute a move towards centralisation in this respect is therefore hardly persuasive (see Weatherill and Beaumont, *EC Law*, Penguin, 69–71). The Maastricht amendments make no reference to the continued existence or otherwise of the so-called Luxembourg compromise whereby a Member State is able to exercise a veto in the Council where its important interests are at stake (see Campbell (1986) 35 I.C.L.Q. 932 and Vasey, "Decision Making in the Agriculture Council and the Luxembourg Compromise" (1988) 25 C.M.L.Rev. 725). While John Major made clear his viewpoint that the compromise still exists (*Hansard*, H.C. Vol. 208, col. 272), there is not a consensus among the Member States on this matter. It is likely that a Member State wishing to actively invoke this veto will find it increasingly difficult as its use generally diminishes (see editorial, (1986) 23 C.M.L.Rev. 744, which discussed the relative rarity of the compromise at the ministerial level and the reluctance of the Member States to continue its application in the Committee of Permanent Representatives (COREPER)). A claim that vital national interests are at stake will be particularly difficult to make in an area where the state concerned has recently agreed to treaty amendments permitting qualified majority voting in that area (see Weatherill and Beaumont, *EC Law*, Penguin, pp. 67–69).

The other factor determinative of the centralising nature of the Community process is the extent to which the European Parliament can influence the content of Community legislation. This influence, minimal prior to the passing of the SEA, grew with the introduction of the co-operation procedure and will do so again as a result of the Maastricht amendments to the E.C.

Treaty. Nonetheless, the Council still remains the pre-eminent institution in the legislative process. Despite the calls for a power of co-decision between the European Parliament and the Council, in part to address the essentially anti-democratic nature of the Council process whereby members of national governments meet in secret to pass legislative measures, the amendments agreed at Maastricht fall far short of such co-decision. The introduction of the new "conciliation and veto" procedure (known imaginatively in the E.C. Treaty as the "procedure referred to in Art. 189b E.C."), while giving the European Parliament for the first time a right of veto over legislation it does not approve of, does not allow the European Parliament to adopt legislation which the Council has expressed a negative opinion on. The Council thus maintains its power to determine the legislative make-up of the Community legal order: the European Parliament having a somewhat greater say in the process than before. This being so, the new procedure is complex and restricted initially to only 13 legislative bases. These include the majority of those areas previously using the co-operation procedure, aimed at the achievement of the internal market and introduced by the SEA (Art. 149(2) E.E.C. replaced by Art. 189c E.C.), as well as the provisions under the "new" Community competences introduced into the E.C. Treaty at Maastricht (examples are education, vocational training and youth measures but excluding any harmonisation of national laws, Art. 126(4); trans-European network guidelines, Art. 129d; incentive measures in the fields of public health and culture, Arts. 129(4) and 128(5) respectively). For a detailed breakdown of the procedure and its scope of application, see the note on Art. 189b.

An important factor in any discussion on the centralising nature of the E.C. Treaty is an analysis of the new competences attributed to the Community; naturally any increase in the scope of Community action means a proportionate decrease in the national sphere of action. This transfer from the Member States to the Community has been kept to the minimum by the TEU. This would not appear to be the case from a cursory glance at Art. 3 of the E.C. Treaty, which would suggest that the increase in the Community's scope of action has been far from minimal; nevertheless, as Tristan Garel-Jones, the Foreign Office Minister responsible for the passage of the Bill through the house made clear: "Article 3 is billed in shock horror terms by some hon. members as containing new competences. It lists the Community activities. The list is longer in the Maastricht Treaty than in the Treaty of Rome, as amended by the SEA. That is because the list has been extended to include references to the new competence chapters included in the Maastricht Treaty for the first time. Nine new policy areas are listed in Art. 3, but that does not mean that there are nine new areas of competence. In all these areas, competence has already been exercised under the Treaty of Rome and the SEA" (see *Hansard*, H.C. Vol. 217, col. 61).

The "new" fields of activity include the following (laid down under the titles by which they will be known): culture; public health; consumer protection; trans-European networks; and industry and development co-operation. The TEU also strengthens the provisions in the Titles on economic and social cohesion and the environment, which were inserted by the SEA. The degree of power given to the Community to adopt actions under the different titles is highly divergent. In the fields of culture and public health, the Community is empowered simply to supplement and encourage national action, with the express proviso that any measures taken at the Community level shall preclude the harmonisation of national laws. On the other hand, the powers attributed to the Community in the field of consumer protection permit the adoption of wide-ranging Community measures aimed at such harmonisation. On this topic see Lane, "New Community Competences under the Maastricht Treaty" (1993) 30 C.M.L.Rev. 939–981.

The preceding discussion has focused on the centralising tendencies of the new Treaty; it is also necessary to look at its decentralising forces. The TEU introduces into the E.C. Treaty the principle of subsidiarity (Art. 3b E.C.) with a view to ensuring a more appropriate use of competences shared between the Member States and the Community institutions. The preamble to the TEU highlights the brake that subsidiarity is intended to place on a centralising Europe. It provides that the Member States are "resolved to continue the process of creating an ever closer union among the peoples of Europe, in which decisions are taken as closely as possible to the citizen in accordance with the principle of subsidiarity". The U.K. Government has placed great reliance on the inclusion of this principle in the Treaty but it will prove very difficult to apply in the judicial context. Subsidiarity's impact will depend upon the degree to which it is absorbed into the institutional culture of the Community. Political rather than legal factors are likely to determine how much restraint the Community institutions exercise in the promulgation of Community legislation (see note on Art. 3b).

Another small decentralising step is the removal of simple majority voting in the Council from substantive areas concerning vocational training (contrast Art. 128 E.E.C. and Arts. 126 and 127 E.C.) and external relations (contrast Art. 228 E.E.C. and Art. 228 E.C.). The shift to qualified majority voting and unanimity prevents the possibility of the Ministers who represent the sizeable majority of the E.C. population being out-voted in Council.

The provisions of the TEU amending the E.E.C. Treaty make some interesting alterations to the Community process in the field of political union; an umbrella term used to convey all areas not specifically covered by economic and monetary union. This being the case, it must be emphasised that the Maastricht amendments do not alter all of the pre-existing E.E.C. Treaty. Many of the most utilised provisions of the Treaty remain almost wholly unaltered; this is the case with regard to the free movement of goods (Arts. 9–37 E.E.C.), agriculture (Arts. 38–47 E.E.C.) and competition policy (Arts. 85–94 E.E.C. but with minor amendments in Arts. 92(3) and 94). The fundamental freedoms of establishment, services and workers are simply amended to provide for the application of a new legislative procedure; something which is quite common in the Maastricht amendments. The areas of the Treaty which have seen the most substantial amendments are the institutional provisions (Arts. 137–198e), the free movement of capital provisions (Arts. 73a–73h), and the community competences chapter (Arts. 110–130y). Elsewhere the amendments are impossible to categorise and range from the simply inconsequential to the essential. The core of the Treaty amendments consists of the substantive provisions governing the move to the third stage of economic and monetary union, with its single currency and independent monetary authority (Arts. 102a–109). This marks a new departure for the Community; the laying down of strict timetables for movement through the three stages highlights the imperative nature of the process. Finally, the only other wholly new addition to the Treaty is a section dealing with the new "Union citizenship", a mixed bag of rights attributable to the status of Union citizenship, something much more noteable for its symbolic value than any substantive content (Arts. 8–8e).

As Curtin has identified, a striking feature of the new Union Treaty is the large number of annexed protocols and declarations (Curtin, The Constitutional Structure of the Union: A Europe of Bits and Pieces (1993) 30 C.M.L.Rev. 17–69, at p. 44). While the use of such instruments is nothing new to the drafters of the Community Treaties, their use in the TEU is often at variance with their generally understood purpose. In this respect it is the protocols annexed to the TEU which have caused the greatest concern; they are an integral part of the E.C. Treaty itself (Art. 239 E.C. (unamended)). While such protocols are ideal instruments to prevent over elaboration of technical or transitional matters in the body of the Treaty (as with the annexed Protocol on the Statutes of the European System of Central Banks and European Central Bank and the Protocol on the excessive deficit procedure in the field of economic and monetary union), they have also been utilised to give effect to opt-outs negotiated by the Member States from fundamental Treaty obligations. This can be seen as a manifestation of the move towards a Europe à la carte. Prime examples of this movement can be seen in the first Protocol annexed to the Treaty which provides for the retention by the Danes of legislation preventing the purchase by nationals of other Member States of second homes in Denmark. This marks an abrogation of the fundamental principle of Community law of free movement for the purpose of securing services and goods. Closer to home, the two opt-outs secured by the U.K. are encompassed in protocols appended to the TEU. The first of these is the opt-out from the move to the third stage of economic and monetary union; enclosed in the vaguely titled Protocol on certain provisions relating to the U.K. and Northern Ireland (Protocol No.11), which makes clear that "the U.K. shall not be obliged or committed to move to the third stage of economic and monetary union without a separate decision to do so by its government and Parliament". The U.K. is therefore given the opportunity permanently to opt-out from the requirements of the third stage of economic and monetary union with its single currency and independent central bank (Denmark has a similar opt-out Protocol). The second opt-out secured by the U.K. is from the development of the social provisions agreed to by the other 11 Member States (see notes later and Curtin, The Constitutional Structure of the Union: A Europe of Bits and Pieces (1993) 30 C.M.L.Rev. 17–69, at pp. 44–59).

Institutional reform

A great number of the changes concern the institutional set-up of the European Union. While the inter-governmental star has risen as regards the new Union competences, where the European Council and Council of Ministers are dominant, in the Community structure itself there has been a modest increase in the powers of the supra-national Parliament and, to a much lesser extent, the Commission.

The European Parliament (Arts. 137–143 E.C.)

The European Parliament will now exercise "the powers conferred upon it by this Treaty" (Art. 137 E.C.) as opposed to the "advisory and supervisory" (Art. 137 E.E.C.) rôle it pursued prior to Maastricht. Most significantly it finds itself the recipient of a new legislative rôle in certain specified areas. Pressure from the more integrationist states led to the creation of this new legislative procedure, under which, for the first time, Parliament has the power to veto certain legislative proposals outright (Art. 189b E.C.). It also sees the formalisation of a number of activities previously carried out by convention, such as the creation of committees of inquiry to investigate alleged contraventions or maladministration in the implementation of Community law (Art. 138c E.C.) and the development of Parliament's rôle in the appointment of the Commission (Art. 158 E.C.). With the development of the European Parliament's rôle in the legislative procedure through the introduction of the conciliation and veto procedure and the extension of the assent procedure (single reading; positive parliamentary approval necessary), the European Parliament is now in the position to apply the brake to the Community legislative process, but cannot press the accelerator without the consent of the Council. Nevertheless, the powers of the European Parliament will be substantially increased in all areas of Community competence, thanks to the potential for cross-bargaining. In other words, the European Parliament will consent to a certain measure under the conciliation and veto or assent procedures on the explicit grounds that in another area where it exercises a great deal less formal influence, its proposals will be given effect to. This will be the price for its consent. Such bargaining will be effective only if the Council is anxious to secure legislation in the area covered by the conciliation and veto or assent procedures; it always has the opportunity simply to let a proposal lapse if European Parliament agreement is not forthcoming. The Maastricht amendments also recognise a limited right of legislative initiative for the European Parliament (Art. 138b); while this falls short of the European Parliament being in a position to require the Commission to submit a legislative proposal on a specific topic, it will give the European Parliament a significant degree of informal leverage. It is quite possible that the European Parliament will select a number of its initiatives as proposals falling under this Article and call the Commission to account until there is some follow-up (Venables, *The Amendment of the Treaties*, Butterworths, (1992), at p. 74). The power of the European Parliament to secure the dismissal of the Commission by passing a motion of censure by a two-thirds majority under Art. 144 E.E.C. is retained and in drastic circumstances could be utilised in this context. The formalisation of the European Parliament vote of confidence in the Commission prior to their taking office may be used as a platform for the European Parliament to make its legislative initiatives quite clear to the incoming Commission.

The Commission (Arts. 156–163 E.C.)

The major amendment as regards the Commission concerns the enhanced rôle of the European Parliament in the appointment of the Commission (Art. 158). Also significant is the Commission's rôle in the economic and monetary union process, *e.g.* its involvement in assessing the Member States' economic performances as a basis for their entering the third stage. Finally, the Commission will have the power to recommend to the E.C.J. the level of sanction it envisages for Member State non-compliance under the new Art. 171 E.C.

A declaration appended to Art. 157 E.C. declares that a review of the number of Commissioners will take place "no later than the end of 1992". While no determinative ruling has yet been made, there is every likelihood that the enlargement process will render the current position of larger Member States, who have two commissioners, untenable. Even the prospect of one state, one commissioner, with the resultant rise in the influence of the smaller Member States, may not prove desirable in a Community of 15 to 20. While the Luxembourg draft mentioned the possibility of deputy commissioners, this was not mooted in the final Treaty.

The European Court of Justice (Arts. 165–184 E.C.)

The most significant innovation concerning the E.C.J. is the new procedure envisaged for enforcement actions under Arts. 169–171 E.C. It is now provided that a financial penalty may be imposed upon states which fail to comply with a judgment of the E.C.J. This development was advocated by the U.K. which has a good record of implementation of Community legislation (see Tenth Annual Report on Commission monitoring of the Application of Community law (COM (93) 320 final). The procedure to be followed in the application of this sanction is long drawn out. In some cases a more immediate remedy may be available under the E.C.'s development of the principle of state liability for non-implementation of Community legislation, enunciated in the landmark case of *Francovich and Boniface* v. *Italy* (Cases C–6, C–9/90) [1991] E.C.R. I-5359, and annotation by Bebr (1992) 29 C.M.L.Rev. 571). For an elaboration of this principle and the new powers of the E.C.J., see note on Art. 171 E.C.

Another important change is the greater range of jurisdictional issues that the Council can agree to transfer from the E.C.J. to the Court of First Instance (see the note on Art. 168a E.C.).

The Committee of the Regions (Arts. 198a–198c E.C.)

The new advisory Committee of the Regions will adopt a similar function to the pre-existing Economic and Social Committee (Arts. 193–198 E.C.). It will be consulted in the legislative process but in a very restricted number of areas, and its powers are purely advisory. While the committee is largely impotent, its inclusion reflects the desire of certain Member States, most notably Germany with its powerful regional bodies (Länder), to see local governments with a much greater say in the Community legislative process; at best the Committee of the Regions marks a symbolic acceptance of this principle.

The Council of Ministers (Arts. 145–154 E.C.)

The Maastricht amendments have made very few alterations to the rôle of the Council, although it has seen the range of its powers increase in the fields of economic and monetary union and in the pillars of justice and home affairs co-operation and common foreign and security policy. The virtual retention of all the powers previously exercised by this body, the Community's principal legislative branch (although see Lenaerts, Some Reflections on the Separation of Powers in the European Communities (1991) 28 C.M.L.Rev. 11–35), is not altogether surprising when one considers that the Treaty amendments were negotiated by the same government ministers who attend the Council.

Legislative procedures

There is no uniform procedure for the making of Community legislation, and the TEU amendments have further added to the procedures applicable (for an overview see Weatherill and Beaumont, *E.C. Law*, Penguin, Chap. 5). The result is a bewildering array of legislative procedures which impedes any real understanding of the Community law making process: "Political accountability, sanctioned by universal suffrage, can indeed only be effective where the actors in the legislative process are known in advance to everyone and when their respective prerogatives and responsibilities can be identified by the public" (Lenaerts, *supra*, at p. 20).

The assent procedure introduced by the SEA is retained but with an increased scope of application. This procedure, which effectively attributes to the European Parliament a right of veto, is now applicable to free movement of citizens (Art. 8a(2) E.C.), legislation increasing the European Central Bank's powers of prudential supervision (Art. 105(6) E.C.), amending certain articles of the Statute of the European System of Central Banks (Art. 106(5) E.C.), the creation of the new cohesion fund and the definition of the tasks of the structural funds (Art. 130d(1) E.C.) and the adoption of a uniform procedure for elections to the European Parliament (Art. 138(2) E.C.). It is also still applicable to the conclusion of certain international agreements (Art. 228(3) E.C.) and the accession of new Member States (Art. O TEU). This procedure avoids the complexities inherent in the new conciliation and veto procedure while still giving the European Parliament a veto. It does not, however, give the European Parliament an opportunity to amend proposals. In an attempt to rectify this the European Parliament has amended its Rules of Procedure to try and create a conciliation process with the Council as part of the assent procedure (see Rule 52G(3), [1993] O.J. C268/51). The parliamentary committee responsible for considering the Council's legislative proposals may make an interim report recommending modifications to them. If any of these modifications are passed by the Parliament by the same majority or is required for final assent then the President of the Parliament will request the Council to open a conciliation procedure. If the Council refuses to engage in conciliation then the implied threat is that the Parliament will refuse to give assent to a proposal in its unmodified form.

The new conciliation and veto procedure introduced by Art. 189b E.C. has certain of the elements of the co-operation procedure (Art. 149(2) E.E.C./Art. 189c E.C.), such as the double reading in the European Parliament, but permits the convening of a third stage conciliation process where an equal number of members of the Council and the European Parliament meet to hammer out their differences. This procedure, permitting the European Parliament to reject legislation it does not approve of, is of Byzantine complexity and lacks legislative transparency. The European Parliament has expressed the opinion that its power to veto legislation is effectively circumscribed by the negative perception which would fall upon this body if it were seen to be blocking legislation which had already spent upwards of six months going through the early stages of the procedure. The then President of the European Parliament, Baron Crespo, was probably exaggerating the "political suicide" of the institution involved in the European Parliament being seen to be exercising such a negative rôle. The European Parliament's powers have increased as a result of the introduction of this procedure, despite its imperfections.

The co-operation procedure, which has, relatively effectively, enabled the European Parliament to secure amendments to the legislation enacted under it, is preserved under the TEU amendments. A number of the measures originally covered by this procedure are promoted to the conciliation and veto procedure. The co-operation procedure will apply to the adoption of social measures between the 11 and a number of the economic and monetary union provisions.

One unwelcome aspect of the E.C. Treaty, as far as the degree of European Parliament involvement is concerned, is the retention of the consultation procedure as one of the prevalent legislative processes. The European Parliament is merely entitled to give an opinion on the measure at hand, and the Commission and Council are then entirely free to disregard this opinion if they so desire. This procedure is retained, along with unanimity in the Council, for a number of politically sensitive areas of Community competence, such as the harmonisation of indirect taxes (Art. 99) and other constitutional matters, including the achievement of Community goals under Art. 235 E.C. One disturbing aspect of the consultation procedure is the Council practice which has grown up of adopting a political position in the Council prior to the consultation of the European Parliament, thus fettering the discretion of the Council as regards any opinion returning from the European Parliament, no matter how meritorious it may be. Even more regrettable is the continuation of some law-making powers in the Community where there is no requirement to consult the European Parliament (see Weatherill and Beaumont, *E.C. Law*, Penguin, pp. 94–95, 125, 130 and 796–797).

A great deal of criticism has been directed at the uncertainties created by what George Robertson, then Labour front bench spokesman on European affairs, called "a cautious compromise among the nation states of Europe". Such comments tend to centre on the disregard which has been paid to institutional efficiency in the interests of national interests. This is of course unavoidable in a Treaty revision process which requires the unanimous agreement of all 12 Member States. This is manifested in the wide variety of legislative procedures now applicable to the adoption of the Community legislation. What is also unavoidable is an increase in the number of challenges being made to the legislative basis of Community law (see, *e.g. Commission* v. *Council* Case C-300/89 (Titanium Dioxide case) [1991] E.C.R. I-2867). With the existence of widely divergent legislative procedures under which each institution's rôle varies greatly, there will undoubtedly be an increase in litigation before the E.C.J. This will further threaten the efficient running of the legislative process.

Economic and monetary union (Arts. 102a–109m E.C.)

The core of the substantive amendments to the E.E.C. Treaty is the section dealing with economic and monetary union; effectively a treaty within a treaty. Agreement upon the route towards eventual economic and monetary union was quickly reached at Maastricht. The existence of a general consensus among the Member States on the main points, as well as the availability of authoritative and influential materials prior to the summit, made the Maastricht negotiations something of a formality. The Delors committee report and the draft statute of the European System of Central Banks drawn up by the Committee of Governors of the Central Banks of the Member States, were among a corpus of materials facilitating discussion throughout.

Article 3a E.C. defines the activities of the Member States and the Community institutions in the realisation of full economic and monetary union. In the economic field, the goal is the adoption of an economic policy which is based on close co-ordination of Member State's economic policies and is conducted in accordance with the principle of an open market economy with free competition. As regards monetary policy, the aim is the irrevocable fixing of exchange rates, leading to the introduction of a single currency, the ECU, and the definition and conduct of a single monetary and exchange rate policy, the primary objective of both of which shall be to maintain price stability.

The treaty goes on to state that the achievement of economic and monetary union shall have the following guiding principles; stable prices, sound public finances and monetary conditions and a sustainable balance of payments (Art. 3a(3) E.C.).

There is a marked difference between the means by which economic union is to be secured under the Treaty and the much stricter progress envisaged for monetary union. This is reflected in their separate treatment in the amended E.C. Treaty. Chapter 1 of the new Title VI (Arts. 102a–104c E.C.) deals with economic policy, while Chap. 2 is dedicated to the monetary policy of the Community (Arts. 105–109 E.C.).

The movement towards the convergence of economic policies remains essentially decentralised. Article 103 highlights the extent to which the pressure for economic convergence rests upon the States themselves. It states that the Council shall, acting by a qualified majority on a recommendation from the Commission, formulate a draft setting out broad guidelines for the economic policies of the Member States and the Community and that it reports to the European Council. After the European Council has discussed a conclusion on the broad guidelines, the Council, acting by a qualified majority, must adopt a recommendation setting out the broad guidelines. Moreover, the Council shall, on the basis of reports from the Commission, monitor economic developments in each of the Member States, as well as the consistency of economic policies with the aforementioned broad guidelines. Should it appear to the Council that the Member State's policies are not consistent with the guidelines, then it may make the necessary recommendations to the Member State concerned, or make its recommendations public and thus apply some political pressure on the State (Art. 103(4) E.C.).

The main goal of the economic co-ordination provisions is the avoidance of excessive government deficits (Art. 104c(1) E.C. and appended Protocol No. 5). No sanctions are envisaged for non-compliance with this obligation during the second stage but, upon the coming into effect of the third stage, punitive measures may be applied in the last resort to states adjudged to have failed in the application of the guidelines (Art. 104c(11)).

In comparison with economic co-ordination, the path towards monetary union is truly deserving of the term "union". The final goal of an independent Central Bank overseeing a single currency will signal an almost absolute transfer of powers in monetary and exchange rate matters from the Member States to the European System of Central Banks and, to a lesser extent, to the Community institutions. The European Central Bank will be based in Frankfurt. It will control the money supply, interest rates and the exchange rate of the ECU. The Bank's decision-making bodies will be made up of bankers rather than politicians. The Bank's primary objective will be price stability. Bankers will not be tempted, or indeed be able, to adjust monetary policy to fit the short-term needs of the electoral cycles in the different Member States which participate in the single currency. The expectation is that low rates of inflation will be preserved more consistently than when politicians control monetary policy. The choice of Frankfurt as the seat of the Bank reflects the hope that it will retain something of the credibility of its forerunner in that city, the Bundesbank. The decision that Frankfurt would be the seat of the Bank was taken at Head of State and Government level in November 1993 (see [1993] O.J. C323/1).

The path mapped out at Maastricht towards economic and monetary union reflects the desire of at least ten of the Member States to move rapidly towards full union, while retaining some of the flexibility of a staged process to give time to achieve the necessary economic convergence. The E.C. Treaty thus lays down a strict timetable for the achievement of economic and monetary union in three stages.

The first stage, already under way, has at its heart the pursuit of greater convergence between the economic performances of the Member States, with the aim of completing the internal market under Art. 8a E.E.C., thus providing the stepping stone towards the stricter convergence of stage two.

The convergence in stage one of economic and monetary union is to be achieved through two inter-related initiatives. Firstly, the liberalisation of capital flows through the dismantling of foreign exchange restrictions which is continuing apace, largely as a result of Directive 88/361 ([1988] O.J. L178/5) implementing Art. 67 E.E.C. Such liberalisation of the flow of capital tends to restrict the ability of national authorities to tinker with economic and monetary policy, thus making for a degree of market led convergence.

Secondly, the Exchange Rate Mechanism (ERM) of the European Monetary System (EMS), which the U.K. joined in June 1989, was an attempt to lock exchange rates within fixed parameters, maintained by interest rate differentials in the Member States. (For a history and explanation of EMS, established in March 1979, see Rey (1980) 17 C.M.L.Rev. 78). However, extreme pressure in the international capital markets in September 1992 led to the suspension of sterling and the lira from the ERM. Subsequent intimations from the U.K. Government on their rejoining ERM have been vague. It remains unclear to what extent this will affect the viability of the ERM and planned progress towards economic and monetary union. While no provision in the Treaty expressly requires membership of the ERM as a precondition of movement to the second stage of economic and monetary union, the Treaty does make exchange rate stability a precursor of such a move. Nevertheless, the decision to alter the normal bandings of the ERM from 2.25 per cent. to fifteen per cent. in the summer of 1993, as a result of further strains on the ERM, may well make compliance with one of the convergence criteria simpler. This states that one of the conditions for the move to the third stage is that the Member State's currency has "respected the normal fluctuation margins provided for by the ERM of the EMS without severe tensions for at least two years before the examination as to suitability for the third stage" (Art. 3 of the Protocol on the Convergence Criteria; Art. 109j E.C.).

The second stage of monetary union, due to commence on January 1, 1994 (Art. 109e(1) E.C.), requires the Member States to complete the free movement of capital and payments, not only between themselves, but also between Member States and third countries (Art. 73b). Any derogations given to Greece and Portugal can continue up to December 31, 1995 at the latest (Art. 73e E.C.). Only Greece has been granted such a derogation ([1992] O.J. L409/33).

As already mentioned, during the second stage Member States are to endeavour to avoid excessive government deficits. No sanctions can be taken to enforce this until the third stage (Art. 109e (3) and (4)). Also relevant in terms of economic policy, the second stage marks the coming into force of other provisions intended to secure improved budgetary discipline in the Member States. These include a prohibition on the granting of credit facilities by the European Central Bank or any central bank, to governmental bodies or Community institutions (Art. 104

E.C.) and the loss of privileged access of governmental and Community bodies to financial institutions (Art. 104a E.C.). Also, the Community and Member States will be precluded from assuming the commitments of governmental bodies or public undertakings (Art. 104 E.C., the no-bailing out rule; see the note on that Article).

In the monetary sphere, the European Monetary Institute will be set up in Frankfurt during the second stage. This body will consist of the Governors of the national central banks, plus a president appointed by common accord of the Member States, from amongst persons of recognised professional experience in economic or monetary matters. The European Monetary Institute, itself without a great number of formal legal powers, will prepare the ground for the much more powerful European Central Bank to come into existence for the move to the third stage. The opinions and recommendations of the European Monetary Institute will have no binding force as regards the orientation of economic and monetary policy, but its rôle in "giving birth" to the European Central Bank will be paramount. The European Monetary Institute will, by December 31, 1996 at the latest, lay down the regulatory, organisational and logistical framework for the European Central Bank. Other functions of the European Monetary Institute will be to strengthen co-operation between the national central banks, monitor the functioning of the EMS and facilitate the use of the existing ECU (made up of a basket of the currencies of the Member States). Finally, as regards the second stage, each Member State is to start the process leading to the independence of its central bank (Art. 109e (5) E.C.).

The E.C. Treaty envisages that the third and final stage of economic and monetary union, with an independent central bank overseeing the single currency, will come into being, at the latest, on January 1, 1999 (Art. 109j (4) E.C.). Prior to this date, but not later than December 31, 1996, the Council, meeting in the composition of the heads of government and state, can decide by a qualified majority to set an earlier date for the commencement of the third stage if a majority of the Member States achieve certain economic targets, which are the convergence criteria required for the third stage (Art. 109j (3) E.C.).

These criteria are laid down in Art. 109j and the annexed Protocol. The four targets, which may be applied with a degree of flexibility, are as follows; first, an average rate of inflation, observed over a period of one year before the examination, which does not exceed by more than 1.5 per cent. the average of the three best performing states (Art. 1 of Protocol No. 6 on the convergence criteria); second, the avoidance of an excessive government budgetary deficit which is defined as meaning an annual budget deficit of less than 3 per cent. of Gross Domestic Product and an overall public debt ratio not exceeding 60 per cent. of Gross Domestic Product (Art. 1 of Protocol No. 5 on the Excessive Deficit Procedure); third, the Member State's currency must have stayed within the normal fluctuation margins in the ERM without severe tensions for at least two years prior to the period of the examination (Art. 3 of Protocol No. 6); and fourth, the Member State's average long-term interest rate, measured over a period of one year before the examination, must not exceed by more than 2 per cent. the average interest rates in the three best performing states in terms of price stability (in other words, inflation rates) (Art. 4 of Protocol No. 6).

The Council must make the determination as to which Member States have fulfilled the criteria by July 1, 1998. The third stage of economic and monetary union will then commence on January 1, 1999. While there is no specified minimum number of states which must have fulfilled these criteria for the move to the third stage to take place, it is unlikely that any system could function effectively without the participation of Germany and at least a core of the other Member States.

While the progress towards economic and monetary union is legally irrevocable, the U.K. and Denmark negotiated opt-outs at Maastricht as regards the third stage of economic and monetary union. In the U.K. this amounts to a proviso that parliamentary approval, based on a comprehensive up-to-date report on the progress of economic and monetary union, must be forthcoming before the U.K. can move towards the third stage (s.2 of the 1993 Act). The Danish opt-out at Maastricht was essentially in the same terms, but the assent required this time in the form of a special referendum. Nevertheless, in the decision taken at the Edinburgh European Council in December 1992, the Danish government committed itself to exercising its right to opt-out. If the Danes were to choose to move to the third stage of economic and monetary union then they are still quite at liberty to apply to the Council under Art. 109k(2) for leave to enter.

1996 and enlargement

A unique feature of the TEU is that it pre-emptively convokes the next set of constitutional talks for 1996 (Art. N.2 TEU). Article B TEU declares that the purpose of this revision process will be to "maintain in full the *acquis communautaire* and build on it with a view to considering to what extent the policies and forms of co-operation introduced by this Treaty may need to be revised with the aim of ensuring the effectiveness of the mechanisms and the institutions of the Community." This wording reflects a concession to the more integrationist Member States, who wished to see the Maastricht inter-governmental conference process go beyond inter-governmental agreements in the fields of justice and home affairs and common foreign and security policy. It is also likely to be relied upon in the next inter-governmental conference as providing a basis for considering the rationalisation of the divergent legislative procedures applicable to the adoption of Community measures. Nevertheless, the inter-governmental conference in 1996 is not confined to these matters but has an open mandate. Certain areas, such as the extension of the conciliation and veto procedure (Art. 189b(8) E.C.), are expressly singled out as meriting attention, but the nature of the inter-governmental conference process precludes nothing from consideration.

Prior even to the Treaty revision process envisaged for 1996, there is a real possibility that the accession of new States to the Community will provide an earlier opportunity for amendment to the Treaties. Given that the TEU will only have been in force for approximately a year, experience as to its practical effectiveness might not yet be determinative. The opportunity for amendments to the Treaties is nonetheless present in any accession settlement (Art. O TEU). The European Parliament may well seek further concessions before assenting to any accession agreement. It is not clear just how far the Parliament would be prepared to pursue this policy and thus risk alienating new Member States. It is still dissatisfied with the "democratic deficit" it perceives in the Community and seeks greater powers for itself as the remedy. At the Edinburgh European Council meeting, the Member States expressed their desire to see the expansion of the Community proceed with all due speed; a strategy long supported by the U.K. government, which had prepared the ground for a number of enlargement negotiations during its Presidency of the European Council in the second half of 1992 (*Hansard*, H.C. Vol. 208, col. 272). The target date for the first wave of applicants to achieve full membership has been set for January 1, 1995 (see E.C. Commission, The Enlargement of the Community, E.C. B15/93). This group consists of the core of European Free Trade Association States, whose membership includes Austria (1989), Sweden (1991), Finland (1992), Norway (1992), Switzerland (1992), Iceland and Liechtenstein—the year in brackets indicates the date of formal application for E.C. membership. Formal negotiations with Austria, Sweden and Finland commenced on February 1, 1993, with Norway joining the discussions on April 5, 1993 immediately after the Commission pronounced a favourable verdict on its application. As of May 1993, the E.C. had received eight formal applications for membership: the five listed European Free Trade Association states, Turkey, Cyprus (see COM (93) 312 final) and Malta (COM (93) 313 final). At least as many again have announced their intention of applying in the future, with the most obvious applicants being some of the Eastern European and Baltic States. The Eastern European states are envisaged as the second wave of new applicants, but accession is unlikely until after the end of the century. The fundamental problems that will be faced by any such enlargement have been well documented elsewhere. In the next stage of constitutional talks, the institutional challenges which enlargement will create, as well as the language and other difficulties, will have to be addressed. One of the primary discussions will concern the feasibility of maintaining the requirement of unanimity in the Council, this being difficult enough to secure in a Community of 12 far less 20, and possible adjustments to the number of votes required in the Council to achieve a qualified majority. (See E.C. Commission, Europe and the Challenge of Enlargement, Bull. E.C. Supplement 3/92 and Ungerer, Institutional Consequences of Broadening and Deepening the Community: The Consequences for the Decision-Making Process, (1993) 30 C.M.L.Rev. 71–83).

On the TEU in general see *Legal Issues of the Maastricht Treaty*, eds. O'Keefe and Twomey, (1993), Chancery, London.

The 1993 Act

The purpose of the 1993 Act is to give domestic legal effect to the changes to the core Community treaties agreed at Maastricht. This is achieved by amending s.1(2) of the European Communities Act 1972 to incorporate the relevant parts of the Treaty on European Union (TEU) into the list of "Community Treaties".

The power to negotiate and ratify international treaties in the U.K. is an exercise of prerogative powers vested in the executive. Theoretically, this can be carried out without reference to Parliament, but in practice many Treaties require changes to domestic legislation or involve public expenditure which necessitates parliamentary approval. Community law is a special case. The accession of the U.K. to the Communities involved accession not just to a set of international obligations, but to a system of law. Thus the entry of the U.K. into the Community, in 1973, followed the passage of the European Communities Act 1972, incorporating E.C. law into the U.K.

The 1993 Act marks the incorporation into U.K. law of the latest stage in the amendment of the Community Treaties. In accordance with U.K. constitutional practice, this was achieved by the passing of a statute amending the 1972 Act and incorporating the changes to Community law accordingly. The practical effect of the amendments which attempted to exclude from the Bill any part of the Treaty which gave rise to Community rights and obligations would have been to render ratification of the Treaty as a whole impossible. Thus the scope for the Government to accept any amendments to the Bill was strictly circumscribed.

The Bill, as originally introduced to the House of Commons, consisted of only two clauses (the forerunners of the current ss.1 and 2). In Committee, the vast majority of the proposed amendments were aimed at removing essential parts of the Treaty from the Bill. Such wrecking amendments from the Euro-sceptics in both Houses, but particularly among the ranks of the Conservative party in the Commons, were generally comfortably defeated thanks to Opposition support.

While the Opposition party expressed approval of the Treaty itself, this was conditioned by a number of specific concerns. These included the U.K. opt-outs from the Social Policy Agreement and the third stage of economic and monetary union, as well as the allegedly undemocratic nature of inter-governmental co-operation in the fields of common foreign and security policy and justice and home affairs. The scope for any amendment to these areas, without effectively preventing ratification, was strictly limited. Sections 3 to 7 of the Act are the result of Opposition amendments introduced at the Committee stage. While not without importance, these amendments deal with U.K. practice only and often do little more than elaborate on Treaty requirements. Sections 3, 4 and 5 are aimed at increased parliamentary scrutiny of economic and monetary matters. Section 6 restricts the categories of appointees to the European Committee of the Regions. Section 7 is now of historical importance only.

The passage of the Bill through Parliament took more than 14 months and the Committee stage in the House of Commons alone amounted to more than 163 hours of debates. While the Treaty itself enjoyed broad cross-party support, political factors transpired to draw out the debate. After the first reading on May 7, 1992 (*Hansard*, H.C. Vol. 207, col. 162), the Bill went on to receive a comfortable majority of 144 on its second reading (*Hansard*, H.C. Vol. 208, col. 597). The Committee stage in front of the whole house was then scheduled to start its consideration of the 400 or so tabled amendments on June 3, 1992. However, the negative vote in the Danish referendum on Maastricht on June 2, led the Government to suspend Parliamentary consideration of the Bill. On November 4 a paving debate was initiated by the Government to assure confidence in the Maastricht issue after the Danish referendum and the withdrawal of sterling from the ERM in September. As with the decision to suspend consideration of the Bill in May, this debate was politically rather than legally or constitutionally necessitated. However it very nearly backfired on the Government with a narrow three vote majority approving a resolution that the Bill progress (*Hansard*, H.C. Vol. 123, col. 283). The price the Government paid for the crucial votes was the promise that the third reading be postponed until after the second Danish referendum in 1993 (*Hansard*, H.C. Vol. 213, col. 410). Such political machinations marked the whole passage of the Bill. Despite a clear majority in the Houses of Parliament for the Treaty, the Government suffered a number of defeats. The first of these concerned appointments to the new advisory Committee of the Regions (Arts. 198a–c E.C.). The Labour party supported the appointment of locally elected persons, rather than unqualified Government discretion in the matter, and a number of Tory Euro-sceptics joined the Opposition in the division lobbies. The Report stage which this amendment necessitated and the attendant delay in passing the Bill were the goals of the Euro-sceptics. Such alliances marked the most important votes on the Bill, with the staunchly anti-European members of the Conservative party joining with the opposition parties. The opposition parties sought to embarrass the Government on key issues, without threatening the ratification of the Treaty, while the Euro-sceptics sought to delay or prevent its ratification.

The most contentious issue during the proceedings was the opt-out negotiated by the U.K. Government from the extension of Community social provisions agreed to by the 11 other Member States. This aspect of the Treaty has caused a great deal of confusion due in part to the inter-changeable use of confusingly similar terms. These include references to the "Social Chapter", the "Social Charter" and the "Social Protocol". It might be helpful to attempt a clarification of the different terms in use, and their origins.

The E.E.C. Treaty, as it stood prior to the Maastricht amendments, contained a chapter on "social provisions" (Title III, Chap. 1, Arts. 117–122). The original "Social Chapter" provides for Member States to "agree on the need to promote improved working conditions and an improved standard of living for workers" (Art. 117 E.E.C.) and for the Commission to promote closer co-operation in the fields of, *inter alia*, employment, labour law and working conditions, vocational training, social security, the prevention of occupational accidents, occupational hygiene and the right of association (Art. 118 E.E.C.). Article 118A (inserted by the SEA) allows the Council, acting by qualified majority vote, to adopt Directives on health and safety issues. Article 119 then lays down the principle of equal pay for equal work. These provisions have provided the base for a large number of Community-wide social measures, but the requirement of unanimity proved a stumbling block to wider developments. Nevertheless, the Commission has made wide use of Arts. 118a and 100a E.E.C. to facilitate decision-making by taking advantage of the qualified majority voting procedure applicable to these provisions. Some of the legal bases chosen have proven controversial. A prime example is the Draft Directive on the organisation of working time (COM(89) 568 final), which the Commission initiated as a "health and safety" measure under Art. 118a. The U.K., currently with no statutory limit to the length of the working week nor any right to holidays, either paid or unpaid, is to challenge the legal base of this measure (*Hansard*, H.C. Vol. 217, col. 1056 and *Financial Times*, June 1, 1993). The Directive was adopted on November 23, 1993 and the U.K. Government confirmed it would seek the amendment of the measure in the E.C.J. under Art. 173 E.C. (see *The Times*, November 24, 1993). The opposition to such legislative initiatives underlines the U.K. Government's stance on what it sees as expensive social provisions which damage the competitiveness of the Country's economy. This approach has been decried as the "sweat shop" approach by many critics of the Government's opt-out.

In December 1989, all the Member States of the Community, except the U.K., signed the Community Charter of the Fundamental Social Rights of Workers (the Social Charter). This charter is purely declaratory in nature and amounts to a political commitment among the signatories to further progress in a number of broadly defined social spheres. Some Commission initiatives under the Action Programme (COM(89) 568 final), on certain of the proposals contained in the Social Charter, have proven successful. These include the recent Directive on the protection at work of pregnant women and on maternity provisions (Dir. 92/85/E.E.C.) passed under Art. 118a E.E.C. The 11 Member States of the Community, apart from the U.K., were still keen to press on further with more concrete reforms.

The TEU gave them this opportunity. While it does not in any significant way amend the Social Chapter in the E.E.C. Treaty, a unique approach was taken by the 11 Member States keen to progress in more ambitious fields of social policy, in the face of outright U.K. opposition to any such development. The Protocol on Social Policy annexed to the TEU (Protocol No. 14, below) records the agreement of all 12 Member States that 11 of them (*i.e.* with the exception of the U.K.) are authorised to utilise the existing European Community institutions to implement a Social Policy Agreement. This Social Policy Agreement, annexed to the Protocol itself, amounts to a revised and updated Social Chapter, providing for wider areas of Community competence in the social field and more importantly an increase in the scope of qualified majority voting. These measures, originally intended by the Dutch Presidency to replace the existing Social Chapter, include qualified majority voting in the areas of workers' health and safety, working conditions, the information and consultation of workers and sexual equality in the labour market and the workplace. Unanimous agreement is required for progress in the fields of social security, protection of workers on termination of their employment, conditions of employment for legally resident non-Community nationals and financial contributions for the promotion of employment and job creation.

These increases in the power of the Community in the social sphere are undeniably modest. While the increase in qualified majority voting from just health and safety to four new areas may well expedite decision-making in these new fields, a number of the provisions merely amount to duplications of pre-existing measures, for example, health and safety measures are already covered by Art. 118a E.E.C. while the equality provision in Art. 119 E.E.C. is essentially rewritten in Art. 6 of the Agreement. The only addition to this Article consists of the controversial provision permitting positive discrimination for women in the labour market. Article 2(6) of the Agreement, in a provision which could well have been drafted for the U.K. Government, declares that the article does not to apply to pay, the right of association, the right to strike or the right to impose lock-outs.

The convoluted legal implications of the existence of two sets of provisions concerning social policy will be dealt with later in these annotations (see the General Note on Chap. 1 of Title VIII of the E.C. Treaty below).

During parliamentary consideration of the Bill, the Labour party attempted to secure the application of the Social Policy Agreement to the U.K. Opposition amendment number 27, passed without a vote, because the Government realised it could not defeat an alliance of Tory Euro-sceptics and the main opposition parties, denied the force of domestic law to the Social Protocol by specifically excluding it from the revised list of Community Treaties under s.1(2) of the European Communities Act 1972. In other words, removing the Social Policy Agreement and the U.K. opt-out from it from the directly effective provisions of domestic law. The original Government legal advice, as enunciated by the minister responsible for the Bill, Tristan Garel-Jones (*Hansard*, H.C. Vol. 217, col. 403), that such an amendment would render the Treaty unratifiable because of the material inconsistency between the Treaty and U.K. law was reversed by the Attorney General. He found that, while inconsistencies ought to be strongly resisted, this principle "was not one of tightest law" (*Hansard*, H.C. Vol. 219, col. 737). The dualist nature of U.K. law, he stated, allowed the ratification of a Treaty protocol without express parliamentary approval for it: domestic incorporating legislation was only necessitated by provisions which affect domestic law. The Social Protocol makes express provision that such domestic effects are excluded. The Social Policy Agreement applies only to the other 11 Member States and does not have any internal effects in the U.K. The existing Social Chapter is in the E.C. Treaty itself, which is given internal effect by s.1(2) of the 1972 Act. The Attorney General did, however, make clear that future inconsistencies, if revealed in subsequent E.C.J. proceedings, would require amendments to domestic law to bring it into line with Community obligations.

The progress of the Bill through Parliament reflected the strength of feeling on all sides over the issues raised. By the time the Bill reached the start of its committee stage in the House of Commons, it had already spent more time before Parliament than the SEA had spent *in toto*. Major concerns over the federal implications of the Bill, the opt-outs from the Social Policy Agreement and the third stage of economic and monetary union, as well as the hold ups passed on from the Danish no vote in June 1992 and the turmoil in the financial markets which led to the withdrawal of sterling from the ERM in September 1992, all served to prolong the passage of the Bill through Parliament.

The Bill finally received Royal Assent on July 20, 1993 and the resolutions on the Social Protocol were passed on July 22 and 23, 1993 (see note on s.7 below).

ABBREVIATIONS

COREPER	:	Committee of Permanent Representatives
E.C.	:	European Community
E.E.C.	:	European Economic Community
E.C.H.R.	:	European Convention on Human Rights
E.C.J.	:	European Court of Justice
ECOFIN	:	Council of Finance Ministers
ECOSOC	:	Economic and Social Committee
ECSC	:	European Coal and Steel Community
EMS	:	European Monetary System
ERM	:	Exchange Rate Mechanism
Euratom	:	European Atomic Energy Community
SEA	:	Single European Act
TEU	:	Treaty on European Union

Treaty on European Union

1.—(1) In section 1(2) of the European Communities Act 1972, in the definition of "the Treaties" and "the Community Treaties", after paragraph (j) (inserted by the European Communities (Amendment) Act 1986) there shall be inserted the words "and

(k) Titles II, III and IV of the Treaty on European Union signed at Maastricht on 7th February 1992, together with the other provisions of the Treaty so far as they relate to those Titles, and the Protocols adopted at Maastricht on that date and annexed to the Treaty establishing the European Community with the exception of the Protocol on Social Policy on page 117 of Cm 1934".

(2) For the purpose of section 6 of the European Parliamentary Elections Act 1978 (approval of treaties increasing the Parliament's powers) the Treaty on European Union signed at Maastricht on 7th February 1992 is approved.

GENERAL NOTE

The purpose of this section is to give the Maastricht amendments to the Community Treaties the force of law in the U.K. This is in line with the U.K. practice of "incorporating all amendments to the Community treaties into domestic law; thus avoiding unnecessary complexity in the implementation of Community obligations" (*per* Tristan Garel-Jones, then Foreign Office Minister with responsibility for European Community Affairs, *Hansard*, H.C. Vol. 217, col. 364).

Subs. (1)

This appends a new para. (k) to s.1(2) of the 1972 Act; thus giving the force of law to Titles II, III and IV of the TEU. The core Community treaties, as amended by the TEU, now stand to be applied in accordance with the well-known principles of the 1972 Act, and E.C.J. jurisprudence.

The Act does not, however, make provision for the incorporation of Titles I, V, VI and VII, except in so far as they relate to Titles II, III and IV. Implementing legislation was only necessitated by measures giving rise to Community obligations. However, the convoluted structure of the Union makes some recourse to the excluded titles unavoidable.

This is especially true as regards Titles I and VII; hybrid provisions covering matters relating to both the Community and the Union. Much of Title VII consists of provisions previously in the E.E.C. Treaty, such as Art. N on the process of Treaty amendments and Art. O regarding accession agreements with new Member States. It is clear that recourse to these provisions is necessary to gain a full picture of the Treaty régime applicable to the European Communities. The inclusion of the words "in so far as they relate to Titles II, III and IV" makes such recourse legally binding. Thus legislative effect is given to operational provisions of the TEU that are necessary for the functioning of the European Communities.

As Tristan Garel-Jones made clear in Committee: "the preamble to Title I, the common provisions and Title VII . . . do not give rise to Community rights and obligations, but the preamble in the common provisions may play a rôle in interpreting other provisions in Titles II, III and IV, under which rights and obligations can arise" (*Hansard*, H.C. Vol. 215, col. 191–192). As regards the operative provisions of Title VII, although the adoption of Community Acts is not permitted, they clearly have an effect on the way in which the Community will operate.

The non-inclusion of Titles V and VI of the TEU on a common foreign and security policy and co-operation in the fields of justice and home affairs respectively, does not mark a departure of principle for the U.K.'s handling of legislation in relation to the European Communities. Under the European Communities (Amendment) Act 1986, the provisions of the SEA were not wholly incorporated into domestic law. Those aspects of the SEA, which were not justiciable by the E.C.J., dealing with the inter-governmental European Council and European Political Co-operation were explicitly not made a part of U.K. law.

Tristan Garel-Jones, explaining the non-inclusion of certain of the Titles of the TEU in the Act, stated that the configuration of the Act was designed to reflect the Treaty structure. Although conceding that the Act does cover the common provisions, the preamble and Titles I and VII, where they are consequential to Titles II, III and IV, he made no such assertion as regards Titles V and VI (*Hansard*, H.C. Vol. 215, col. 192). Nevertheless, the wording of the Act does not preclude reference to Titles V and VI in the same manner. Thus a U.K. court could take notice of matters under Titles V and VI if they related to Community activities. This is likely to be of only academic concern for domestic law, given the nature of the essentially inter-governmental process under these pillars.

The protocols adopted at Maastricht

Article 239 E.C., unrevised by the TEU, provides that protocols annexed to the E.C. Treaty are to be considered as an "integral part" of it. Their express inclusion as a part of the amended "Community treaties" in this section might thus appear superfluous. Nevertheless, the unprecedented utilisation of protocols in the TEU might well justify such reinforcement of their existence. There are 17 protocols annexed to the E.C. Treaty (one of these, Protocol No. 17 or the "Irish Abortion Protocol" is annexed to the TEU and all three of the Treaties establishing the European Communities). Of the 17 protocols, a number are in-depth elaborations of Treaty Articles, such as the Statutes of the European System of Central Banks and the European Monetary Institute (Protocols Nos. 3 and 4 respectively). The use of protocols in these circumstances prevents excessive cluttering of the Treaty itself and permits the well-known numbering system to remain relatively intact. Other protocols amount to little more than opt-outs by certain Member States. These explicit derogations from the *acquis communautaire* include Protocol No.1— the Danish "second home" Protocol and Protocol No. 17—the Irish Abortion Protocol. The emergence of such measures is profoundly damaging to the legal structure of the Communities, built upon the principle of uniform supremacy over national law. The possibility of Member States selecting which areas of their laws ought to remain outwith the scope of Community influence prejudices the unique nature of the Community system. Any derogation from the uniform application of Community law in each Member State makes a mockery of the TEU's expressed desire to "maintain in full the *acquis communautaire* and build on it" (Arts. B and C of the TEU). This is equally true of the opt-outs negotiated at Maastricht in the fields of economic and monetary union and social policy. The Danish and U.K. opt-outs from the third stage of economic and monetary union and the U.K. opt-out from the Social Policy Agreement are contained in protocols annexed to the E.C. Treaty. While such derogations have been witnessed in the past, they generally concerned specific time periods of derogation, during which the Member State was to equip itself for subsequent compliance. The Maastricht derogations are potentially timeless, and only changed political conditions in the Member States concerned will alter the situation. In the meantime, the risk of the damaging scenario of a two-speed Community is all too apparent. See Curtin, (1993) 30 C.M.L.Rev. 17–69 at 44.

With the exception of the Protocol on Social Policy on page 117 of Cm. 1934

This clause is present as a result of political machinations in the parliamentary stages. The U.K. opt-out from the Social Policy Agreement in Protocol No. 14 marked the agreement of all 12 Member States that 11 of them, with the exception of the U.K., could use Community institutions to develop the social principles contained in the agreement annexed to the Protocol. Opposition amendment no. 27 inserted the words "with the exception of the Protocol on Social Policy". The aim of the Labour and Liberal Parties was that the Government would find it necessary to convene a rapid fire inter-governmental conference to amend the TEU to permit U.K. admittance to the Social Policy Agreement. Tory rebels on the other hand, aware of the political capital made by Prime Minister John Major out of his opt-out from the Social Policy Agreement, hoped to force the non-ratification of the Treaty.

The original s.1 reflected the U.K. practice of matching every part of the core Community Treaties with provisions in the European Communities Act 1972 (as amended), in order to avoid potential conflicts between U.K. and E.C. law. This practice meant that the Protocol on Social Policy was included in the measures to be given effect to in domestic law. The original Government legal advice was in accordance with this traditional U.K. practice; the effect of the adoption of the amendment would be "that U.K. law would not conform to the treaty's provisions, so it would be impossible for the U.K. to ratify the treaty" (*Hansard,* H.C. Vol. 217, col. 403).

On February 15, 1993, the Foreign Secretary made a statement to the House of Commons where he made it clear that this assertion was not correct: "while incorporation of the Protocol in domestic law is desirable, it is not necessary for ratification or implementation of the Maastricht Treaty. In other words, there would be no impediment to ratification if the amendment were carried because acts adopted under the Protocol would still not apply to the U.K." (*Hansard,* H.C. Vol. 219, col. 27). The Attorney General reiterated such arguments in a special statement to the Commons on February 22, 1993 (*Hansard,* H.C. Vol. 219, col. 738).

Despite this subsequent legal advice, the Labour party still pushed the issue to a vote. The inclusion of the amendment means that the Protocol is not a part of domestic law and, while this did not prevent ratification of the treaty which was the duty of the executive, it might lead to subsequent legal conflicts between E.C. and U.K. law. The potential for, and effects of, any such challenges are assessed in the notes on the Treaty social provisions themselves (Arts. 117–122 E.C. and see Curtin, (1993) 30 C.M.L.Rev. 17, 52–61). The advice of the Attorney General with regard to amendments to the Bill in general was that: "Any amendment to the Bill that, by preventing incorporation of a treaty provision into our domestic law, makes it impossible for the U.K. to implement its Community obligations would cause us to regard ourselves as unable to ratify the Treaty and would mean that if we did ratify the Treaty we should be in breach of our Treaty obligations as soon as the Treaty came into effect" (*Hansard,* H.C. Vol. 219, col. 737). The U.K. Government felt able to continue with the ratification of the Treaty, despite amendment 27, because the piece of law not incorporated into U.K. law simply permits the other 11 Member States to use the Community institutions for the purpose of developing their own Social Policy Agreement; it therefore ought not to give rise to domestic obligations.

In *R.* v. *Secretary of State for Foreign and Commonwealth Affairs, ex p. Rees-Mogg* [1993] 3 C.M.L.R. 101, counsel for Lord Rees-Mogg, David Pannick Q.C., argued that the failure to incorporate the Social Protocol into domestic law by s.1(1) of the Act meant that, if the U.K. ratified the Protocol, the Treaty would affect domestic law without parliamentary approval. This might happen because the European Court's interpretation of the E.C. Treaty may be influenced by provisions of the Social Policy Agreement between the 11 Member States other than the U.K., provided for by the Social Protocol. The example given was that the interpretation of Art. 119 E.C. could be altered due to the impact of Art. 6 of the Social Policy Agreement. The Queen's Bench Division stated that: "this possible indirect effect is far too slender a basis on which to support Mr Pannick's argument. We conclude that the Government would not, by ratifying the Protocol, be altering or affecting the content of domestic law without Parliamentary approval" (at p. 113).

Subs. (2)

The European Parliamentary Elections Act 1978, passed in order to permit elections to the European Parliament by direct universal suffrage, contains, in s.6, a statutory fetter on the prerogative power to conclude treaties. Section 6 of the 1978 Act was introduced by the Government at the committee stage to subdue concerns from back-benchers over the possibility that powers of the European Parliament might be increased at the expense of Westminster without the consent of the latter body (*Hansard,* H.C. Vol. 940, col. 820). Section 6 states that: "no treaty which provides for any increase in the powers of the parliament shall be ratified unless it has been approved by an Act of Parliament".

Section 1(2) attempts to provide the explicit parliamentary authorisation necessitated by the 1978 Act and mirrors s.3 of the European Communities (Amendment) Act 1986 which approved the SEA for the same purpose.

In *R.* v. *Secretary of State for Foreign and Commonwealth Affairs, ex p. Rees-Mogg* [1993] 3 C.M.L.R. 101, Lord Rees-Mogg's counsel argued that s.6 of the 1978 Act had not been satisfied in relation to the Protocol on Social Policy, because that Protocol increased the powers of the European Parliament and s.1(2) only referred to the "Treaty on European Union" and not to the protocols attached to the E.C. Treaty. He argued that the Social Protocol was annexed to the E.C. Treaty and not to the TEU and could not therefore be authorised by any reference to the TEU. Lord Justice Lloyd, giving the judgment of the Queen's Bench Division, noted that the only provision relating to ratification of the TEU and the protocols was Art. R of the TEU. The reference in that Article to "this Treaty" included the protocols annexed by the TEU to the E.C. Treaty. Indeed the instruments of ratification already lodged by France, Spain, Portugal, Ireland, the Netherlands and Denmark contained no reference to the protocols, they simply ratified the TEU. The Queen's Bench Division concluded that ratification of the TEU automatically involves ratification of the Protocols annexed to the E.C. Treaty (see pp. 109–110).

Mr Pannick's second line of argument for construing "Treaty on European Union" in s.1(2) of the Act as not including the protocols was the fact that those words as utilised in s.1(1) of the Act clearly did not include the protocols. The Queen's Bench Division noted that the Treaty and the protocols had to be referred to separately in s.1(1) in order to indicate which parts of the Treaty and which protocols were to be incorporated into domestic law and which were not. Its conclusion that the meaning of "Treaty on European Union" varied according to where it was used in the Act and did not always exclude the protocols was reinforced by reference to the long title of the Act. The court concluded that "Treaty on European Union" in s.1(2) included the protocols, and therefore s.6 of the 1978 Act was satisfied in relation to the Social Protocol. The court noted, *obiter*, that if s.1(2) had been ambiguous, this would have been an appropriate case to resort to *Hansard*, in accordance with the principles stated in *Pepper (Inspector of Taxes)* v. *Hart* [1992] 3 W.L.R. 1032. Statements by the Foreign Secretary in the House of Commons and the Lord Privy Seal in the House of Lords supported the construction of s.1(2) arrived at by the court. Lord Justice Lloyd said, "Parliament has enacted s.1(2) in the light of clear statements made in both Houses as to its intended scope" (at p. 112). It is a little worrying that statements made by the executive in Parliament on the meaning of a section in a highly controversial Bill are to be taken as indicative of the meaning Parliament intended to give to the Act. Judges should be very careful not to impute the intentions of the executive onto the legislature.

During the course of the debate on February 22, 1993, several members raised the possibility that an amendment very similar to amendment 27, excepting the Social Protocol, might have an altogether different effect if it were attached to cl. 1(2) instead of cl. 1(1). An amendment in these terms, number 443, was then tabled. While this amendment did not get to a vote, its potential implications are worth some consideration. The Social Protocol has an annex which contains the Social Policy Agreement. In accordance with this Agreement the 11 Member States other than the U.K. could introduce social policy directives using the co-operation procedure provided for thereunder (Art. 189c E.C.). This would therefore give new powers to the European Parliament in the field of social policy. In certain other areas, listed under Art. 2(3) of the Agreement, the 11 state Council would decide by unanimity with a right of consultation for the European Parliament over any such measures. Therefore, the Social Protocol, by virtue of the Agreement annexed to it, does increase the powers of the European Parliament. Indeed, this point was accepted by counsel for the Foreign Secretary in *R.* v. *Secretary of State for Foreign and Commonwealth Affairs*, ex p. *Rees-Mogg, supra,* at p. 107. It therefore follows that, if removal of the Protocol from the approved measures under cl. 1(2) had been effected, the requirements of the 1978 Act might not have been satisfied.

Economic and monetary union

2. No notification shall be given to the Council of the European Communities that the United Kingdom intends to move to the third stage of economic and monetary union (in accordance with the Protocol on certain provisions relating to the United Kingdom adopted at Maastricht on 7th February 1992) unless a draft of the notification has first been approved by Act of Parliament and unless Her Majesty's Government has reported to Parliament on its proposals for the co-ordination of economic policies, its role in the European Council of Finance Ministers (ECOFIN) in pursuit of the objectives of Article 2 of the Treaty establishing the European Community as provided for in

Articles 103 and 102a, and the work of the European Monetary Institute in preparation for economic and monetary union.

GENERAL NOTE

The opt-out negotiated by the U.K. Government from the third stage of economic and monetary union, encompassed in the Protocol on certain provisions relating to the U.K., makes it quite clear that the U.K. will not pass onto the third stage of economic and monetary union automatically. The move to this stage, with a single European currency and the independent European Central Bank overseeing the money supply, is conditional on a subsequent decision of the U.K. John Major made clear that in his opinion the Treaty did not make it a legal requirement that an Act of Parliament be passed to approve a move to the third stage (*Hansard*, H.C. Vol. 208, col. 264). This viewpoint is probably the correct one. Parliamentary authorisation of the transition to the third stage seems to be politically rather than legally necessitated, given the gravity of full economic and monetary union. Early Governmental acceptance of the rôle of Parliament is inferred from the wording of the protocol preamble, which talks of a decision of "Government and Parliament". The requirement set out in s.2 of the 1993 Act that an Act of Parliament will be needed to authorise the move to the third stage of economic and monetary union was part of the original Bill and not a concession forced upon the Government by Parliament.

The requirement that the Government report to Parliament on its proposals for the co-ordination of economic policies and its rôle in the Council of Finance Ministers (ECOFIN) was added as a result of an opposition amendment. It adds little of substance, given that it is Government practice to report to Parliament on Council matters. This merely represents a formalisation of convention. However the secrecy of Council negotiations means that there is no independent method of checking the governmental assertions on the proceedings of the Council meetings. This section appears to be in line with the desire of the opposition to see ECOFIN develop as a politically accountable counterpart of any European Central Bank (*Hansard*, H.C. Vol. 221, col. 965). ECOFIN's rôle in setting the economic framework, through its responsibilities for the broad guidelines of economic policy and for multilateral surveillance under Art. 103 E.C., gives it an enhanced status during the transition stage to full economic and monetary union. It will have further powers in the third stage, including the setting of exchange rate system agreements with non-Community countries (Art. 109 E.C.) and imposing sanctions on Member States who maintain excessive Government deficits (Art. 104c(9) E.C.).

Annual report by Bank of England

3. In implementing Article 108 of the Treaty establishing the European Community, and ensuring compatibility of the statutes of the national central bank, Her Majesty's Government shall, by order, make provision for the Governor of the Bank of England to make an annual report to Parliament, which shall be subject to approval by a Resolution of each House of Parliament.

GENERAL NOTE

During the second stage of economic and monetary union, each Member State is to start the process leading to the independence of its central bank, in accordance with Art. 108 E.C. (Art. 109e(5) E.C.). The completion of this process requires the compliance of national law with the E.C. Treaty and the Statute of the European System of Central Banks. Chapter III, Art. 7 of the Statute declares that the bank shall not "seek or take instructions from the Community institutions or from any government of a Member State or other body". This provision means that if the U.K. were to join the single currency, s.4 of the Bank of England Act 1946 would have to be repealed, given its assertion that the Treasury may "from time to time give such directions to the Bank . . . [as] they think necessary in the public interest". However, the Bank of England is only legally required to be independent of the Treasury if the U.K. moves to the third stage of economic and monetary union (see para. 5 of the U.K. opt-out Protocol exempting the U.K. from Art. 108 E.C.). It would seem that Art. 109e(5) E.C.'s requirement to start the process towards central bank independence during the second stage can be satisfied by the U.K. simply by talking about how an independent Bank of England might operate.

Section 3 requires the Governor of the Bank of England to make an annual report to Parliament, which shall be subject to approval by a Resolution of each House. Mr George Robertson, then Labour spokesperson on European Affairs, speaking on the amendment, hailed it as historic, being the first time in British history that the Governor of the Bank of England will be required to report to the House (*Hansard*, H.C. Vol. 224, col. 244). Earlier in the proceedings, the possibility of parliamentary rejection of the Report was similarly lauded (*Hansard*, H.C. Vol. 150, col. 965). The effect of such a negative resolution is open to question. Politically, the rejection by either House of the report of the Governor would certainly be significant, but in legal terms it might be less than determinative. If the U.K. becomes a party to the single currency, the Bank would be under an obligation to maintain its independence and this would certainly include not bowing to parliamentary pressure in the form of a negative resolution on the Bank's report.

The major opportunity the section offers is for increased parliamentary scrutiny of the workings of the independent European System of Central Banks. The Bank of England, as a component part of that system, will be legally bound to report to Parliament and thus a degree of accountability is assured. This provision thus mirrors Art. 109b(3) E.C. which requires the European Central Bank to report on the activities of the European System of Central Banks and on monetary policy to the European Parliament, the Council and the Commission. The European Parliament can then hold a debate on the report. The independent European Central Bank need not pay any heed to the views of the European Parliament. One of the key issues if the U.K. Parliament is asked to opt-in to the third stage of economic and monetary union will be the democratic accountability of the Central Bank.

The clause introduced at the committee stage required only the approval of the House of Commons but was amended at the report stage to encompass both houses (*Hansard*, H.C. Vol. 172, col. 246), it being common practice that when votes on free standing resolutions are called for in one house, the same opportunity is provided to the other House.

Information for Commission

4. In implementing the provisions of Article 103(3) of the Treaty establishing the European Community, information shall be submitted to the Commission from the United Kingdom indicating performance on economic growth, industrial investment, employment and balance of trade, together with comparisons with those items of performance from other member States.

GENERAL NOTE

This provision, introduced by opposition amendment, merely elaborates on the requirement of Art. 103(3) E.C. that the Member States submit such information to the Commission as they deem necessary to assist in the process of multilateral surveillance of the economic policies of Member States. It would seem again to reflect the opposition desire to see emphasis placed on factors such as employment and industrial investment, as well as more monetarist factors such as the level of government deficit. The provisions of this section are quite in keeping with the Treaty itself, simply putting meat on the bones of Art. 103(3) E.C. in the U.K. context. The section's requirement of a comparative assessment of the U.K.'s economic performance goes further than the Treaty necessitates. Such a survey of the European economic situation will provide the U.K. Parliament with a useful overview of the U.K.'s position in Europe but is unlikely to prove particularly influential in the Commission, which already keeps close track of such figures.

Convergence criteria: assessment of deficits

5. Before submitting the information required in implementing Article 103 (3) of the Treaty establishing the European Community, Her Majesty's Government shall report to Parliament for its approval an assessment of the medium term economic and budgetary position in relation to public investment expenditure and to the social, economic and environmental goals set out in Article 2, which report shall form the basis of any submission to the Council and Commission in pursuit of their responsibilities under Articles 103 and 104c.

GENERAL NOTE

Under Art. 103(3) E.C., the convergence of the Member States' economic performances is to be assessed on the basis of information forwarded to the Commission by the Member States on any important measures taken by them in the field of their economic policy and such other information as they deem necessary. On the basis of this information the Commission will forward reports to the Council, which will be utilised to assess the degree of compliance with the broad guidelines on economic policy set down by the Council under Art. 103(2) E.C. Section 5, included at the Committee stage by an opposition back-bencher, Mr Andrew Smith, was described as "a modest success on the economic front". It reflects opposition concern at the patently monetarist characteristics of the planned path to economic union, with its primary goal of price stability (Art. 3a E.C.). The section emphasises the existence of the general goals of the Treaty set out in Art. 2, which tie the achievement of a high degree of economic convergence with "a high level of employment and of social protection and the raising of the standard of living and quality of life". While this section may have admirable aims, its existence will have little effect on the application of the E.C. Treaty and, in particular, the weight to be attached to the particular goals of the Community. That will be a matter for subsequent political practice and judicial pronouncement at the European level. Scepticism at the legal effect of the "social" provisions under Art. 2 was voiced in the Commons. The reference in Art. 102a E.C. that "Member States shall conduct their economic policies with a view to contributing to the objectives of the Community, as defined in Art. 2" was declared to be prejudiced by the "monetarist imperatives" to be found in the other clauses of the Treaty (*Hansard*, H.C. Vol. 224, col. 88). The often quoted example is the excessive Government deficit level of 3 per cent. as set out in Art. 104c E.C. and the annexed Protocol, as well as the pre-eminent pursuit of price stability under the new monetary provisions of the Treaty (Art. 105 E.C.).

The section simply provides for enhanced parliamentary scrutiny of the economic criteria being passed to the Commission. Information relating to the multilateral surveillance process in the fields of government deficit (Art. 104c E.C.) and the convergence of economic performances (Art. 103 E.C.) will come before Parliament.

It is unclear what form the parliamentary approval will take. Moreover, the effect of such consultation for effective parliamentary scrutiny is ambiguous. While there is little doubt over the importance of the information to be submitted to the Commission, it is then up to the Commission to interpret it and pass it on to the Council. As regards the excessive deficit procedure and the convergence of economic criteria, the U.K. will not be subject to sanctions for failure to comply with the Community guidelines. At most, it will be subject to moral pressure by the publication of Council recommendations. It is only during the third stage of economic and monetary union that majority-imposed sanctions for non-compliance will come into being. Such sanctions can apply only to States which have joined the single currency and only in relation to excessive government deficits (see Art. 104c(11)).

Committee of the Regions

6. A person may be proposed as a member or alternate member for the United Kingdom of the Committee of the Regions constituted under Article 198a of the Treaty establishing the European Community only if, at the time of the proposal, he is an elected member of a local authority.

GENERAL NOTE

This section, inserted despite Government opposition, alters the appointment process to the newly established Committee of the Regions (Art. 198a E.C.). As with its sister body, the Economic and Social Committee (ECOSOC) (Arts. 193–198 E.C.), the Committee of the Regions will consist of 189 members sitting in an advisory capacity in restricted areas of the legislative process. The appointment of members to the ECOSOC and to the Committee of the Regions is by unanimous Council approval of Member State nominees. The unfettered discretion enjoyed by the Government in its selection of members to the ECOSOC is to be restricted marginally with regard to the Committee of the Regions. "The U.K. is limiting the category of persons who can be nominated for appointment to serve on the Committee of the Regions, not purporting to fetter the Council's power of appointment itself" (*Hansard*, H.C. Vol. 224, col. 29). This section requires all those persons proposed by the Government for appointment to the Committee of the Regions to be elected members of a local authority. The definition appears to be a wide one. It includes "any person who was properly elected under the democratic process to any local government authority in Britain" (*Hansard*, H.C. Vol. 224, col. 30). This definition is to include parish councils.

The clause, as originally drafted, could have been read as obliging any member of the Committee of the Regions, upon the termination of their locally elected status to give up their position on the Committee of the Regions also. This would have been in breach of Art. 189a, which provides for a four year renewable period of office for members. The addition of the words "if at the time of the proposal he is an elected member of a local authority", removes the possibility of any such conflict between U.K. and E.C. law and makes provision for the potentially common situation where a U.K. member of the Committee of the Regions is subsequently removed from local office during their European appointment. While local councillors generally serve for a similar four year period of office, their terms are unlikely to be congruent.

While the term of office of Committee members is renewable, it would appear that a member of the Committee no longer in local office will be ineligible for reappointment for a further term.

A Government proposal that members making a worthwhile contribution to the Committee could be renominated, regardless of their ceasing to be a local government representative, was removed in the face of parliamentary opposition (*Hansard*, H.C. Vol. 224, col. 29).

The Government has recently announced the split of the 24 U.K. seats: England is to get 14, Scotland five, Wales three and Northern Ireland two (*The Times*, July 30, 1993).

Commencement (Protocol on Social Policy)

7. This Act shall come into force only when each House of Parliament has come to a Resolution on a motion tabled by a Minister of the Crown considering the question of adopting the Protocol on Social Policy.

GENERAL NOTE

This provision was introduced by the Opposition at the Committee stage, marking their open disapproval of the U.K. opt-out from the Social Policy Agreement (*Hansard*, H.C. Vol. 223, col. 529). In his speech on the new clause, Opposition spokesman George Robertson described it as "the ticking bomb" (at col. 530). He explained that the clause would oblige the Government to table a motion on the Social Protocol, but more importantly it would permit the Labour party to table an amendment withholding Parliament's authorisation for ratification of the Treaty unless the Government subscribed to the Social Policy Agreement.

The Government, faced with certain defeat over the adoption of this measure, accepted it without debate, but the Foreign Secretary, Douglas Hurd, refused to be drawn on the implications of the Labour motion prevailing (*Hansard*, H.C. Vol. 223, col. 548).

During the report stage, the Government successfully altered the wording of the clause to provide for a resolution in both Houses, as opposed to the House of Commons alone (*Hansard*, H.C. Vol. 224, col. 250).

The debate on the Government resolution and the Opposition amendment took place on July 22 and 23, 1993, two months after the third reading in the House of Commons.

The wording of s.7 did not require either House of Parliament actually to approve the Social Protocol, but merely to come to a resolution. This was reflected in the Government motion for debate which ran "this House notes the policy of Her Majesty's government on the adoption of the Protocol on Social Policy". The voting itself could not have been closer. The Labour amendment calling for the postponement of ratification until the U.K. acceded to the Social Policy Agreement was defeated only by the Speaker's casting vote and thus thorny constitutional questions over the ability of the Government to go ahead and ratify the Treaty regardless were narrowly avoided (the next day it was revealed that there had been a miscount and the Government had, in fact, secured a majority of one). However, the Government failed to secure parliamentary approval for its own neutral motion. The Tory rebels swelling the Opposition ranks in these votes succumbed to party pressure and backed the Government the next day, when the adoption of the motion was tied to a general vote of confidence in the Government. For critical commentary on the legality of the resolution passed by the House of Commons on July 23, 1993, see Marshall, "The Maastricht Proceedings" (1993) Pub. Law 402–407.

Section 7 is now of purely historical interest. (For debates and votes on this resolution see *Hansard*, H.C. Vol. 229, cols. 521–612; 623–725).

Short title

8. This Act may be cited as the European Communities (Amendment) Act 1993.

TREATY ESTABLISHING THE EUROPEAN COMMUNITY
(previously the European Economic Community)

ADOPTED BY THE E.C. MEMBER-STATES

(Done at Rome)   25 March 1957

(as amended, most recently at Maastricht by the Treaty on European Union)   7 February 1992

GENERAL NOTE
Entry into force (in amended form): November 1, 1993
Territorial application: E.C. Member States

ARRANGEMENT OF ARTICLES

TITLE V: COMMON RULES ON COMPETITION, TAXATION AND APPROXIMATION OF LAWS

CHAPTER 1 (RULES ON COMPETITION)

SECTION 1: RULES APPLYING TO UNDERTAKINGS

85. Prohibited agreements and concerted practices; conditions for exemption.
86. Prohibition of abuse of a dominant position.
87. Legislative priorities and procedures.
88. Transitional enforcement powers of national authorities.
89. Transitional enforcement powers of the Commission.
90. Public undertakings.

SECTION 2: DUMPING

91. Protective measures within the Community; free reimportation of goods in free circulation.

SECTION 3: AIDS GRANTED BY STATES

92. Prohibited and permissible State aids.
93. Policing and enforcement powers of the Commission; referral to the Council; obligation on Member States to notify aids.
94. Legislative powers and procedures.

CHAPTER 2 (TAX PROVISIONS)

95. Prohibition on discriminatory taxation; cessation of existing discrimination.
96. Prohibition on excessive export refunds.
97. Establishment of average rates for turnover taxes.
98. Prohibition on unauthorised export refunds or countervailing import charges.
99. Harmonisation of legislation for indirect taxes.

CHAPTER 3 (APPROXIMATION OF LAWS)

100. Legislative powers and procedure; unanimity.
100a. Alternative legislative powers and procedure for completing the internal market; majority voting; laws relating to fiscal matters or those relating to the free movement of person and workers' rights excepted; notification of post-harmonisation national protectionist measures.
100b. Inventory of national laws not harmonised.
100c. Visa requirements for non-Community nationals; uniform format for visas.
100d. Role of the Co-ordinating Committee set up under Article K.4 of the European Union Treaty.
101. Elimination of distortions of competition in the common market caused by differing national laws.
102. Consultation on national legislative proposals likely to distort competition in the common market.

TITLE VI: ECONOMIC AND MONETARY POLICY

CHAPTER 1 (ECONOMIC POLICY)

102a. Economic policies of the Member States.
103. Co-ordination of economic policies; establishment of guidelines for economic policies; monitoring of developments in the Member States; action on diverging policies.
103a. Power of the Council to adapt to the economic situation; Community financial assistance to Member States.
104. Prohibition on any public entity having credit facilities with the European Central Bank (ECB) or any national central bank.
104a. Prohibition on any public entity having favoured access to financial institutions.
104b. Prohibition on Community liability for the commitments of national public entities and on one Member State being liable for the commitments of public entities in another.
104c. Avoidance of excessive government deficits; monitoring of budgetary discipline; enforcement by the Council.

CHAPTER 2 (MONETARY POLICY)

105. Objectives and tasks of the European System of Central Banks (ESCB); consultation with the ECB.
105a. Authorisation for issuing bank notes and coins; harmonisation of denominations and specifications of coins.
106. Composition and control of the ESCB; adoption and amendment of the Statute of the ESCB; legal personality of the ECB.
107. Independence of the ECB and national central banks.
108. Compatibility of national legislation with the Treaty and the Statute of the ESCB.
108a. Legislative and enforcement powers of the ECB.
109. Powers of the Council as regards monetary and foreign exchange matters; treaty-making powers; adjustment of ECU central rates; competence of Member States.

CHAPTER 3 (INSTITUTIONAL PROVISIONS)

109a. Composition of the governing council and executive board of the ECB.
109b. Right of representation to the Council and the ECB; ESCB annual report.
109c. Establishment of a Monetary Committee; establishment of an Economic and Financial Committee and liquidation of the Monetary Committee.
109d. Consultation with the Commission.

CHAPTER 4 (TRANSITIONAL PROVISIONS)

109e. Second stage of economic and monetary union.
109f. Establishment of the European Monetary Institute.
109g. Composition of the ECU.
109h. Authorisation of protective measures for balance of payments difficulties.
109i. Independent protective measures.
109j. Progress reports on economic and monetary union.
109k. Member States with a derogation.
109l. Third stage of economic and monetary union; establishment of the ESCB and the ECB; liquidation of the EMI; introduction of the ECU as single currency.
109m. Exchange rate policy of Member States with a derogation.

TITLE VII: COMMON COMMERCIAL POLICY

110. World trade and the competitive strength of Community undertakings.
111. [*repealed at Maastricht*]
112. Aid for exports to third countries.
113. Implementation of the common commercial policy; treaties.
114. [*repealed at Maastricht*]
115. Protective measures.
116. [*repealed at Maastricht*]

TITLE VIII: SOCIAL POLICY, EDUCATION, VOCATIONAL TRAINING AND YOUTH

CHAPTER 1 (SOCIAL PROVISIONS)

117. Need to improve working conditions.
118. Promotion of inter-State co-operation in specified areas.
118a. Power to legislate on labour matters.
118b. Dialogue between the social partners.
119. Equal pay for equal work.
120. Paid holiday schemes.
121. Implementation of common measures, particularly on social security.
122. Chapter on social developments in Commission's annual report to the European Parliament.

CHAPTER 2 (THE EUROPEAN SOCIAL FUND)

123. Establishment of European Social Fund.
124. Administration of Fund.
125. Implementing decisions relating to the Fund.

CHAPTER 3 (EDUCATION, VOCATIONAL TRAINING AND YOUTH)

126. Education.
127. Vocational training.

THE AMENDED E.C. TREATY

PREAMBLE

[THE HEADS OF STATE]

DETERMINED to lay the foundations of an ever closer union among the peoples of Europe,

RESOLVED to ensure the economic and social progress of their countries by common action to eliminate the barriers which divide Europe,

AFFIRMING as the essential objective of their efforts the constant improvement of the living and working conditions of their peoples,

RECOGNISING that the removal of existing obstacles calls for concerted action in order to guarantee steady expansion, balanced trade and fair competition,

ANXIOUS to strengthen the unity of their economies and to ensure their harmonious development by reducing the differences existing between the various regions and the backwardness of the less favoured regions,

DESIRING to contribute, by means of a common commercial policy, to the progressive abolition of restrictions on international trade,

INTENDING to confirm the solidarity which binds Europe and the overseas countries and desiring to ensure the development of their prosperity, in accordance with the principles of the Charter of the United Nations, peace and liberty, and calling upon the other peoples of Europe who share their ideal to join in their efforts,

HAVE DECIDED to create a European Community and to this end . . . have agreed as follows.

GENERAL NOTE
Articles which have been altered (other than mere renumbering) have the heading italicised (*e.g. Article 3*). In some cases (*e.g.* new *Art. 128*) the whole text of the Article is new; in others there are only minor drafting changes.

PART ONE (PRINCIPLES)

Article 1

By this Treaty, the HIGH CONTRACTING PARTIES establish among themselves a EUROPEAN COMMUNITY.

GENERAL NOTE
The changed nomenclature from the European Economic Community to the more general European Community is not entirely symbolic. It marks a significant realisation by the Member States that the Community is now more than a strictly economic entity. This is highlighted by the expansion of Art. 3 E.C. to cover 20 different areas of Community interest; including some which are far from specifically economic in nature. This is reflected in the amendment of Art. 3, below, to include a policy in the sphere of the environment, in the promotion of research and technological development and a policy in the social sphere. Also indicative of the broader

scope of the new Community is the inclusion of new legislative bases in the fields of education, culture, public health, consumer protection and development co-operation.

The change in name increases the scope for European Court rulings supporting disputed Community action in spheres without an obvious economic flavour, in, for example, Art. 235 cases. The European Court in the past, however, has not seen the E.C. as an exclusively economic entity ((Case 43/75) *Defrenne (Gabrielle)* v. *Société Anonyme Belge de Navigation Aérienne (SABENA)* [1976] E.C.R. 455 at 472) and as a result, it is not clear to what extent, if any, the change in name will affect its jurisprudence. What is clear is that the E.C.J. has always given Art. 235 E.E.C. a very broad interpretation and has not shied away from ruling in favour of legislation purportedly based on Art. 235 E.E.C. but with, at best, tenuous links with the fulfilment of the then Treaty objectives (see note on Art. 235 E.C. and Usher in *Current Issues in European and International Law*, Ch. 2, (eds. White and Smythe)).

One result of the name change may be increased confusion regarding the different Community bodies: in the past, the combined European Coal and Steel Community, Euratom and E.E.C. were collectively known as the European Community or Communities.

Article 2

The Community shall have as its task, by establishing a common market and an economic and monetary union and by implementing the common policies or activities referred to in Articles 3 and 3a, to promote throughout the Community a harmonious and balanced development of economic activities, sustainable and non-inflationary growth respecting the environment, a high degree of convergence of economic performance, a high level of employment and of social protection, the raising of the standard of living and quality of life, and economic and social cohesion and solidarity among Member States.

GENERAL NOTE

Article 2 is a broadly phrased declaration of the Community's intent. The original provision, drawn up in 1957, was in need of revision to take account of the Community's developing rôle; not least in the light of the further evolution of the Community agreed at Maastricht. Article 2 E.E.C. provided for the promotion throughout the Community of "a harmonious development of economic activities, a continuous and balanced expansion, an increase in stability, an accelerated standard of living and closer relations between the states belonging to it". The amended version of Art. 2, to take account of the new, more diverse Community activities, makes reference to the broadened Art. 3 and the new Art. 3a on economic and monetary union, as well as setting out a number of less specific and more politically oriented declarations of intent.

The existence of such mixed, and even contradictory, declarations will mean a great deal rests on the interpretation of the provisions, and on the political will to see them implemented. The E.C.J., in interpreting an individual Article of the Treaty or provision of Community law will often set it in its context in the Treaty and construe it in the light of the objectives set out in the preamble and Arts. 2 and 3 E.C. The task of the Court in "reconciling and prioritising these objectives" will not be made any easier by the amendments enunciated in the new Art. 2 E.C. (Plender (1982) 2 YEL 57, 75). The Court will have to make the determinative rulings on the application of these provisions. It has not shrunk from this task in the past. Its approach was summarised in Case 28/66 *Netherlands* v. *Commission* [1968] E.C.R. 1, 12 and 13: "Although the general objectives of the Treaty, set out in Arts. 2 and 3, cannot always be pursued simultaneously in their totality, the Community must continuously reconcile these objectives when considered individually and, when conflict arises, must grant such priority to certain general objectives as appear necessary, having regard to the economic facts or circumstances in the light of which it adopts its decisions". Subjective application of the new Art. 2 would appear unavoidable.

Nevertheless, Member States are required to conduct their economic policies with a view to contributing to the achievement of the objectives of the Community as defined in Art. 2 (Art. 102a E.C.). This will not be made any easier by the fact that, in this sphere, the objectives of the Treaty can be regarded as contradictory. Article 2 requires "a high level of employment and of social protection" yet the U.K. Government has repeatedly asserted that the adoption of a high level of social protection makes for uncompetitiveness and thus leads to higher unemployment. On the other hand, some politicians on the left have argued that "non-inflationary growth with the essential goal of price stability" (Art. 3a E.C.) is incompatible with a high level of employment and the provision of wide-ranging social services by the State.

Article 2 also forms the basis for the application of the law-making power of Art. 235 E.C. It could be argued that the expanded Art. 2 provides the Community with a much broader law-making power, but this is questionable in two respects. Firstly, the potentially unlimited legislative power of Art. 235 is constrained by the requirement of unanimity in Council for any legislative measure under that Article and this will tend to prevent agreement on any development of the politically sensitive generalities espoused in the new Art. 2. Secondly, the wording of the original Art. 2 that the Community should seek to promote "closer relations between the states belonging to it" justified the propagation of legislation in a very wide number of areas not specifically covered by the Treaty (see notes on Art. 235 E.C.). Whether or not the more specific provisions in the new Art. 2 permit action under Art. 235 will depend more on political pressures than legal justification.

The new Community *vires* rule in Art. 3b that "any action by the Community must not go beyond what is necessary to achieve the objectives of this Treaty" must also be read in the light of Art. 2.

Article 3

For the purposes set out in Article 2, the activities of the Community shall include, as provided in this Treaty and in accordance with the timetable set out therein:
- (a) the elimination, as between Member States, of customs duties and of quantitative restrictions on the import and export of goods, and of all other measures having equivalent effect;
- (b) a common commercial policy;
- (c) an internal market characterised by the abolition, as between Member States, of obstacles to the free movement of goods, persons, services and capital;
- (d) measures concerning the entry and movement of persons in the internal market as provided for in Article 100c;
- (e) a common policy in the sphere of agriculture and fisheries;
- (f) a common policy in the sphere of transport;
- (g) a system of ensuring that competition in the internal market is not distorted;
- (h) the approximation of the laws of Member States to the extent required for the proper functioning of the common market;
- (i) a policy in the social sphere comprising a European Social Fund;
- (j) the strengthening of economic and social cohesion;
- (k) a policy in the sphere of the environment;
- (l) the strengthening of the competitiveness of Community industry;
- (m) the promotion of research and technological development;
- (n) encouragement for the establishment and development of trans-European networks;
- (o) a contribution to the attainment of a high level of health protection;
- (p) a contribution to education and training of quality and to the flowering of the cultures of the Member States;
- (q) a policy in the sphere of development co-operation;
- (r) the association of the overseas countries and territories in order to increase trade and promote jointly economic and social development;
- (s) a contribution to the strengthening of consumer protection;
- (t) measures in the spheres of energy, civil protection and tourism.

GENERAL NOTE

This Article, setting out in detail the scope of the Communities' activities, highlights the development of the Community. Numerically, the 11 areas of Community competence in the original E.E.C. Treaty have been expanded to 20 diverse Community concerns. The jurisprudence of the E.C.J. on the Art. 5 "fidelity" clause means that the Member States are committed to "facilitate the achievement of the Community's tasks" (Art. 5 E.C., unamended) and in this respect the existence of a common policy at Community level requires the Member States to participate in the furtherance of that policy (Case 805/79 *E.C. Commission* v. *U.K.* [1981] E.C.R. 1045 at 1047). However, as Weatherill has pointed out: "the jurisprudence dealing with the use of Art. 5 to commit Member States to act in accordance with Community policies is rather underdeveloped" (Research Paper, 1993, No. 6, University of Nottingham).

The objectives of the Treaty laid down here must still be read in the light of the developing Art. 5 jurisprudence of the E.C.J. (see Temple Lang (1990) 27 C.M.L.Rev. 645). The Court is increasingly using Art. 5 to draw different agencies into the shaping of the Community. This has been particularly shown in the obligations imposed on the Member State courts to ensure the effective application of Community law, which reached new lengths in the case of *Francovich and Boniface* v. *Italy* (Cases C-6 and C-9/90) [1991] E.C.R. 5359 (see notes on Art. 171). The Court has also ruled that the duty imposed by Art. 5 is applicable to the Community institutions (Case 2/88, *Zwartveld*, [1990] E.C.R. I-3365). This duty was found to require the Commission to take action to support the enforcement of Community law at the national level. It is highly unlikely that the E.C.J. would utilise similar reasoning to force the Commission to adopt legislation in one of the listed policy fields of the Community, unless of course there existed a specific time-frame for the adoption of any such measures. For the E.C.J. to step in in any other situation would amount to an implicit breach of the "separation of powers in the Community", especially the Commission's right of legislative initiative.

Nevertheless, a number of the additions to the list of Community activities in this Article are flattered by a cursory glance. The provisions on culture, education, and public health leave little scope for Community activity, with the emphasis on action at national level. In the majority of these fields, harmonisation is specifically excluded and the Community is simply to support Member State initiatives. These matters will be dealt with in the notes on their respective titles.

In terms of amendments to existing provisions of the section, Arts. 3(a) and (h) E.C. on the functioning of the common market remain unchanged. The variation in the usage of the terms "common" and "internal" markets is worthy of mention here. The amended version of Art. 3(c) contains a specific reference to the creation of an internal market and might give some indication of the scope of the "internal market" in so far as the achievement of the four freedoms of goods, persons, services and capital is to "characterise" the internal market. It is quite possible to argue that the wording of this provision and its express reference to the abolition, *between Member States*, of these restrictions to trade implies that the internal market is wholly concerned with intra-Community matters and cannot impinge on external affairs [emphasis added]. If this approach is taken and a distinction is recognised between the concepts of the common as opposed to the internal market, then the amended Art. 3(g) E.C. (previously Art. 3(h) E.E.C.) on competition distortion is made more interesting. Article 3(g) E.C. now talks of the avoidance of competition in the internal market; the only alteration from Art. 3(h) E.E.C. being the change from "common market" to internal market. The reason for this alteration is unclear. Nowhere in the Treaty is the notion of the "common market" actually defined but, as Wyatt and Dashwood point out, its primary meaning can be gathered from Art. 2 E.E.C. where it is one of the two means by which the Community is to achieve the objectives laid out in the rest of that Article (the other now being the achievement of economic and monetary union). Since the objectives laid out in this Article (and Arts. 3 and 3a E.C. which are now referred to in Art. 2 E.C.) include a number which entail action beyond the Community borders, it would seem that the common market is a wider concept than the internal market (see notes on these Articles and Wyatt and Dashwood, *EC Law* (1993, 3rd ed.), pp. 357–358).

Article 3(b) reflects the new stage in the development of the Communities. The wording, which previously referred to the "establishment of a common customs tariff and a common commercial policy" is altered to reflect the continuing progress of the commercial policy. The reference to the common customs tariff is dropped, presumably because it is an acknowledged part of the common commercial policy and no longer requires an explicit reference in the Treaty.

Similar amendments are made to Arts. 3(e), (f) and (g). Article 3(e) is also amended to provide the first mention of fisheries as part of a common Community policy. This is long overdue. The original definition of agriculture in the E.E.C. Treaty included fisheries as an element of the agriculture sector, covered by Arts. 38–46 (see Annex II to the Treaty). The importance of fisheries to the Community led to the building up of a detailed body of law covering this area. This took place through many Community initiatives and the developing E.C.J. jurisprudence in the field (*e.g.* Case 32/79 *Fishery Conservation Measures, Re; E.C. Commission* v. *U.K. (Danish, French, Irish and Dutch Governments Intervening)* [1980] E.C.R. 2403 and Case 804/79 *Fishery Conservation Measures (No. 2); E.C. Commission* v. *United Kingdom* [1981] E.C.R. 1045). The inclusion of the reference to fisheries as an autonomous Community policy merely confirms current practice. Regulation 3760/92 sets out the principal provisions of the Common Fisheries Policy, see [1992] O.J. L389/1. For earlier developments of that policy see Mathijsen, *A Guide to European Community Law* (5th ed.), at pp. 181–186).

Article 3(d), inserted by the TEU, gives the status of a Community objective to the controversial Art. 100c E.C., which establishes a new procedure for the adoption of measures regarding visas for persons crossing the external borders of the Community. Article 3(d) also elevates to the level of a Community objective the adoption of a common format for visas. Prior to January

1, 1996, decisions as to which third countries' nationals will require visas can be taken by the Council only by unanimity (Art. 100c(1) E.C.), but temporary measures not lasting more than six months can be taken by qualified majority (Art. 100c(2) E.C.). After January 1, 1996 all decisions in this area will be taken by qualified majority.

The old Art. 3(g) E.E.C. on the "co-ordination of the economic policies of the Member States" is removed, having been rendered obsolete by the new provisions on economic and monetary union.

Article 3(i) is updated to cover a social policy and not just the European Social Fund, as was the case following the SEA amendments. The specific provisions in the original Art. 3(i) on the "improved employment opportunities" and the raising of workers' standards of living are removed. Although social policy is elevated to an activity of the Community, the substantive provisions on social policy in the E.C. Treaty were not widened at Maastricht because the U.K. refused to permit any such changes. Instead, the Social Protocol provides for all the Member States except the U.K. to make some modest changes in the social field.

Article 3(j) E.E.C., inserted by the SEA, simply made reference to the European Investment Bank and its rôle in the economic expansion of the Community, whereas the new provision is much broader, referring to the strengthening of economic and social cohesion. The latter concept was introduced into the Treaty by the SEA in Arts. 130a to 130e. It refers to the Structural Funds in the Community, which seek to lessen the disparities between the levels of development in the various regions of the Community. The TEU introduced provision for a new Structural Fund, the so-called Cohesion Fund (Art. 130d E.C.), to aid the four poorest States in the Community (Greece, Ireland, Portugal and Spain). Further details are given in the note on Art. 130d.

Articles 3(k) and (m) E.C. on the environment and research and development respectively are additions to Art. 3. Nevertheless, both spheres have been included in the Treaty since the SEA amendments. The environment has been elevated from an area of Community action to a Community policy, to reflect its slightly more dynamic rôle. One of the changes to its set-up is the recognition that "environmental protection requirements must be integrated into the definition and implementation of other Community policies" (Art. 130r(2) E.C.). While the old Art. 130r (2) E.E.C. stated that "environmental protection requirements shall be a component of the Community's other policies", this was a less rigorous guarantee that environmental issues would be an important part of the Community's policies in areas such as transport and agriculture.

The addition of new objectives to the Treaty may appear impressive in strict numerical terms but the substance is not quite so grand. Many of the areas covered by this article, and dealt with in new provisions in the Treaty itself, are essentially codifying measures. A prime example of a "new" area that was, in fact, already being dealt with, admittedly on a more ad hoc basis, is development co-operation (Art. 3(q) E.C.). Its inclusion in the policy sphere of the Community is, however, indicative of the new general Community competence in this field under the new Title XVII of the amended Treaty. This also marks some progress away from the old development régime under Art. 3(r) E.C. (previously Art. 3(k) E.E.C.), whereby special relationships were envisaged with overseas countries and territories of the Member States (Arts. 131–136a E.C. unamended). The Community has used its powers under Art. 113 E.E.C. to conclude international agreements as part of the common commercial policy; often with development co-operation as a key element (see Case 45/86, *Commission* v. *Council (Generalised Tariff Preferences Case)* [1987] E.C.R. 1493, 1522). Such measures have naturally not been restricted to the strict geographical boundaries laid down in Arts. 131 to 136a E.E.C. Article 3(q) codifies this application of the development provisions.

Articles 3(n), (o) and (p) on trans-European networks, health protection and education, and training and culture respectively, while marking the inclusion of these spheres as part of the Community policies laid down in Part Three of the Treaty, do not create a great deal of scope for Community action. This is reflected in the wording of Art. 3; Community activity in these areas is confined to "encouragement" and "contribution" rather than the harmonisation of the laws and regulations of Member States (except to ensure the inter-operability of trans-European networks in transport, telecommunications and energy infrastructure—see Art. 129c(1)). The inclusion of these areas in Art. 3 is somewhat ambiguous at this stage of the Community's development, given that they remain essentially national competences.

The new Art. 3(l) E.C. on the strengthening of the competitiveness of Community industry (see also Art. 130 E.C.) is an enigmatic provision and, as the Select Committee on European Legislation on its first consideration of the Treaty made clear, could give scope for considerable Community expenditure on measures currently financed by Member States (15th Report, Session 1991–1992, 24, pp. xxxix–lx at p. xlvii). Whether or not this will be the case is dependent on the achievement of unanimity in the Council (Art. 130(3)) and on budgetary constraints.

The final list of Community policies as espoused in the TEU marks something of a watering down of the original Luxembourg draft Treaty. In particular, the Luxembourg proposal included consumer protection, energy, civil protection, and tourism. While consumer protection was retained in the negotiations (see Art. 3(s) E.C. and Art. 129a E.C.), energy, civil protection and tourism are left in the anomalous position of being included in the list of Community objectives (Art. 3(t) E.C.) without corresponding operative provisions in the Treaty itself. Declaration no. 1 on civil protection, tourism and energy appended to the Treaty, provides that these matters will be examined in the 1996 round of Treaty negotiations, to decide upon their potential inclusion as Titles within the Treaty. It remains to be seen whether the political difficulties that prevented their inclusion at Maastricht will be resolved by then.

Article 3a

1. For the purposes set out in Article 2, the activities of the Member States and the Community shall include, as provided in this Treaty and in accordance with the timetable set out therein, the adoption of an economic policy which is based on the close co-ordination of Member States' economic policies, on the internal market and on the definition of common objectives, and conducted in accordance with the principle of an open market economy with free competition.
2. Concurrently with the foregoing, and as provided in this Treaty and in accordance with the timetable and the procedures set out therein, these activities shall include the irrevocable fixing of exchange rates leading to the introduction of a single currency, the ECU, and the definition and conduct of a single monetary policy and exchange rate policy the primary objective of both of which shall be to maintain price stability and, without prejudice to this objective, to support the general economic policies in the Community, in accordance with the principle of an open market economy with free competition.
3. These activities of the Member States and the Community shall entail compliance with the following guiding principles: stable prices, sound public finances and monetary conditions and a sustainable balance of payments.

GENERAL NOTE
   The centre-piece of the TEU amendments is the establishment of a timetable for the progress towards economic and monetary union. This timetable has, however, subsequently been called into question by recessionary pressures in the European economy and the fluctuations in the ERM of the EMS (see Introduction and General Note above and the General Note on Title VI below).
   Article 3a sets out the broad goals of the progress envisaged towards economic and monetary union. It lays down the principles and tasks of the Community in pursuit of the specific provisions in Arts.102a–109m E.C.
   Article 3a(1) lays down the principles underlying the economic aspect of the union. The wording of this provision reflects the essentially decentralised nature of the progress towards economic union. The Community economic policy is to be based on the co-ordination of the Member States' own policies rather than on a single policy applicable to all Member States.
   Article 3a(2) sets out the more specific and definite proposals underlying the achievement of the monetary side of the union process. The wording "irrevocable" and "single" highlight the nature of this process.
   As with Art. 3a(1), this process is to take place in accordance with the timetable set out in the Treaty. It is possible that that timetable may be altered at the inter-governmental conference in 1996. Whatever happens to the specific details of the economic and monetary union process, including the convergence criteria or the timetable itself, the fundamental principles of the process laid down in this Article are likely to remain. The ideas of an open market economy and stable prices, sound public finances, and a sustainable balance of payments are essential prerequisites of any effective convergence of the Member State economies. Article 3a(2) does not apply to the U.K., see para. 5 of the U.K. opt-out Protocol (No. 11).

Article 3b

   The Community shall act within the limits of the powers conferred upon it by this Treaty and of the objectives assigned to it therein.

In areas which do not fall within its exclusive competence, the Community shall take action, in accordance with the principle of subsidiarity, only if and in so far as the objectives of the proposed action cannot be sufficiently achieved by the Member States and can therefore, by reason of the scale or effects of the proposed action, be better achieved by the Community.

Any action by the Community shall not go beyond what is necessary to achieve the objectives of this Treaty.

GENERAL NOTE

This marks the latest stage in the ongoing debate on the allocation of regulatory competences in the Community. The extension of the Community in the TEU provided a forum for the rehashing of the old and unsettled problems of who should do what within the Community, an issue that has been present since the very inception of the E.E.C. The second paragraph of Art. 3b, encompassing the principle of subsidiarity, is the most significant attempt to date, and aims to lay down a guiding framework for the effective exercise of regulatory competences (see on this topic, Wilke and Wallace, Approaches to Subsidiarity and Power Sharing in the European Community, RIIA Discussion Papers No. 27, London, Royal Institute of International Affairs, 1990).

The principle of subsidiarity is implicit in Art. A of the TEU, where it is stated that "This Treaty marks a new stage in the process of creating an ever closer union among the peoples of Europe, *in which decisions are taken as closely as possible to the citizen*" [emphasis added]. The inclusion of the principle in its current format was particularly championed by the U.K. which tends to perceive it as a means of renationalising, and reclaiming competences currently exercised by the Community or, more graphically, as a "prophylactic against the contagion of Brussels" (Mackenzie Stuart in *Constitutional Adjudication in E.C. Law and National Law*, Curtin and O'Keefe (eds.) at p. 21).

Attempts to attach a date to the emergence of the principle have been taken *ad absurdia*; most commentators distinguish the first explicit reference in a Papal Edict in the 1930's: "Let the public authority leave to the lower groupings the care of lesser matters where it would expend an inordinate effort. It will thus be able to carry out more freely and more effectively those functions which belong only to it because it alone can perform them".

Whatever the minutiae of its origins it is a basic tenet of a democratic system that the decision-making process be carried out as close to the citizen as is viable. In so far as it relates to a layered decision-making process, there is little doubt that the principle of subsidiarity is the expression of a particular type of political culture—that of federal states (RTDE (1990) 441, esp. 453). The division of competences between the Länders and the Federal authority in Germany is an example of "subsidiarity" in action in a federal context (Santer in Subsidiarity: The Challenge of Change, EIPA, (Maastricht) 1991, Proceedings of Jacques Delors Colloquium, at p. 19).

The second paragraph of this Article, containing the Community definition of subsidiarity is an attempt to rationalise the division of competences in the Community. This rationalisation will not take place as a direct result of an application of the principle laid down in this Article. Subsidiarity is best understood as a political or constitutional convention, rather than as a legal principle (Europe after Maastricht: Interim Report of Foreign Affairs Select Committee H.C. 205, Session 92/93 at p. vi). It is not, therefore, readily capable of any concrete legal interpretation; the subjectivities inherent in its wording are manifestly evident. All questions on the topic hinge on two factors; subsequent political practice in the Member States and, in particular, the Community institutions; and upon the interpretation of the principle by the E.C.J.

Para. 1

This Paragraph would seem to be an express formulation of the *ultra vires* rule. The first clause: "the Community shall act within the limits of the powers conferred under this Treaty", reiterates the first ground of review under Art. 173 E.C. that the Community shall act only in those areas where it is competent to do so. The reason for the inclusion of the phrase "and of the objectives assigned to it therein" is, as Hartley points out, somewhat more ambiguous. He reasons that it marks another reformulation of an Art. 173 ground of review, that of the misuse of powers (42 I.C.L.Q. 213–237 at 215). Where the Community is acting within the powers assigned to it, it must use those powers only to attain the objectives assigned to it. As the Court puts it "a decision may amount to a misuse of powers if it appears to have been taken for purposes other than those stated" Cases 18, 35/65 *Gutmann* v. *Commission* [1966] E.C.R. 103.

The paragraph, taken as a whole, may not be particularly significant in legal terms. Its inclusion, however, symbolises the desire of certain Member States to be reassured of the specific and limited nature of the Community's sphere of action.

Para. 2

The ambiguities surrounding the Community concept of subsidiarity found in this paragraph make the subsequent examination necessarily subjective. Reference must thus be made to the plethora of literature on the subject: Emiliou, Subsidiarity: An Effective Barrier against the Enterprises of Ambition? (1992) 17 E.L.Rev. 383; Toth, The Principle of Subsidiarity in the Maastricht Treaty (1992) 29 C.M.L.Rev. 1107; Lasok, (1992) 142 New L.J. 1228; Foreign Affairs Committee, Europe after Maastricht, Interim Report, Session 1992–1993; Subsidiarity: the Challenge of Change, Proceedings of Jacques Delors Colloquium, EIPA, 1991; Mackenzie-Stuart in *Constitutional Adjudication in the E.C. and National Law*, Curtin and O'Keefe (eds.) and Cass, The word that saves Maastricht? The Principle of Subsidiarity and the division of powers within the European Community (1992) 29 C.M.L.Rev. 1107–1136.

The first sentence of this paragraph indicates that the subsidiarity principle is not applicable to areas "within the exclusive competence of the Community". The dichotomy between areas of exclusive and concurrent jurisdiction is one well known to students of federalism. Matters within the former category are to be exempt from the application of subsidiarity. They are to be carried out by the Community and there will be no burden on the Community institutions to justify any exercise of their regulatory competences in these areas. Unfortunately, nowhere in the Treaty is any explicit recognition given to the categorisation of particular areas into either exclusive or concurrent competences. This has led some commentators to assert that the result will be that the subsidiarity test will be utilised only in a very restricted number of areas. This viewpoint, which is essentially based on pre-Maastricht European Court jurisprudence, involves two main predicates.

Firstly, there is the doctrine of supremacy of Community law, whereby the enactment of Community legislation in a specified area automatically precludes the application of any conflicting provisions of national law. This is not however an expression of exclusive competence and does not take account of the myriad of areas where both the Community and the Member States exercise complementary competences; conflicting legislation is a special case.

More cogently, opponents of an unquantified "exclusive competences" exception, point to the E.C.J.'s practice in declaring "Community exclusive jurisdiction" in fields where the Community has exercised the right conferred by the Treaty to take binding measures in that area. As Toth makes clear, once the Community has "occupied the field" by taking legislative action in certain areas, any national measure not expressly authorised by the Community or which exceeds the limits of the powers delegated back to the Member State is illegal. The concern is that the continued utilisation of such jurisprudence in the application of Art. 3b will mean that subsidiarity would be applicable only when the Community legislated for the first time in a new field (Hartley, *supra*, at p. 216). The current practice of the Community would tend to suggest that the notion of the Community "occupying the field" is a little archaic. More and more the Community is moving towards minimum harmonisation, which specifically leaves the Member States with the power to adopt stricter laws or set higher standards, provided they satisfy the minimum laid down by the Community (see, *e.g.* Martelmans, Minimum Harmonisation and Consumer Protection [1988] ECLJ 2). A great deal of the internal market operates on this principle; a tacit acknowledgement of the impossibility of legislating for every eventuality and also the need to permit differences in Member States with different attitudes and traditions. The development of this Community practice was alluded to in the case of *R. v. London Boroughs Transport Committee, ex p. Freight Transport Association* [1991] 1 W.L.R. 828 where the House of Lords, and Lord Templeman in particular, looked to the new régime of Community environmental regulation, placing great reliance on the Commission Green Paper on the Environment COM(90)218, with its emphasis on the avoidance of strict Community harmonisation. On this basis, the Court concluded that the environmental legislation promulgated by the London Boroughs' Transport Committee to regulate freight noise was permissible. Unfortunately, this case did not turn on the notion of minimum harmonisation but rather on the misplaced preconception that the Community "had not occupied the field". In reality, the directives being relied on by the Freight Transport Association were of the traditional harmonisation type which precluded Member State action not specifically detailed in the Community measure (for criticism of the decision see Weatherill, (1992) 17 E.L.Rev. 299).

It is to be regretted that no definitive list of measures coming within the exclusive jurisdiction of the Community was laid down by the Treaty. A draft on subsidiarity submitted to the European Parliament by Giscard D'Estaing followed the German Federal Constitution and set out clearly defined areas of Community and Member State competence. The Commission, in its Communication to the Council and Parliament (SEC (92) 1990 final, CONS DOC 9649/92), admitted that the Maastricht Treaty had confused the Member States by drawing a distinction between exclusive competences and concurrent competences shared with the Member States without clarifying the content of each category. In response, the Commission laid down a list of measures it considered fell within the exclusive competence of the Community. These measures centre on the four fundamental freedoms, and other common policies essential for the completion of the internal market, including: the removal of barriers to the free movement of goods, persons, services and capital (Art. 8a); the common commercial policy (Art. 113); the general rules on competition; the common organisation of agricultural markets (Art. 39); the conservation of fishery resources (Art. 102) and organisation of fishery markets; the essential elements of transport policy (Art. 75); and measures necessitated by the third stage of economic and monetary union (CONS DOC *supra* at p. 7). This list is not "fixed indefinitely" but will have to change as "European integration progresses". To this list of exclusive competences must be added specific Community obligations, including, *inter alia*, competition policy, enforcement of Community law and Community expenditure (conclusions of the Presidency, Edinburgh Summit 12/10/92, SN 456/92). It could thus be argued that the definition of exclusive competences simply marks an *a priori* assessment of the relative efficiency and necessity of Community action.

The opinions of the Commission on the matter, while certainly indicative of its likely future practice are not binding. It must be presumed that the E.C.J. will be called upon to rule on the exact scope of those measures which fall under the exclusive competences of the Community.

Turning now to the subsidiarity principle proper, it will apply to all areas in which regulatory competence is to be shared between the Community and Member States. The burden of proof appears to rest on the Community institutions to demonstrate the need to legislate at the Community level, rather than at the national level. Not only must the Community demonstrate the necessity of Community action as opposed to national measures, the Community must also satisfy a second requirement, that the measures it takes will be a better response to the requirements of the situation than national action.

Thus, for the Community to justify its actions, it must make clear the necessity of Community action and also assert that it is more efficient for the Community to act, having regard to the "scale or effects of the proposed action". The Commission has laid down draft guidelines on the assessment of the fulfilment of these tests, while acknowledging "an inevitable lack of precision" and the need to treat each case on an individual basis.

More helpfully, the Commission laid down a number of areas where it determined that the efficiency test would seem to point towards action at the Community level. These included: the cross-border implications of the proposed action; the consequences of failure to act within the Community; and the need to avoid the distortion of competition within the Community. The influence of "cross-border implications" on the assessment of the competent regulatory body was recognised in the Spinelli Draft Treaty on European Union of 1984 (Bull.E.C. 2–1984, 14/2/ 84). Given today's highly market-integrated Community, it is very difficult for measures to pertain to one Member State alone. The jurisprudence of the Court has occasionally tended towards an artificial definition of "effects on the common market". In Case C-159/90 *Society for the Protection of the Unborn Child (Ireland)* v. *Grogan (Stephen)* [1991] 3 C.M.L.R. 689, the E.C.J. found that abortion amounted to "a service within the meaning of Art. 60 of the Treaty". The Court therefore implicitly ruled that the Irish constitution's prohibition of abortion could amount to a restriction on the freedom to travel to receive economic services protected by Art. 59 E.E.C. Protocol No. 17 annexed to the Maastricht Treaty aims to forestall further challenges to the Irish constitution on these grounds. Whether or not this will be successful is a matter of some debate (see, *e.g.* (1992) 29 C.M.L.Rev. 686). The result of the 1992 "abortion" referendum in Ireland was the addition to the constitution of provisos that nothing in the Irish constitution (Art. 40.3.3—the anti-abortion clause) prevented the dissemination of information about abortion services available in other countries or the freedom to travel. The result is that there is currently no conflict between the E.C. law on services and the Irish constitution, although it is not clear whether future developments might not bring the systems into conflict. Whatever the result, the *Grogan* case illustrates the attribution of Community market effects to the highly contentious issue of abortion.

It will not be in the application of nebulous tests of efficiency and necessity that the principle of subsidiarity will prove its worth. In the political sphere it may make the Commission more restrained in the measures it proposes and the Council more cautious in the measures it adopts. Subsidiarity depends for its political effectiveness on its acceptance into the "institutional culture" of the Community. The European Parliament has committed itself to paying particular attention to whether a legislative proposal respects the principle of subsidiarity (see Rule 36E of the European Parliament's Rules of Procedure as amended subsequent to the TEU in [1993] O.J. C268/51).

There are already examples of such acceptance. The application of a *de minimis* attitude to regulatory measures is implicit in both the Edinburgh summit conclusions and the Commission Communication. Where possible, the imposition of legislative harmonisation is to be avoided and replaced by the least obtrusive alternative, for example, mutual recognition, the adoption of recommendations, the provision of financial support or the promotion of co-operation between

Member States. Moreover, the withdrawal of proposed legislative measures at the Edinburgh summit and similar subsequent action, while not dealing with any matters of great substance would tend to suggest that at least the principle is being noted by the institutions (see Weatherill and Beaumont, *EC Law*, Penguin, pp. 779–782).

In legal terms, the major question as regards the subsidiarity principle is the rôle of the E.C.J. in its application. Despite many protestations that the essentially political nature of the concept ought to preclude judicial consideration of what will be little more than political value judgements, the inclusion of subsidiarity as one of the principles of the Community means that it is the duty of the E.C.J. under Art. 164, to rule on its application and interpretation. Subsidiarity is a legal principle; it is merely very difficult to interpret. The existence of so many imponderables makes it impossible to predict the approach of the E.C.J. Much discussion has of course centred on the Court's past predilection for the expansion of the Community's power and of its own jurisdiction.

It would seem that it will be very difficult to succeed in any action for the annulment of a piece of Community legislation on the grounds of infringement of the subsidiarity principle. This is particularly so for individuals, who would need to fulfil the strict *locus standi* requirements of Art. 173 E.C.

The Commission reported to the December 1993 European Council on a review of certain Community rules with a view to adapting them to the subsidiarity principle. An inter-institutional agreement on the application of the principle is also envisaged in the near future (conclusions of the Presidency, Birmingham European Council, point iii).

Another very important aspect of the subsidiarity principle concerns the number of levels to which the principle will be applicable. A literal reading of the Article suggests that the lowest level at which the matter might be dealt with efficiently is the correct one. This has led to a great deal of debate about the future rôle of the regions and other such bodies in the regulation of the Community. The official U.K. view, while not denying the potential for such devolution of powers, is that it is for each Member State to decide how these competences should be distributed within its own country (*Hansard*, H.C. Vol. 216, col. 911).

Para. 3

The third paragraph of this Article is open to different interpretations. It might well simply be an expression of the general principle of Community law of proportionality and thus is merely an extension of the *vires* condition in the first paragraph. The E.C.J. will have to apply the proportionality test to any Community action (see Weatherill and Beaumont, *EC Law*, Penguin, pp. 225–226).

Article 4

1. The tasks entrusted to the Community shall be carried out by the following institutions:

    a EUROPEAN PARLIAMENT,

    a COUNCIL,

    a COMMISSION,

    a COURT OF JUSTICE,

    a COURT OF AUDITORS.

Each institution shall act within the limits of the powers conferred upon it by this Treaty.

2. The Council and the Commission shall be assisted by an Economic and Social Committee and a Committee of the Regions acting in an advisory capacity.

GENERAL NOTE

Para. 1

This article has been amended to take account of the elevation of the Court of Auditors to the status of a fully fledged Community institution. The Court was set up by the Financial Provisions Treaty in 1975 and held its first session in 1977. The membership of the court is roughly equivalent to the E.C.J. Its main responsibility lies in the examination of the Community accounts and the submission of an annual report on the sound management of the Community finances.

The upgrading of the Court will not affect its duties, which are now laid down in Arts. 188a–c. The provisions governing the Court have been moved to Part Five of the amended Treaty, dealing with the institutions. The original Art. 206 E.C. which contained essentially similar provisions, is now dedicated to the budgetary procedure in general.

The upgrading of the Court of Auditors was welcomed by the U.K. Government who see it as an essential element in the development of stricter and more effective financial controls in the Community. This goal is highlighted by the insertion of Art. 209a E.C. on the combating of the fraudulent use of Community funds.

Para. 2

This paragraph has been amended to take account of the creation of the new Committee of the Regions (Art. 198a–c E.C.). Its inclusion alongside the Economic and Social Committee reflects the two bodies' similar tasks and make-up. Moreover, Protocol 16, appended to the Treaty, states that the two committees are to have a common institutional structure.

Article 4a

A European System of Central Banks (hereinafter referred to as 'ESCB') and a European Central Bank (hereinafter referred to as 'ECB') shall be established in accordance with the procedures laid down in this Treaty; they shall act within the limits of the powers conferred upon them by this Treaty and by the Statute of the ESCB and of the ECB (hereinafter referred to as 'Statute of the ESCB') annexed thereto.

GENERAL NOTE

This Article gives effective institutional status to the new monetary organs of the Community. The start of the third stage of economic and monetary union will bring into being the European System of Central Banks and the European Central Bank to carry out the tasks entrusted to them, in particular the definition and implementation of a Community monetary policy.

The governing Statute of the European Central Bank and the European System of Central Banks is laid down in the Protocol on the Statute of the European System of Central Banks and the European Central Bank (Protocol Number 3), supplementing the institutional provisions in the Treaty itself (Arts. 109a–d E.C.).

The failure to include the European Central Bank and the European System of Central Banks in Art. 4 (institutions of the Community) would appear to be due to the fact that these bodies will come into force at a later date. Nevertheless, the European Central Bank and European System of Central Banks are for all practical purposes Community institutions. The European Central Bank will have legal personality (Art. 9 of Protocol No. 3) and may be a party to legal proceedings in Member State courts. Moreover, European Central Bank legislation will be subject to the usual procedures for judicial review under Art. 173 E.C.

Article 4b

A European Investment Bank is hereby established, which shall act within the limits of the powers conferred upon it by this Treaty and the Statute annexed thereto.

GENERAL NOTE

Under the E.E.C. Treaty, the European Investment Bank was given the task of facilitating the economic expansion of the Community by opening up new resources (Art. 3j E.E.C., repealed). Reflecting the European Investment Bank's position as an element of Community policy, the provisions governing the organisation, tasks and working methods of the European Investment Bank were located in Arts. 129 and 130 E.E.C. The Maastricht amendments have moved these provisions into the institutional title at Arts. 198d and 198e E.C. They remain largely unaltered and the Protocol on the Statute of the European Investment Bank annexed to the Treaty is untouched.

The status of the European Investment Bank as an institution of the Community is merely an acknowledgement of its *de facto* institutional status prior to the Maastricht amendments. The European Investment Bank has enjoyed legal personality under Art. 129 E.E.C. and, under Art. 180 E.E.C. (unamended in relation to European Investment Bank), the E.C.J. has jurisdiction in disputes concerning the fulfilment of the Member States' obligations under the Statute of the European Investment Bank or regarding any measures adopted by the Governors of the European Investment Bank.

Article 5

Member States shall take all appropriate measures, whether general or particular, to ensure fulfilment of the obligations arising out of this Treaty or resulting from action taken by the institutions of the Community. They shall facilitate the achievement of the Community's tasks.

They shall abstain from any measure which could jeopardise the attainment of the objectives of this Treaty.

Article 6

Within the scope of application of this Treaty, and without prejudice to any special provisions contained therein, any discrimination on grounds of nationality shall be prohibited.

The Council, acting in accordance with the procedure referred to in Article 189c, may adopt rules designed to prohibit such discrimination.

GENERAL NOTE

This Article, previously Art. 7 E.E.C., replaces the obsolete Art. 6 E.E.C. on economic policy co-ordination. The content of the original Art. 7 E.E.C. is preserved, continuing the application of the co-operation procedure to measures in this area (as introduced by the SEA Arts. 6 and 7/Art. 149 E.E.C.). The only alteration is to take account of the changed nomenclature for this procedure (the simple terminology "co-operation" has been replaced by the "procedure referred to in Art. 189c E.C.").

In pursuing measures under this Article, the Community institutions are permitted to enact regulations, directives and recommendations at their discretion. However, the actual promulgation of measures under this provision is rare. Measures under the more specific provisions on the four freedoms are much more common.

In the case of Case C-295/90 *European Parliament* v. *E.C. Council, Financial Times*, July 14, 1992, however, the European Court found that the adoption of a Directive under Art. 235 E.E.C., on the right of residence of students, was invalid and the Council ought to have relied instead on Art. 7 E.E.C. The E.C.J. went on to record that "measures adopted under the second paragraph of Art. 7 E.E.C. (now Art. 6 E.C.) did not necessarily have to be limited to regulating the rights derived from the first paragraph of that Article, but could also deal with aspects where regulation appeared necessary to enable those rights to be exercised effectively". This ruling would seem to open up further the potential for Art. 6 E.C. to be utilised as a legislative basis (see O'Leary, (1992) 30 C.M.L.Rev. 639–651 for analysis of the implications of this case).

More important than the enactment of Community legislation, is the potential this Article affords those alleging discrimination to take their cases before the relevant national court. Such actions are common, but rest on the alleged discrimination not falling under one of the more specific anti-discriminatory Articles such as the provisions on the four freedoms, competition rules, or special anti-discrimination rules in the fields of agriculture or transport. The case law in this field is vast. For an overview see Kapteyn, *The Law of the European Communities* (2nd ed. 1989) at pp. 92–97.

In the interests of clarity, it is to be regretted that such an important and well known Article has been renumbered. The inclusion of the new provisions which reputedly necessitated such alterations could have been carried out much less clumsily.

Article 7

1. The common market shall be progressively established during a transitional period of 12 years.

This transitional period shall be divided into three stages of four years each; the length of each stage may be altered in accordance with the provisions set out below.

2. To each stage there shall be assigned a set of actions to be initiated and carried through concurrently.

3. Transition from the first to the second stage shall be conditional upon a finding that the objectives specifically laid down in this Treaty for the first stage have in fact been attained in substance and that, subject to the exceptions and procedures provided for in this Treaty, the obligations have been fulfilled.

This finding shall be made at the end of the fourth year by the Council, acting unanimously on a report from the Commission. A Member State may not, however, prevent unanimity by relying upon the non-fulfilment of its own obligations. Failing unanimity, the first stage shall automatically be extended for one year.

At the end of the fifth year, the Council shall make its finding under the same conditions. Failing unanimity, the first stage shall automatically be extended for a further year.

At the end of the sixth year, the Council shall make its finding, acting by a qualified majority on a report from the Commission.

4. Within one month of the last-mentioned vote any Member State which voted with the minority or, if the required majority was not obtained, any Member State shall be entitled to call upon the Council to appoint an arbitration board whose decision shall be binding upon all Member States and upon the institutions of the Community. The arbitration board shall consist of three members appointed by the Council acting unanimously on a proposal from the Commission.

If the Council has not appointed the members of the arbitration board within one month of being called upon to do so, they shall be appointed by the Court of Justice within a further period of one month.

The arbitration board shall elect its own Chairman.

The board shall make its award within six months of the date of the Council vote referred to in the last subparagraph of paragraph 3.

5. The second and third stages may not be extended or curtailed except by a decision of the Council, acting unanimously on a proposal from the Commission.

6. Nothing in the preceding paragraphs shall cause the transitional period to last more than 15 years after the entry into force of this Treaty.

7. Save for the exceptions or derogations provided for in this Treaty, the expiry of the transitional period shall constitute the latest date by which all the rules laid down must enter into force and all the measures required for establishing the common market must be implemented.

GENERAL NOTE

Again, this Article represents a renumbering of an existing provision rather than a substantive amendment to the Community Treaties. This Article, previously Art. 8 E.E.C., deals with the transitional period to the original goal of a common market as set out by the E.E.C. Treaty. The reason for its continued inclusion in the Treaty is unclear, given that its provisions are universally obsolete.

Article 7a

The Community shall adopt measures with the aim of progressively establishing the internal market over a period expiring on 31 December 1992, in accordance with the provisions of this Article and of Articles 7b, 7c, 28, 57(2), 59, 70(1), 84, 99, 100a and 100b and without prejudice to the other provisions of this Treaty.

The internal market shall comprise an area without internal frontiers in which the free movement of goods, persons, services and capital is ensured in accordance with the provisions of this Treaty.

Article 7b

The Commission shall report to the Council before 31 December 1988 and again before 31 December 1990 on the progress made towards achieving the internal market within the time limit fixed in Article 7a.

The Council, acting by a qualified majority on a proposal from the Commission, shall determine the guidelines and conditions necessary to ensure balanced progress in all the sectors concerned.

Article 7c

When drawing up its proposals with a view to achieving the objectives set out in Article 7a, the Commission shall take into account the extent of the effort that certain economies showing differences in development will have to sustain during the period of establishment of the internal market and it may propose appropriate provisions.

If these provisions take the form of derogations, they must be of a temporary nature and must cause the least possible disturbance to the functioning of the common market.

GENERAL NOTE
Articles 7a–7c originally introduced by the SEA, are unchanged but have been renumbered from Arts. 8a–c E.E.C. to their current titles.

PART TWO (CITIZENSHIP OF THE UNION)

GENERAL NOTE
Part Two of the E.C. Treaty is now concerned exclusively with the new provisions on the citizenship of the Union. Article 8 E.C. lays down the fundamental basis of this concept, while the specific rights attached to the status of Community citizenship are laid down in Arts. 8a–d E.C. The rights included in Part Two of the Treaty and related Articles are restrictive and far from the wide scope envisaged by some of the Member States in the run-up to the Maastricht summit. Nevertheless, the mere inclusion of such a politically sensitive topic within the Community structure itself is important, not least in terms of the symbolism for the new Union (for a general analysis of this part of the Treaty see Closa, The Concept of Citizenship in the Treaty on European Union (1992) 29 C.M.L.Rev. 1137–1169).

As an inherently political concept, the Member States were significantly divided over the nature and scope of any notion of Union citizenship. The conferral of rights and duties on persons as citizens of the Union was seen by many national parliaments as a challenge to national sovereignty. The inclusion of political, social, economic and human rights were all mooted in the subsequent negotiations.

The first reference to the inclusion of a concept of citizenship in the inter-governmental negotiations came from the Spanish Prime Minister Felipe Gonzalez (*Agence Europe* No. 5252 May 11, 1990 p. 3). The basis for his assertion was the political determination to see the creation of the new Union structure backed up by a proper definition of the rights and duties of the citizens of this new entity. In pursuit of this goal he sought, *inter alia*, unlimited freedom of movement and the right to vote and stand for election regardless of country of residence.

The European Parliament, in its contribution on the matter, called for a comprehensive catalogue of fundamental rights and freedoms attributable to Union citizens. This catalogue, essentially based on the Council of Europe's European Convention on Human Rights, contained rights specific to the Community process, including the right to move freely as well as certain social rights (See European Parliament Resolution of November 22, 1990, Rapporteur D. Martin). The Commission, having already recorded its desire to see the Community sign up to the European Convention on Human Rights, requested the consideration of broader issues such as a specific right to equal opportunities and equal enjoyment of social rights.

Human rights do not appear to have been specifically dealt with by the European Council in its deliberations on citizenship. The only reference to the European Convention on Human Rights is contained in the expressly non-justiciable Art. F of the Common Provisions of the TEU; any development of Community human rights will continue instead through E.C.J. jurisprudence. It is not desirable to restrict fundamental human rights to those who are citizens of the Union but rather, on the model of the European Convention on Human Rights, to apply those rights to all who are present within the Union (*cf.* Closa, *supra*, at pp. 1156–1157).

The final enunciation of the concept of Union citizenship in the TEU falls far short of many expectations, and not just in terms of human rights. The European Council's conclusions from the Rome summit called for the development of citizenship rights in three areas ([1990] E.C. Bull. 12 at p. 10). Firstly, civic rights, including the participation of non-nationals in municipal and European Parliamentary elections. Secondly, social and economic rights, such as the freedom of movement and equality of opportunities and treatment for all Union citizens. Thirdly, the Council looked to Union co-operation in the protection of citizens outwith the Community. Fourthly, it raised the possibility of the development of the defence of citizen's rights through some form of administrative officer in the Community. These areas are all reflected in the new provisions.

Two fundamental points must be made. Firstly, the majority of the rights espoused in Part Two of the Treaty are simply additional to existing rights already found elsewhere in the Treaty; they are supplementing current protections rather than creating new ones. This is especially true as regards Art. 8a where the free movement of citizens is reiterated. This adds very little to the situation under current Community law. Secondly, as Hartley is keen to point out (Constitutional and Institutional Implications of the Maastricht Agreement (1993) 42 I.C.L.Q. 213, 219–220), those provisions which do seem to create new citizenship rights, such as the minor foray into political issues in Art. 8b, are subject to subsequent inter-governmental agreement as to their content. This is equally true of Art. 8c, where negotiations will be required with third countries as well as intra-Member State agreements.

Article 8

1. Citizenship of the Union is hereby established.

Every person holding the nationality of a Member State shall be a citizen of the Union.

2. Citizens of the Union shall enjoy the rights conferred by this Treaty and shall be subject to the duties imposed thereby.

GENERAL NOTE

Para. (1)

This paragraph, duplicating the wording of the Commission draft, establishes the principle of Union citizenship. The second sentence however is the operative provision. This lays down the basic principle for the conferral of Union citizenship that "every person holding the nationality of a Member State shall be a citizen of the Union". Thus the nationality laws of the Member States will implicitly decree those persons who are eligible for Union citizenship. While this will generally attribute the rights of citizenship to all Member State nationals there is nothing to stop Member States from making declarations defining those persons who qualify as their nationals for Community law purposes. The U.K. have such a declaration in force, laid down after the passing of the British Nationality Act 1981 (see [1983] O.J. C23/1). It is a moot point as to whether or not the E.C.J. could overrule the nationality provisions of a Member State for failure to comply with Treaty obligations. The fact that the vast majority of Community rights fall to be conferred on individuals solely by virtue of their status as Community nationals (exceptions, *e.g.* Arts. 30 and 95 E.C.) makes these nationality provisions very important, but because this citizenship is conferred by the Member States acting at their own discretion, European Court action would seem to be inapplicable. Indeed, the inclusion in the 1981 Act of a special provision for the descendants of British E.E.C. employees born outwith the U.K. was not to prevent a conflict between U.K. and Community law but rather to prevent anomalies in U.K. law. The European Parliament, which had also been pushing for such a provision in U.K. law, stated in its resolution on the matter, with notably uncharacteristic reserve, that the definition of nationality for the purposes of Community law was the responsibility of each Member State ([1981] O.J. C260/100).

More importantly, Declaration Number 2 to the Treaty on the nationality of a Member State states that: "the question whether an individual possesses the nationality of a Member State shall be settled solely by reference to the national law of the Member State concerned".

Nevertheless it has been suggested that, when defining the persons who qualify as its nationals for the purposes of free movement, Member States must satisfy the requirements of Community law (Evans, Nationality Law and European Integration, (1991) 16 E.L.Rev. 192).

The approach of the Treaty here reflects the continuing national state dominance in such matters. The prospect for any harmonisation of the European rules for decreeing nationality is remote for two reasons. Firstly, the conferral of the status of citizen is entwined with the basic principles of state sovereignty and unlikely to be given up to the Community institutions. Secondly, the pressure to give up such powers is unlikely to be forthcoming. If the Member States' rules on the conferral of citizenship were divergent, then those states with stricter conditions might well press for tighter Community wide controls. The reality is that, although the Member States do exercise different tests for conferring citizenship, all the Member States exercise generally strict controls. Many of the problems which have arisen are the subject of inter-governmental agreement, such as the Convention on the Crossing of External Borders.

Any codification of the law on citizenship is unlikely unless the rights exercisable by virtue of this status become much more important and, as a result, the Member States find it necessary to reach an agreement on exactly who should be a citizen and thus benefit from these rights.

Para. (2)

This seemingly innocuous section has created a great deal of controversy as well as highlighting the nature of the citizenship process. As regards the latter achievement, the Article makes it quite clear that the rights and duties of the Union are to be additional to the national rights and responsibilities stemming from the citizenship of a Member State, and additional to the Community rights and responsibilities stemming from the core Community Treaties. The interplay of these different rights and duties will be a matter for the E.C.J. It is unlikely that, even in the event of the E.C.J. conferring direct effect on Art. 8, the resultant litigation will have any determinative effect on current practice. This is a direct result of the fact that many of the Union citizenship provisions add little to existing rights in the Community sphere. Litigation is most likely to assert the right of free movement within the Member States, under Art. 8a(1), but the wording of that provision specifically retains the exceptions to the principle found in existing Community law (see note on that Article).

The controversy on this Article surrounds the inclusion of the reference to the obligation of Union citizen to comply with the "duties imposed" on such citizenship. The current provisions on citizenship confer only rights and entitlements so this reference to indistinct future duties caused concern in many of the Member States prior to ratification, not least due to scare mongering over the potential of conscription as one of the potential duties to be imposed on Union citizens. Such fears are essentially ungrounded, given that any development of the citizenship provisions requires unanimity in Council and their adoption by the Member States in accordance with their respective constitutional practice (Art. 8e E.C.). Thus nothing can be added without the effective equivalent of an inter-governmental conference on the subject, with no legal potential for the imposition on a Member State of an undesired Treaty addition. Section A of the Decision Concerning Denmark adopted at the Edinburgh European Council makes it clear that any addition to the citizenship provisions in that country will require, as well as unanimity in Council, either a majority of five-sixths of the Parliament or a majority in Parliament and in a popular referendum. This adds nothing new to the provisions of Art. 8e but was felt necessary by the Danish government to quell concerns in their country over potentially unwelcome developments in the field of citizenship being forced on the Danes.

Article 8a

1. Every citizen of the Union shall have the right to move and reside freely within the territory of the Member States, subject to the limitations and conditions laid down in this Treaty and by the measures adopted to give it effect.

2. The Council may adopt provisions with a view to facilitating the exercise of the rights referred to in paragraph 1; save as otherwise provided in this Treaty, the Council shall act unanimously on a proposal from the Commission and after obtaining the assent of the European Parliament.

GENERAL NOTE

Para. (1)
This Article deals with the principle of free movement of citizens in the Union. The original Treaty, in particular Arts. 48–52 E.E.C., enshrined the rights of freedom of movement and residence for Community nationals. This did not, however, lead to the creation of a systematic régime of freedom of movement for all Community nationals. This position is continued by the new Article which, while seeming to create a generalised right to free movement for Union (as opposed to Community) citizens, must be read in terms of the pre-existing exceptions to that freedom as embodied in the secondary legislation on the subject.

Prior to June 30, 1992, the exercise of the freedom of movement and residence was dependent on the person's economic status. Under the old provisions, Member State nationals who were workers or dependants of workers, enjoyed a right to live in any Member State and to claim state benefits on the same conditions as nationals of the host state. The specifics of this general right were laid down in a number of regulations and directives (*e.g.* Reg. 1612/68 on the eligibility of nationals of Member States to take employment in another state "with the same priority as nationals of that state" and to be joined by their families; Reg. 1251/70 on the right to remain in the state after the period of employment has terminated; Dir. 68/369 on the abolition of restrictions on free movement and residence in the Community and Dirs. 75/34 and 75/35 extending similar rights to self-employed persons).

The three new Directives taking effect from June 30, 1992 still do not create a general right of free movement and residence as desired by the Commission. Nevertheless, they do come very close to such an achievement, attributing such rights to students (Dir. 90/366/E.E.C., [1990] O.J. L180/30), retired workers (Dir. 90/365/E.E.C., [1990] O.J. L180/28) and all "non-economically active persons" (Dir. 90/364/E.E.C., [1990] O.J. L180/26). The latter of these provisions which attributes the right of residence to all those nationals of Member States (now, read as Union citizens) who do not already enjoy that right under an existing provision of Community law means that virtually all Community nationals are now covered. Thus it has been argued, quite credibly, that little is added by the new Art. 8a (Hartley, (1993) 42 I.C.L.Q. 213, 219).

Moreover, the exceptions laid down in the secondary legislation outlined above will continue to apply as regards the new Art. 8a. Thus the application of Art. 8a will be open only to those with sufficient resources, who will not become a burden on the Member State, and have sickness insurance where relevant. These requirements apply to both nationals and dependants alike and aim to prevent nationals "shopping" for the most generous social security provisions in the Community. (See *Hansard*, H.C. Vol. 166, cols. 1101–2 for the debate on these Directives). The citizenship freedoms in Art. 8a are also subject to derogations on the grounds of public policy, public security and health, probably to be applied in accordance with the jurisprudence built up around the existing Dir. 64/221 E.E.C.

Para. (2)
This Article permits the adoption of measures facilitating the exercise of these rights by Council adoption of a Commission proposal. While this procedure is less arduous than that laid down in Art. 8e E.C. it still requires Council unanimity and the Parliament is given a power of veto over any measure by virtue of the assent procedure.

Article 8b

1. Every citizen of the Union residing in a Member State of which he is not a national shall have the right to vote and to stand as a candidate at municipal elections in the Member State in which he resides, under the same conditions as nationals of that State. This right shall be exercised subject to detailed arrangements to be adopted before 31 December 1994 by the Council, acting unanimously on a proposal from the Commission and after consulting the European Parliament; these arrangements may provide for derogations where warranted by problems specific to a Member State.
2. Without prejudice to Article 138(3) and to the provisions adopted for its implementation, every citizen of the Union residing in a Member State of which he is not a national shall have the right to vote and to stand as a candidate in elections to the European Parliament in the Member State in which he resides, under the same conditions as nationals of that State. This right shall be exercised subject to detailed arrangements to be adopted before 31 December 1993 by the Council, acting unanimously on a proposal from the Commission and after consulting the European Parliament; these arrangements may provide for derogations where warranted by problems specific to a Member State.

GENERAL NOTE
This Article recognises the right of every citizen of the Union to vote and stand for election in the European Parliament and municipal elections in the Member State in which he resides. This is a large symbolic step for the Community, the first time that political rights as such have been laid down in the Treaty. The attribution of such rights to all citizens of the Union means that factors external to the Member State will determine eligibility to vote and stand for election. The practical application of the principles will only become clear after the conclusion of detailed arrangements among the Member States. Many problems will need to be addressed and the reference to the potential for Member State derogations is indicative of the difficulties envisaged.

Para. (1)
Under this Article, citizens of the Union are to be eligible to vote in municipal elections in the Member State in which they are resident "under the same conditions as the nationals of that state". Concerns were voiced in the House of Commons as to the scope of the term "municipal". To allay the fears of a number of M.P.'s, the Government made clear that the designation "municipal" had been chosen so as to expressly exclude the application of this Article to national elections (*Hansard*, H.C. Vol. 218, col. 34). More importantly, this right is to be exercised subject to detailed arrangements adopted before December 31, 1994. Issues which will have to be addressed in these negotiations will be the regulation of the voters to ensure that they only vote once and also the determination of what constitutes residence. The Commission's draft Treaty text (Art. X.5, see E.C. Bull. Supp. 2/91 at p. 85) and many of the Member State submissions to the inter-governmental conference referred to a minimum period of residence

(Closa, The Concept of Citizenship in the Treaty on European Union (1992) 29 C.M.L.Rev. 1137, 1163). It is quite possible that no harmonisation of the periods of residence will take place and this ought not significantly affect the exercise of this right. Article 8b does not prejudge the content of the negotiations.

The inclusion of a requirement of unanimity in Council for the adoption of these detailed arrangements means that derogations from the rules are likely to be unavoidable. The wording "where warranted by the problems specific to a Member State" is generally taken as a reference to Luxembourg, where over 25 per cent. of the resident population consists of non-Luxembourg national Union citizens. Thus the attribution of voting rights to these persons would significantly alter the makeup of the Luxembourg electorate and is opposed by the Luxembourg Government.

Nevertheless, the specific reference to the potential of derogations may encourage other Member States to assert their own national problems as grounds for special treatment, thus threatening the degree of uniformity necessary to ensure the effective operation of this right. This might well be made more likely due to the strict timetable under which the states will be working. The aim is to have the necessary rules in force in time for the 1995 round of local elections.

Para. (2)

Similar provisions are envisaged as regards the conferral of electoral rights for the European Parliamentary elections. Again the provision is subject to the adoption by unanimity of detailed arrangements by December 31, 1993. This is a year earlier than the timetable envisaged under Art. 8b(1) because of the desire to see the rules in force prior to the 1994 European Parliamentary elections.

This Article is to have no bearing on the specific rules to be drawn up by the European Parliament under Art. 138(3) E.C. on a uniform electoral procedure to the European Parliament. There is still no deadline on the drawing up of these proposals.

Article 8c

Every citizen of the Union shall, in the territory of a third country in which the Member State of which he is a national is not represented, be entitled to protection by the diplomatic or consular authorities of any Member State, on the same conditions as the nationals of that State.

Before 31 December 1993, Member States shall establish the necessary rules among themselves and start the international negotiations required to secure this protection.

GENERAL NOTE

This Article projects the principle of Union citizenship to situations outwith the Community borders. The citizens of the Union are to be entitled to diplomatic protection in the territory of a third country by another Member States' external authorities "on the same conditions as the nationals of that state".

The scope of this Article is narrower than envisaged in the Commission draft Treaty (Art. X8, E.C. Bull. Supp. 2/91 at p. 85), where the national could have relied on the protection of any Member State and this was not conditional on his/her own Member State being represented in the third country. The final draft as contained in this Article marks the continuation of national concerns in this area. The protection of another Member State is afforded solely where the national's own Member State is not represented in the third country. This derogates from the spirit of a true Union and fails to take account of the situation where a national is in one part of a large country, a vast distance from his own Member States' diplomatic facilities but legally excluded from having reliance on a more conveniently located diplomatic authority of another Member State. This is particularly relevant as regards the smaller Member States, who do not have the resources to maintain a diplomatic presence throughout the world; even the larger states are consistently cutting back on their external representation. Thus, these provisions again give lip-service to the idea of a Union without going to the logical extent of actual Union representation in third countries, which is an idea manifestly sound in practical terms but spurned by the Member States, concerned at such a visible loss of national "sovereignty".

A great deal will rest on actual governmental practice in the setting up of the rules between the Member States and the negotiation of the international agreements which will be necessary to secure the effective implementation of this right. Issues that will have to be addressed include the determination of which Member State will represent the citizen of the Union if more than one Member State has a diplomatic presence in that state. Will this depend on the existence of a bilateral agreement between the unrepresented national's Member State and the diplomatic authority he seeks to rely on or will an overall agreement among all 12 Member States be negotiated?

It also remains to be seen the extent to which the E.C.J. will be able to intervene in this area, given the predominance of inter-governmental agreements. Nevertheless, the jurisdiction of the European Court is not explicitly excluded from any of the citizenship provisions and Art. 164 E.C. thus makes it the duty of the E.C.J. to ensure the application of the law in this field.

Article 8d

Every citizen of the Union shall have the right to petition the European Parliament in accordance with Article 138d.

Every citizen of the Union may apply to the Ombudsman established in accordance with Article 138e.

GENERAL NOTE

Para. (1)
The right of every citizen of the Union to petition the European Parliament adds very little to current practice. This right has been available since 1953, under Rule 128 of the European Parliament's Rules of Procedure. Its constitutionalisation may well cause greater use to be made of what is an increasingly popular means of redress by disaffected parties. Its inclusion among the Treaty citizenship rights is something of a misnomer, however, given that the right is not exclusive to Union citizens but is rather a general right available to all those residing within the Community. It is available to a much broader group of people than Union citizens *per se*, including, as well as resident natural persons, legal persons with a statutory seat in a Member State. The detailed provisions governing the right are laid down in the new Art. 138d E.C.

Although the right of petition is expressly open to all citizens of the Union; it would appear that the right has been intentionally circumscribed to exclude petitions on the inter-governmental pillars of Union competence (Closa, *supra*, at 1164). Article 138d E.C. restricts the area of competence of petitions to "matters within the Community's fields of activity". It may well fall upon the E.C.J. to rule on the exact scope of this right.

Para. (2)
The new office of Community ombudsman, set up by Art. 138e of the E.C. Treaty, gives Union citizens the right to address complaints concerning instances of maladministration in the Community institutions to an independent ombudsman appointed by the European Parliament.

Once again the right is not exclusive to Union citizens and applies to the same categories of person as for petitioning the European Parliament.

The detailed arrangements governing the performance of the ombudsman's duties are to be laid down by the European Parliament, after consulting the Commission and pending acceptance, by a qualified majority, of the Council.

One of the matters to be addressed will have to be the relationship between the office of ombudsman and the right of petition to the European Parliament. The latter body expressed its dismay at the relatively limited powers attributed to the ombudsman and the clash of functions it envisaged with its Committee of Petitions (European Parliament Interim Report on European Citizenship, European Parliament Document A3-0139/91).

Article 8e

The Commission shall report to the European Parliament, to the Council and to the Economic and Social Committee before 31 December 1993 and then every three years on the application of the provisions of this Part. This report shall take account of the development of the Union. On this basis, and without prejudice to the other provisions of this Treaty, the Council, acting unanimously on a proposal from the Commission and after consulting the European Parliament, may adopt provisions to strengthen or to add to the rights laid down in this Part, which it shall recommend to the Member States for adoption in accordance with their respective constitutional requirements.

GENERAL NOTE
This Article lays down the procedure governing the future modification of the citizenship provisions of the Treaty. The first paragraph provides for the production of a Commission report on the application of the citizenship provisions. This report is to form the basis of any

legislative initiative aimed at strengthening or adding to the catalogue of citizenship rights currently laid out in the Treaty. As Closa points out, the only modifications envisaged to this part of the Treaty are positive in that they must "strengthen or add to" the existing rights. Member States might well retain the current restricted list of citizenship provisions. While the Commission has the right of initiative to put forward proposals in this field, any progress is dependent upon unanimity in the Council and furthermore any such measures must be adopted in accordance with the constitutional requirements of the respective Member States.

PART THREE (COMMUNITY POLICIES)

GENERAL NOTE

Community policies
   The addition of the new provisions establishing a Union citizenship under the heading Part Two has led to a renumbering of the remaining E.E.C. titles. The original Parts Two and Three of the E.E.C. Treaty on the "Foundations of the Community" and "Policy of the Community" are now regrouped under the single heading of "Community Policies" in Part Three of the E.C. Treaty (Arts. 9–130y E.C.).

TITLE I: Free Movement of Goods

Article 9

1. The Community shall be based upon a customs union which shall cover all trade in goods and which shall involve the prohibition between Member States of customs duties on imports and exports and of all charges having equivalent effect, and the adoption of a common customs tariff in their relations with third countries.
2. The provisions of Chapter 1, Section 1, and of Chapter 2 of this Title shall apply to products originating in Member States and to products coming from third countries which are in free circulation in Member States.

Article 10

1. Products coming from a third country shall be considered to be in free circulation in a Member State if the import formalities have been complied with and any customs duties or charges having equivalent effect which are payable have been levied in that Member State, and if they have not benefited from a total or partial drawback of such duties or charges.
2. The Commission shall, before the end of the first year after the entry into force of this Treaty, determine the methods of administrative co-operation to be adopted for the purpose of applying Article 9(2), taking into account the need to reduce as much as possible formalities imposed on trade.
   Before the end of the first year after the entry into force of this Treaty, the Commission shall lay down the provisions applicable, as regards trade between Member States, to goods originating in another Member State in whose manufacture products have been used on which the exporting Member State has not levied the appropriate customs duties or charges having equivalent effect, or which have benefited from a total or partial drawback of such duties or charges.
   In adopting these provisions, the Commission shall take into account the rules for the elimination of customs duties within the Community and for the progressive application of the common customs tariff.

Article 11

Member States shall take all appropriate measures to enable Governments to carry out, within the periods of time laid down, the obligations with regard to customs duties which devolve upon them pursuant to this Treaty.

Chapter 1 (The Customs Union)

SECTION 1: Elimination of customs duties between Member States

Article 12

Member States shall refrain from introducing between themselves any new customs duties on imports or exports or any charges having equivalent effect, and from increasing those which they already apply in their trade with each other.

Article 13

1. Customs duties on imports in force between Member States shall be progressively abolished by them during the transitional period in accordance with Articles 14 and 15.
2. Charges having an effect equivalent to customs duties on imports, in force between Member States, shall be progressively abolished by them during the transitional period. The Commission shall determine by means of directives the timetable for such abolition. It shall be guided by the rules contained in Article 14(2) and (3) and by the directives issued by the Council pursuant to Article 14(2).

Article 14

1. For each product, the basic duty to which the successive reductions shall be applied shall be the duty applied on 1 January 1957.
2. The timetable for the reductions shall be determined as follows:
   (a) during the first stage, the first reduction shall be made one year after the date when this Treaty enters into force; the second reduction, eighteen months later; the third reduction, at the end of the fourth year after the date when this Treaty enters into force;
   (b) during the second stage, a reduction shall be made eighteen months after that stage begins; a second reduction, eighteen months after the preceding one; a third reduction, one year later;
   (c) any remaining reductions shall be made during the third stage; the Council shall, acting by a qualified majority on a proposal from the Commission, determine the timetable therefor by means of directives.
3. At the time of the first reduction, Member States shall introduce between themselves a duty on each product equal to the basic duty minus 10 per cent.

At the time of each subsequent reduction, each Member State shall reduce its customs duties as a whole in such manner as to lower by 10 per cent. its total customs receipts as defined in paragraph 4 and to reduce the duty on each product by at least 5 per cent. of the basic duty.

In the case, however, of products on which the duty is still in excess of 30 per cent., each reduction must be at least 10 per cent. of the basic duty.

4. The total customs receipts of each Member State, as referred to in paragraph 3, shall be calculated by multiplying the value of its imports from other Member States during 1956 by the basic duties.
5. Any special problems raised in applying paragraphs 1 to 4 shall be settled by directives issued by the Council acting by a qualified majority on a proposal from the Commission.
6. Member States shall report to the Commission on the manner in which effect has been given to the preceding rules for the reduction of duties. They

shall endeavour to ensure that the reduction made in the duties on each product shall amount:

— at the end of the first stage, to at least 25 per cent. of the basic duty;
— at the end of the second stage, to at least 50 per cent. of the basic duty.

If the Commission finds that there is a risk that the objectives laid down in Article 13, and the percentages laid down in this paragraph, cannot be attained, it shall make all appropriate recommendations to Member States.

7. The provisions of this Article may be amended by the Council, acting unanimously on a proposal from the Commission and after consulting the European Parliament.

Article 15

1. Irrespective of the provisions of Article 14, any Member State may, in the course of the transitional period, suspend in whole or in part the collection of duties applied by it to products imported from other Member States. It shall inform the other Member States and the Commission thereof.

2. The Member States declare their readiness to reduce customs duties against the other Member States more rapidly than is provided for in Article 14 if their general economic situation and the situation of the economic sector concerned so permit.

To this end, the Commission shall make recommendations to the Member States concerned.

Article 16

Member States shall abolish between themselves customs duties on exports and charges having equivalent effect by the end of the first stage at the latest.

Article 17

1. The provisions of Articles 9 to 15(1) shall also apply to customs duties of a fiscal nature. Such duties shall not, however, be taken into consideration for the purpose of calculating either total customs receipts or the reduction of customs duties as a whole as referred to in Article 14(3) and (4).

Such duties shall, at each reduction, be lowered by not less than 10 per cent. of the basic duty. Member States may reduce such duties more rapidly than is provided for in Article 14.

2. Member States shall, before the end of the first year after the entry into force of this Treaty, inform the Commission of their customs duties of a fiscal nature.

3. Member States shall retain the right to substitute for these duties an internal tax which complies with the provisions of Article 95.

4. If the Commission finds that substitution for any customs duty of a fiscal nature meets with serious difficulties in a Member State, it shall authorise that State to retain the duty on condition that it shall abolish it not later than six years after the entry into force of this Treaty. Such authorisation must be applied for before the end of the first year after the entry into force of this Treaty.

SECTION 2: Setting up of the common customs tariff

Article 18

The Member States declare their readiness to contribute to the development of international trade and the lowering of barriers to trade by entering into agreements designed, on a basis of reciprocity and mutual advantage, to reduce customs duties below the general level of which they could avail themselves as a result of the establishment of a customs union between them.

Article 19

1. Subject to the conditions and within the limits provided for hereinafter, duties in the common customs tariff shall be at the level of the arithmetical average of the duties applied in the four customs territories comprised in the Community.

2. The duties taken as the basis for calculating this average shall be those applied by Member States on 1 January 1957.

In the case of the Italian tariff, however, the duty applied shall be that without the temporary 10 per cent. reduction. Furthermore, with respect to items on which the Italian tariff contains a conventional duty, this duty shall be substituted for the duty applied as defined above, provided that it does not exceed that latter by more than 10 per cent. Where the conventional duty exceeds the duty applied as defined above by more than 10 per cent., the latter duty plus 10 per cent. shall be taken as the basis for calculating the arithmetical average.

With regard to the tariff headings in List A, the duties shown in that List shall, for the purpose of calculating the arithmetical average, be substituted for the duties applied.

3. The duties in the common customs tariff shall not exceed:

(a) 3 per cent. for products within the tariff headings in List B;
(b) 10 per cent. for products within the tariff headings in List C;
(c) 15 per cent. for products within the tariff headings in List D;
(d) 25 per cent. for products within the tariff headings in List E;

where in respect of such products, the tariff of the Benelux countries contains a duty not exceeding 3 per cent., such duty shall, for the purpose of calculating the arithmetical average, be raised to 12 per cent.

4. List F prescribes the duties applicable to the products listed therein.

5. The Lists of tariff headings referred to in this Article and in Article 20 are set out in Annex I to this Treaty.

Article 20

The duties applicable to the products in List G shall be determined by negotiation between the Member States. Each Member State may add further products to this List to a value not exceeding 2 per cent. of the total value of its imports from third countries in the course of the year 1956.

The Commission shall take all appropriate steps to ensure that such negotiations shall be undertaken before the end of the second year after the entry into force of this Treaty and be concluded before the end of the first stage.

If, for certain products, no agreement can be reached within these periods, the Council shall, on a proposal from the Commission, acting unanimously until the end of the second stage and by a qualified majority thereafter, determine the duties in the common customs tariff.

Article 21

1. Technical difficulties which may arise in applying Articles 19 and 20 shall be resolved, within two years of the entry into force of this Treaty, by directives issued by the Council acting by a qualified majority on a proposal from the Commission.

2. Before the end of the first stage, or at latest when the duties are determined, the Council shall, acting by a qualified majority on a proposal from the Commission, decide on any adjustments required in the interests of the internal consistency of the common customs tariff as a result of applying the rules set out in Articles 19 and 20, taking account in particular of the degree

of processing undergone by the various goods to which the common tariff applies.

Article 22

The Commission shall, within two years of the entry into force of this Treaty, determine the extent to which the customs duties of a fiscal nature referred to in Article 17(2) shall be taken into account in calculating the arithmetical average provided for in Article 19(1). The Commission shall take account of any protective character which such duties may have.

Within six months of such determination, any Member State may request that the procedure provided for in Article 20 should be applied to the product in question, but in this event the percentage limit provided in that Article shall not be applicable to that State.

Article 23

1. For the purpose of the progressive introduction of the common customs tariff, Member States shall amend their tariffs applicable to third countries as follows:

(a) in the case of tariff headings on which the duties applied in practice on 1 January 1957 do not differ by more than 15 per cent. in either direction from the duties in the common customs tariff, the latter duties shall be applied at the end of the fourth year after the entry into force of this Treaty;

(b) in any other case, each Member State shall, as from the same date, apply a duty reducing by 30 per cent. the difference between the duty applied in practice on 1 January 1957 and the duty in the common customs tariff;

(c) at the end of the second stage this difference shall again be reduced by 30 per cent;

(d) in the case of tariff headings for which the duties in the common customs tariff are not yet available at the end of the first stage, each Member State shall, within six months of the Council's action in accordance with Article 20, apply such duties as would result from application of the rules contained in this paragraph.

2. Where a Member State has been granted an authorisation under Article 17(4), it need not, for as long as that authorisation remains valid, apply the preceding provisions to the tariff headings to which the authorisation applies. When such authorisation expires, the Member State concerned shall apply such duty as would have resulted from application of the rules contained in paragraph 1.

3. The common customs tariff shall be applied in its entirety by the end of the transitional period at the latest.

Article 24

Member States shall remain free to change their duties more rapidly than is provided for in Article 23 in order to bring them into line with the common customs tariff.

Article 25

1. If the Commission finds that the production in Member States of particular products contained in Lists B, C and D is insufficient to supply the demands of one of the Member States, and that such supply traditionally depends to a considerable extent on imports from third countries, the Council shall, acting by a qualified majority on a proposal from the Commission, grant the Member State concerned tariff quotas at a reduced rate of duty or duty free.

Such quotas may not exceed the limits beyond which the risk might arise of activities being transferred to the detriment of other Member States.

2. In the case of the products in List E, and of those in List G for which the rates of duty have been determined in accordance with the procedure provided for in the third paragraph of Article 20, the Commission shall, where a change in sources of supply or shortage of supplies within the Community is such as to entail harmful consequences for the processing industries of a Member State, at the request of that Member State, grant it tariff quotas at a reduced rate of duty or duty free.

Such quotas may not exceed the limits beyond which the risk might arise of activities being transferred to the detriment of other Member States.

3. In the case of the products listed in Annex II to this Treaty, the Commission may authorise any Member State to suspend, in whole or in part, collection of the duties applicable or may grant such Member State tariff quotas at a reduced rate of duty or duty free, provided that no serious disturbance of the market of the products concerned results therefrom.

4. The Commission shall periodically examine tariff quotas granted pursuant to this Article.

Article 26

The Commission may authorise any Member State encountering special difficulties to postpone the lowering or raising of duties provided for in Article 23 in respect of particular headings in its tariff.

Such authorisation may only be granted for a limited period and in respect of tariff headings which, taken together, represent for such State not more than 5 per cent. of the value of its imports from third countries in the course of the latest year for which statistical data are available.

Article 27

Before the end of the first stage, Member States shall, in so far as may be necessary, take steps to approximate their provisions laid down by law, regulation or administrative action in respect of customs matters. To this end, the Commission shall make all appropriate recommendations to Member States.

Article 28

Any autonomous alteration or suspension of duties in the common customs tariff shall be decided by the Council acting by a qualified majority on a proposal from the Commission.

Article 29

In carrying out the tasks entrusted to it under this Section the Commission shall be guided by:
  (a) the need to promote trade between Member States and third countries;
  (b) developments in conditions of competition within the Community in so far as they lead to an improvement in the competitive capacity of undertakings;
  (c) the requirements of the Community as regards the supply of raw materials and semi-finished goods; in this connection the Commission shall take care to avoid distorting conditions of competition between Member States in respect of finished goods;

(d) the need to avoid serious disturbances in the economies of Member States and to ensure rational development of production and an expansion of consumption within the Community.

Chapter 2 (Elimination of Quantitative Restrictions between Member States)

Article 30

Quantitative restrictions on imports and all measures having equivalent effect shall, without prejudice to the following provisions, be prohibited between Member States.

Article 31

Member States shall refrain from introducing between themselves any new quantitative restrictions or measures having equivalent effect.

This obligation shall, however, relate only to the degree of liberalisation attained in pursuance of the decisions of the Council of the Organisation for European Economic Co-operation of 14 January 1955. Member States shall supply the Commission, not later than six months after the entry into force of this Treaty, with lists of the products liberalised by them in pursuance of these decisions. These lists shall be consolidated between Member States.

Article 32

In their trade with one another Member States shall refrain from making more restrictive the quotas and measures having equivalent effect existing at the date of the entry into force of this Treaty.

These quotas shall be abolished by the end of the transitional period at the latest. During that period, they shall be progressively abolished in accordance with the following provisions.

Article 33

1. One year after the entry into force of this Treaty, each Member State shall convert any bilateral quotas open to any other Member States into global quotas open without discrimination to all other Member States.

On the same date, Member States shall increase the aggregate of the global quotas so established in such a manner as to bring about an increase of not less than 20 per cent. in their total value as compared with the preceding year. The global quota for each product, however, shall be increased by not less than 10 per cent.

The quotas shall be increased annually in accordance with the same rules and in the same proportions in relation to the preceding year.

The fourth increase shall take place at the end of the fourth year after the entry into force of this Treaty; the fifth, one year after the beginning of the second stage.

2. Where, in the case of a product which has not been liberalised, the global quota does not amount to 3 per cent. of the national production of the State concerned, a quota equal to not less than 3 per cent. of such national production shall be introduced not later than one year after the entry into force of this Treaty. This quota shall be raised to 4 per cent. at the end of the second year, and to 5 per cent. at the end of the third. Thereafter, the Member State concerned shall increase the quota by not less than 15 per cent. annually.

Where there is no such national production, the Commission shall take a decision establishing an appropriate quota.

3. At the end of the tenth year, each quota shall be equal to not less than 20 per cent. of the national production.

4. If the Commission finds by means of a decision that during two successive years the imports of any product have been below the level of the quota

opened, this global quota shall not be taken into account in calculating the total value of the global quotas. In such case, the Member State shall abolish quota restrictions on the product concerned.

5. In the case of quotas representing more than 20 per cent. of the national production of the product concerned, the Council may, acting by a qualified majority on a proposal from the Commission, reduce the minimum percentage of 10 per cent. laid down in paragraph 1. This alteration shall not, however, affect the obligation to increase the total value of global quotas by 20 per cent. annually.

6. Member States which have exceeded their obligations as regards the degree of liberalisation attained in pursuance of the decisions of the Council of the Organisation for European Economic Co-operation of 14 January 1955 shall be entitled, when calculating the annual total increase of 20 per cent. provided for in paragraph 1, to take into account the amount of imports liberalised by autonomous action. Such calculation shall be submitted to the Commission for its prior approval.

7. The Commission shall issue directives establishing the procedure and timetable in accordance with which Member States shall abolish, as between themselves, any measures in existence when this Treaty enters into force which have an effect equivalent to quotas.

8. If the Commission finds that the application of the provisions of this Article, and in particular of the provisions concerning percentages, makes it impossible to ensure that the abolition of quotas provided for in the second paragraph of Article 32 is carried out progressively, the Council may, on a proposal from the Commission, acting unanimously during the first stage and by a qualified majority thereafter, amend the procedure laid down in this Article and may, in particular, increase the percentages fixed.

Article 34

1. Quantitative restrictions on exports, and all measures having equivalent effect, shall be prohibited between Member States.

2. Member States shall, by the end of the first stage at the latest, abolish all quantitative restrictions on exports and any measures having equivalent effect which are in existence when this Treaty enters into force.

Article 35

The Member States declare their readiness to abolish quantitative restrictions on imports from and exports to other Member States more rapidly than is provided for in the preceding Articles, if their general economic situation and the situation of the economic sector concerned so permit.

To this end, the Commission shall make recommendations to the Member States concerned.

Article 36

The provisions of Articles 30 to 34 shall not preclude prohibitions or restrictions on imports, exports or goods in transit justified on grounds of public morality, public policy or public security; the protection of health and life of humans, animals or plants; the protection of national treasures possessing artistic, historic or archaeological value; or the protection of industrial and commercial property. Such prohibitions or restrictions shall not, however, constitute a means of arbitrary discrimination or a disguised restriction on trade between Member States.

Article 37

1. Member States shall progressively adjust any State monopolies of a commercial character so as to ensure that when the transitional period has

ended no discrimination regarding the conditions under which goods are procured and marketed exists between nationals of Member States.

The provisions of this Article shall apply to any body through which a Member State, in law or in fact, either directly or indirectly supervises, determines or appreciably influences imports or exports between Member States. These provisions shall likewise apply to monopolies delegated by the State to others.

2. Member States shall refrain from introducing any new measure which is contrary to the principles laid down in paragraph 1 or which restricts the scope of the Articles dealing with the abolition of customs duties and quantitative restrictions between Member States.

3. The timetable for the measures referred to in paragraph 1 shall be harmonised with the abolition of quantitative restrictions on the same products provided for in Articles 30 to 34.

If a product is subject to a State monopoly of a commercial character in only one or some Member States, the Commission may authorise the other Member States to apply protective measures until the adjustment provided for in paragraph 1 has been effected; the Commission shall determine the conditions and details of such measures.

4. If a State monopoly of a commercial character has rules which are designed to make it easier to dispose of agricultural products or obtain for them the best return, steps should be taken in applying the rules contained in this Article to ensure equivalent safeguards for the employment and standard of living of the producers concerned, account being taken of the adjustments that will be possible and the specialisation that will be needed with the passage of time.

5. The obligations on Member States shall be binding only in so far as they are compatible with existing international agreements.

6. With effect from the first stage the Commission shall make recommendations as to the manner in which and the timetable according to which the adjustment provided for in this Article shall be carried out.

TITLE II: Agriculture

Article 38

1. The common market shall extend to agriculture and trade in agricultural products. 'Agricultural products' means the products of the soil, of stock-farming and of fisheries and products of first-stage processing directly related to these products.

2. Save as otherwise provided in Articles 39 to 46, the rules laid down for the establishment of the common market shall apply to agricultural products.

3. The products subject to the provisions of Articles 39 to 46 are listed in Annex II to this Treaty. Within two years of the entry into force of this Treaty, however, the Council shall, acting by a qualified majority on a proposal from the Commission, decide what products are to be added to this list.

4. The operation and development of the common market for agricultural products must be accompanied by the establishment of a common agricultural policy among the Member States.

Article 39

1. The objectives of the common agricultural policy shall be:
(a) to increase agricultural productivity by promoting technical progress and by ensuring the rational development of agricultural production and the optimum utilisation of the factors of production, in particular labour;
(b) thus to ensure a fair standard of living for the agricultural community, in particular by increasing the individual earnings of persons engaged in agriculture;

   (c) to stabilise markets;

   (d) to assure the availability of supplies;

   (e) to ensure that supplies reach consumers at reasonable prices.

2. In working out the common agricultural policy and the special methods for its application, account shall be taken of:

   (a) the particular nature of agricultural activity, which results from the social structure of agriculture and from structural and natural disparities between the various agricultural regions;

   (b) the need to effect the appropriate adjustments by degrees;

   (c) the fact that in the Member States agriculture constitutes a sector closely linked with the economy as a whole.

Article 40

1. Member-States shall develop the common agricultural policy by degrees during the transitional period and shall bring it into force by the end of that period at the latest.

2. In order to attain the objectives set out in Article 39 a common organisation of agricultural markets shall be established.

This organisation shall take one of the following forms, depending on the product concerned:

   (a) common rules on competition;

   (b) compulsory co-ordination of the various national market organisations:

   (c) a European market organisation.

3. The common organisation established in accordance with paragraph 2 may include all measures required to attain the objectives set out in Article 39, in particular regulation of prices, aids for the production and marketing of the various products, storage and carryover arrangements and common machinery for stabilising imports or exports.

The common organisation shall be limited to pursuit of the objectives set out in Article 39 and shall exclude any discrimination between producers or consumers within the Community.

Any common price policy shall be based on common criteria and uniform methods of calculation.

4. In order to enable the common organisation referred to in paragraph 2 to attain its objectives, one or more agricultural guidance and guarantee funds may be set up.

Article 41

To enable the objectives set out in Article 39 to be attained, provision may be made within the framework of the common agricultural policy for measures such as:

   (a) an effective co-ordination of efforts in the spheres of vocational training, of research and of the dissemination of agricultural knowledge; this may include joint financing of projects or institutions;

   (b) joint measures to promote consumption of certain products.

Article 42

The provisions of the Chapter relating to rules on competition shall apply to production of and trade in agricultural products only to the extent determined by the Council within the framework of Article 43(2) and (3) and in accordance with the procedure laid down therein, account being taken of the objectives set out in Article 39.

The Council may, in particular, authorise the granting of aid:

   (a) for the protection of enterprises handicapped by structural or natural conditions;

   (b) within the framework of economic development programmes.

Article 43

1. In order to evolve the broad lines of a common agricultural policy, the Commission shall, immediately this Treaty enters into force, convene a conference of the Member States with a view to making a comparison of their agricultural policies, in particular by producing a statement of their resources and needs.

2. Having taken into account the work of the conference provided for in paragraph 1, after consulting the Economic and Social Committee and within two years of the entry into force of this Treaty, the Commission shall submit proposals for working out and implementing the common agricultural policy, including the replacement of the national organisations by one of the forms of common organisation provided for in Article 40(2), and for implementing the measures specified in this Title.

These proposals shall take account of the interdependence of the agricultural matters mentioned in this Title.

The Council shall, on a proposal from the Commission and after consulting the European Parliament, acting unanimously during the first two stages and by a qualified majority thereafter, make regulations, issue directives, or take decisions, without prejudice to any recommendations it may also make.

3. The Council may, acting by a qualified majority and in accordance with paragraph 2, replace the national market organisations by the common organisation provided for in Article 40(2) if:

(a) the common organisation offers Member States which are opposed to this measure and which have an organisation of their own for the production in question equivalent safeguards for the employment and standard of living of the producers concerned, account being taken of the adjustments that will be possible and the specialisation that will be needed with the passage of time;

(b) such an organisation ensures conditions for trade within the Community similar to those existing in a national market.

4. If a common organisation for certain raw materials is established before a common organisation exists for the corresponding processed products, such raw materials as are used for processed products intended for export to third countries may be imported from outside the Community.

Article 44

1. In so far as progressive abolition of customs duties and quantitative restrictions between Member States may result in prices likely to jeopardise the attainment of the objectives set out in Article 39, each Member State shall, during the transitional period, be entitled to apply to particular products, in a non-discriminatory manner and in substitution for quotas and to such an extent as shall not impede the expansion of the volume of trade provided for in Article 45(2), a system of minimum prices below which imports may be either:

— temporarily suspended or reduced; or

— allowed, but subjected to the condition that they are made at a price higher than the minimum price for the product concerned.

In the latter case the minimum prices shall not include customs duties.

2. Minimum prices shall neither cause a reduction of the trade existing between Member States when this Treaty enters into force nor form an obstacle to progressive expansion of this trade. Minimum prices shall not be applied so as to form an obstacle to the development of a natural preference between Member States.

3. As soon as this Treaty enters into force the Council shall, on a proposal from the Commission, determine objective criteria for the establishment of minimum price systems and for the fixing of such prices.

These criteria shall in particular take account of the average national production costs in the Member State applying the minimum price, of the position of the various undertakings concerned in relation to such average production costs, and of the need to promote both the progressive improvement of agricultural practice and the adjustments and specialisation needed within the common market.

The Commission shall further propose a procedure for revising these criteria in order to allow for and speed up technical progress and to approximate prices progressively within the common market.

These criteria and the procedure for revising them shall be determined by the Council acting unanimously within three years of the entry into force of this Treaty.

4. Until the decision of the Council takes effect, Member States may fix minimum prices on condition that these are communicated beforehand to the Commission and to the other Member States so that they may submit their comments.

Once the Council has taken its decision, Member States shall fix minimum prices on the basis of the criteria determined as above.

The Council may, acting by a qualified majority on a proposal from the Commission, rectify any decisions taken by Member States which do not conform to the criteria defined above.

5. If it does not prove possible to determine the said objective criteria for certain products by the beginning of the third stage, the Council may, acting by a qualified majority on a proposal from the Commission, vary the minimum prices applied to these products.

6. At the end of the transitional period, a table of minimum prices still in force shall be drawn up. The Council shall, acting on a proposal from the Commission and by a majority of nine votes in accordance with the weighting laid down in the first subparagraph of Article 148(2), determine the system to be applied within the framework of the common agricultural policy.

Article 45

1. Until national market organisations have been replaced by one of the forms of common organisation referred to in Article 40(2), trade in products in respect of which certain Member States:

— have arrangements designed to guarantee national producers a market for their products; and

— are in need of imports,

shall be developed by the conclusion of long-term agreements or contracts between importing and exporting Member States.

These agreements or contracts shall be directed towards the progressive abolition of any discrimination in the application of these arrangements to the various producers within the Community.

Such agreements or contracts shall be concluded during the first stage; account shall be taken of the principle of reciprocity.

2. As regards quantities, these agreements or contracts shall be based on the average volume of trade between Member States in the products concerned during the three years before the entry into force of this Treaty and shall provide for an increase in the volume of trade within the limits of existing requirements, account being taken of traditional patterns of trade.

As regards prices, these agreements or contracts shall enable producers to dispose of the agreed quantities at prices which shall be progressively approximated to those paid to national producers on the domestic market of the purchasing country.

This approximation shall proceed as steadily as possible and shall be completed by the end of the transitional period at the latest.

Prices shall be negotiated between the parties concerned with the framework of directives issued by the Commission for the purpose of implementing the two preceding subparagraphs.

If the first stage is extended, these agreements or contracts shall continue to be carried out in accordance with the conditions applicable at the end of the fourth year after the entry into force of this Treaty, the obligation to increase quantities and to approximate prices being suspended until the transition to the second stage.

Member States shall avail themselves of any opportunity open to them under their legislation, particularly in respect of import policy, to ensure the conclusion and carrying out of these agreements or contracts.

3. To the extent that Member States require raw materials for the manufacture of products to be exported outside the Community in competition with products of third countries, the above agreements or contracts shall not form an obstacle to the importation of raw materials for this purpose from third countries. This provision shall not, however, apply if the Council unanimously decides to make provision for payments required to compensate for the higher price paid on goods imported for this purpose on the basis of these agreements or contracts in relation to the delivered price of the same goods purchased on the world market.

Article 46

Where in a Member State a product is subject to a national market organisation or to internal rules having equivalent effect which affect the competitive position of similar production in another Member State, a countervailing charge shall be applied by Member States to imports of this product coming from the Member State where such organisation or rules exist, unless that State applies a countervailing charge on export.

The Commission shall fix the amount of these charges at the level required to redress the balance; it may also authorise other measures, the conditions and details of which it shall determine.

Article 47

As to the functions to be performed by the Economic and Social Committee in pursuance of this Title, its agricultural section shall hold itself at the disposal of the Commission to prepare, in accordance with the provisions of Articles 197 and 198, the deliberations of the Committee.

TITLE III: Free Movement of Persons, Services and Capital

Chapter 1 (Workers)

Article 48

1. Freedom of movement for workers shall be secured within the Community by the end of the transitional period at the latest.

2. Such freedom of movement shall entail the abolition of any discrimination based on nationality between workers of the Member States as regards employment, remuneration and other conditions of work and employment.

3. It shall entail the right, subject to limitations justified on grounds of public policy, public security or public health:

(a) to accept offers of employment actually made;
(b) to move freely within the territory of Member States for this purpose;
(c) to stay in a Member State for the purpose of employment in accordance with the provisions governing the employment of nationals of that State laid down by law, regulation or administrative action;
(d) to remain in the territory of a Member State after having been employed in that State, subject to conditions which shall be embodied in implementing regulations to be drawn up by the Commission.

4. The provisions of this Article shall not apply to employment in the public service.

Article 49

As soon as this Treaty enters into force, the Council shall, acting in accordance with the procedure referred to in Article 189b and after consulting the Economic and Social Committee, issue directives or make regulations setting out the measures required to bring about, by progressive stages, freedom of movement for workers, as defined in Article 48, in particular:

(a) by ensuring close co-operation between national employment services;
(b) by systematically and progressively abolishing those administrative procedures and practices and those qualifying periods in respect of eligibility for available employment, whether resulting from national legislation or from agreements previously concluded between Member States, the maintenance of which would form an obstacle to liberalisation of the movement of workers;
(c) by systematically and progressively abolishing all such qualifying periods and other restrictions provided for either under national legislation or under agreements previously concluded between Member States as imposed on workers of other Member States conditions regarding the free choice of employment other than those imposed on workers of the State concerned;
(d) by setting up appropriate machinery to bring offers of employment into touch with applications for employment and to facilitate the achievement of a balance between supply and demand in the employment market in such a way as to avoid serious threats to the standard of living and level of employment in the various regions and industries.

GENERAL NOTE
This is the operative provision under which the majority of the secondary legislation giving effect to the freedom of movement of workers under Art. 48 has been passed. The amendment relates purely to the post-Maastricht legislative procedure applicable to the adoption of such legislation. The relevant procedure is now the conciliation and veto procedure (Art. 189b E.C.). In common with the majority of the provisions dealing with the achievement of the single market, this marks an upgrading from the co-operation procedure introduced by the SEA (Art. 149(2) E.E.C., now Art. 189c E.C.).

Article 50

Member States shall, within the framework of a joint programme, encourage the exchange of young workers.

Article 51

The Council shall acting unanimously on a proposal from the Commission, adopt such measures in the field of social security as are necessary to provide freedom of movement for workers; to this end, it shall make arrangements to secure for migrant workers and their dependants:

(a) aggregation, for the purpose of acquiring and retaining the right to benefit and of calculating the amount of benefit, of all periods taken into account under the laws of the several countries;

(b) payment of benefits to persons resident in the territories of Member States.

Chapter 2 (Right of Establishment)

Article 52

Within the framework of the provisions set out below, restrictions on the freedom of establishment of nationals of a Member State in the territory of another Member State shall be abolished by progressive stages in the course of the transitional period. Such progressive abolition shall also apply to restrictions on the setting up of agencies, branches or subsidiaries by nationals of any Member State established in the territory of any Member State.

Freedom of establishment shall include the right to take up and pursue activities as self-employed persons and to set up and manage undertakings, in particular companies or firms within the meaning of the second paragraph of Article 58, under the conditions laid down for its own nationals by the law of the country where such establishment is effected, subject to the provisions of the Chapter relating to capital.

Article 53

Member States shall not introduce any new restrictions on the right of establishment in their territories of nationals of other Member States, save as otherwise provided in this Treaty.

Article 54

1. Before the end of the first stage, the Council shall, acting unanimously on a proposal from the Commission and after consulting the Economic and Social Committee and the European Parliament, draw up a general programme for the abolition of existing restrictions on freedom of establishment within the Community. The Commission shall submit its proposal to the Council during the first two years of the first stage.

The programme shall set out the general conditions under which freedom of establishment is to be attained in the case of each type of activity and in particular the stages by which it is to be attained.

2. In order to implement this general programme or, in the absence of such programme, in order to achieve a stage in attaining freedom of establishment as regards a particular activity, the Council, acting in accordance with the procedure referred to in Article 189b and after consulting the Economic and Social Committee, shall act by means of directives.

3. The Council and the Commission shall carry out the duties devolving upon them under the preceding provisions, in particular:
   (a) by according, as a general rule, priority treatment to activities where freedom of establishment makes a particularly valuable contribution to the development of production and trade;
   (b) by ensuring close co-operation between the competent authorities in the Member States in order to ascertain the particular situation within the Community of the various activities concerned;
   (c) by abolishing those administrative procedures and practices, whether resulting from national legislation or from agreements previously concluded between Member States, the maintenance of which would form an obstacle to freedom of establishment;
   (d) by ensuring that workers of one Member State employed in the territory of another Member State may remain in that territory for the purpose of taking up activities therein as self-employed persons, where they satisfy the conditions which they would be required to satisfy if they were entering that State at the time when they intended to take up such activities;

(e) by enabling a national of one Member State to acquire and use land and buildings situated in the territory of another Member State, in so far as this does not conflict with the principles laid down in Article 39(2);

(f) by effecting the progressive abolition of restrictions on freedom of establishment in every branch of activity under consideration, both as regards the conditions for setting up agencies, branches or subsidiaries in the territory of a Member State and as regards the subsidiaries in the territory of a Member State and as regards the conditions governing the entry of personnel belonging to the main establishment into managerial or supervisory posts in such agencies, branches or subsidiaries;

(g) by co-ordinating to the necessary extent the safeguards which, for the protection of the interests of members and others, are required by Member States of companies or firms within the meaning of the second paragraph of Article 58 with a view to making such safeguards equivalent throughout the Community;

(h) by satisfying themselves that the conditions of establishment are not distorted by aids granted by Member States.

GENERAL NOTE

Article 54 permits the adoption of legislation aimed at the achievement of the freedom of establishment (Art. 52 E.E.C./E.C.). The only change in the Article is that the co-operation procedure, operating in this field since the coming into force of the SEA (Art. 149(2) E.E.C., now Art. 189c E.C.) is now replaced by the conciliation and veto procedure (Art. 189b E.C.).

Article 55

The provisions of this Chapter shall not apply, so far as any given Member State is concerned, to activities which in that State are connected, even occasionally, with the exercise of official authority.

The Council may, acting by a qualified majority on a proposal from the Commission, rule that the provisions of this Chapter shall not apply to certain activities.

Article 56

1. The provisions of this Chapter and measures taken in pursuance thereof shall not prejudice the applicability of provisions laid down by law, regulation or administrative action providing for special treatment for foreign nationals on grounds of public policy, public security or public health.

2. Before the end of the transitional period, the Council shall, acting unanimously on a proposal from the Commission and after consulting the European Parliament, issue directives for the co-ordination of the abovementioned provisions laid down by law, regulation or administrative action. After the end of the second stage, however, the Council shall, acting in accordance with the procedure referred to in Article 189b, issue directives for the co-ordination of such provisions as, in each Member State, are a matter for regulation or administrative action.

GENERAL NOTE

This Article is aimed at the co-ordination of the constraints within Member States on the freedom of establishment due to public policy, public health and public security. The passing of directives with this purpose is now to be carried out under the conciliation and veto procedure (Art. 189b E.C. replacing the co-operation procedure Art. 149(2) E.E.C., now Art. 189c E.C.). The remainder of the Article is unamended.

Article 57

1. In order to make it easier for persons to take up and pursue activities as self-employed persons, the Council shall, acting in accordance with the procedure referred to in Article 189b, issue directives for the mutual recognition of diplomas, certificates and other evidence of formal qualifications.

2. For the same purpose, the Council shall, before the end of the transitional period, issue directives for the co-ordination of the provisions laid down by law, regulation or administrative action in Member States concerning the taking up and pursuit of activities as self-employed persons. The Council, acting unanimously on a proposal from the Commission and after consulting the European Parliament, shall decide on directives the implementation of which involves in at least one Member State amendment of the existing principles laid down by law governing the professions with respect to training and conditions of access for natural persons. In other cases the Council shall act in accordance with the procedure referred to in Article 189b.

3. In the case of the medical and allied and pharmaceutical professions, the progressive abolition of restrictions shall be dependent upon co-ordination of the conditions for their exercise in the various Member States.

GENERAL NOTE

The amendment of this Article alters the legislative procedure for the adoption of Directives aimed at the mutual recognition of diplomas. The co-operation procedure is replaced by the new conciliation and veto procedure under Art. 189b E.C.

Article 57(2) provides for the co-ordination of the legislative and administrative procedures laid down by Member States concerning the taking-up and pursuit of activities by self-employed persons. The principle that unanimity be required to adopt Directives which, in at least one Member State, would require amendment to existing legislation on the taking-up of and access to a particular profession is retained. The applicable process in the absence of a need for such national legislation is now the conciliation and veto procedure (Art. 189b E.C.). See Weatherill and Beaumont, *EC Law*, Penguin, pp. 526–529 and Kapteyn, *The Law of European Communities*, pp. 536–540.

Article 58

Companies or firms formed in accordance with the law of a Member State and having their registered office, central administration or principal place of business within the Community shall, for the purposes of this Chapter, be treated in the same way as natural persons who are nationals of Member States.

'Companies or firms' means companies or firms constituted under civil or commercial law, including co-operative societies, and other legal persons governed by public or private law, save for those which are non-profit-making.

Chapter 3 (Services)

Article 59

Within the framework of the provisions set out below, restrictions on freedom to provide services within the Community shall be progressively abolished during the transitional period in respect of nationals of Member States who are established in a State of the Community other than that of the person for whom the services are intended.

The Council may, acting by a qualified majority on a proposal from the Commission, extend the provisions of the Chapter to nationals of a third country who provide services and who are established within the Community.

Article 60

Services shall be considered to be 'services' within the meaning of this Treaty where they are normally provided for remuneration, in so far as they are not governed by the provisions relating to freedom of movement for goods, capital and persons.

'Services' shall in particular include:

(a) activities of an industrial character;
(b) activities of a commercial character:
(c) activities of craftsmen;
(d) activities of the professions.

Without prejudice to the provisions of the Chapter relating to the right of establishment, the person providing a service may, in order to do so, temporarily pursue his activity in the State where the service is provided, under the same conditions as are imposed by that State on its own nationals.

Article 61

1. Freedom to provide services in the field of transport shall be governed by the provisions of the title relating to transport.

2. The liberalisation of banking and insurance services connected with movements of capital shall be effected in step with the progressive liberalisation of movement of capital.

Article 62

Save as otherwise provided in this Treaty, Member States shall not introduce any new restrictions on the freedom to provide services which have in fact been attained at the date of the entry into force of this Treaty.

Article 63

1. Before the end of the first stage, the Council shall, acting unanimously on a proposal from the Commission and after consulting the Economic and Social Committee and the European Parliament, draw up a general programme for the abolition of existing restrictions on freedom to provide services within the Community. The Commission shall submit its proposal to the Council during the first two years of the first stage.

The programme shall set out the general conditions under which and the stages by which each type of service is to be liberalised.

2. In order to implement this general programme or, in the absence of such programme, in order to achieve a stage in the liberalisation of a specific service, the Council shall, on a proposal from the Commission and after consulting the Economic and Social Committee and the European Parliament, issue directives, acting unanimously until the end of the first stage and by a qualified majority thereafter.

3. As regards the proposals and decisions referred to in paragraphs 1 and 2, priority shall as a general rule be given to those services which directly affect production costs or the liberalisation of which helps to promote trade in goods.

Article 64

The Member States declare their readiness to undertake the liberalisation of services beyond the extent required by the directives issued pursuant to Article 63(2), if their general economic situation and the situation of the economic sector concerned so permit.

To this end, the Commission shall make recommendations to the Member States concerned.

Article 65

As long as restrictions on freedom to provide services have not been abolished, each Member State shall apply such restrictions without distinction on grounds of nationality or residence to all persons providing services within the meaning of the first paragraph of Article 59.

Article 66

The provisions of Articles 55 to 58 shall apply to the matters covered by this Chapter.

Chapter 4 (Capital and Payments)

GENERAL NOTE

The provisions on capital and payments in Arts. 67–73 E.E.C. will remain in force until January 1, 1994 (Art. 73a E.C.) when they will be superseded by the new rules encompassed in Arts. 73b–g E.C.

The changes made to this chapter by the TEU are designed to further liberalise free movement of capital, following the coming into force of the second stage of economic and monetary union on January 1, 1994. The overall aim is to secure the outright freedom of movement for capital and payments between the Member States and between Member States and third countries (Art. 73b E.C.).

The free movement of capital between the Member States has already been secured to a large extent thanks to Dir. 88/361 E.E.C., which came into force between nine of the Member States on July 1, 1990 (see below).

The free movement of capital was included in the original E.E.C. Treaty as one of the four freedoms deemed necessary for the creation of a common European market (Arts. 67–73 E.E.C.). The European Court in *Casati* (Case 203/80), [1981] E.C.R. 2595) reiterated that the free movement of capital is a key element of the market integration process.

Nevertheless, the unequivocal rules that characterise the other freedoms were long absent in this field. The movement of capital across borders causes greater implications for national economies than related provisions on the freedom of movement of workers, goods and services. Capital can be moved much more easily than people, and major outflows could take place from the relatively weak economies of the Community, further weakening their economies.

The provisions of the E.E.C. Treaty dealing with capital reflect these qualifications. The requirement in Art. 67 E.E.C. that capital movement be freed "only to the extent necessary to ensure the proper functioning of the common market" sets Art. 67 apart from its companion provisions in the areas of free movement of workers, goods and services. It also deprives Art. 67 E.E.C. of direct effect (Case 203/80, *Casati, supra*).

The amplification of the restricted rights included in this chapter was dependent on the promulgation of legislation by the Council under Art. 69 E.E.C. Developments in this area were very slow and restrictive until the passing of Dir. 88/361 E.E.C. ([1988] O.J. L178/5) aimed at achievement of the internal market called for by Art. 8a E.E.C. (now Art. 7a E.C.) inserted by the SEA (for examination of pre-1988 legislation and an assessment of Dir. 88/361 see Oliver and Bache, Free Movement of Capital: Recent Developments (1989) 26 C.M.L.Rev. 61).

The objective of Dir. 88/361 is to implement Art. 67 by abolishing the remaining restrictions on movements of capital between persons resident in Member States. The Directive came into effect as regards the majority of the Member States at the start of July 1990 (Art. 6(1)). Spain, Ireland, Greece and Portugal were granted an extension until the end of 1992 before full compliance was required, and in the cases of Greece and Portugal further extensions until the end of 1995 may be granted in the event of balance of payments difficulties or the failure of their financial systems to adapt sufficiently (Art. 73e E.C.). Any such further derogations must be agreed according to the procedure laid down in Art. 69 E.E.C. A derogation in relation to Greece, applicable until January 1, 1995, was agreed by Council Dir. 92/122 ([1992] O.J. L409/33).

The Directive itself contains certain exceptions. Member States may take safeguard measures where short-term capital movements of exceptional magnitude impose serious strains on the foreign exchange markets, leading to serious disturbances in the conduct of monetary and exchange rate policies (Art. 3). The Council were due to review the continued application of this exception by the end of 1992 but no alteration was made. With the pressures being encountered in the capital markets during that year, any move to revoke the latitude afforded by Art. 3 was always going to be unlikely. The turmoil in the ERM brought the issue of currency restrictions to the fore, with huge quantities of capital flowing out of the beleaguered countries. While Ireland and Spain reintroduced currency controls, this did not prevent the sustained attacks on their and other ERM currencies.

Member States were also given some room for fiscal manoeuvre by the provision under Art. 108 E.E.C. relating to serious balance of payments disequilibrium. The Member State could take restricted measures to ensure that the problems it faced would not endanger the other goals of the Community, such as the achievement of the common market or the common commercial policy. This provision ceased to be applicable when the TEU came into force, but is replaced by Arts. 109h and 109i E.C. which are similar and will apply until the single currency is operative in the state(s) concerned (see notes on these Articles).

Article 67

1. During the transitional period and to the extent necessary to ensure the proper functioning of the common market, Member States shall progressively abolish between themselves all restrictions on the movement of capital belonging to persons resident in Member States and any discrimination based on the nationality or on the place of residence of the parties or on the place where such capital is invested.

2. Current payments connected with the movements of capital between Member States shall be freed from all restrictions by the end of the first stage at the latest.

Article 68

1. Member States shall, as regards the matters dealt with in this Chapter, be as liberal as possible in granting such exchange authorisations as are still necessary after the entry into force of this Treaty.

2. Where a Member State applies to the movements of capital liberalised in accordance with the provisions of this Chapter the domestic rules governing the capital market and the credit system, it shall do so in a non-discriminatory manner.

3. Loans for the direct or indirect financing of a Member State or its regional or local authorities shall not be issued or placed in other Member States unless the States concerned have reached agreement thereon. This provision shall not preclude the application of Article 22 of the Protocol on the Statute of the European Investment Bank.

Article 69

The Council shall, on a proposal from the Commission, which for this purpose shall consult the Monetary Committee provided for in Article 105, issue the necessary directives for the progressive implementation of the provisions of Article 67, acting unanimously during the first two stages and by a qualified majority thereafter.

Article 70

1. The Commission shall propose to the Council measures for the progressive co-ordination of the exchange policies of Member States in respect of the movement of capital between those States and third countries. For this purpose the Council shall issue directives, acting by a qualified majority. It shall endeavour to attain the highest possible degree of liberalisation. Unanimity shall be required for measures which constitute a step back as regards the liberalisation of capital movements.

2. Where the measures taken in accordance with paragraph 1 do not permit the elimination of differences between the exchange rules of Member States and where such differences could lead persons resident in one of the Member States to use the freer transfer facilities within the Community which are provided for in Article 67 in order to evade the rules of one of the Member States concerning the movement of capital to or from third countries, that

State may, after consulting the other Member States and the Commission, take appropriate measures to overcome these difficulties.

Should the Council find that these measures are restricting the free movement of capital within the Community to a greater extent than is required for the purpose of overcoming the difficulties, it may, acting by a qualified majority on a proposal from the Commission, decide that the State concerned shall amend or abolish these measures.

Article 71

Member States shall endeavour to avoid introducing within the Community any new exchange restrictions on the movement of capital and current payments connected with such movements, and shall endeavour not to make existing rules more restrictive.

They declare their readiness to go beyond the degree of liberalisation of capital movements provided for in the preceding Articles in so far as their economic situation, in particular the situation of their balance of payments, so permits.

The Commission may, after consulting the Monetary Committee, make recommendations to Member States on this subject.

Article 72

Member States shall keep the Commission informed of any movements of capital to and from third countries which come to their knowledge. The Commission may deliver to Member States any opinions which it considers appropriate on this subject.

Article 73

1. If movements of capital lead to disturbances in the functioning of the capital market in any Member State, the Commission shall, after consulting the Monetary Committee, authorise that State to take protective measures in the field of capital movements, the conditions and details of which the Commission shall determine.

The Council may, acting by a qualified majority, revoke this authorisation or amend the conditions or details thereof.

2. A Member State which is in difficulties may, however, on grounds of secrecy or urgency, take the measures mentioned above, where this proves necessary, on its own initiative. The Commission and the other Member States shall be informed of such measures by the date of their entry into force at the latest. In this event the Commission may, after consulting the Monetary Committee, decide that the State concerned shall amend or abolish the measures.

GENERAL NOTE

The new provisions (Arts. 73a–h E.C.)

While the freedom of movement of capital has been largely secured under Dir. 88/361, from January 1, 1994 this protection will become subject to the unequivocally worded provisions of Art. 73b E.C. whereby all restrictions on the freedom of movement of capital and payments between Member States and between Member States and third countries will be prohibited.

There will be an absolute prohibition on restrictions on capital movements between Member States but there will still possibly be restrictions between Member States and third countries. The majority of the new provisions are concerned with the conditions for such derogations as regards third countries and would seem to permit extensive exceptions to the general rule in Art. 73b E.C. Article 73c(1) E.C. permits the continued application of national or Community law, existing prior to January 1, 1994, which restricts the movement of capital to or from third countries. There is thus nothing to stop the Community or Member States from "stocking up" protections prior to this deadline; neither Art. 71 E.E.C. or Dir. 88/361 E.E.C. deal with extra-Community transfers (see Art. 1 of the Directive). Under Art. 72 E.E.C. the Member

States are simply under an obligation to keep the Commission informed of capital movements to or from third countries. Protections against capital moving to non-Member States will be ineffective if capital can be moved to a Member State which has no such restrictions on capital movement and from there moved to a non-Member State.

The result of the new capital provisions may be limited, at least in the short-term. As regards capital and payments freedoms between the Member States, little has been added to the protections afforded by Dir. 88/361. The major alteration is the removal of the potential derogations afforded by this provision including the short-term safeguard measures permitted by Art. 3 of the Directive. Also to be removed is the potential derogation afforded by Art. 73 E.E.C., whereby if movements of capital lead to disturbances in the functioning of the capital market in any Member State, it may take emergency measures on its own initiative (Art. 73(2) E.E.C.) or with the authorisation of the Commission (Art. 73(1) E.E.C.). The removal of this protective measure from January 1, 1994 may well prove less than welcome if the move towards economic and monetary convergence of the Member State economies is behind schedule. The lack of any meaningful convergence could open up further problems of pressures being applied on Member State currencies, especially if the commitment to narrow ERM bands is reiterated. Whatever the pressures, the commitment to free movement of capital appears virtually absolute; exceptions are permitted in Arts. 73d(1) and 73d(2) concerning, *inter alia*, taxation matters and statistical analysis of capital flows but with the express proviso that these do not constitute a disguised restriction on the free movement of capital (Art. 73(d)(3) E.C.). The vexed matter of taxation could well prove one of the major stumbling blocks to the free movement of capital both intra-Community and vis-à-vis third countries. There is a potential contradiction between the wording of Art. 73d E.C. and the appended declaration which will require to be clarified. The current divergent interpretations on the scope of permissible tax measures with regard to Community and non-Community nationals is discussed in the note on Art. 73d.

Returning to the effects of the new provisions, the significant change from the legislation applicable prior to the TEU coming into force is the commitment to freedom of capital and payments between the Member States and third countries. Nevertheless, this commitment is subject to a wide variety of potential derogations. As already mentioned there is the proviso that existing restrictive measures may remain in force after the January 1, 1994 deadline (Art. 73c(1) E.C.). There is also a provision permitting the Council, acting on a qualified majority, to enact safeguard measures for a maximum of six months where capital movements to or from third countries threaten or cause serious difficulties for the operation of economic and monetary union (Art. 73f E.C.). Other potential restrictions which may be applied by the Member States are included in Art. 73g(2) E.C., which permits the imposition of unilateral measures against a third country for serious political reasons or on the grounds of urgency. The Community is likewise permitted to take such measures as are agreed under the common foreign and security policy pillar (Art. 73g(1) E.C.).

Nowhere in these new provisions is there any provision for the formal involvement of the European Parliament in the legislative process. (Article 73g makes it necessary for the European Parliament to be consulted after the event, should the Council strike down any Member State's economic sanction in force against a third state.)

Article 73a

As from 1 January 1994, Articles 67 to 73 shall be replaced by Articles 73b, c, d, e, f and g.

GENERAL NOTE
This article sets the time-scale for the coming into force of the new provisions on the freedom of movement of capital and payments. Articles 73(b)–(g) are the operative provisions which will dictate the policy governing this area from January 1, 1994. Prior to that date, the existing legislation in the field, primarily Dir. 88/361, must be read in the light of the new Art. 73h E.C. The intermediate provisions contained in this Article will take effect on the coming into force of the Treaty and fall into desuetude on January 1, 1994. The Treaty thus provides for a transitional phase during which the liberalisation of capital movements and payments will continue to be tied to the liberalisation of the other freedoms enshrined in the E.C. Treaty.

Article 73b

1. Within the framework of the provisions set out in this Chapter, all restrictions on the movement of capital between Member States and between Member States and third countries shall be prohibited.

2. Within the framework of the provisions set out in this Chapter, all restrictions on payments between Member States and between Member States and third countries shall be prohibited.

GENERAL NOTE
The division of this section into two sub-paragraphs reflects the practice under the existing Treaty provisions of dealing with the freedom of movement of capital and payments separately (Art. 67(1) E.E.C. on capital and 67(2) E.E.C. on payments). This dichotomy has only now been expressly recognised in the Titles of the Treaty, whereby the new heading to Chap. 4 reads "capital and payments" as opposed to its old single word title of "capital". Nevertheless, this change is purely cosmetic. The E.C.J., in the few cases on this topic, developed a distinction between the free movement of capital and the free movement of payments. The Court accepted that capital movements are not the only transactions that involve transfers of currency. Currency may be transferred in order to invest the funds themselves or it may be transferred to make a specific purchase. In the latter case, currency movement is a precondition for the exercise of other freedoms, such as those relating to goods, persons and services (see Cases 203/80 *Casati* [1981] E.C.R. 2595; 308/86 *Lambert* [1988] E.C.R. 4369; and 286/82, 26/83 *Luisi and Carbone* [1984] E.C.R. 377). The result was the protection for the free movement of payments analogous to the protection attributed to the other freedoms.

With the gradual removal of restrictions on the free movement of capital, any distinction between the treatment of capital and payments has been steadily removed. Article 73b E.C. would seem to have taken this to its logical conclusion with the prohibition of any restrictions to the free movement of capital ensured by para. 1 and with regard to payments in para. 2. In both cases this prohibition is absolute, but with regard to the freedom of movement of capital with third countries it is crucial to note the qualifying phrase: "within the framework of the provisions set out in this chapter". Due to the potentially more "injurious" effects of capital transfers, several of the restrictions do not apply to payments: Arts. 73c(1) and (2) and 73f E.C. make reference only to "capital". It is difficult to regard the omission of any reference to "payments" in these Articles as an oversight, in so far as Art. 73g E.C. makes explicit allusion to the potential restriction of both capital and payments. It would therefore seem that the distinction drawn by the European Court between capital and payments in Community matters will continue to be applicable, but only in cases with an external third country element.

The wording of this Article and the prohibitions which it enunciates ought to be capable of direct effect and thus permit the enforcement of its obligations before the national courts. Those Member States which maintain restrictions on this freedom, not justified under any other heading, will probably find themselves the subject of Art. 169 E.C. proceedings.

Article 73c

1. The provisions of Article 73b shall be without prejudice to the application to third countries of any restrictions which exist on 31 December 1993 under national or Community law adopted in respect of the movement of capital to or from third countries involving direct investment (including investment in real estate), establishment, the provision of financial services or the admission of securities to capital markets.

2. Whilst endeavouring to achieve the objective of free movement of capital between Member States and third countries to the greatest extent possible and without prejudice to the other Chapters of this Treaty, the Council may, acting by a qualified majority on a proposal from the Commission, adopt measures on the movement of capital to or from third countries involving direct investment (including investment in real estate), establishment, the provision of financial services or the admission of securities to capital markets.

Unanimity shall be required for measures under this paragraph which constitute a step back in Community law as regards the liberalisation of the movement of capital to or from third countries.

GENERAL NOTE

Para. (1)
This Article permits measures restricting the flow of capital to or from third countries, in existence on December 31, 1993, to remain applicable after the deadline for the abolition of restrictions on capital movements has come into being. As already mentioned, this seems to

render the supposed prohibition on measures preventing the free movement of capital between third states and the Community somewhat otiose. The scope of areas in which national or Community legislation derogating from the free movement of capital to or from third countries is permissible is large, including any form of direct investment, establishment, the provision of financial services or the admission of securities to the capital markets. The majority of these appear to be aimed at preventing extra-Community competition in these fields, notably as regards the provision of financial services. Moreover, the Article concerns both the inflow and outflow of capital, thus permitting national laws preventing internal investment, as well as permitting rules aimed at preventing the outflow of capital from a Member State to a third country. Moreover, there is no deadline set by the Treaty for the abolition of such restrictions. So long as they were in existence on December 31, 1993, then they may continue, *ad infinitum*, unless the Community adopts legislation on the matter under Art. 73(2) E.C.

Para. (2)

This paragraph lays down the legislative procedure applicable to the promulgation of measures dealing with the movement of capital to and from third countries in the four areas listed, encompassing direct investment, establishment, the provision of financial services or the admission of securities to capital markets. Those measures which "constitute a step back in Community law" as regards the liberalisation of the movement of capital must be approved by a unanimous Council, while other measures (not specifically defined but presumably all other measures apart from those already mentioned) are subject to qualified majority acceptance. This reflects the wording and purpose of Art. 70 E.E.C., which it will supersede on January 1, 1994.

Article 73d

1. The provisions of Article 73b shall be without prejudice to the right of Member States:
   (a) to apply the relevant provisions of their tax law which distinguish between tax-payers who are not in the same situation with regard to their place of residence or with regard to the place where their capital is invested;
   (b) to take all requisite measures to prevent infringements of national law and regulations, in particular in the field of taxation and the prudential supervision of financial institutions, or to lay down procedures for the declaration of capital movements for purposes of administrative or statistical information, or to take measures which are justified on grounds of public policy or public security.

2. The provisions of this Chapter shall be without prejudice to the applicability of restrictions on the right of establishment which are compatible with this Treaty.

3. The measures and procedures referred to in paragraphs 1 and 2 shall not constitute a means of arbitrary discrimination or a disguised restriction on the free movement of capital and payments as defined in Article 73b.

GENERAL NOTE

This Article gives some discretion to Member States to derogate from the absolute requirement of free movement of capital in Art. 73b E.C. This is achieved by setting out in paras. 1 and 2 the specific areas where this is permissible, but making them subject to the proviso contained in para. 3.

Para. (1)(a)

The issue of taxation is one of the most contentious as regards the influence of the Community. This Article preserves the right of the Member States to charge tax within its own boundaries at different levels, which are dependent on the residence of the tax-payer. Dassesse suggests that the wording of this Article is potentially in conflict with the appended declaration on Art. 73d E.C. The original wording of the declaration provided that the Member States would have the right to apply the relevant provisions of their tax laws "only with respect to the relevant provisions which existed at the end of 1993". However, the declaration was later substantially amended by the addition of a new second clause which reads "this declaration shall apply only to capital movements between Member States and to payments effected between Member States". Dassesse argues that while Art. 73d E.C. appears to permit the Member States to discriminate between local residents, other Member State nationals and nationals of third countries, the declaration would seem to permit differentiation between taxpayers only as regards those measures which are in force at the end of 1993 and only for operations concerning residents of other Member States. Some Member States, reading the declaration together with Art. 73d E.C., see this as imposing a duty on all Member States not to adopt tax measures which treat residents of other Member States more favourably than their own residents. In other words a prohibition on the adoption of measures making the Member State a "tax haven" for residents of other Member States. Other Member States have interpreted the provisions as permitting a Member State to treat residents of third countries less favourably than nationals of other Member States. This is particularly asserted with regard to the refusal to refund a withholding tax on securities held by a third country resident, even though such refunds are granted to Community residents (see Dassesse, The TEU, Implications for the Free Movement of Capital [1992] 6 *Journal of International Banking Law*, pp. 238–243). While this argument does carry some weight, it fails to place enough emphasis on the ambivalent legal status of declarations appended to the core Community Treaties. These measures are legally non-binding, collective declarations of intent or declarations of a purely political nature. Toth, referring to the SEA, described the declarations appended to that instrument as "having no effect on the interpretation of the SEA by the E.C.J." (Toth, The Legal Status of Declarations Appended to the SEA (1986) 23 C.M.L.Rev. 811.) There is no reason to question the applicability of these statements to the TEU declarations. It will nevertheless be up to the E.C.J. to rule on the effect of this provision of the Treaty.

Para. (1)(b)

This paragraph permits checks applied to the movement of capital to continue, for example to ensure the proper supervision of financial institutions or for the compilation of administrative or statistical information (reiteration of Art. 4 of Dir. 88/361/E.E.C.) and allows the Member States to take measures justified on the grounds of public policy or public security.

The exception in relation to "public policy" or "public security" would appear to afford a potentially wide let-out clause to the otherwise absolute prohibition on measures preventing the flow of capital and payments between Member States. While it is impossible to predict to what extent Member States might rely on this provision, it is easier to predict the tests which will have to be fulfilled in order to justify such actions. In any challenge to legislation derogating from free movement of capital or payments on any of the grounds listed in this Article, the Member State will have to prove that its actions are proportionate to the goals sought. Ultimately, the European Court would determine the lawfulness of any such derogations (see Case 42/82 *E.C. Commission* v. *French Republic* [1983] E.C.R. 1013, in the context of Art. 36 E.E.C.). It has always, as regards other fundamental freedoms, refused to accept a broad definition of this exception (as regards the free movement of goods under Art. 36 E.E.C., see Weatherill and Beaumont, *EC Law*, pp. 399–404).

Para. (2)

This paragraph permits the continued reliance by Member States on the existing restrictions applicable to the freedom of establishment (Arts. 52–66 E.C.). The provisions in this chapter are to have no effect on the continued reliance on such derogations. While Art. 52 E.C. makes it clear that the right of establishment must be exercised "subject to the provisions of the chapter on capital", this paragraph makes it clear that the exceptions to the freedom of establishment continue to be applicable regardless. These restrictions include the exception in the case of activities concerned with the exercise of official authority (Art. 55 E.C. and Case 2/74, *Reyners* v. *Belgium* [1974] E.C.R. 631), as well as the permissible restrictions laid down in Art. 56 E.C. that special measures may be taken as regards foreign nationals on the grounds of public policy, public health or public security. See Weatherill and Beaumont, *EC Law*, Penguin, pp. 511–513 and 517–521; Wyatt and Dashwood, *EC Law*, (1993, 3rd ed., Sweet & Maxwell), pp. 291–293 and 307–312. This paragraph ensures that such restrictions as still apply on January 1, 1994 will not be subject to attack on the grounds that they do not comply with the absolute freedom of capital laid down in Art. 73b E.C.

This paragraph must be read in the light of para. 3 which dictates that any measures must not constitute a means of arbitrary discrimination or a disguised restriction on the free movement of capital (see note on that paragraph).

While dealing with the free movement of services as opposed to establishment, the E.C.J. recently laid down an important ruling, of ambiguous legal relevance to the present article, on the permissible scope of restrictions to one of the fundamental freedoms. This took place in *Bachmann (Hans-Martin)* v. *Belgium* and *E.C. Commission* v. *Belgium* (cases 204 and 300/90, judgments of January 28, 1992), in which the E.C.J., in contrast to its previous jurisprudence on the topic, found that Member States were permitted to take measures which restrict the free provision of cross-border services where such measures are necessary to ensure "the coherence of their national tax system". It is impossible to predict the potential of the E.C.J. developing such a derogation in the establishment field and thus accruing further derogations from the free movement of capital through the present article.

Para. (3)

This paragraph reiterates the provision common to Community law, emphasising the restricted scope within which any derogations to the fundamental freedoms in the Treaty are to be exercised. Such a test inevitably involves a delicate balancing of the derogation and its purpose. Article 36 E.C. contains an identically worded provision as regards measures derogating from the free movement of goods. As this type of provision is new to the field of capital movement, it is likely that the jurisprudence of the European Court as regards Art. 36 E.C. will prove illuminating. The measures will only be justified where they are no more restrictive than is strictly necessary, in other words, in accordance with the principle of proportionality (see Cases 5/77 *Tedeschi (Carlo) Denkavit Commerciale SRL* [1977] E.C.R. 1556 and 251/78 *Denkavit* [1979] E.C.R. 3327 at para. 21). The requirements that the restriction be proportionate, not constitute a disguised restriction on trade nor be a means of arbitrary discrimination cannot be considered in isolation. For example, the test of proportionality may well indicate the existence of a disguised restriction on trade (see Wyatt and Dashwood, at *supra* p. 229). For an overview of this field as regards Art. 36, see Weatherill and Beaumont, *supra*, Chap. 16.

Given that any measures are to be assessed in terms of their compliance with the free movement of capital and payments as defined in Art. 73b, it is highly likely that the E.C.J. will apply strict tests to any derogation measures.

Article 73e

By way of derogation from Article 73b, Member States which, on 31 December 1993, enjoy a derogation on the basis of existing Community law, shall be entitled to maintain, until 31 December 1995 at the latest, restrictions on movements of capital authorised by such derogations as exist on that date.

GENERAL NOTE

This Article allows those Member States who are permitted to maintain restrictions on the movement of capital on December 31, 1993 to maintain these restrictions in force until December 31, 1995 at the latest. Under Dir. 88/361/E.E.C., transitional arrangements were made permitting four Member States (Spain, Greece, Ireland and Portugal) to continue the application of certain restrictions to the liberalised provisions until the end of 1992. Provision was also made for the possibility of further extension of the transitional arrangements by up to three years for Greece and Portugal (Art. 6(2) Dir. 88/361/E.E.C.). Such arrangements must be subject to agreement by the Council, in accordance with the procedure laid down in Art. 69 E.E.C. Dir. 92/122/E.E.C. authorises Greece to defer the liberalisation of certain capital movements pursuant to Art. 6(2) of Dir. 88/361/E.E.C., O.J. 1992 L407/1 until January 1, 1995.

Article 73f

Where, in exceptional circumstances, movements of capital to or from third countries cause, or threaten to cause, serious difficulties for the operation of economic and monetary union, the Council, acting by a qualified majority on a proposal from the Commission and after consulting the ECB, may take safeguard measures with regard to third countries for a period not exceeding six months if such measures are strictly necessary.

GENERAL NOTE

This Article permits the Council, acting by a qualified majority on a proposal from the Commission, to enact safeguard measures with regard to third countries, for a period not exceeding six months. The wording of this Article makes it quite clear that such measures must not be taken lightly. The words "exceptional circumstances", "serious difficulties", and "strictly necessary" make this provision appear very much a last resort measure.

Also relevant in this respect are the provisions in Arts. 109h and 109i E.C. on serious balance of payments difficulties in the Member States (see notes on those articles).

No express provision is made as to the date at which this provision is to come into effect but the reference to the consultation of the European Central Bank and to economic and monetary union makes it seem that it may not take effect until the coming into force of the third stage of economic and monetary union.

Article 73g

1. If, in the case envisaged in Article 228a, action by the Community is deemed necessary, the Council may, in accordance with the procedure provided for in Article 228a, take the necessary urgent measures on the movement of capital and on payments as regards the third countries concerned.

2. Without prejudice to Article 224 and as long as the Council has not taken measures pursuant to paragraph 1, a Member State may, for serious political reasons and on grounds of urgency, take unilateral measures against a third country with regard to capital movements and payments. The Commission and the other Member States shall be informed of such measures by the date of their entry into force at the latest.

The Council may, acting by a qualified majority on a proposal from the Commission, decide that the Member State concerned shall amend or abolish such measures. The President of the Council shall inform the European Parliament of any such decision taken by the Council.

GENERAL NOTE

This Article gives authority to further derogations from the outright freedom of capital espoused in this chapter. These derogations are based on essentially political considerations, including the imposition of economic sanctions on third countries (para. 1). It also permits unilateral derogations by Member States in their relations with third countries, but subject to Community revocation (para. 2).

Para. (1)

This paragraph gives weight to the new Art. 228a E.C. added at Maastricht. Under Art. 228a E.C., the Council is to take the necessary urgent measures required to interrupt or reduce, in part or completely, economic relations with one or more third countries. Such measures, to be adopted by qualified majority in the Council, are incorporated into Community law by virtue of Art. 228a E.C. and are based on common positions or joint actions taken under the inter-governmental foreign and security policy pillar (Title V TEU). The political agreement to impose economic sanctions on a third country is taken under the common foreign and security policy pillar but the necessary legal measures to suspend free movement of capital or payments with that country are taken under Arts. 228a E.C. and 73g(1) of the E.C. Treaty. Article 73g(1) authorises such economic sanctions in so far as they represent a derogation from the free movement of capital. It must be observed that this Article permits the derogation from the freedom of movement of payments as well as capital, thus permitting very wide-ranging sanctions against the countries involved.

Para. (2)

This paragraph permits a Member State to take unilateral measures against a third country, with regard to capital movements and payments, for serious political reasons and on grounds of urgency. The scope of this measure is far from clear. The existence of Community action under Art. 228a E.C. precludes the application of unilateral measures. Article 73g(2) is without prejudice to Art. 224 E.C., which requires Member States to consult each other with a view to taking the steps needed to prevent the functioning of the common market being affected by certain unilateral measures being taken by a Member State due to war, terrorism or United Nations economic or military sanctions.

Whatever the scope of the Member State action, it is obviously preferable to have Community action. Any unilateral measures must be referred to the Commission and other Member States prior to its entry into force, thus permitting its discussion under the aegis of the common foreign and security policy which is based on such inter-governmental negotiations. Moreover, the Council, acting by a qualified majority, may decide to abolish or amend any such measure. This constitutes quite a significant step as regards Community oversight of the Member States' foreign policy operations. Economic sanctions by a Member State on a non-Member State can be overturned by the Community, acting by qualified majority in Council. The European Parliament is to be informed of any action taken by the Council under this article.

Article 73h

Until 1 January 1994, the following provisions shall be applicable:
(1) Each Member State undertakes to authorise, in the currency of the Member State in which the creditor or the beneficiary resides, any

payments connected with the movement of goods, services or capital, and any transfers of capital and earnings, to the extent that the movement of goods, services, capital and persons between Member States has been liberalised pursuant to this Treaty.

The Member States declare their readiness to undertake the liberalisation of payments beyond the extent provided in the preceding subparagraph, in so far as their economic situation in general and the state of their balance of payments in particular so permit.

(2) In so far as movements of goods, services and capital are limited only by restrictions on payments connected therewith, these restrictions shall be progressively abolished by applying, *mutatis mutandis*, the provisions of this Chapter and the Chapters relating to the abolition of quantitative restrictions and to the liberalisation of services.

(3) Member States undertake not to introduce between themselves any new restrictions on transfers connected with the invisible transactions listed in Annex III to this Treaty.

The progressive abolition of existing restrictions shall be effected in accordance with the provisions of Articles 63 to 65, in so far as such abolition is not governed by the provisions contained in paragraphs 1 and 2 or by the other provisions of this Chapter.

(4) If need be, Member States shall consult each other on the measures to be taken to enable the payments and transfers mentioned in this Article to be effected; such measures shall not prejudice the attainment of the objectives set out in this Treaty.

GENERAL NOTE

This Article consists of transitional provisions which applied until the new Arts. 73b–g E.C. came into force on January 1, 1994. These provisions are a motley collection of declarations and measures ancillary to the on-going liberalisation of payments and capital freedoms, in essence, an exercise in spring cleaning. These provisions will not be analysed in detail.

Para. (1)

This paragraph aims to ensure the freedom of payments by laying down that the Member States must authorise payments in the currency of the creditor where the transaction is in relation to the free movement of goods, services and capital. The Member States thus cannot fetter the movement of payments on the ground that a certain currency is not acceptable for the transaction. The currency must be that of the creditor's Member State, which excludes the application of this provision to third country residents or non-Community currencies. The last sentence indicates that this provision will exist only in those areas which have already been liberalised by the Treaty, thus adding little to current practice.

The second section of this Article amounts to little more than a political declaration of intent thanks to the wording "in so far as their economic situation in general and the state of their balance of payments in particular so permit" which robs this provision of all binding force. It merely signals the desire to see the continued liberalisation of the free movement of payments prior to the deadline of January 1, 1994 when all such restrictions (between the Member States) are to be prohibited.

Para. (2)

Once again, this symbolises the desire to see the progressive removal of all restrictions on the free movement of payments, where these restrictions are impeding the other market freedoms. This adds little to current practice, and the only devices open to pursue such goals are those provisions of the Treaty already in existence.

Para. (3)

As regards the invisible transactions listed in Annex III to the Treaty, the Member States are to avoid the introduction of any new restrictions on such transfers.

Para. (4)

This Article simply provides for non-obligatory consultation between the Member States on the measures deemed necessary for achievement of the freedoms envisaged under Art. 73h E.C.

TITLE IV: Transport

Article 74

The objectives of this Treaty shall, in matters governed by this Title, be pursued by Member States within the framework of a common transport policy.

Article 75

1. For the purpose of implementing Article 74, and taking into account the distinctive features of transport, the Council shall, acting in accordance with the procedure referred to in Article 189c and after consulting the Economic and Social Committee, lay down:

    (a) common rules applicable to international transport to or from the territory of a Member State or passing across the territory of one or more Member States;

    (b) the conditions under which non-resident carriers may operate transport services within a Member State;

    (c) measures to improve transport safety;

    (d) any other appropriate provisions.

2. The provisions referred to in (a) and (b) of paragraph 1 shall be laid down during the transitional period.

3. By way of derogation from the procedure provided for in paragraph 1, where the application of provisions concerning the principles of the regulatory system for transport would be liable to have a serious effect on the standard of living and on employment in certain areas and on the operation of transport facilities, they shall be laid down by the Council acting unanimously on a proposal from the Commission, after consulting the European Parliament and the Economic and Social Committee.

In so doing, the Council shall take into account the need for adaptation to the economic development which will result from establishing the common market.

GENERAL NOTE

Para. (1)

This Article, which constitutes the core of the transport provisions in the E.C. Treaty, is amended slightly. The legislative procedure for the promulgation of measures, as listed in sub-paras. (a)–(d) is altered from a requirement of qualified majority in Council, after consulting the European Parliament, to the application of the co-operation procedure (Art. 189c E.C.). This gives the European Parliament a greater say in the legislative process (see note on Art. 189c E.C. For analysis of transport policy itself, see Mathijsen, *A Guide to European Community Law*, (5th ed.) Sweet & Maxwell, pp. 186–192.

The Article is also amended to include the new sub-para. (c) on "measures to improve transport safety". Community action, in line with the procedure outlined above, is now available in this field. This power probably existed already under the catch-all provision, previously Art. 73(1)(c) E.E.C., which is retitled (d) to make way for the new, specific provision (see 31st Report of the Select Committee on European Legislation, Session 1988–89 (H.C. 15–xxxi) para. 11).

Para. (3)

While the adoption of transport measures under Art. 75(1) is altered from the consultation procedure to the co-operation procedure, the consultation procedure is to be applied to the creation of legislation under Art. 75(3), whereas previously the Council could act without consulting the Parliament. Unanimity in the Council is preserved.

Article 76

Until the provisions referred to in Article 75(1) have been laid down, no Member State may, without the unanimous approval of the Council, make the various provisions governing the subject when this Treaty enters into force less favourable in their direct or indirect effect on carriers of other Member States as compared with carriers who are nationals of that State.

Article 77

Aids shall be compatible with this Treaty if they meet the needs of co-ordination of transport or if they represent reimbursement for the discharge of certain obligations inherent in the concept of a public service.

Article 78

Any measures taken within the framework of this Treaty in respect of transport rates and conditions shall take account of the economic circumstances of carriers.

Article 79

1. In the case of transport within the Community, discrimination which takes the form of carriers charging different rates and imposing different conditions for the carriage of the same goods over the same transport links on grounds of the country of origin or of destination of the goods in question, shall be abolished, at the latest, before the end of the second stage.

2. Paragraph 1 shall not prevent the Council from adopting other measures in pursuance of Article 75(1).

3. Within two years of the entry into force of this Treaty, the Council shall, acting by a qualified majority on a proposal from the Commission and after consulting the Economic and Social Committee, lay down rules for implementing the provisions of paragraph 1.

The Council may in particular lay down the provisions needed to enable the institutions of the Community to secure compliance with the rule laid down in paragraph 1 and to ensure that users benefit from it to the full.

4. The Commission shall, acting on its own initiative or on application by a Member State, investigate any cases of discrimination falling within paragraph 1 and, after consulting any Member State concerned, shall take the necessary decisions within the framework of the rules laid down in accordance with the provisions of paragraph 3.

Article 80

1. The imposition by a Member State, in respect of transport operations carried out within the Community, of rates and conditions involving any element of support or protection in the interest of one or more particular undertakings or industries shall be prohibited as from the beginning of the second stage, unless authorised by the Commission.

2. The Commission shall, acting on its own initiative or on application by a Member State, examine the rates and conditions referred to in paragraph 1, taking account in particular of the requirements of an appropriate regional economic policy, the needs of underdeveloped areas and the problems of areas seriously affected by political circumstances on the one hand, and of the effects of such rates and conditions on competition between the different modes of transport on the other.

After consulting each Member State concerned, the Commission shall take the necessary decisions.

3. The prohibition provided for in paragraph 1 shall not apply to tariffs fixed to meet competition.

Article 81

Charges or dues in respect of the crossing of frontiers which are charged by a carrier in addition to the transport rates shall not exceed a reasonable level after taking the costs actually incurred thereby into account.

Member States shall endeavour to reduce these costs progressively.

The Commission may make recommendations to Member States for the application of this Article.

Article 82

The provisions of this Title shall not form an obstacle to the application of measures taken in the Federal Republic of Germany to the extent that such measures are required in order to compensate for the economic disadvantages caused by the division of Germany to the economy of certain areas of the Federal Republic affected by that division.

Article 83

An Advisory Committee consisting of experts designated by the Governments of Member States, shall be attached to the Commission. The Commission, whenever it considers it desirable, shall consult the Committee on transport matters without prejudice to the powers of the transport section of the Economic and Social Committee.

Article 84

1. The provisions of this Title shall apply to transport by rail, road and inland waterway.

2. The Council may, acting by a qualified majority, decide whether, to what extent and by what procedure appropriate provisions may be laid down for sea and air transport.

The procedural provisions of Article 75(1) and (3) shall apply.

TITLE V: Common Rules on Competition, Taxation and Approximation of Laws

GENERAL NOTE

The alteration to the heading of this section of the Treaty (previously Title I on "Common Rules" under the main heading of Part Three: "Policy of the Community") is entirely cosmetic. Where it used to read "common rules" we now have "common rules on competition, taxation and the approximation of laws"; exactly what this section had dealt with in the past, without any necessity to make this explicit in the Title. The substantive provisions under this title have changed very little.

Chapter 1 (Rules on Competition)

SECTION 1: Rules applying to undertakings

Article 85

1. The following shall be prohibited as incompatible with the common market: all agreements between undertakings, decisions by associations of undertakings and concerted practices which may affect trade between Member States and which have as their object or effect the prevention, restriction or distortion of competition within the common market, and in particular those which:
   (a) directly or indirectly fix purchase or selling prices or any other trading conditions;
   (b) limit or control production, markets, technical development, or investment;
   (c) share markets or sources of supply;
   (d) apply dissimilar conditions to equivalent transactions with other trading parties, thereby placing them at a competitive disadvantage;
   (e) make the conclusion of contracts subject to acceptance by the other parties of supplementary obligations which, by their nature or according to commercial usage, have no connection with the subject of such contracts.

2. Any agreements or decisions prohibited pursuant to this Article shall be automatically void.

3. The provisions of paragraph 1 may, however, be declared inapplicable in the case of:

— any agreement or category of agreements between undertakings;
— any decision or category of decisions by associations of undertakings;
— any concerted practice or category of concerted practices;

which contributes to improving the production or distribution of goods or to promoting technical or economic progress, while allowing consumers a fair share of the resulting benefit, and which does not:

(a) impose on the undertakings concerned restrictions which are not indispensable to the attainment of these objectives;
(b) afford such undertakings the possibility of eliminating competition in respect of a substantial part of the products in question.

Article 86

Any abuse by one or more undertakings of a dominant position within the common market or in a substantial part of it shall be prohibited as incompatible with the common market in so far as it may affect trade between Member States.

Such abuse may, in particular, consist in:

(a) directly or indirectly imposing unfair purchase or selling prices or other unfair trading conditions;
(b) limiting production, markets or technical development to the prejudice of consumers;
(c) applying dissimilar conditions to equivalent transactions with other trading parties, thereby placing them at a competitive disadvantage;
(d) making the conclusion of contracts subject to acceptance by the other parties of supplementary obligations which, by their nature or according to commercial usage, have no connection with the subject of such contracts.

Article 87

1. Within three years of the entry into force of this Treaty the Council shall, acting unanimously on a proposal from the Commission and after consulting the European Parliament, adopt any appropriate regulations or directives to give effect to the principles set out in Articles 85 and 86.

If such provisions have not been adopted within the period mentioned, they shall be laid down by the Council, acting by a qualified majority on a proposal from the Commission and after consulting the European Parliament.

2. The regulations or directives referred to in paragraph 1 shall be designed in particular:

(a) to ensure compliance with the prohibitions laid down in Article 85(1) and in Article 86 by making provision for fines and periodic penalty payments;
(b) to lay down detailed rules for the application of Article 85(3), taking into account the need to ensure effective supervision on the one hand, and to simplify administration to the greatest possible extent on the other;
(c) to define, if need be, in the various branches of the economy, the scope of the provisions of Articles 85 and 86;
(d) to define the respective functions of the Commission and of the Court of Justice in applying the provisions laid down in this paragraph;

(e) to determine the relationship between national laws and the provisions contained in this Section or adopted pursuant to this Article.

Article 88

Until the entry into force of the provisions adopted in pursuance of Article 87, the authorities in Member States shall rule on the admissibility of agreements, decisions and concerted practices and on abuse of a dominant position in the common market in accordance with the law of their country and with the provisions of Article 85, in particular paragraph 3, and of Article 86.

Article 89

1. Without prejudice to Article 88, the Commission shall, as soon as it takes up its duties, ensure the application of the principles laid down in Articles 85 and 86. On application by a Member State or on its own initiative, and in co-operation with the competent authorities in the Member States, who shall give it their assistance, the Commission shall investigate cases of suspected infringement of these principles. If it finds that there has been an infringement, it shall propose appropriate measures to bring it to an end.

2. If the infringement is not brought to an end, the Commission shall record such infringement of the principles in a reasoned decision. The Commission may publish its decision and authorise Member States to take the measures, the conditions and details of which it shall determine, needed to remedy the situation.

Article 90

1. In the case of public undertakings and undertakings to which Member States grant special or exclusive rights, Member States shall neither enact nor maintain in force any measure contrary to the rules contained in this Treaty, in particular to those rules provided for in Article 6 and Articles 85 to 94.

2. Undertakings entrusted with the operation of services of general economic interest or having the character of a revenue-producing monopoly shall be subject to the rules contained in this Treaty, in particular to the rules on competition, in so far as the application of such rules does not obstruct the performance, in law or in fact, of the particular tasks assigned to them. The development of trade must not be affected to such an extent as would be contrary to the interests of the Community.

3. The Commission shall ensure the application of the provisions of this Article and shall, where necessary, address appropriate directives or decisions to Member States.

Section 2: Dumping

Article 91

1. If during the transitional period, the Commission, on application by a Member State or by any other interested party, finds that dumping is being practised within the common market, it shall address recommendations to the person or persons with whom such practices originate for the purpose of putting an end to them.

Should the practices continue, the Commission shall authorise the injured Member State to take protective measures, the conditions and details of which the Commission shall determine.

2. As soon as this Treaty enters into force, products which originate in or are in free circulation in one Member State and which have been exported to another Member State shall, on reimportation, be admitted into the territory of the first-mentioned State free of all customs duties, quantitative restrictions or measures having equivalent effect. The Commission shall lay down appropriate rules for the application of this paragraph.

SECTION 3: Aids granted by States

Article 92

1. Save as otherwise provided in this Treaty, any aid granted by a Member State or through State resources in any form whatsoever which distorts or threatens to distort competition by favouring certain undertakings or the production of certain goods shall, in so far as it affects trade between Member States, be incompatible with the common market.

2. The following shall be compatible with the common market.

(a) aid having a social character, granted to individual consumers, provided that such aid is granted without discrimination related to the origin of the products concerned;

(b) aid to make good the damage caused by natural disasters or exceptional occurrences;

(c) aid granted to the economy of certain areas of the Federal Republic of Germany affected by the division of Germany, in so far as such aid is required in order to compensate for the economic disadvantages caused by that division.

3. The following may be considered to be compatible with the common market:

(a) aid to promote the economic development of areas where the standard of living is abnormally low or where there is serious underemployment;

(b) aid to promote the execution of an important project of common European interest or to remedy a serious disturbance in the economy of a Member State;

(c) aid to facilitate the development of certain economic activities or of certain economic areas, where such aid does not adversely affect trading conditions to an extent contrary to the common interest. However, the aids granted to shipbuilding as of 1 January 1957 shall, in so far as they serve only to compensate for the absence of customs protection, be progressively reduced under the same conditions as apply to the elimination of customs duties, subject to the provisions of this Treaty concerning common commercial policy towards third countries;

(d) aid to promote culture and heritage conservation where such aid does not affect trading conditions and competition in the Community to an extent that is contrary to the common interest;

(e) such other categories of aid as may be specified by decision of the Council acting by a qualified majority on a proposal from the Commission.

GENERAL NOTE

Para. (3)

A minor amendment is made to this Article; the new sub-para. (d) on the granting of state aid to promote culture and heritage conservation, subject to the provisos listed therein, has been inserted. The existing sub-para. (d) is therefore moved to (e). On state aid in general, see Weatherill and Beaumont, *EC Law*, Penguin, Chap. 27.

Article 93

1. The Commission shall, in co-operation with Member States, keep under constant review all systems of aid existing in those States. It shall propose to the latter any appropriate measures required by the progressive development or by the functioning of the common market.

2. If, after giving notice to the parties concerned to submit their comments, the Commission finds that aid granted by a State or through State resources is not compatible with the common market having regard to Article 92, or that such aid is being misused, it shall decide that the State concerned shall

abolish or alter such aid within a period of time to be determined by the Commission.

If the State concerned does not comply with this decision within the prescribed time, the Commission or any other interested State may, in derogation from the provisions of Articles 169 and 170, refer the matter to the Court of Justice direct.

On application by a Member State, the Council, may, acting unanimously, decide that aid which that State is granting or intends to grant shall be considered to be compatible with the common market, in derogation from the provisions of Article 92 or from the regulations provided for in Article 94, if such a decision is justified by exceptional circumstances. If, as regards the aid in question, the Commission has already initiated the procedure provided for in the first subparagraph of this paragraph, the fact that the State concerned has made its application to the Council shall have the effect of suspending that procedure until the Council has made its attitude known.

If, however, the Council has not made its attitude known within three months of the said application being made, the Commission shall give its decision on the case.

3. The Commission shall be informed, in sufficient time to enable it to submit its comments, of any plans to grant or alter aid. If it considers that any such plan is not compatible with the common market having regard to Article 92, it shall without delay initiate the procedure provided for in paragraph 2. The Member State concerned shall not put its proposed measures into effect until this procedure has resulted in a final decision.

Article 94

The Council, acting by a qualified majority on a proposal from the Commission and after consulting the European Parliament, may make any appropriate regulations for the application of Articles 92 and 93 and may in particular determine the conditions in which Article 93(3) shall apply and the categories of aid exempted from this procedure.

GENERAL NOTE

This Article is amended to make provision for the consultation of the European Parliament in the adoption of measures under this head.

Chapter 2: (Tax Provisions)

Article 95

No Member State shall impose, directly or indirectly, on the products of other Member States any internal taxation of any kind in excess of that imposed directly or indirectly on similar domestic products.

Furthermore, no Member State shall impose on the products of other Member States any internal taxation of such a nature as to afford indirect protection to other products.

Member States shall, not later than at the beginning of the second stage, repeal or amend any provisions existing when this Treaty enters into force which conflict with the preceding rules.

Article 96

Where products are exported to the territory of any Member State, any repayment of internal taxation shall not exceed the internal taxation imposed on them whether directly or indirectly.

Article 97

Member States which levy a turnover tax calculated on a cumulative multi-stage tax system may, in the case of internal taxation imposed by them on imported products or of repayments allowed by them on exported products, establish average rates for products or groups of products, provided that there is no infringement of the principles laid down in Articles 95 and 96.

Where the average rates established by a Member State do not conform to these principles, the Commission shall address appropriate directives or decisions to the State concerned.

Article 98

In the case of charges other than turnover taxes, excise duties and other forms of indirect taxation, remissions and repayments in respect of exports to other Member States may not be granted and countervailing charges in respect of imports from Member States may not be imposed unless the measures contemplated have been previously approved for a limited period by the Council acting by a qualified majority on a proposal from the Commission.

Article 99

The Council shall, acting unanimously on a proposal from the Commission and after consulting the European Parliament and the Economic and Social Committee, adopt provisions for the harmonisation of legislation concerning turnover taxes, excise duties and other forms of indirect taxation to the extent that such harmonisation is necessary to ensure the establishment and the functioning of the internal market within the time-limit laid down in Article 7a.

GENERAL NOTE

This Article, on the harmonisation of indirect taxes, as befitting its nationally contentious status, remains the subject of unanimity in Council. The amendments to this Article, in keeping with those to the topic in general, are negligible. It is amended to provide for the consultation of the Economic and Social Committee (ECOSOC) but it is difficult to envisage why this change has come about at this stage in the development of the Community. Political disagreement prevented any meaningful change taking place to this Article. Article 7a is referred to, rather than Art. 8a, reflecting the fact that the latter Article was renumbered into the former by the TEU.

Chapter 3 (Approximation of Laws)

Article 100

The Council shall, acting unanimously on a proposal from the Commission and after consulting the European Parliament and the Economic and Social Committee, issue directives for the approximation of such laws, regulations or administrative provisions of the Member States as directly affect the establishment or functioning of the common market.

GENERAL NOTE

This Article, central to the approximation of the laws of the Member States for the purpose of the achievement of the common market, is updated but no significant alterations made.

The requirement of unanimity in the Council is upheld, but European Parliament and Economic and Social Committee consultation is widened to cover all matters under this Article. This rationalises an unduly complicated situation whereby consultation was necessitated only where the implementation of Community measures would have involved the amendment of one or more Member States' domestic legislation.

Article 100a

1. By way of derogation from Article 100 and save where otherwise provided in this Treaty, the following provisions shall apply for the achievement of the objectives set out in Article 7a. The Council shall, acting in accordance with the procedure referred to in Article 189b and after consulting the Economic and Social Committee, adopt the measures for the approximation of

the provisions laid down by law, regulation or administrative action in Member States which have as their object the establishment and functioning of the internal market.

2. Paragraph 1 shall not apply to fiscal provisions, to those relating to the free movement of persons nor to those relating to the rights and interests of employed persons.

3. The Commission, in its proposals envisaged in paragraph 1 concerning health, safety, environmental protection and consumer protection, will take as a base a high level of protection.

4. If, after the adoption of a harmonisation measure by the Council acting by a qualified majority, a Member State deems it necessary to apply national provisions on grounds of major needs referred to in Article 36, or relating to protection of the environment or the working environment, it shall notify the Commission of these provisions.

The Commission shall confirm the provisions involved after having verified that they are not a means of arbitrary discrimination or a disguised restriction on trade between Member States.

By way of derogation from the procedure laid down in Articles 169 and 170, the Commission or any Member State may bring the matter directly before the Court of Justice if it considers that another Member State is making improper use of the powers provided for in this Article.

5. The harmonisation measures referred to above shall, in appropriate cases, include a safeguard clause authorising the Member States to take, for one or more of the non-economic reasons referred to in Article 36, provisional measures subject to a Community control procedure.

GENERAL NOTE

This Article, introduced by the SEA as a base for the adoption of legislation for the achievement of the objectives set out in Art. 8a E.E.C. (now Art. 7a E.C.), the completion of the internal market, is altered as regards the legislative procedure necessary for the promulgation of such measures. The conciliation and veto procedure (Art. 189b E.C.) is introduced to replace the co-operation procedure. Questions may be asked about the effect of altering the legislative procedure as regards a process deemed to have been completed by the end of 1992. The nature of the internal market process, however, means that the need for Community legislation is ever present. While the great majority of those measures deemed necessary for the completion of the internal market are in place, the development of technology and changing circumstances mean that legislation will continually be necessary under this heading. Moreover, the objectives laid down under what is now Art. 7a E.C. are a wide base for any further legislative action that may be deemed necessary for the proper functioning of the internal market. The granting of real legislative power to the Parliament in the area of the internal market is one of the most significant changes made by the Maastricht Treaty in the gradual evolution of that body into a genuine legislature.

Article 100b

1. During 1992, the Commission shall, together with each Member State, draw up an inventory of national laws, regulations and administrative provisions which fall under Article 100a and which have not been harmonised pursuant to that Article.

The Council, acting in accordance with the provisions of Article 100a, may decide that the provisions in force in a Member State must be recognised as being equivalent to those applied by another Member State.

2. The provisions of Article 100a(4) shall apply by analogy.

3. The Commission shall draw up the inventory referred to in the first subparagraph of paragraph 1 and shall submit appropriate proposals in good time to allow the Council to act before the end of 1992.

Article 100c

1. The Council, acting unanimously on a proposal from the Commission and after consulting the European Parliament, shall determine the third

countries whose nationals must be in possession of a visa when crossing the external borders of the Member States.

2. However, in the event of an emergency situation in a third country posing a threat of a sudden inflow of nationals from that country into the Community, the Council, acting by a qualified majority on a recommendation from the Commission, may introduce, for a period not exceeding six months, a visa requirement for nationals from the country in question. The visa requirement established under this paragraph may be extended in accordance with the procedure referred to in paragraph 1.

3. From 1 January 1996, the Council shall act by a qualified majority on the decisions referred to in paragraph 1. The Council shall, before that date, acting by a qualified majority on a proposal from the Commission and after consulting the European Parliament, adopt measures relating to a uniform format for visas.

4. In the matters referred to in this Article, the Commission shall examine any request made by a Member State that it submit a proposal to the Council.

5. This Article shall be without prejudice to the exercise of the responsibilities incumbent upon the Member States with regard to the maintenance of law and order and the safeguarding of internal security.

6. This Article shall apply to other matters if so decided pursuant to Article K.9 of the provisions of the Treaty on European Union which relate to co-operation in the fields of justice and home affairs, subject to the voting conditions determined at the same time.

7. The provisions of the conventions in force between the Member States governing matters covered by this Article shall remain in force until their content has been replaced by directives or measures adopted pursuant to this Article.

GENERAL NOTE

This is a new addition to the Treaty, bringing matters of visa policy within the Community sphere of action for the first time. The U.K. Government were insistent prior to the Maastricht agreement that all matters in the broad field of what was to become the "justice and home affairs pillar" ought to remain within the scope of the national governments. In particular, it cited immigration and asylum policy as exclusively determinable by the individual Member States as opposed to the Community. In the end, the setting up of the separate justice and home affairs pillar reflects the prevalence of the U.K.'s viewpoint. Nevertheless, the inclusion of visa matters within the Community sphere marks an admission, urged by the practical experience of the Benelux countries, that the creation of an area without internal frontiers requires the creation of some form of common policy towards third country nationals. This was agreed to as regards visa policy, but the treatment of third country nationals will still take place on two levels. While visa policy will be ascertained at the Community level, the remainder of essential matters governing third country nationals, such as asylum and immigration policy, will continue to be dealt with at the inter-governmental level, in accordance with the procedures envisaged by the justice and home affairs pillar of the TEU.

A number of relatively novel procedures are envisaged in Art. 100c, reflecting the uneasy alliance of Community and national influences, in what is a sensitive field for Member State authorities.

The scope of the areas to be dealt with under the Treaty is restricted to the determination of which third countries' nationals will be required to be in possession of a visa when crossing the external borders of the Community (Art. 100c(1) E.C.). Tied to this is the marginal issue of the creation of a uniform format for visas (Art. 100c(3) E.C.). The original process of determining which third countries' nationals require visas is to be carried out by a unanimous vote in Council (but changing to qualified majority from January 1, 1996 (Art. 100c(3) E.C.)).

The remainder of topics in this area, such as asylum policy, extradition, judicial co-operation, etc. (see the list of headings under the justice and home affairs pillar, Art. K.1 TEU), remain in the inter-governmental arena. Nevertheless, certain of these matters may be transferred into the Community sphere without the necessity of a further inter-governmental conference (Art. 100c (6) E.C.). Asylum policy is a prime candidate for such a transfer (see Declaration No.31 to the TEU). It is not, however, a simple matter to increase the scope of Art. 100c, as the decision to do so requires unanimity in the Council and the adoption of the measures in accordance with the constitutional requirements of each Member State (Art. K.9 TEU).

Moreover, the application of the conventions governing areas covered by this Article, in force between the Member States, will remain in force until their content has been replaced by Directives or measures adopted pursuant to this Article (Art. 100c(7) E.C.).

Para. (1)

This paragraph provides for the determination of which third countries' nationals shall require visas before crossing the external borders of the Community. Such harmonisation of visa policy is deemed essential in order to permit the opening up of internal frontiers; certain Member States are reluctant to see all internal frontiers come down with no guarantee that other Member States might be operating less stringent external controls than their own indigenous policies. This is particularly true as regards the U.K., with its unique island status.

All decisions in this field will have to be taken by unanimous vote in Council until January 1, 1996 when qualified majority voting will take over (Art. 100c(3) E.C.). Express provision is made for the consultation of the European Parliament prior to the adoption of any measure.

Para. (2)

This paragraph permits the adoption of emergency measures to impose visa requirements on third country nationals not previously covered by the visa requirement but who threaten to flood the Community. Such measures may be adopted by qualified majority vote and remain in force for a maximum of six months initially, but are subject to potentially unlimited extension under the applicable Art. 100c(1) E.C. voting procedure. Significantly, no provision is made for any consultation of the European Parliament. The latter body was a staunch opponent of this form of visa policy, viewing it as an unjustified manifestation of the "fortress Europe" mentality. The problem envisaged by the European Parliament was that the imposition of a visa requirement on a country facing an internal emergency, requires persons who wish to leave that country to visit a Member State's diplomatic premises there to request a visa. In time of war or civil unrest, these diplomatic facilities may not be left in operation and the time taken to process such applications prevents the rapid assessment of cases deserving of a visa. In other words, the imposition of a visa requirement upon a warring state or during severe civil disturbances is an effective barrier to refugees fleeing such areas, even if they are genuine political refugees.

Para. (4)

This adds little to the current practice as regards the initiation of legislation in the Community sphere. The Commission retains its monopoly of legislative initiative but express provision is made that it must examine any request made by a Member State that it submit a proposal to the Council. In other matters the Commission would normally examine any such request, and this Article merely formalises the process. There is no duty on the Commission to submit a proposal.

Para. (5)

This paragraph highlights the sensitivity of the Community competence in relation to visas, with its close relationship to the typically jealously guarded national competence in the areas of internal security and law and order. This paragraph permits a potentially wide exception to the application of this Article in the Member States. It is impossible to predict the scope of measures which the Member States will rely on as falling under this exception. As visas are within Community competence, it is within the jurisdiction of the E.C.J. to rule on the breadth of exception allowed under this paragraph. The matter could either come before the court for a preliminary ruling under Art. 177 or in an action brought against the Member State under Arts. 169 or 170. Thus the E.C.J. has an opportunity to rule on the acceptability of such measures in an area where national government discretion has largely been left unchecked.

Para. (6)

This is one of the most interesting and novel provisions of the new amended Treaty. It provides for the transfer of competences currently dealt with at the inter-governmental level, under the justice and home affairs pillar, into the Community sphere. Article K.9 TEU lays down the procedure for this transfer, known also as passarelle. The process is applicable to the activities laid down in Art. K.1(1)–(6) TEU, which are: asylum policy; rules governing the crossing by persons of the external borders of the Member States; immigration policy including conditions of entry, residence, work and movement; combating drug addiction; combating international fraud; and judicial co-operation in civil matters. Those matters not open to any transfer under this process are: judicial co-operation in criminal matters (K.1(7) TEU); customs co-operation (K.1(8) TEU) and international police co-operation (K.1(9) TEU). The majority of these matters, be they in the former or latter categories, are currently covered by international conventions and multilateral agreements which have sprung up on an ad hoc basis, when and where perceived necessary (see note on Art. 100c(7) E.C.). At present, asylum policy is the prime candidate for a transfer into the Community sphere (Declaration No.31 to the TEU).

The achievement of any such transfer will prove very difficult and, while it may take place without an inter-governmental conference being convened under Art. N TEU, it has the same requirement of unanimous agreement by government ministers from each of the Member States, followed by approval in accordance with the appropriate constitutional process in each of these States. Kenneth Clark, then Home Secretary, making clear the opposition of the U.K. Government to any transfer of these areas into the Community sphere, talked of the "double lock" which had been placed on any such development in this area. He stated that the approval of the U.K. Government, coupled with the express approval of Parliament would make for an effective lock; the equivalent of a double veto existing in both these bodies. (See *Hansard*, H.C. Vol. 295, col. 26). In Denmark, a majority of five-sixths of members of the Danish Parliament or both a majority of members of the Parliament and a majority of votes in a referendum is required. See the Danish Declaration on Co-operation in the fields of justice and home affairs published at the Edinburgh European Council in December 1992, and Weatherill and Beaumont, *E.C. Law* (1993), Penguin, p. 777.

Para. (7)

There are a plethora of multilateral agreements existing at present in this field, but co-operation at the inter-governmental level on an ad hoc basis has not been followed up by comprehensive progress in the completion of international conventions. Article 100c(7) E.C. makes provision for the continued existence of these multilateral instruments until they are replaced by directives or measures adopted pursuant to this Article. One of the most important agreements in this field is the Schengen accord. Initiated by the Benelux countries, France and Germany, this agreement provided for the gradual elimination of all border and customs formalities between the countries concerned. Nine of the E.C. Member States are now affiliated to the Schengen convention of June 19, 1990 which elaborates on the earlier agreement (for text see 30 International Legal Materials 1991 at 68–147) and makes provision for, *inter alia*, action on visa policy, asylum seekers, police and security measures, and extradition (see Schutte, Schengen: Its Meaning for the Free Movement of Persons in Europe, (1991) 28 C.M.L.Rev. 549–570; European Parliament Report 336/92; Spencer, *1992 and all That*, Chap. 2 and NJCM Bulletin, Schengen Special 16 NJCM Bulletin 745–839). The U.K., Ireland and Denmark are the only Community Member States which are not members of the agreement. An E.C.-wide deal to abolish all internal borders, as envisaged by the SEA (Art. 8a E.E.C. Art. 7a E.C. on the free movement of persons throughout the Community by the end of 1992) has not materialised. The nine Schengen Member States are, however, to remove all the remaining stumbling blocks to the elimination of internal borders by February 1, 1994.

Another key agreement in this field is the draft Convention on the Crossing of External Borders which is currently being held up by the dispute between the U.K. and Spain over the status of Gibraltar (see the discussion on the Convention in *Hansard*, H.C. Vol. 193, col. 242). National interests in these fields have proven a real handicap to the conclusion of any such agreements. The introduction of qualified majority voting in 1996 in the limited fields provided for under this Article will thus mark something of a watershed.

The other main prospect for international agreement in this area is the Dublin Convention, signed in 1990 (Cmnd 1623 and text in 30 International Legal Materials 1991, 425–444), which deals with the problem of determining the state responsible for examining applications for asylum lodged in one of the Member States. It provides for the controversial first stop asylum policy, whereby the country at which the asylum seeker arrived first or first made his claim is responsible for the processing of the claim. In particular it calls for the setting up of an exchange of information about applicants, thus attempting to highlight false or multiple asylum claims. The Convention has not yet entered into force. Two of the stumbling blocks are the civil liberties implications of the information exchange and, more importantly, the worries from states such as Germany with many land borders that the first stop rule will require them to consider an unduly high proportion of all asylum claims.

Article 100d

The Co-ordinating Committee consisting of senior officials set up by Article K.4 of the Treaty on European Union shall contribute, without prejudice to the provisions of Article 151, to the preparation of the proceedings of the Council in the fields referred to in Article 100c.

GENERAL NOTE

This Article makes provision for the Co-ordinating Committee of senior officials, set up under the justice and home affairs pillar (Art. K.4 TEU), to act alongside COREPER in the matters to be dealt with under Art. 100c. This shadowy body of senior civil servants, active in this field in their respective Member States, will prepare the ground for Council meetings. This Article is necessary to give Community effect to the actions of this body. These officials, accountable only to the national governments, will prove most influential, and yet their work will be largely invisible to the scrutiny of both the national and European Parliaments. The speed with which this body has moved is highlighted by the convening of at least 60 meetings under its auspices during the U.K. Presidency alone (July–December 1992) (*The Guardian* February 2, 1993). It has rapidly taken over the work of the diverse groups previously operating in this area, such as the Ad Hoc Group on Immigration, etc. Both Arts. 100d E.C. and K.4 of the TEU provide that the co-ordinating committee is to operate without prejudice to Art. 151 E.C., thus signalling an unclear relationship with COREPER.

Article 101

Where the Commission finds that a difference between the provisions laid down by law, regulation or administrative action in Member States is distorting the conditions of competition in the common market and that the resultant distortion needs to be eliminated, it shall consult the Member States concerned.

If such consultation does not result in an agreement eliminating the distortion in question, the Council shall, on a proposal from the Commission, acting unanimously during the first stage and by a qualified majority thereafter, issue the necessary directives. The Commission and the Council may take any other appropriate measures provided for in this Treaty.

Article 102

1. Where there is reason to fear that the adoption or amendment of a provision laid down by law, regulation or administrative action may cause distortion within the meaning of Article 101, a Member State desiring to proceed therewith shall consult the Commission. After consulting the Member States, the Commission shall recommend to the States concerned such measures as may be appropriate to avoid the distortion in question.

2. If a State desiring to introduce or amend its own provisions does not comply with the recommendation addressed to it by the Commission, other Member States shall not be required, in pursuance of Article 101, to amend their own provisions in order to eliminate such distortion. If the Member State which has ignored the recommendation of the Commission causes distortion detrimental only to itself, the provisions of Article 101 shall not apply.

TITLE VI: Economic and Monetary Policy

GENERAL NOTE

The section on economic and monetary union is one of the most complicated parts of the Treaty, by virtue not only of its content, but also of its lay-out. The subject matter is necessarily detailed and, in order to prevent the body of the Treaty becoming too lengthy and technical, many of the more complex provisions are included in protocols annexed to the Treaty. The application of the Treaty Articles requires frequent cross-reference to these protocols.

Firstly, it is necessary to make a few points on the process towards economic and monetary union, specifically the means envisaged by this Treaty, and the Delors Committee Report (Report on Economic and Monetary Union in the European Community, Luxembourg, Office for Official Publications of the European Communities, 1989). In keeping with the Delors Report, the TEU Treaty envisages a gradual progress towards the achievement of full economic and monetary union. This is deemed to consist of a single currency overseen by an independent monetary authority. Nevertheless, this should be seen as two separate unification processes. On the one hand, the achievement of economic union can be seen as a natural progression of the SEA, in which goods, services, assets and production factors are freely traded. With markets for goods already largely integrated, the completion of economic union requires the elimination of the remaining constraints on the mobility of services, capital and labour in the E.C. On the other hand, the economic unification of the Community is to be tied to the achievement of a monetary union. This process was defined by the Delors Report as requiring: "a currency area in which policies are managed jointly, with the single most important condition for a monetary union being fulfilled only when the decisive step was taken to lock exchange rates irrevocably". This process will be achieved through: "a new monetary institution necessary because a single monetary policy cannot result from independent decisions and actions by different central banks" (paras. 22 and 33 of the Delors Report). In other words, the Report envisaged the introduction of a single currency and the transfer of responsibility for monetary policy from the national to the European level. The reasoning behind the decision to adopt this parallel approach of economic and monetary union is open to some debate in economic circles. It has been asserted that, while monetary union does add some value to the achievement of economic union, it is far from essential for its success. Nevertheless, the achievement of monetary union, as well as bolstering economic union, marks a very important step towards a true European Union, with its centralised decision making structure. Thus, the achievement of full economic and monetary union has long been seen by the Commission as a vital part of the political unification of Europe.

The achievement of economic union simply envisages co-ordination of economic policies, rather than centralised control (other than to prevent excessive government deficits) and thus the Community will not take control of taxation or public spending policies in the Member States. The only "control" it will exercise is the indirect power to ensure that the Member State shall not maintain an excessive government deficit.

One of the fundamental problems in designing a strategy for economic and monetary union arose with regard to the speed of the process. The Delors Report, like the TEU itself, envisaged a three stage process towards full economic and monetary union. The Delors Report insisted that the first stage would commence on July 1, 1990 (para. 30) but gave no further dates for the achievement of the later steps. The TEU does not give any specific date for the start of the first stage, which is presumed to have commenced already, but it does lay down strict and irrevocable dates for the achievement of the second and third stages. The second stage is to commence on January 1, 1994 and is envisaged as the stage during which the Member States will take the steps necessary to permit the achievement of full economic and monetary union at the beginning of the third stage. The second stage is seen as a period of rapid transition, during which the Member States still make the determinative decisions but, with the common goal of full union in mind. The third stage is due to commence, at the latest, by January 1, 1999.

Not all the Member States will make the transition to the third stage by this date. Political derogations were permitted at the Maastricht summit, which saw the U.K. and Denmark exercise their right to opt-out of the otherwise inevitable move towards the third stage. The other states which will not progress towards the third stage will be those who fail to fulfil the necessary economic criteria laid down in the Treaty.

The achievement of full economic and monetary union in the Community by the date envisaged is somewhat open to question, given the current economic and political climate in Europe. One result of the gradual nature of the progress towards the third stage of economic and monetary union is that the political and practical costs of withdrawal are relatively minimal at all stages prior to the building of the common institutions (see Fratianni, Von Hagen *et al*, The Maastricht Way to Economic and Monetary Union, *Essays in International Finance*, No. 187, 1992, Princeton University at pp.10–15). The key building block in the creation of the single currency was to be the ERM of the EMS. It was expected that the maintenance of relatively tight bands (2.25 per cent.) would create economic convergence and act as a driving force in the securing of the Member States' commitment to full economic and monetary union. With the recent problems in the ERM, the forced withdrawal of Italy and the U.K. in 1992 and the widening of the bands to 15 per cent. in 1993, that may seem more of a hope than a realistic expectation. Moreover, the achievement of economic convergence criteria as a prerequisite to the move to the third stage, permits national "discretion", through the level of effort put in by the Member State in achieving the necessary convergence. For example, a state could deliberately increase its borrowing beyond the 3 per cent. ratio of Gross Domestic Product mentioned in Art. 1 of the Protocol on the Excessive Deficit Procedure if it did not wish to join the single currency.

Returning to the structure of the economic and monetary union provisions themselves, the new Arts. 102a–104c E.C. deal with economic policy, and lay down the process for the gradual convergence of the economic policies of the Member States. This is to be achieved by the conferral of duties on the Member States and Community institutions, in a manner not wholly unfamiliar as regards other areas of the Treaty. Article 102a E.C. lays down the general guiding principles of the process, while the main means of achieving the co-ordination of economic policies, through the surveillance of the Member States' economic policies, is found in Art. 103 E.C. The Council is to exercise a general monitoring role, acting on the basis of reports from the Commission, to assess Member State compliance with the broad guidelines on economic policy laid down under Art. 103(2) E.C. Article 104–104b E.C. sets out a small number of prohibited practices in the area of public sector finance, including the favouring of public authorities in the provision of credit facilities by central banks (Art. 104 E.C.). Article 104c contains the critical duty on Member States that they "avoid excessive government deficits". It is up to the Commission to monitor the budgetary situation and government debt in Member States and to identify "gross errors" (Art. 104c(2) E.C.). The basic criteria are specified, involving the ratio of government deficit, and of government debt, to Gross Domestic Product in relation to a reference value. These reference values are set out in Art. 1 of the Protocol on the Excessive Deficit Procedure annexed to the Treaty and are defined as (a) 3 per cent. for the ratio of planned or actual government deficit to Gross Domestic Product, and (b) 60 per cent. for the ratio of government debt to Gross Domestic Product. Articles 104c(3)–(14) E.C. then deal with the enforcement measures applicable in this area. The scale of sanction is progressively stepped up as the process continues, but the punitive sanctions laid down in Art. 104c(11) E.C. will not be applicable until the third stage comes into force and will only apply as regards states who have made the transition to the single currency. The sanctions will not apply to the U.K. unless the U.K. abrogates its opt-out from the single currency and meets the economic convergence criteria to enable it to join that currency. The basis of the enforcement measures prior to the coming into force of the third stage is the adverse publicity of a negative Council report. Nevertheless, the criteria for judging the excessive deficit may not be applied in a strict fashion, as Art. 104c(2) E.C. makes clear. A judgmental element is implicit, whereby the non-compliance with the reference values in the Protocol is less important than the overall trend in the figures.

The provisions on monetary policy laid down in Arts. 105–109m E.C. are very different from the preceding economic provisions. They introduce new bodies and structures which will come into operation progressively and in accordance with a pre-determined timetable. National competences in this field will be progressively removed into the hands of an independent monetary authority overseeing a single currency. The major problem with the Treaty provisions in this field, is that they are laid out in a manner which will appear a great deal more logical upon the coming into force of the third stage of economic and monetary union. At all stages prior to that, the governing provisions are structured in a far from coherent way. Article 105 E.C. is a prime example of this. It lays down the primary objective of the European System of Central Banks as the maintenance of price stability. It goes on to elaborate on the basic tasks of this body which include: the definition and implementation of the monetary policy of the Community; the conducting of foreign exchange operations; the holding and management of the official foreign reserves of the Member States; and the promotion of the smooth operation of payment systems. Despite the appearance of this Article at the forefront of the section on monetary policy, it will only come into force at the outset of the third stage of economic and monetary union, when the European System of Central Banks and the European Central Bank itself will take over the running of the Community monetary policy. Article 106 E.C. lays down the composition of the European System of Central Banks, as well as making reference to the governing statute of this body, which is included in the detailed Protocol on the Statute of the European System of Central Banks and of the European Central Bank, annexed to the Treaty. The remainder of this chapter of the Treaty (Arts. 107–109 E.C.) concerns the European System of Central Banks and the European Central Bank; including the enjoining of their independence from national and Community authorities (Art. 107 E.C.). For an excellent comparison of the European System of Central Banks and the German Bundesbank see Fratianni et al, *supra*, at pp. 28–42.

The chapter on "institutional provisions" under Arts. 109a–d E.C. marks a further lack of transparency in this area. Articles 109a and b E.C. shed some light on the composition of the European Central Bank and its ruling bodies, but must be read alongside the Statute of the European System of Central Banks and European Central Bank as well as the preceding paragraphs on the Bank system. Article 109c E.C. provides for the creation of an advisory Monetary Committee, which will be superseded at the start of the third stage by an analogous body, the Economic and Financial Committee. Article 109d, mysteriously included in the institutional provisions, lays down a list of areas where the Council or a Member State may request the Commission to make a recommendation or proposal.

Articles 109e–109m contain the so-called "Transitional Provisions". Included in this section are all those Articles dealing with the first and second stages of the economic and monetary union process. The first stage gives way to the second stage on January 1, 1994 (Art. 109e(1) E.C.). The duties of each Member State in the period up to this transition are laid down in Art. 109e(2) E.C. Article 109e(3) E.C. adds to the general confusion by dictating which of the foregoing provisions on economic and monetary union are to apply from the beginning of the second stage and which from the start of the third stage; in other words it aims to unscramble the transitional from the permanent. Article 109f E.C. provides for the establishment of the European Monetary Institute as from January 1, 1994. The Statute of this body is laid down in a Protocol to the Treaty and its tasks are to be, *inter alia*, the strengthening of co-operation between national central banks; the monitoring of the EMS; and the easing of the development of the single currency, the ECU (see Art. 109f(2) E.C.). The central feature of the European Monetary Institute is that it performs an essentially consultative and co-ordinating rôle, during a stage at which policy responsibilities will generally remain at the national level. Article 109f(3) E.C. lays out the tasks of the European Monetary Institute in preparation for the third stage. The European

Monetary Institute is the midwife for the birth of the much more powerful European Central Bank which is to oversee the single currency.

No set date is envisaged for the move to the third stage but it is provided that, if no date has been set by the end of 1997, then the third stage is to start on January 1, 1999 (Art. 109j(4) E.C.). Whether or not this fall back date is needed depends on the convergence of the Member States' economic performances prior to this date. The achievement of some degree of sustainable convergence is seen as essential to ensure effective and lasting union, with the minimum of economic hardship. Article 109j(1) requires the Commission and the European Monetary Institute to report to the Council on the progress made by the Member States towards economic and monetary union. This progress report is based on the achievement of the four convergence criteria laid down in this article, and elaborated in the Protocol on the Convergence Criteria and on the Excessive Deficit Procedure. Article 109j(2) then requires the Council, by qualified majority vote, and on the basis of the reports prepared under Art. 109j(1), to assess for each Member State whether it fulfils the conditions necessary for the adoption of a single currency. If a majority of the Member States (excluding Denmark and the U.K. if they exercise their opt-outs) fulfil these four conditions then it is up to the Council, prior to December 31, 1996, to decide if it is appropriate for the Community to enter the third stage. If so, it will then set the date (Art. 109j(3) E.C.).

All those Member States who do not fulfil the conditions laid down in the Treaty are then classed as "Member States with a derogation". The status of such countries must be reviewed every two years and, in the meantime, specified Articles will apply to them. There is no specific number of countries required for the move to the third stage if the fall back date of January 1, 1999 is invoked (see Art. 109j(4) E.C.). The irrevocability of this move is highlighted by the Protocol on the transition to the third stage of economic and monetary union. It provides that no Member State shall prevent the entering into the third stage and that all states shall expedite the preparatory work aimed at this goal. It will, nevertheless, remain to be seen whether or not the Treaty timetable will be retained at the inter-governmental conference scheduled for 1996.

The specific provisions governing the U.K. opt-out from the third stage of economic and monetary union are included in the Protocol on certain provisions relating to the U.K. This provides that the U.K. shall not be obliged to move to the third stage without a separate decision by its government and parliament. The Decision concerning Denmark, passed at the Edinburgh European Council, recognised that Denmark had exercised its right under the Protocol on certain provisions relating to Denmark, not to move to the third stage. Thus, unless specific notification is given to the Council by the U.K. and Denmark they will be classed as "Member States with a derogation" on the coming into force of the third stage. The respective Protocols contain intricate details excluding the two countries from various economic and monetary union provisions.

Chapter 1 (Economic Policy)

Article 102a

Member States shall conduct their economic policies with a view to contributing to the achievement of the objectives of the Community, as defined in Article 2, and in the context of the broad guidelines referred to in Article 103(2).

The Member States and the Community shall act in accordance with the principle of an open market economy with free competition, favouring an efficient allocation of resources, and in compliance with the principles set out in Article 3a.

GENERAL NOTE

This Article amounts to little more than a broad statement of general policy, as regards the conduct of the Member States' economic policies. These policies are to be co-ordinated with a view to the achievement of the objectives of the Community, set out in Art. 2 of the Treaty, the broad guidelines referred to in Art. 103(2) E.C. and in compliance with the principles set out in Art. 3a. Article 2 E.C. has been updated to take account of the new Community competences in the pursuit of economic and monetary union and thus talks of "a high degree of convergence of economic performances", the core feature of the economic policy provisions of the Treaty. Some scepticism has been voiced about the likelihood of achievement of all of the objectives laid out in Art. 2 E.C. (see note on that Article). The co-ordination of economic policies to achieve "a high level of employment and social protection, and the raising of the standard of living" will not be easy, given the divergent economic and political opinion as to how these goals can be achieved (*e.g.* greater deregulation to provide growth and higher employment levels or regulation to ensure better social protection for workers). In other words, the pursuit of all these goals may require contradictory economic strategies. Nevertheless, Art. 2 must be taken for what it is, a statement of intent; the relevant part for the purposes of Art. 102a E.C. is the goal of "a high degree of convergence of economic performances". Article 3a E.C. duplicates the wording of this Article when it talks of "the adoption of an economic policy based on the close co-ordination of the Member States' economic policies". The most cogent and clear-cut reference in this Article as to the background factors determining the economic policy of the Community is the reference to the guidelines laid down in Art. 103(2) E.C. These broad guidelines laid down by the Council will act as the tangible basis of the Member States' economic policies (see note on that Article).

Article 103

1. Member-States shall regard their economic policies as a matter of common concern and shall co-ordinate them within the Council, in accordance with the provisions of Article 102a.

2. The Council shall, acting by a qualified majority on a recommendation from the Commission, formulate a draft for the broad guidelines of the economic policies of the Member States and of the Community, and shall report its findings to the European Council.

The European Council shall, acting on the basis of this report from the Council, discuss a conclusion on the broad guidelines of the economic policies of the Member States and of the Community.

On the basis of this conclusion, the Council shall, acting by a qualified majority, adopt a recommendation setting out these broad guidelines. The Council shall inform the European Parliament of its recommendation.

3. In order to ensure closer co-ordination of economic policies and sustained convergence of the economic performances of the Member States, the Council shall, on the basis of reports submitted by the Commission, monitor economic developments in each of the Member States and in the Community as well as the consistency of economic policies with the broad guidelines referred to in paragraph 2, and regularly carry out an overall assessment.

For the purpose of this multilateral surveillance, Member States shall forward information to the Commission about important measures taken by them in the field of their economic policy and such other information as they deem necessary.

4. Where it is established, under the procedure referred to in paragraph 3, that the economic policies of a Member State are not consistent with the broad guidelines referred to in paragraph 2 or that they risk jeopardising the proper functioning of economic and monetary union, the Council may, acting by a qualified majority on a recommendation from the Commission, make the necessary recommendations to the Member State concerned.

The Council may, acting by a qualified majority on a proposal from the Commission, decide to make its recommendations public.

The President of the Council and the Commission shall report to the European Parliament on the results of multilateral surveillance. The President of the Council may be invited to appear before the competent Committee of the European Parliament if the Council has made its recommendations public.

5. The Council, acting in accordance with the procedure referred to in Article 189c, may adopt detailed rules for the multilateral surveillance procedure referred to in paragraphs 3 and 4 of this Article.

GENERAL NOTE

Para. (1)
    This Article forms the core of the economic component of economic and monetary union. The Member States' economic policies are to be *co-ordinated* within the Council [emphasis added]. This indicates the relatively weak nature of this process. Given the wide scope for interpretation of the meaning of Art. 102a E.C., it is difficult to predict what economic policy guidelines will be adopted by the Council.

Para. (2)

This lays out the apparatus for the co-ordination of the Member States' economic policies. The Council, acting on a recommendation from the Commission, will formulate a draft of the broad guidelines of the economic policies of the Member States and the Community. This draft then passes to the European Council who prepare a conclusion on the topic. It is strange that the European Council is given a rôle to play under the E.C. Treaty. It would have been more consistent and institutionally appropriate to follow the pattern in Art. 109j E.C. and have the guidelines adopted by the Council in the composition of the heads of state or government. The conclusion of the European Council will then pass back to the Council before the latter body adopts, by a qualified majority vote, a recommendation setting out these guidelines. Being a recommendation, the Treaty is quite explicit that it has "no binding force" (Art. 189 E.C.).

One matter of some confusion is that no guidance is given as to the voting rights in the European Council in the adoption of their "conclusions". The Treaty does not indicate whether the heads of government and of state have to be unanimous as to the "conclusions" adopted or whether some form of majority voting will suffice. The President of the Commission is a full member of the European Council and it is far from clear if he has any voting rights.

Another unusual factor in the process envisaged under this Article is that, normally, matters coming under the Community competences which are discussed at the level of the European Council return to the Commission for it to prepare legislative proposals. In this case, and probably emphasising the sensitive governmental nature of these guidelines, no provision is made for the return of the recommendation to the Commission before its adoption by the Council.

This paragraph provides that the European Parliament is to be informed by the Council of its recommendation. This would seem to give the European Parliament no scope for any debate on the matter prior to its entry into force, and was the subject of criticism in the European Parliament in the report on the Maastricht inter-governmental conference (European Parliament Report A3–123). There is no requirement that the European Parliament be informed prior to the entry into force of the recommendation and even if there was, the notion of "informing" the European Parliament leaves it with no real power. This is in contrast to the Commission's draft, which had proposed the formal consultation of the European Parliament on general recommendations and on the adoption of recommendations specific to a Member State, but with a time-limit of two months imposed on the European Parliament's consideration of any matter under the latter heading to prevent delay (Arts. 102c/102d, see E.C. Bull. Supp. 2/91, pp. 41–42).

Para. (3)

This deals with the so-called multilateral surveillance procedure. This surveillance, carried out by the Council on the basis of Commission reports, will assess both the Member States' economic performances and the compliance of the Member States' economic policies with the broad guidelines laid down under Art. 103(2) E.C.

The requirement of para. 2 that the Member States shall forward relevant information to the Commission to assist in this surveillance process must be read, as regards the U.K., in the light of s.4 of the 1993 Act, which lays down a list of what is considered to be relevant information. This includes information on economic growth, industrial investment, employment and balance of trade figures, as well as a comparison, based on these factors, with the performances of the other Member States. Nothing in s.4, however, precludes the Commission requesting other information or the U.K. being required to pass on information not covered in this section. The wording of Art. 103(3) E.C. makes clear the wide scope of material expected.

Para. (4)

This contains the very limited "sanctions" envisaged for those Member States whose economic policies "are not consistent with the broad guidelines referred to in para. 2" or more vaguely, whose economic policies "risk jeopardising the proper functioning of economic and monetary union". In the event of a perceived breach, the Council may, by a qualified majority vote, make the necessary recommendations to the Member State involved. Any such action by the Council must be based, in the first instance, on a Commission recommendation. If the Commission makes a proposal to do so, the Council can, by qualified majority vote, make its recommendations public. Such public censure is the maximum "penalty" available in this field, and is only available where the Member State concerned has the opportunity to vote in its own defence. Unanimity in Council is required to amend a Commission proposal (see Art. 189a E.C.) but no such Treaty restraint is imposed on the Council in amending a Commission recommendation.

The President of the Council and the Commission are to report to the European Parliament on the results of the multilateral surveillance, and this is stepped up where the Council has made its recommendations public. In this situation, the President of the Council may be invited before the relevant Committee of the European Parliament. While this paragraph does not indicate any compulsion on the President to attend, it is politically very likely that he would attend, if requested. It also marks the first Treaty recognition of the important rôle played by Committees in the European Parliament (see also Art. 109b(3) E.C.).

Para. (5)
This lays down the procedure for the adoption of the detailed rules for the multilateral surveillance process, which is to be the co-operation procedure (Art. 189c E.C.). No specific timeframe is envisaged for this taking place.

Article 103a

1. Without prejudice to any other procedures provided for in this Treaty, the Council may, acting unanimously on a proposal from the Commission, decide upon the measures appropriate to the economic situation, in particular if severe difficulties arise in the supply of certain products.

2. Where a Member State is in difficulties or is seriously threatened with severe difficulties caused by exceptional occurrences beyond its control, the Council may, acting unanimously on a proposal from the Commission, grant, under certain conditions, Community financial assistance to the Member State concerned. Where the severe difficulties are caused by natural disasters, the Council shall act by qualified majority. The President of the Council shall inform the European Parliament of the decision taken.

GENERAL NOTE
The first paragraph permits the derogation from the co-ordination guidelines laid down above. The specific situation envisaged is serious supply difficulties as regards certain products, but derogation can apply in other situations, subject to the proviso that the measures taken be "appropriate to the economic situation". The effective limitation on any abuse of this procedure is that its application requires the unanimous vote of the Council. This replaces the analogous provisions in Art. 103 E.E.C. on conjunctural policy. That Article permitted a limited amount of qualified majority voting in the Council, which has not been retained in the E.C. Treaty.

Paragraph 2 permits, by the same procedure, the granting of financial assistance to a Member State faced with "severe difficulties caused by exceptional occurrences beyond its control". In the event of these severe difficulties being the result of natural disasters (*e.g.* earthquakes), then qualified majority voting will apply. Paragraph 2 of this Article shall apply only from the start of the third stage (Art. 109e(3) E.C.).

The European Parliament has no formal rôle in measures adopted under the first paragraph and is merely informed of the outcome of the process under para. 2.

Article 104

1. Overdraft facilities or any other type of credit facility with the ECB or with the central banks of the Member States (hereinafter referred to as 'national central banks') in favour of Community institutions or bodies, central governments, regional, local or other public authorities, other bodies governed by public law or public undertakings of Member States shall be prohibited, as shall the purchase directly from them by the ECB or national central banks of debt instruments.

2. The provisions of paragraph 1 shall not apply to publicly-owned credit institutions, which in the context of the supply of reserves by central banks shall be given the same treatment by national central banks and the ECB as private credit institutions.

GENERAL NOTE
This Article, and the subsequent Arts. 104a and 104b E.C., lay down a number of practices which are to be forbidden in the field of public sector finance. These prohibitions will take effect from the coming into force of the second stage of economic and monetary union on January 1, 1994 (see Art. 109e(3) E.C.). Firstly, overdraft facilities or any other type of credit facility with the European Central Bank or the national central banks in favour of public sector bodies are to be forbidden. The direct purchase of debt instruments from the European Central Bank or national central banks by public sector bodies is also prohibited. Paragraph 2 sets out an exemp-

tion to this prohibition for publicly owned credit institutions, where the supply of reserves by central banks is concerned. For some reason, the adoption of more specific definitions as regards the prohibition in this Article, appear under Art. 104b(2) E.C. (see note on that Article. These definitions are to be decided upon by the co-operation procedure).

It is expressly provided in the Protocol on certain provisions relating to the U.K. that, so long as the U.K. does not move to the third stage, then the Government may maintain its Ways and Means facility with the Bank of England, irrespective of the provisions of this Article (Protocol No.11 at para. 11).

Article 104a

1. Any measure, not based on prudential considerations, establishing privileged access by Community institutions or bodies, central governments, regional, local or other public authorities, other bodies governed by public law or public undertakings of Member States to financial institutions shall be prohibited.

2. The Council, acting in accordance with the procedure referred to in Article 189c, shall, before 1 January 1994, specify definitions for the application of the prohibition referred to in paragraph 1.

GENERAL NOTE

This Article, applicable from the start of the second stage, seeks to prohibit the privileged access to financial institutions by national authorities. Acting under the co-operation procedure, the Council is to determine the specific definitions for the application of this provision by January 1, 1994. Central to the discussion in Council will be the determination of what constitutes "prudential considerations".

Article 104b

1. The Community shall not be liable for or assume the commitments of central governments, regional, local or other public authorities, other bodies governed by public law, or public undertakings of any Member State, without prejudice to mutual financial guarantees for the joint execution of a specific project. A Member State shall not be liable for or assume the commitments of central governments, regional, local or other public authorities, other bodies governed by public law or public undertakings of another Member State, without prejudice to mutual financial guarantees for the joint execution of a specific project.

2. If necessary, the Council, acting in accordance with the procedure referred to in Article 189c, may specify definitions for the application of the prohibitions referred to in Article 104 and in this Article.

GENERAL NOTE

This Article, again applicable from the start of the second stage, lays out the details of the so-called "no-bailing out" rule. It makes it clear that the Community shall neither be responsible for, nor assume, the commitments of central governments or other national public authorities. A similar duty is imposed on the Member States as regards the commitments of central governments and of other national authorities in other Member States. A proviso is made in the case of both Community and national authorities, that mutual financial guarantees for the joint execution of a specific project will still be permissible. This was included because such joint guarantees constitute one of the most common means of Community funding under the Cohesion funds, etc.

Paragraph 2 asserts that definitions for this Article and for Art. 104 E.C., *supra*, will be specified under the co-operation procedure. Unlike Art. 104a(2) E.C. on the adoption of specific definitions in the field of privileged access to financial institutions, the current Article does not specify any time-limit for the adoption of definitions. As both measures are due to come into force at the same time, the reason for this discrepancy is unclear.

Article 104c

1. Member States shall avoid excessive government deficits.

2. The Commission shall monitor the development of the budgetary

situation and of the stock of government debt in the Member States with a view to identifying gross errors. In particular it shall examine compliance with budgetary discipline on the basis of the following two criteria:
  (a) whether the ratio of the planned or actual government deficit to gross domestic product exceeds a reference value, unless
    — either the ratio has declined substantially and continuously and reached a level that comes close to the reference value;
    — or, alternatively, the excess over the reference value is only exceptional and temporary and the ratio remains close to the reference value;
  (b) whether the ratio of government debt to gross domestic product exceeds a reference value, unless the ratio is sufficiently diminishing and approaching the reference value at a satisfactory pace.
The reference values are specified in the Protocol on the excessive deficit procedure annexed to this Treaty.
  3. If a Member State does not fulfil the requirements under one or both of these criteria, the Commission shall prepare a report. The report of the Commission shall also take into account whether the government deficit exceeds government investment expenditure and take into account all other relevant factors, including the medium term economic and budgetary position of the Member State.
The Commission may also prepare a report if, notwithstanding the fulfilment of the requirements under the criteria, it is of the opinion that there is a risk of an excessive deficit in a Member State.
  4. The Committee provided for in Article 109c shall formulate an opinion on the report of the Commission.
  5. If the Commission considers that an excessive deficit in a Member State exists or may occur, the Commission shall address an opinion to the Council.
  6. The Council shall, acting by a qualified majority on a recommendation from the Commission, and having considered any observations which the Member State concerned may wish to make, decide after an overall assessment whether an excessive deficit exists.
  7. Where the existence of an excessive deficit is decided according to paragraph 6, the Council shall make recommendations to the Member State concerned with a view to bringing that situation to an end within a given period. Subject to the provisions of paragraph 8, these recommendations shall not be made public.
  8. Where it establishes that there has been no effective action in response to its recommendations within the period laid down, the Council may make its recommendations public.
  9. If a Member State persists in failing to put into practice the recommendations of the Council, the Council may decide to give notice to the Member State to take, within a specified time limit, measures for the deficit reduction which is judged necessary by the Council in order to remedy the situation.
In such a case, the Council may request the Member State concerned to submit reports in accordance with a specific timetable in order to examine the adjustment efforts of that Member State.
  10. The rights to bring actions provided for in Articles 169 and 170 may not be exercised within the framework of paragraphs 1 to 9 of this Article.
  11. As long as a Member State fails to comply with a decision taken in accordance with paragraph 9, the Council may decide to apply or, as the case may be, intensify one or more of the following measures:
    — to require that the Member State concerned shall publish additional information, to be specified by the Council, before issuing bonds and securities;
    — to invite the European Investment Bank to reconsider its lending policy towards the Member State concerned;

— to require that the Member State concerned makes a non-interest-bearing deposit of an appropriate size with the Community until the excessive deficit has, in the view of the Council, been corrected;
— to impose fines of an appropriate size.

The President of the Council shall inform the European Parliament of the decisions taken.

12. The Council shall abrogate some or all of its decisions as referred to in paragraphs 6 to 9 and 11 to the extent that the excessive deficit in the Member State concerned has, in the view of the Council, been corrected.

If the Council previously has made public recommendations, it shall, as soon as the decision under paragraph 8 has been abrogated, make a public statement that an excessive deficit in the Member State concerned no longer exists.

13. When taking the decisions referred to in paragraphs 7 to 9, 11 and 12, the Council shall act on a recommendation from the Commission by a majority of two thirds of the votes of its members weighted in accordance with Article 148(2) and excluding the votes of the representative of the Member State concerned.

14. Further provisions relating to the implementation of the procedure described in this Article are set out in the Protocol on the excessive deficit procedure annexed to this Treaty.

The Council shall, acting unanimously on a proposal from the Commission and after consulting the European Parliament and the ECB, adopt the appropriate provisions which shall then replace the said Protocol.

Subject to the other provisions of this paragraph the Council shall, before January 1994, acting by a qualified majority on a proposal from the Commission and after consulting the European Parliament, lay down detailed rules and definitions for the application of the provisions of the said Protocol.

GENERAL NOTE

Para. (1)

Article 104c(1) states, in no uncertain terms, that the main task of the co-ordination of the Member States' economic policies is to be the avoidance of excessive government deficits. Article 104c(2) sets out the criteria for determining the "excessiveness" or otherwise of the deficit. The remainder of the Article concerns the procedures for sanctioning non-complying States. Unlike the procedure for the co-ordination of economic policies under Art. 103 E.C., the sanctions envisaged under this Article may, after an ascending course of adverse publicity and warnings, become punitive in nature (Art. 104c(11) E.C.). This shall take place, however, once the third stage has come into force and will apply only to States who have joined the single currency. The coming into force of the Article as a whole is somewhat convoluted. According to Art. 109e(3) E.C., Art. 104c will take effect from the start of the second stage but Arts. 104c(1), (9) and (11) will come into operation only during the third stage. Articles 104c(9) and (11) deal with the punitive aspects of the process and the result is that, while the basis of the excessive deficit procedure operates during the second stage, there are less rigorous sanctions in place. As with Art. 103 E.C. the maximum penalty during the second stage is adverse publicity. The postponement of Art. 104c(1) E.C., on the other hand, frees the States from the imperative "States *shall* avoid excessive government deficits". During the second stage, the Member States have a somewhat lower target to meet. Article 109e(4) E.C. simply states that "the Member States shall *endeavour* to avoid excessive government deficits" [emphasis added].

One source of confusion is that the core provision on the punitive sanctions applicable in the third stage, Art. 104c(14), is not included under Art. 109e(3) as coming into force on the commencement of the third stage. This is probably a legislative oversight rather than an intentional omission.

Para. (2)

This paragraph sets out the criteria for assessing the scale of the government deficit and more lucidly, sets the levels at which this is deemed to become excessive. The duty to monitor the development of the budgetary situations in the Member States falls on the Commission. The Commission must pay particular heed to two factors: (a) whether the ratio of the planned or actual government deficit to Gross Domestic Product exceeds a reference value; and (b) whether the ratio of government debt to Gross Domestic Product exceeds a specific reference value. The reference values themselves are laid down in the Protocol on the Excessive Deficit Procedure. The Protocol defines these reference values as (a) 3 per cent. for the ratio of planned or actual government deficit to Gross Domestic Product and (b) 60 per cent. for the ratio of government debt to Gross Domestic Product.

This Article is markedly different from that in the Luxembourg draft. The latter document was seen by many Member States, including the U.K., as being too inflexible, concentrating heavily on one year's budgetary figures. This Article allows a great deal more flexibility in the analysis. As regards the ratio of government deficit to Gross Domestic Product; even if the figure exceeds 3 per cent., if the ratio has declined substantially and continuously and reached a level that comes close to the reference value, then it will be acceptable. This is also the case where the excess over the reference value is only exceptional and temporary, and the ratio remains close to the reference value. Similar conditions apply as regards the ratio of government debt to Gross Domestic Product.

This emphasis on the direction in which the debt and borrowing levels are moving, rather than their absolute levels, might well prove essential in so far as current economic trends make rigid compliance with the figures unlikely in the near future in all but a few Member States. The latest estimates for government borrowing as a per cent. of Gross Domestic Product are as follows (1993 figures followed by 1994 figures in brackets): Belgium 7.0 per cent. (6.1 per cent.); Denmark 4.4 per cent. (4.9 per cent.); France 5.9 per cent. (5.9 per cent.); Germany 4.1 per cent. (3.8 per cent.); Greece 13.1 per cent. (11.1 per cent.); Ireland 3.4 per cent. (3.9 per cent.); Italy 10.4 per cent. (9.1 per cent.); Luxembourg 2.0 per cent. (1.7 per cent.); Netherlands 3.8 per cent. (3.0 per cent.); Portugal 5.7 per cent. (4.7 per cent.); Spain 4.7 per cent. (4.6 per cent.); U.K. 7.7 per cent. (6.9 per cent.). Source: European Economy, E.C. Publications, June/July 1993. Belgium, Greece and Italy had public debt ratios of over 100 per cent. of Gross Domestic Product in 1992 and will need several years of budget surpluses to come anywhere near the 60 per cent. target (see the House of Commons Library Research Paper 93/25, The Maastricht Debate: Central Banking and Monetary Union, of March 5, 1993 by Edmonds).

The downside of such subjective analysis of the compliance is that the exercise of discretion becomes inevitable in what is a relatively sensitive area. The Commission will initially make such decisions but at all levels of the decision-making process some form of discretion is present.

Para. (3)

This marks the commencement of the provisions dealing with the enforcement procedure and will take effect from the start of the second stage. It empowers the Commission to prepare a report where a Member State has failed to fulfil the requirements under one or both of the criteria discussed in the note on para. (2) above. This report is to take into account all other relevant factors, including the medium term economic and budgetary position of the Member State. It ensures that the next stage of the enforcement procedure is equipped with adequate background information. The exercise of some form of discretion is unavoidable in this field and the Commission is permitted, under the second paragraph of this Article, to prepare a report even where the Member State is currently complying with the criteria, "if it is of the opinion that there is a risk of an excessive deficit".

Para. (4)

The Monetary Committee, set up under Art. 109c, and which will come into being on January 1, 1994, is to formulate an opinion on the report of the Commission. This is in keeping with the general rôle of this body, which has as its major task the review of the monetary and financial situation in the Member States (see note on Art. 109c(1) E.C.). Nowhere in this Article or in Art. 109c(1) E.C. is there any indication as to the procedures to be followed by this Committee. The only evidence which can be adduced is that it is to operate "without prejudice to Art. 151 E.C." which would suggest that it will work alongside COREPER, but sheds little light on the manner in which it will adopt the opinion expected of it under this Article. An examination of the governing provisions of the Economic and Financial Committee (Art. 109c(2) E.C.) which will take over from the Monetary Committee at the start of stage three, is equally unilluminating in this respect.

Para. (5)

This provision gives an important discretion to the Commission. The Council cannot consider whether there is an excessive deficit unless the Commission addresses an opinion to the Council. According to Fratianni, this gives the Commission a critical rôle in the future political economy of the Community, as it will be for the Commission to determine in the first instance whether or not a country's fiscal policy is subject to Community scrutiny. There is, however, no duty upon the Council to act upon the Commission's recommendations (Fratianni et al, *Essays in International Finance*, No. 187, 1992, Princeton University, pp. 40–41).

Para. (6)

The Council is to decide, on a qualified majority vote, whether an excessive deficit exists in the Member State. This vote takes place after the Member State has had an opportunity to put its own case in defence. One ambiguity in this stage of the process is the type of proposal expected from the Commission. In Art. 104c(5) the Commission is to address an opinion to the Council but, under this Article, the Commission would seem to have to make a recommendation to the Council. It is not clear whether or not this is merely an unfortunate discrepancy in the use of words. If it is not it would seem to be another example of the unduly complicated nature of the process. Whether it is an opinion or a recommendation, the Council is not constrained by the Treaty as to the voting requirements for any amendments it may wish to make. It is not a Commission "proposal" and therefore the unanimity requirement for amendment is not applicable (see Art. 189a(1) E.C.). The Council acts by a qualified majority, with the "accused" State retaining a vote. The Council has a wide discretion in deciding whether an excessive deficit exists, given the wording of Art. 104c(2). If the Council has reached such a decision, then the State concerned cannot qualify to participate in the third stage of economic and monetary union (see Art. 2 of the Protocol on the Convergence Criteria and the note on Art. 109j).

Para. (7)

If the Council makes the determination that an excessive government deficit does in fact exist, then it shall make recommendations to the Member State concerned, with a view to bringing the situation to an end within a given period. This decision is to be taken in accordance with the voting procedure laid down in Art. 104c(13) (see note on that paragraph below).

Para. (8)

This paragraph permits the Council to make its recommendations public if it establishes that there has not been an adequate response to its recommendations in the specified period. This is the strongest sanction available during the second stage. Unlike the equivalent sanction in relation to a Member State breaching the economic guidelines, it is not contingent on a proposal from the Commission (see Art. 103(4) E.C.). The decision is to be taken in accordance with the procedure laid down in Art. 104c(13). This requires two-thirds of the votes in Council, weighted in accordance with Art. 148(2) E.C., and excluding the vote of the Member State concerned.

Para. (9)

On the coming into force of the third stage, the Council may give the Member State a specific list of measures deemed necessary by the Council for the reduction of the excessive deficit. Once again, this is to be determined in accordance with the procedure laid down in Art. 104c(13).

Para. (10)

This paragraph excludes the application of Arts. 169 and 170 E.C. from matters within the scope of paras. (1) to (9) above. The Commission is therefore precluded from its normal rôle as guardian of the Treaties. Under Art. 169 E.C. the Commission can bring proceedings against a Member State before the E.C.J. when it alleges in a reasoned opinion that the State has failed to fulfil its obligations under Community law and the State fails to comply with that opinion within the time-limit. In relation to Art. 104c, paras. (1) to (9) the Council takes over the Commission's powers of notification to the Member State in the event of an envisaged breach and the E.C.J. has no rôle to play. The exclusion of Art. 170 means that other Member States are precluded from initiating proceedings before the E.C.J. where they feel that another Member State has failed to fulfil its obligations under Art. 104c(1) to (9) of the E.C. Treaty. On Arts. 169 and 170 generally see Weatherill and Beaumont, *EC Law*, Chap. 7.

Para. (11)

This is the key Article once the third stage comes into force. The Council may apply, at its discretion, any of the listed sanctions to States persisting with an excessive deficit. The Council may apply any or all of these measures and is quite at liberty to step up the sanction if it so desires. The only requirement for the latter course of action is, as for any action taken under this heading, that the voting requirements in Art. 104c(13) are complied with. The power to impose fines on a Member State is an important one but no mechanism is provided for dealing with Member States that fail to pay the sums due. No power is given to reduce the amount paid to that State under the Common Agricultural Policy or under the structural funds. There is therefore at least a theoretical risk, that a Member State which is a party to the single currency could destabilise the currency union by failing to reduce an excessive government deficit. Such a State would find it very difficult to obtain any favourable outcomes in decisions taken by the Council which impinge on their interests.

The European Parliament is to be informed of any action taken, but has no formal rôle. Before any sanction may be imposed the Commission must have made a recommendation (see Art. 104c(13)) but as such a recommendation is not a "proposal" the Council is not restricted by the Treaty to making any amendments only by unanimity. The Council could choose to permit amendments to a Commission recommendation by simple or qualified majority.

It must be emphasised that the U.K., by virtue of its opt-out (see para. 5 of the Protocol relating to the U.K.), is exempt from the imperative in Art. 109c(1) as well as any application of the punitive provisions in paras. 9 and 11.

Para. (12)

This paragraph makes provision for the Council to revoke an earlier decision, where it believes that an excessive deficit has been corrected. Alternatively, if the earlier decision has been made public, the Council will make a public statement to the effect that the deficit no longer exists. The voting procedure applicable to the original adoption of the sanctions against the Member State is also applicable to any revocations under this section (Art. 104c(13)).

Para. (13)

The voting procedure is to be a form of qualified majority vote, with the individual weightings determined by Art. 148(2) E.C. The requisite majority is to be two-thirds of the Member States' votes, excluding the votes of the Member State concerned. This is a relatively strict requirement but does not give any real advantage to specific Member States. If the Member State concerned is one of the big four (U.K., Germany, France or Italy) then the exclusion of their 10 votes from the equation requires 44 of the remaining 66 votes to pass any sanctioning (or revoking) measure. Thus 23 votes are required to veto any action. If the non-compliant State were to be one of the smaller Member States with three votes, Ireland or Denmark, then the number of votes required to veto the application of sanctions is 25.

Para. (14)

This paragraph deals with the Protocol on the excessive deficit procedure, already referred to as regards the reference values for determining the excessive deficits under Art. 104c(2) E.C. (Art. 1 of the Protocol). The Protocol also contains: definitions of certain key concepts including "government", "investment", "deficit" and "debt" (Art. 2 of the Protocol); a reiteration of the duty of the Member States to "ensure that national procedures in the budgetary area enable them to meet their obligations deriving from the Treaty (Art. 3 of the Protocol); and finally, a provision that the statistical data to be used in the application of the Protocol is to come from the Commission (Art. 4).

The coming into force of this provision of the Treaty is left in some doubt by virtue of Art. 109e(3) which states that, while Art. 104c is to come into force from the start of the second stage, certain paragraphs are excluded, including Art. 104c(14). However, no provision is made in the second sentence of Art. 109e(3) that para. (14) will come into force at the start of the third stage either. This makes for a very unclear situation as regards the application of para. 14. The Protocol itself is to come into operation from the start of the second stage, and the third paragraph of this Article specifies that action be taken prior to January 1994 for the adoption of the detailed rules and provisions allowing for the application of the Protocol. Nevertheless, the second paragraph would seem to be applicable only from the start of the third stage, in so far as reference is made to the European Central Bank. The whole situation is far from clear. This matter is far from academic, given that this paragraph permits the adoption of new measures to replace the Protocol on the excessive deficit procedure and, most importantly, permits the alteration of the reference values contained therein. The Council, acting by unanimity on a Commission proposal, is to adopt the appropriate provisions for such a replacement. The Protocol itself sheds no light on the envisaged time-scale for this taking place. Moreover, this process of replacing the provisions of the Protocol appears not to be a matter of discretion on the part of the Council but a necessary step; the wording of the paragraph appears imperative, with the requirement that the Council "shall adopt the appropriate provisions".

Chapter 2 (Monetary Policy)

Article 105

1. The primary objective of the ESCB shall be to maintain price stability. Without prejudice to the objective of price stability, the ESCB shall support

the general economic policies in the Community with a view to contributing to the achievement of the objectives of the Community as laid down in Article 2.

The ESCB shall act in accordance with the principle of an open market economy with free competition, favouring an efficient allocation of resources, and in compliance with the principles set out in Article 3a.

2. The basic tasks to be carried out through the ESCB shall be:
— to define and implement the monetary policy of the Community;
— to conduct foreign exchange operations consistent with the provisions of Article 109;
— to hold and manage the official foreign reserves of the Member States;
— to promote the smooth operation of payment systems.

3. The third indent of paragraph 2 shall be without prejudice to the holding and management by the governments of Member States of foreign exchange working balances.

4. The ECB shall be consulted:
— on any proposed Community act in its fields of competence;
— by national authorities regarding any draft legislative provision in its fields of competence, but within the limits and under the conditions set out by the Council in accordance with the procedure laid down in Article 106(6).

The ECB may submit opinions to the appropriate Community institutions or bodies or to national authorities on matters within its fields of competence.

5. The ESCB shall contribute to the smooth conduct of policies pursued by the competent authorities relating to the prudential supervision of credit institutions and the stability of the financial system.

6. The Council may, acting unanimously on a proposal from the Commission and after consulting the ECB and after receiving the assent of the European Parliament, confer upon the ECB specific tasks concerning policies relating to the prudential supervision of credit institutions and other financial institutions with the exception of insurance undertakings.

GENERAL NOTE

The importance of this Article should not be underestimated. From the start of the third stage of economic and monetary union, when this provision enters into force, the European System of Central Banks is to take over the running of the Community monetary policy. While there are separate currencies, national governments have, at least in theory, a substantial degree of flexibility of action. They may keep their central banks under political control and decide their own monetary policy and dictate their own fiscal policies. With the creation of a common currency, these freedoms are vitiated. A common monetary policy is thereby required.

The overriding objective of this policy is the maintenance of price stability (Art. 105(1)). While the European System of Central Banks may look to the objectives of the Community in Arts. 2 and 3a in the determination of its actions, pursuit of these objectives must be "without prejudice to" the achievement of price stability. This policy reflects that of the Bundesbank on which the European Central Bank is substantially modelled, and is frequently reiterated in other provisions of the Treaty. The Bundesbank does not, however, have a statutory duty to maintain "price stability" but rather to safeguard the "stability of the currency", but in practice it does give much greater weight to keeping a tight rein on inflation (Fratianni *et al*, *supra*, at 33).

The tasks of the European System of Central Banks are set out in Art. 105(2) and reflect to a large extent those encompassed in the Central Banker's suggested draft. The European System of Central Banks is to define and implement the monetary policy of the Community (presumably in accordance with the provisions of Art. 105(1)), to conduct foreign exchange operations consistent with the provisions of Art. 109, to hold and manage the official foreign reserves of the Member States and to promote the smooth operation of the payments system.

As regards the duty to conduct foreign exchange operations, the European System of Central Banks will act as a consultative partner to the Council rather than as an autonomous agent. While the European Central Bank will have the operational responsibility, the definition of the exchange rate policy will fall to the Council (see Art. 109 E.C.). Prior to the Maastricht European Council this was one of the more contentious topics in the economic and monetary union negotiations. It is generally accepted that it is very difficult for an independent monetary authority to pursue alternative goals; either it concentrates on keeping inflation down (as the Bundesbank has done) or it concentrates on maintaining an exchange rate policy. The decision to make price stability the goal was taken very early on in the negotiations, and this meant that a great deal of debate centred on the institutional control of the exchange rate policy. The eventual decision to utilise the Council will make the future relations of the European Central Bank and the Council very important and often complicated.

The third task set out in para. 2 was the subject of much debate, and its final form not determined until the Maastricht summit itself. The controversy surrounded the degree of European Central Bank control over the Member States' foreign reserves. The final draft, stating that the European Central Bank shall hold and manage the foreign exchange reserves suggests that *all* the reserves will be under the control of the European Central Bank. The rejected version simply contained a reference to "exchange reserves". On the other hand, Art. 30.1 of the Statute of the European System of Central Banks and the European Central Bank (set out in Protocol No. 3 below) provides that the European Central Bank shall be provided, by the national central banks, with foreign reserve assets up to an amount equivalent to 50,000 million ECUs. In most countries these reserves are currently held by the national governments rather than the central banks, although Germany is a well-known exception. Their transfer to the Central Bank and their pooling under its authority are essential in order to permit the European Central Bank to maintain the external value of the ECU. Article 105(3) does allow Member States to hold and manage "foreign exchange working balances"; Art. 31.2 of the European System of Central Banks and European Central Bank Statute permits the national central banks to retain some foreign reserve assets, but any operations in those assets above a certain limit are subject to approval by the European Central Bank.

Article 105(4) provides for the incorporation of the European Central Bank into the legislative arena. It is to be consulted on any proposed Community act in its field of competence. Even if this were to be interpreted relatively narrowly, the European Central Bank, given the wide scope of matters which will have a bearing on its actions, will find itself consulted on a huge variety of matters. Because this consultation process is to take place at the proposal stage, the European Central Bank is given scope for exercising its influence over the legislation in question. The Member States are also required to submit draft legislation to the European Central Bank if this legislation falls within its area of competence. This provision duplicates Art. 4 of the Statute of the European Central Bank annexed to the Treaty. Its application is to be determined by virtue of the procedure in Art. 106(6) E.C. The European Central Bank is also empowered to submit opinions to the appropriate Community institutions or national authorities on matters in its field of competence.

Article 105(5) gives the European System of Central Banks (as opposed to the European Central Bank) the duty to contribute to the smooth conduct of policies pursued by the competent authorities relating to the prudential supervision of credit institutions and the stability of the financial system. Thus the European System of Central Banks is to take an ancillary rôle in this field, leaving the actual supervisory duties to other unspecified bodies (but likely to be the Central Banks themselves). It has been suggested, however, that the European Central Bank itself will play a much stronger rôle in the prudential supervision as time passes. It will be the only organisation in Europe with the ability to provide sufficient funds at short notice to bail out any institution in financial difficulties (Lomax, National Westminster Bank Quarterly Review, May 1991). This delegation of duties to the European Central Bank in the area of prudential supervision is specifically catered for in Art. 105(6), whereby the Council, acting unanimously on a proposal from the Commission, and after receiving the assent of the European Parliament, may confer upon the European Central Bank specific tasks relating to the prudential supervision of financial and credit institutions, with the exception of insurance undertakings. Until the U.K. opts to join the single currency, Art. 105(1) to (5) is not applicable to it (see para. 5 of the U.K. opt-out Protocol).

Article 105a

1. The ECB shall have the exclusive right to authorise the issue of bank notes within the Community. The ECB and the national central banks may issue such notes.

The bank notes issued by the ECB and the national central banks shall be the only such notes to have the status of legal tender within the Community.

2. Member States may issue coins subject to approval by the ECB of the volume of the issue. The Council may, acting in accordance with the procedure referred to in Article 189c and after consulting the ECB, adopt measures to harmonise the denominations and technical specifications of all

coins intended for circulation to the extent necessary to permit their smooth circulation within the Community.

GENERAL NOTE

This Article contains further material consequential on the move to a single currency, specifically the issue of the new currency units. The Article is inapplicable to the U.K. as long as it opts not to join the single currency (para. 5 of the U.K. opt-out). The European Central Bank is to have the exclusive right to authorise the issue of banknotes within the Community, but any of the national banks, subject to this authorisation, may issue such notes. One area of some interest concerns the position of the Scottish banks which currently have statutory authority to issue their own banknotes. This was the subject of a written answer in the House of Commons where it was stated that: "Article 16 of the Protocol on the Statute of the European Central Bank requires the European Central Bank to respect, as far as possible, existing practices regarding the issue and design of banknotes. If the U.K. were to participate in Stage Three of economic and monetary union these Articles would permit the European Central Bank to authorise the Scottish banks to continue to issue their own banknotes. In stage two of economic and monetary union, and in stage three were the U.K. not to participate, the U.K. could continue to maintain its own arrangements" (*Hansard*, H.C. Vol. 216, cols. 60–61).

Article 105a(2) deals with the issue of coins. This is to be the duty of the Member States, subject to the approval of the European Central Bank. The harmonisation of the denominations and technical specifications of the coins is to be carried out under the co-operation procedure. Although this would appear at first sight to be a relatively trivial matter, it will be very complicated in practice. The coins will have to be acceptable in coin operated machines throughout the Community, as well as being sufficiently similar to prevent confusion in different Member States. It is not a field easily susceptible to the application of the subsidiarity principle (Art. 36 E.C.).

Article 106

1. The ESCB shall be composed of the ECB and of the national central banks.

2. The ECB shall have legal personality.

3. The ESCB shall be governed by the decision-making bodies of the ECB which shall be the Governing Council and the Executive Board.

4. The Statute of the ESCB is laid down in a Protocol annexed to this Treaty.

5. Articles 5.1, 5.2, 5.3, 17, 18, 19.1, 22, 23, 24, 26, 32.2, 32.3, 32.4, 32.6, 33.1(a) and 36 of the Statute of the ESCB may be amended by the Council, acting either by a qualified majority on a recommendation from the ECB and after consulting the Commission or unanimously on a proposal from the Commission and after consulting the ECB. In either case, the assent of the European Parliament shall be required.

6. The Council, acting by a qualified majority either on a proposal from the Commission and after consulting the European Parliament and the ECB, or on a recommendation from the ECB and after consulting the European Parliament and the Commission, shall adopt the provisions referred to in Articles 4, 5.4, 19.2, 20, 28.1, 29.2, 30.4 and 34.3 of the Statute of the ESCB.

GENERAL NOTE

This Article lays down certain institutional provisions relating to the European System of Central Banks and the European Central Bank. Article 106(1) indicates the composition of the European System of Central Banks. It is to consist of the European Central Bank and the national central banks, but will be governed by the decision-making bodies of the European Central Bank (Art. 106(3)). The full operative provisions governing the European System of Central Banks are to be found in the Protocol on the Statute of the European System of Central Banks and European Central Bank annexed to the Treaty. The seat of the European Central Bank will be in Frankfurt (see [1993] O.J. C323/1).

Para. (5)

Article 106(5) permits the amendment of the listed Articles of the Statute of the European Central Bank. Reflecting the vested interest of the latter body in any such amendments, two different procedures are envisaged, and the choice between the two is dependent on the degree of European Central Bank involvement. If the amendment is proposed by the European Central

Bank, then the Council may adopt the measure by qualified majority; if on the other hand the proposal originates with the Commission, then unanimity is needed. In either case, the assent of the European Parliament is required.

There is no common denominator to the Articles of the Statute open to amendment. Rather, they cover a wide variety of areas and scale from the trivial to the more weighty. They include the collection of statistical information (Art. 5.1–5.3), accounts with the European Central Bank and national central banks (Art. 17), open market and credit operations (Art. 18), minimum reserves (Art. 19.1), clearing and payment systems (Art. 22), external and other operations (Arts. 23 and 24), financial accounts (Art. 26), allocation of monetary income of national central banks (Art. 32.2, 32.4 and 32.6), allocation of net profits and losses of the European Central Bank (Art. 33.1(a)) and staff provisions (Art. 36). The major features of the system, such as the organisation of the European System of Central Banks (Chap. III, Arts. 7–16), its objectives and tasks (Arts. 2–3), and the adoption of legal acts by the European Central Bank (Art. 34) are inalienable except by the normal Treaty amendment process.

Para. (6)

This paragraph, at first glance seemingly very similar to the preceding paragraph, lays out the applicable procedure for the adoption of provisions, under certain specified Articles, of the Protocol on the Statute of the European System of Central Banks. These matters, explicitly left incomplete by the TEU, are to be dealt with by the Council, acting on a recommendation from either the European Central Bank or the Commission and subject to consultation with the other body. The Council is to act by qualified majority vote and the process is to start in all these areas immediately after the decision on the date for the beginning of the third stage is taken. This procedure is reiterated in Art. 42 of the Protocol. Matters included under this heading are: advisory functions (Art. 4); the collection of statistical information (Art. 5.4); the setting of minimum and maximum reserves levels (Art. 19.2); the scope of operational methods of monetary control imposing obligations on third parties (Art. 20); the limits on the capital of the European Central Bank (Art. 28.1); statistical data for capital subscription (Art. 29.2); the transfer of additional foreign reserve assets to the European Central Bank (Art. 30.4); and, finally, the setting of the conditions for the imposition of fines and penalty payments for failure to comply with European Central Bank regulations and decisions (Art. 34.3).

Article 107

When exercising the powers and carrying out the tasks and duties conferred upon them by this Treaty and the Statute of the ESCB, neither the ECB, nor a national central bank, nor any member of their decision-making bodies shall seek or take instructions from Community institutions or bodies, from any government of a Member State or from any other body.

The Community institutions and bodies and the governments of the Member States undertake to respect this principle and not to seek to influence the members of the decision-making bodies of the ECB or of the national central banks in the performance of their tasks.

GENERAL NOTE

This Article enjoins the absolute independence of the European System of Central Banks, the European Central Bank, the national central banks and members of their decision-making authorities, from the Community institutions, Member States or any other related body. The language is very similar to that used under Art. 157(2) E.C. to ensure the independence of the Commission. The independence of the bank has been a matter of some debate, especially in this country, with its history of Treasury control over Bank of England policy. Nevertheless, this Article is of limited significance for the U.K. unless it moves to the third stage of economic and monetary union (see its non-applicability by virtue of para. 5 of the U.K. opt-out Protocol). The only duty falling on the U.K. is that it does not seek to influence the members of the decision-making bodies of the European Central Bank. The theoretical justification for an independent central bank is that it will respect its duty to maintain price stability, whereas politicians may engineer short-term growth prior to an election, despite the long-term inflation which such a move may cause. The rôle model for the European Central Bank is the Bundesbank. Studies indicate that governments attempt to influence the Bundesbank's policies at the stage of appointing its members, but cannot thereby create a bank that will engineer pre-electoral monetary expansion. The eight-year appointment period, followed in the European Central Bank, is one reason why the Bundesbank has not become the puppet of the German government (see Fratianni, Von Hagen *et al*, *supra*, pp. 33–38). The chances of political control of the European Central Bank are even less than in relation to the Bundesbank, because the Council is made up of people whose eight year appointments are not renewable (they are renewable in the Bundesbank) and who are either appointed collectively by the Governments of the Member States (up to six members of the board) or by each Government (the governors of the national central banks). Given the diverse interests of the Member States, it seems inevitable that the Bank will be genuinely independent. It will hardly be able to engineer monetary expansion to suit the electoral cycle in all of the Member States, even if it wished to do so.

Article 108

Each Member State shall ensure, at the latest at the date of the establishment of the ESCB, that its national legislation including the statutes of its national central bank is compatible with this Treaty and the Statute of the ESCB.

GENERAL NOTE

This Article requires each Member State to take all necessary steps to ensure that their national legislation, including the statute of the national central bank, is compatible with the Treaty and the Statute of the European System of Central Banks. This is to take place prior to the establishment of the latter body. The degree of action required in each Member State will depend on existing national practice, especially as regards the independence of the national central bank, but the obligations imposed by the Treaty during the third stage are diverse and often complex. The Protocol on certain provisions relating to the U.K. expressly provides that, in the absence of a decision to move to the third stage, this Article will not apply to the U.K. (see para. 5). Nevertheless, the coming into force of the third stage does not free Member States with a derogation from certain obligations. The U.K. will therefore have to ensure that its legislation permits compliance with these, albeit limited, obligations, such as the payment of subscription to the European Central Bank to cover operational expenditure (para. 9 of the Protocol on the U.K.).

Article 108a

1. In order to carry out the tasks entrusted to the ESCB, the ECB shall, in accordance with the provisions of this Treaty and under the conditions laid down in the Statute of the ESCB:
    — make regulations to the extent necessary to implement the tasks defined in Article 3.1, first indent, Articles 19.1, 22 or 25.2 of the Statute of the ESCB and in cases which shall be laid down in the acts of the Council referred to in Article 106(6);
    — take decisions necessary for carrying out the tasks entrusted to the ESCB under this Treaty and the Statute of the ESCB;
    — make recommendations and deliver opinions.
2. A regulation shall have general application. It shall be binding in its entirety and directly applicable in all Member States.

Recommendations and opinions shall have no binding force.

A decision shall be binding in its entirety upon those to whom it is addressed.

Articles 190 to 192 shall apply to regulations and decisions adopted by the ECB.

The ECB may decide to publish its decisions, recommendations and opinions.

3. Within the limits and under the conditions adopted by the Council under the procedure laid down in Article 106(6), the ECB shall be entitled to impose fines or periodic penalty payments on undertakings for failure to comply with obligations under its regulations and decisions.

GENERAL NOTE

This Article endows the European Central Bank with legislative powers (in the carrying out of its tasks) analogous to those of Art. 189 E.C. The European Central Bank is also given a limited power to fine undertakings for non-compliance. For as long as the U.K. chooses not to move to the third stage, this Article will not apply to it (para. 5 of the U.K. opt-out Protocol).

The first paragraph indicates the scope of the European Central Bank's powers. It may only adopt legislative provisions in order to carry out the tasks entrusted to the European System of

Central Banks and subject to the conditions laid down in the Statute. This must be read in the light of the amended Art. 173 E.C. which permits the E.C.J. to review the legality of acts of the European Central Bank. The European Central Bank legislation is subject to the usual procedures for judicial review.

The European Central Bank is permitted to pass regulations in four areas of European System of Central Banks statutory competence, and in any other areas to be selected by the Council acting under Art. 106(6). The topics in the original category include: the definition and implementation of the monetary policy of the Community (Art. 3.1); the calculation and determination of the required minimum reserves to be held on account with the European Central Bank and national central banks by credit institutions established in the Member States (Art. 19.1); clearing and payment systems (Art. 22); and specific tasks concerning policies relating to the prudential supervision of credit institutions and other financial institutions in accordance with the powers conferred by the Council under Art. 105(6) (Art. 25.2). The Articles referred to in brackets are those of the Statute of the European System of Central Banks and of the European Central Bank contained in the third Protocol annexed to the E.C. Treaty at Maastricht (see below for the text). The definition of regulations laid down in para. 2 is analogous to that contained in Art. 189 E.C., which indicates that they will be binding in their entirety and directly applicable in all Member States. One of the most novel aspects of this process is that the European Central Bank can pass such measures without the necessity of a proposal or recommendation from the Commission. The principle underlying the Commission's monopoly of legislative initiative, that it will act in the interests of the Community and not specific Member States, is obviously taken as read as regards the European Central Bank.

The European Central Bank is also empowered to take decisions necessary for the carrying out of the tasks entrusted to the European System of Central Banks, and to make recommendations and deliver opinions. The major difference from Art. 189 E.C., which governs other Community institutions, is that the European Central Bank is not empowered to pass directives.

The reference to Arts. 190 to 192 E.C. signals the requirement that the European Central Bank must state the reasons upon which the regulations and decisions it promulgates are based (Art. 190 E.C.), as well as clarifying the publication requirements of regulations in the Official Journal. Regulations passed by the European Central Bank will be published in the Official Journal and come into force on the twentieth day following publication (unless specified otherwise in the regulation). Decisions of the European Central Bank must be notified to those addressed and take effect upon such notification.

Paragraph 3 is an example of a Community institution being in a position to apply sanctions for non-compliance with Community obligations (see also the E.C.J. under Art. 171 E.C. and the Commission under Reg. 17/62/E.E.C.). The independent European Central Bank is empowered to impose fines or periodic penalty payments on undertakings. This power will be exercised in accordance with the detailed rules to be decided by the Council under Art. 106(6). Given that the European Central Bank will be acting entirely on its own discretion in the application of these sanctions, it is likely that the Member States, in setting the ground rules, will ensure that the procedure will be rigorous and the sanctions not easily enforced. Once the rules are up and running, the Member States will have no say whatsoever in their application. The Council may adopt a regulation giving the E.C.J. unlimited jurisdiction under Art. 172 E.C. to review any penalties imposed by the European Central Bank.

Article 109

1. By way of derogation from Article 228, the Council may, acting unanimously on a recommendation from the ECB or from the Commission, and after consulting the ECB in an endeavour to reach a consensus consistent with the objective of price stability, after consulting the European Parliament, in accordance with the procedure in paragraph 3 for determining the arrangements, conclude formal agreements on an exchange rate system for the ECU in relation to non-Community currencies.

The Council may, acting by a qualified majority on a recommendation from the ECB or from the Commission, and after consulting the ECB in an endeavour to reach a consensus consistent with the objective of price stability, adopt, adjust or abandon the central rates of the ECU within the exchange rate system.

The President of the Council shall inform the European Parliament of the adoption, adjustment or abandonment of the ECU central rates.

2. In the absence of an exchange rate system in relation to one or more non-Community currencies as referred to in paragraph 1, the Council, acting

by a qualified majority either on a recommendation from the Commission and after consulting the ECB, or on a recommendation from the ECB, may formulate general orientations for exchange rate policy in relation to these currencies.

These general orientations shall be without prejudice to the primary objective of the ESCB to maintain price stability.

3. By way of derogation from Article 228, where agreements concerning monetary or foreign exchange regime matters need to be negotiated by the Community with one or more States or international organisations, the Council, acting by a qualified majority on a recommendation from the Commission and after consulting the ECB, shall decide the arrangements for the negotiation and for the conclusion of such agreements.

These arrangements shall ensure that the Community expresses a single position. The Commission shall be fully associated with the negotiations.

Agreements concluded in accordance with this paragraph shall be binding on the institutions of the Community, on the ECB and on Member States.

4. Subject to paragraph 1, the Council shall, on a proposal from the Commission and after consulting the ECB, acting by a qualified majority decide on the position of the Community at international level as regards issues of particular relevance to economic and monetary union and, acting unanimously, decide its representation in compliance with the allocation of powers laid down in Articles 103 and 105.

5. Without prejudice to Community competence and Community agreements as regards economic and monetary union, Member States may negotiate in international bodies and conclude international agreements.

GENERAL NOTE

This Article, applicable from the start of the third stage, lays down the procedure for the adoption and amendment of an exchange rate system for the ECU as against non-Community currencies. As noted under Art. 105 E.C., the Council has the responsibility for the adoption of such measures, acting in consultation with, or on a recommendation from, the European Central Bank in an "endeavour to reach a consensus consistent with the objective of price stability".

The creation of such an exchange rate system will necessitate the conclusion of international agreements. The first sentence of this Article recognises that the normal process for the conclusion of such agreements is that they are negotiated by the Commission (Art. 228 E.C.). In contrast, under this Article, it will be the Council which will decide how any exchange rate agreement is negotiated and the Commission need only be "fully associated" with the negotiations. Article 228 will be effectively displaced in monetary matters. The conclusion of formal arrangements is to be carried out by a unanimous vote in Council, of Member States without a derogation (Art. 109k(4)), and may be based on either a recommendation from the European Central Bank or the Commission, after consulting the European Parliament. If the recommendation comes from the Commission, then the Council must consult the European Central Bank to try to reach an agreement consistent with the objective of price stability. The procedure envisaged for the adoption, adjustment or abandonment of the central rates of the ECU within the exchange rate system is identical, except for the voting conditions in the Council. In this area a qualified majority vote will suffice. The actual definition of qualified majority will depend on the existence of "Member States with a derogation". The votes of such Member States will be suspended and the requisite majority will be two-thirds of the votes cast, weighted in accordance with Art. 148(2) (see Art. 109k(3) and (5)). The wording of Art. 109(1) is such that the Council can override the European Central Bank and adopt or change an exchange rate agreement with third countries even though the Bank thinks that the measure will endanger price stability in the Member States that have adopted the single currency.

The President of the Council shall inform the European Parliament of any adoption, adjustment or abandonment of the ECU central rates and, although it is not expressly provided for, probably will inform the Parliament of the conclusion of formal arrangements on an exchange rate system, given the scale of importance of such a decision.

A special procedure is envisaged as regards non-Community currencies with which no exchange rate system (as under para. 1 above) is in operation (para. 2). In such a situation the Council may, by a qualified majority vote, formulate general orientations for exchange rate policy in relation to these currencies. No pre-conditions are set as to the content of these orientations. Once again, the Commission and the European Central Bank are to be involved in the process. The general orientations on exchange rate policy cannot weaken the independence of the Bank in deciding on interest rates and money supply, because the Bank's primary objective remains the maintenance of price stability.

Paragraph 3 lays down the procedure for determining the arrangements for the negotiation and conclusion of agreements on foreign exchange or monetary matters. While the detailed arrangements are to be laid down by the Council, acting by a qualified majority, this paragraph lays down the pre-condition that the Commission will "be fully associated with the negotiations".

In the first three paragraphs the Commission does not make a proposal for the Council to adopt but rather a recommendation. This frees the Council from the requirement in Art. 189a(1) that it can only amend a Commission "proposal" by unanimity. It also means that the Commission is not free to alter the recommendations at any time up to the adoption of the act by the Council (*cf.* Art. 189a(2) E.C.). Clearly the idea of "recommendation" is used here, and elsewhere in the provisions on economic and monetary union, to shift the balance of power further in favour of the Council in its relationship with the Commission.

Paragraph 4 empowers the Council to decide, on a qualified majority vote of Member States without a derogation, the position which the Community should take at the international level as regards issues of particular relevance to economic and monetary union. The significance of this provision will rest on subsequent political developments. The potential afforded to open up Community decision-making in the many international fora in which the Member States are currently represented is manifest, but will depend entirely on the desire of the Member States to surrender the prestige and influence afforded by such national representation. This paragraph would operate to regulate any such surrender, but is worded to provide for much less significant developments and is awash with ambiguities. The phrase "position of the Community at international level" might well indicate that the Member States are to adopt these positions in the different international organisations, but could also be taken as a simple desire to express the Community position without a requirement that this position be adopted by the Member State in its actings. There is no analogous provision to that in Art. K.5 of the TEU concerning the common foreign and security policy, whereby the Member States are obliged to uphold the Community common position in international negotiations.

Representation of the Community at the international level must be decided upon by unanimous vote in Council, of Member States without a derogation, and in accordance with the allocation of powers laid down in Arts. 103 and 105. The reference to Arts. 103 and 105 will mean that the rôles attributed to the Community bodies will depend on the specific international body. If the body is dealing with monetary matters it would be expected, according to the tasks of the European System of Central Banks laid down in Art. 105, that the European Central Bank would be the natural Community representative. In the fora where the national central banks and national governments are currently represented, such as the Bank for International Settlements, the meetings of the Group of Seven, IMF meetings and the World Bank, the European Central Bank would seem to be the natural representative of a third stage Community. Nevertheless, this will again depend on the desire of the Member States to cede responsibility in this field. The key words in para. 5 are "without prejudice". The paragraph preserves the power of Member States to negotiate in international bodies and conclude international agreements in the economic and monetary sphere, provided that they do not contradict Community competence and Community agreements as regards monetary union. The E.C.J. may become involved in resolving the respective competences of the Community and the Member States in that area of international relations.

Chapter 3 (Institutional Provisions)

GENERAL NOTE

This chapter, read alongside the relevant Protocols to the Treaty, lays down the institutional backdrop to the second and third stages. It does not however deal with all the specific institutions envisaged during the process to economic and monetary union. In this respect, the heading "institutional provisions" is not so much misleading as incomplete. Those provisions governing the European Monetary Institute, which will prepare the ground for the third stage, are laid down under the chapter on "Transitional Provisions" (Chap. 4) but the other new institution designed for the second stage, the Monetary Committee, is dealt with under the present chapter (Art. 109c(1)).

Article 109a

1. The Governing Council of the ECB shall comprise the members of the Executive Board of the ECB and the Governors of the national central banks.

2. (a) The Executive Board shall comprise the President, the Vice-President and four other members.

(b) The President, the Vice-President and the other members of the Executive Board shall be appointed from among persons of recognised standing and professional experience in monetary or banking matters by common accord of the Governments of the Member States at the level of Heads of State or of Government, on a recommendation from the Council, after it has consulted the European Parliament and the Governing Council of the ECB.

Their term of office shall be eight years and shall not be renewable. Only nationals of Member States may be members of the Executive Board.

GENERAL NOTE

This Article lays down the composition of the European Central Bank's governing and executive council. Given that the bank is to have legal personality (Art. 106(2)) and be independent of Community and Member State influence (Art. 107), the personnel of these bodies have a hugely important position.

The Executive Board members, including the President and Vice-President, shall be appointed by common accord of the governments of the Member States at the level of heads of state or government. These persons are to be independent in the pursuit of their duties and thus they are to be appointed for a non-renewable eight-year period. The eight year time-scale, uncommon in most institutions, is intended to remove the appointees from the influence of generally shorter term governmental majorities. The non-renewable term of office is designed to obviate any advantage of appeasing a governmental authority with the aim of securing another term. The Executive Board members have eight years to exercise their independent powers, free from any influence by Member State governments or any desire to be reappointed. Given that the Executive Board has a maximum of six members, the governments cannot each have their own appointee. The decision-making process will have the collective quality of the appointment of the President of the Commission, rather than the simple rubber stamping of each country's nominee(s) that happens when appointing the rest of the Commission. The Governing Council of the European Central Bank, and the European Parliament, are merely consulted on the choice made by the Member States, and the Commission is given no formal rôle in the process. Rule 29D of the European Parliament's Rules of Procedure (amended subsequent to the TEU, see [1993] O.J. C268/51) provides that the candidates for President, Vice President and Executive Board members of the European Central Bank will be invited to appear before the parliamentary committee responsible. The committee will recommend to the Parliament acceptance or rejection of the candidate. If the vote is against a candidate the President of the Parliament will ask the council to withdraw the candidate. The Council can ignore this request, but it would put any candidate in a very weak position to be appointed after being rejected by the European Parliament.

The Executive Board of the Bank will have day to day responsibility for the single currency and, unless otherwise provided, will take decisions by a simple majority, with the President having a casting vote in the event of a tie (Art. 11 of the Protocol on the Statute of the European System of Central Banks, referred to in Art. 106). The members of the Executive Board are joined by the governors of the national central banks of Member States without a derogation, to form the Governing Council of the European Central Bank, which will formulate the monetary policy of the States party to the single currency, including intermediate monetary objectives, key interest rates and the supply of reserves (Arts. 10 and 12 of the Protocol on the Statute of the European System of Central Banks). The Governing Council meets at least 10 times a year and, unless otherwise provided, takes decisions by a simple majority with the President having a casting vote.

Article 109b

1. The President of the Council and a member of the Commission may participate, without having the right to vote, in meetings of the Governing Council of the ECB.

The President of the Council may submit a motion for deliberation to the Governing Council of the ECB.

2. The President of the ECB shall be invited to participate in Council meetings when the Council is discussing matters relating to the objectives and tasks of the ESCB.

3. The ECB shall address an annual report on the activities of the ESCB and on the monetary policy of both the previous and current year to the European Parliament, the Council and the Commission, and also to the European Council.

The President of the ECB shall present this report to the Council and to the European Parliament, which may hold a general debate on that basis.

The President of the ECB and the other members of the Executive Board may, at the request of the European Parliament or on their own initiative, be heard by the competent Committees of the European Parliament.

GENERAL NOTE

This Article lays down the limited interaction between the European Central Bank and the other Community institutions. It reflects the necessity of some co-ordination between the bodies while maintaining respect for the independence of the monetary authority.

Therefore, the President of the Council and a member of the Commission may participate in the meetings of the Governing Council of the European Central Bank, but have no voting rights. Their influence will no doubt depend on the particular matter under discussion and upon a variety of other variables not susceptible to legal analysis. The President of the Council may submit a motion for deliberation to the Governing Council; the emphasis that the Governing Council gives it is entirely at their own discretion.

The President of the European Central Bank shall be invited to participate in Council meetings where matters within the discretion of the European Central Bank are being discussed. Again his or her influence will depend on many diverse political factors.

Further means of ensuring the accountability of the bank are laid down in para. (3). The European Central Bank is to address an annual report on the activities of the European System of Central Banks, and on the monetary policy of both the previous and current year, to the European Parliament, the Council, the Commission and also to the European Council. It is open to the European Parliament to hold a debate on the report. Although the President of the European Central Bank will present an annual report to Parliament and the President and the other Executive Board members may be heard by the competent committees of Parliament, it is not clear how forthcoming they will be in answering any questions put to them. If the European Central Bank's accountability to the political institutions were increased it might lose its independence and therefore risk losing the benefits of sustained low inflation.

Article 109c

1. In order to promote co-ordination of the policies of Member States to the full extent needed for the functioning of the internal market, a Monetary Committee with advisory status is hereby set up.

It shall have the following tasks:

— to keep under review the monetary and financial situation of the Member States and of the Community and the general payments system of the Member States and to report regularly thereon to the Council and to the Commission;

— to deliver opinions at the request of the Council or of the Commission, or on its own initiative for submission to those institutions;

— without prejudice to Article 151, to contribute to the preparation of the work of the Council referred to in Articles 73f, 73g, 103(2), (3), (4) and (5), 103a, 104a, 104b, 104c, 109e(2), 109f(6), 109h, 109i, 109j(2) and 109k(1);

— to examine, at least once a year, the situation regarding the movement of capital and the freedom of payments, as they result from the application of this Treaty and of measures adopted by the Council; the examination shall cover all measures relating to capital movements and payments; the Committee shall report to the Commission and to the Council on the outcome of this examination.

The Member States and the Commission shall each appoint two members of the Monetary Committee.

2. At the start of the third stage, an Economic and Financial Committee shall be set up. The Monetary Committee provided for in paragraph 1 shall be dissolved.

The Economic and Financial Committee shall have the following tasks:
— to deliver opinions at the request of the Council or of the Commission, or on its own initiative for submission to those institutions;
— to keep under review the economic and financial situation of the Member States and of the Community and to report regularly thereon to the Council and to the Commission, in particular on financial relations with third countries and international institutions;
— without prejudice to Article 151, to contribute to the preparation of the work of the Council referred to in Articles 73f, 73g, 103(2), (3), (4) and (5), 103a, 104a, 104b, 104c, 105(6), 105a(2), 106(5) and (6), 109, 109h, 109i(2) and (3), 109k(2), 109l(4) and (5), and to carry out other advisory and preparatory tasks assigned to it by the Council;
— to examine, at least once a year, the situation regarding the movement of capital and the freedom of payments, as they result from the application of this Treaty and of measures adopted by the Council; the examination shall cover all measures relating to capital movements and payments; the Committee shall report to the Commission and to the Council on the outcome of this examination.

The Member States, the Commission and the ECB shall each appoint no more than two members of the Committee.

3. The Council shall, acting by a qualified majority on a proposal from the Commission and after consulting the ECB and the Committee referred to in this Article, lay down detailed provisions concerning the composition of the Economic and Financial Committee. The President of the Council shall inform the European Parliament of such a decision.

4. In addition to the tasks set out in paragraph 2, if and as long as there are Member States with a derogation as referred to in Articles 109k and 109l, the Committee shall keep under review the monetary and financial situation and the general payments system of those Member States and report regularly thereon to the Council and to the Commission.

GENERAL NOTE

This Article makes provision for the creation of the Monetary Committee and its successor, the Economic and Financial Committee. The Monetary Committee (para. 1) is an advisory body with the main task of monitoring the Member States' budgetary performance and monetary situation (first indent). In addition, it can deliver opinions to the Council or the Commission on its own initiative or at their request and, at least once a year, it will look at the position regarding the freedom of movement of capital between the Member States (second and fourth indents). It will also take on a rôle alongside COREPER in the preparation of material for the Council in certain specified areas (third indent).

On the coming into force of the third stage, the Monetary Committee will be dissolved and replaced by the Economic and Financial Committee, provided for in para. 2. This body will take an essentially similar rôle to the Monetary Committee, with marginal differences regarding its make-up and its tasks. Detailed provisions are to be drawn up by the Council, acting by a qualified majority, on the composition of the Committee. All that exists at present is the assertion that the Member States, the Commission and the European Central Bank shall each appoint no more than two members of the Committee. Rules governing eligibility, periods of office and removal will be necessary. In the realm of the Monetary Committee, no provision was made for the adoption of such rules. The preconception was that the members would serve until the dissolution of the Committee. The lack of attention to detail as regards the second stage may come to be regretted, given the possibility of its prolongation.

Article 109d

For matters within the scope of Articles 103(4), 104c with the exception of paragraph 14, 109, 109j, 109k and 109l(4) and (5), the Council or a Member State may request the Commission to make a recommendation or a proposal, as appropriate. The Commission shall examine this request and submit its conclusions to the Council without delay.

GENERAL NOTE
This Article permits the Member States or the Council to request the Commission to make a recommendation or proposal. Thus the Commission's right of initiative in the specified areas is preserved, but the aforementioned parties are permitted to exercise a degree of influence over the process. This influence is however only as powerful as the Commission chooses it to be. The Commission's sole obligation is to examine any such request and report its conclusions to the Council. The areas where this prompting of the Commission is permitted include: recommendations to a Member State that its economic policies are not consistent with the broad economic guidelines laid down by Council (Art. 103(4)); the excessive deficit procedure in Art. 104c (with the exception of para. 14 on the amendment of the Protocol on the excessive deficit procedure); all matters on the external exchange rate of the ECU (Art. 109); matters relating to the convergence criteria (Art. 109j); the time-frame for the move to the third stage and the determination of Member States with a derogation (Art. 109k); and, finally, matters relating to the adoption of the conversion rates for national currencies for the change to the ECU (Art. 109l(4) and (5)). The Council already had the power to make such requests under Art. 152 E.E.C./E.C. but Art. 109d extends the power to each Member State in the specific cases listed.

Chapter 4 (Transitional Provisions)

GENERAL NOTE
These Articles, as the name would suggest, deal with the second stage of economic and monetary union, known as the transitional stage given its intended short life. During this second stage of economic and monetary union, the necessary steps are to be taken to permit the adoption of a single currency and an independent monetary authority overseeing the whole process.

Article 109e

1. The second stage for achieving economic and monetary union shall begin on 1 January 1994.
2. Before that date
   (a) each Member State shall:
      — adopt, where necessary, appropriate measures to comply with the prohibitions laid down in Article 73b, without prejudice to Article 73e, and in Articles 104 and 104a(1);
      — adopt, if necessary, with a view to permitting the assessment provided for in subparagraph (b), multiannual programmes intended to ensure the lasting convergence necessary for the achievement of economic and monetary union, in particular with regard to price stability and sound public finances;
   (b) the Council shall, on the basis of a report from the Commission, assess the progress made with regard to economic and monetary convergence, in particular with regard to price stability and sound public finances, and the progress made with the implementation of Community law concerning the internal market.
3. The provisions of Articles 104, 104a(1), 104b(1) and 104c with the exception of paragraphs 1, 9, 11 and 14 shall apply from the beginning of the second stage.
   The provisions of Articles 103a(2), 104c(1), (9) and (11), 105, 105a, 107, 109, 109a, 109b and 109c(2) and (4) shall apply from the beginning of the third stage.
4. In the second stage, Member States shall endeavour to avoid excessive government deficits.
5. During the second stage, each Member State shall, as appropriate, start the process leading to the independence of its central bank, in accordance with Article 108.

GENERAL NOTE

Para. (1)
This clearly sets the date for the coming into force of the second stage. All Member States will move to this level irrespective of their economic position, degree of convergence, or economic policies.

Para. (2)

This paragraph is the only indication in the Treaty of the tasks envisaged during the first stage but it operated only from November 1, 1993 to December 31, 1993.

The duties incumbent on the Member States include: the adoption of appropriate measures to ensure the removal of all restrictions on the free movement of capital between the Member States and third countries (Art. 73b and see note on that Article); compliance with Arts. 104 and 104a on the prohibition of certain aspects of public sector finance and the adoption of multi-annual programmes, intended to ensure the lasting convergence necessary for the achievement of economic and monetary union. Paragraph 2 also makes it clear that the progress towards the single market, and in particular the implementation of the necessary Community law, is another key feature of the first stage.

Para. (3)

This delimits those provisions of the Treaty which will take effect from the start of the second stage and those which shall take effect from the commencement of the third stage.

Para. (4)

This is the key aspect of the second stage. The Member States are to endeavour to avoid excessive government deficits. This is in contrast to the third stage imperative that the Member States shall avoid such deficits (see note on Art. 104c).

Para. (5)

During the second stage, the Member States are to start the process leading to the independence of their central banks. The words "as appropriate" would seem to have been inserted at the bequest of the U.K. as they mean that Member States with an express derogation from the third stage do not have to comply. The U.K. is under no obligation to pursue an independent national central bank, provided that it complies with all the other provisions dealing with the progress towards the third stage. The specific details governing the U.K.'s position in relation to the relevant Treaty Articles is laid out in the Protocol on certain provisions relating to the U.K., paras. 3–10.

Article 109f

1. At the start of the second stage, a European Monetary Institute (hereinafter referred to as 'EMI') shall be established and take up its duties; it shall have legal personality and be directed and managed by a Council, consisting of a President and the Governors of the national central banks, one of whom shall be Vice-President.

The President shall be appointed by common accord of the Governments of the Member States at the level of Heads of State or of Government, on a recommendation from, as the case may be, the Committee of Governors of the central banks of the Member States (hereinafter referred to as 'Committee of Governors') or the Council of the EMI, and after consulting the European Parliament and the Council. The President shall be selected from among persons of recognised standing and professional experience in monetary or banking matters. Only nationals of Member States may be President of the EMI. The Council of the EMI shall appoint the Vice-President.

The Statute of the EMI is laid down in a Protocol annexed to this Treaty.

The Committee of Governors shall be dissolved at the start of the second stage.

2. The EMI shall:
— strengthen co-operation between the national central banks;
— strengthen the co-ordination of the monetary policies of the Member States, with the aim of ensuring price stability;
— monitor the functioning of the European Monetary System;
— hold consultations concerning issues falling within the competence of the national central banks and affecting the stability of financial institutions and markets;

— take over the tasks of the European Monetary Co-operation Fund, which shall be dissolved; the modalities of dissolution are laid down in the Statute of the EMI;

— facilitate the use of the ECU and oversee its development, including the smooth functioning of the ECU clearing system.

3. For the preparation of the third stage, the EMI shall:

— prepare the instruments and the procedures necessary for carrying out a single monetary policy in the third stage;

— promote the harmonisation, where necessary, of the rules and practices governing the collection, compilation and distribution of statistics in the areas within its field of competence;

— prepare the rules for operations to be undertaken by the national central banks in the framework of the ESCB;

— promote the efficiency of cross-border payments;

— supervise the technical preparation of ECU bank notes.

At the latest by 31 December 1996, the EMI shall specify the regulatory, organisational and logistical framework necessary for the ESCB to perform its tasks in the third stage. This framework shall be submitted for decision to the ECB at the date of its establishment.

4. The EMI, acting by a majority of two thirds of the members of its Council may:

— formulate opinions or recommendations on the overall orientation of monetary policy and exchange rate policy as well as on related measures introduced in each Member State;

— submit opinions or recommendations to Governments and to the Council on policies which might affect the internal or external monetary situation in the Community and, in particular, the functioning of the European Monetary System;

— make recommendations to the monetary authorities of the Member States concerning the conduct of their monetary policy.

5. The EMI, acting unanimously, may decide to publish its opinions and its recommendations.

6. The EMI shall be consulted by the Council regarding any proposed Community act within its field of competence.

Within the limits and under the conditions set out by the Council, acting by a qualified majority on a proposal from the Commission and after consulting the European Parliament and the EMI, the EMI shall be consulted by the authorities of the Member States on any draft legislative provision within its field of competence.

7. The Council may, acting unanimously on a proposal from the Commission and after consulting the European Parliament and the EMI, confer upon the EMI other tasks for the preparation of the third stage.

8. Where this Treaty provides for a consultative rôle for the ECB, references to the ECB shall be read as referring to the EMI before the establishment of the ECB.

Where this Treaty provides for a consultative rôle for the EMI, references to the EMI shall be read, before 1 January 1994, as referring to the Committee of Governors.

9. During the second stage, the term 'ECB' used in Articles 173, 175, 176, 177, 180 and 215 shall be read as referring to the EMI.

GENERAL NOTE

This is a comprehensive provision laying down the structure and tasks of the primary second stage body, the European Monetary Institute. At the special European Council in Brussels in November 1993, held to mark the coming into force of the TEU, it was agreed that the European Monetary Institute will have its seat in Frankfurt (see [1993] O.J. C323/1).

Paragraph 1 lays down the organisational structure of the European Monetary Institute and designates it as having legal personality. The European Monetary Institute's rôle is mainly advisory: exhorting the Member States and the national central banks to strengthen their co-operation and their co-ordination of monetary policy. It can, however, take legally binding decisions under Arts. 15.1 and 15.4 of the Statute of the European Monetary Institute. Its organisation is very similar to that envisaged for the European Central Bank; its direction and management will be determined by a Council, consisting of all the Governors of the national central banks and a President selected from among persons of recognised standing and appointed by common accord of the governments of the Member States. As with the members of the Executive Council of the European Central Bank, the President of the European Monetary Institute must be a national of one of the Member States. He or she is appointed on a full time basis for three years. The appointment can be renewed. The President proposes and chairs meetings of the Council of the European Monetary Institute, presents the views of the European Monetary Institute externally and is responsible for its day to day management (Art. 9 of the Statute of the European Monetary Institute). No explicit provision is made for the other members of either the European Central Bank or the European Monetary Institute governing bodies; such matters are presumably the domain of the Member State when it appoints its national governors. The detailed provisions governing the European Monetary Institute are laid down in the Protocol on the Statute of the European Monetary Institute annexed to the Treaty.

Upon the coming into force of the second stage, the Committee of Governors is to be dissolved. This body, established in 1964, has been the main forum for co-operation of the central banks of the Community and has seen an exponential rise in its workload since the movement towards full economic and monetary union started. Its tasks will be taken over, in the first instance, by the Monetary Committee and the European Monetary Institute.

Paragraph 2 lays down the tasks of the European Monetary Institute. The emphasis is on strengthening co-operation, and monitoring and overseeing the different aspects of the second stage. It will, nevertheless, be responsible for the running of the European Monetary Co-operation Fund until its dissolution.

Paragraph 3 asserts the preparatory tasks of the European Monetary Institute in laying the groundwork for the third stage. One of the most significant tasks is to be found in the last indent of this paragraph. At the latest by December 31, 1996, the European Monetary Institute is to specify the regulatory, organisational, and logistical framework necessary for the European Central Bank to perform its tasks. In effect, the European Monetary Institute will act as a midwife for the birth of the European Central Bank.

Paragraph 4 provides for the adoption of non-binding measures by the European Monetary Institute, aimed again at the smoothing of progress towards the third stage. These measures, to be adopted by the Council of the European Monetary Institute by a two-thirds majority, are laid down in the three indents to this paragraph. They cover a broad sphere of activities and permit the addressing of opinions and recommendations to the Member States, the Council and the monetary authorities of the Member States. The Council of the European Monetary Institute may decide to publish its recommendations and opinions and thus ensure some form of adverse publicity, if it so wishes, for bodies it considers unco-operative. Whatever the motives of the European Monetary Institute, it must act by unanimity if it wishes to take this step (para. 5). In a provision mirroring the analogous European Central Bank Article, para. 6 requires that the European Monetary Institute is to be consulted by the Council regarding any proposed Community act within its fields of competence. Paragraph 6 also provides that the European Monetary Institute is to be consulted by the Member States on any draft national legislation in its field of competence, but this is to be subject to any limitations and conditions set by the Council, acting by a qualified majority on a proposal from the Commission. The tasks of the European Monetary Institute in the preparation for the third stage are not exhaustively listed; it is possible for the Council to add any further tasks it considers necessary, but any such addition must be decided upon by unanimity (para. 7). Although the national central banks may not be independent of their national governments during stage two, when the governors of the central banks meet in the Council of the European Monetary Institute they must act independently of their governments (see Art. 8 of the Statute of the European Monetary Institute).

Paragraph 8 highlights the close relationship between the European Central Bank and the European Monetary Institute, in that it states that references to a consultative rôle for the European Central Bank in the Treaty must be read as referring to the European Monetary Institute prior to the establishment of the European Central Bank. Similar provision is made for references to the European Monetary Institute in the period up to January 1, 1994 to be taken as applying to the Committee of Governors. Paragraph 9 lays out specific instances where the European Central Bank reference is to be replaced by a reference to the European Monetary Institute. This seemingly innocuous provision gives wide "hidden" powers to the European Monetary Institute in the period up till the establishment of the European Central Bank. The substitution of the reference to the European Central Bank by a reference to the European Monetary Institute in the Articles specified means that: the European Monetary Institute will be able to take Art. 173 action for the purpose of protecting its prerogatives (but most measures adopted by the European Monetary Institute will not be subject to Art. 173 review because they do not produce legal effects vis-à-vis third parties—see Art. 173); the European Monetary Institute may take actions against the other institutions for failure to act and is subject to the same sanction itself (Art. 175); the European Monetary Institute must take steps to comply with any decision of the E.C.J. rendering one of its acts void or after a ruling that it has failed to act (Art. 176); and the validity and interpretation of acts of the European Monetary Institute will be open to preliminary rulings under the Art. 177 procedure. Damage caused by the European Monetary Institute or its servants in the performance of their duties will require to be made good (Art. 215) and the E.C.J. will have jurisdiction to determine the liability of the European Monetary Institute (Art. 178). Finally, this paragraph alludes to Art. 180 E.C., whereby the E.C.J. will have jurisdiction in disputes concerning the fulfilment by national central banks of obligations under the Statute of the European Monetary Institute. In this connection, the powers of the Council of the European Monetary Institute in respect of national central banks shall be the same as those conferred upon the Commission in respect of Member States by Art. 169. In other words, where the Governing Council of the European Monetary Institute considers that a national central bank has failed to fulfil an obligation under the statute of the European Monetary Institute, it shall deliver a reasoned opinion on the matter, after giving the bank a chance to submit its observations. Should the bank concerned not comply with this opinion within the period laid down by the European Monetary Institute, then the latter may bring the matter before the E.C.J.

All the above provisions shall apply to the European Central Bank from the start of the third stage.

Article 109g

The currency composition of the ECU basket shall not be changed.

From the start of the third stage, the value of the ECU shall be irrevocably fixed in accordance with Article 109l(4).

GENERAL NOTE

This Article makes reference to the ECU in terms of the transitional phases. The first paragraph ensures that the currency composition of the ECU basket shall not be changed at any stage in the run-up to the adoption of the ECU as the single currency of the E.C. This measure is likely to be of limited significance; its greatest impact will be on ECU denominated deposits, loans and marketable securities. The second paragraph makes reference to the irrevocable fixing of currency values, when the single currency is adopted, under Art. 109l(4).

Article 109h

1. Where a Member State is in difficulties or is seriously threatened with difficulties as regards its balance of payments either as a result of an overall disequilibrium in its balance of payments, or as a result of the type of currency at its disposal, and where such difficulties are liable in particular to jeopardise the functioning of the Common Market or the progressive implementation of the common commercial policy, the Commission shall immediately investigate the position of the State in question and the action which, making use of all the means at its disposal, that State has taken or may take in accordance with the provisions of this Treaty.

The Commission shall state what measures it recommends the State concerned to take.

If the action taken by a Member State and the measures suggested by the Commission do not prove sufficient to overcome the difficulties which have arisen or which threaten, the Commission shall, after consulting the Committee referred to in Article 109c, recommend to the Council the granting of mutual assistance and appropriate methods therefor.

The Commission shall keep the Council regularly informed of the situation and of how it is developing.

2. The Council, acting by a qualified majority, shall grant such mutual assistance; it shall adopt directives or decisions laying down the conditions and details of such assistance, which may take such forms as:

    (a) a concerted approach to or within any other international organisations to which Member States may have recourse;

(b) measures needed to avoid deflection of trade where the State which is in difficulties maintains or reintroduces quantitative restrictions against third countries;

(c) the granting of limited credits by other Member States, subject to their agreement.

3. If the mutual assistance recommended by the Commission is not granted by the Council or if the mutual assistance granted and the measures taken are insufficient, the Commission shall authorise the State which is in difficulties to take protective measures, the conditions and details of which the Commission shall determine.

Such authorisation may be revoked and such conditions and details may be changed by the Council acting by a qualified majority.

4. Subject to Article 109k(6), this Article shall cease to apply from the beginning of the third stage.

GENERAL NOTE

Article 109h makes provision, effective during the second stage only, for the benefit of a Member State whose balance of payments difficulties risk jeopardising the functioning of the common market or the progressive implementation of the common commercial policy. The Commission can investigate and recommend measures to the Member State. If these are insufficient, the Commission can recommend to the Council that it should grant mutual assistance to the Member State concerned. The Council can act by qualified majority vote. This may take one of the specified forms laid down in the Article but this would not appear to be an exhaustive list. The Commission can, as a last resort, authorise the Member State to take protective measures, the conditions and details of which the Commission shall predetermine. This is one of the Commission's more significant powers, which can be amended or overridden by the Council only if it can do so by a qualified majority.

This Article must be read in the light of the existing power under Council regulation 1969/88 of June 24, 1988, which established a single facility providing medium-term financial assistance for Member States' balance of payments. The European Monetary Institute has a function under Art. 11 of that regulation (see Art. 6.1 of the European Monetary Institute Statute).

This Article will continue to apply to Member States with a derogation after the coming into force of the third stage (Art. 109k(6)).

Article 109i

1. Where a sudden crisis in the balance of payments occurs and a decision within the meaning of Article 109h(2) is not immediately taken, the Member State concerned may, as a precaution, take the necessary protective measures. Such measures must cause the least possible disturbance in the functioning of the Common Market and must not be wider in scope than is strictly necessary to remedy the sudden difficulties which have arisen.

2. The Commission and the other Member States shall be informed of such protective measures not later than when they enter into force. The Commission may recommend to the Council the granting of mutual assistance under Article 109h.

3. After the Commission has delivered an opinion and the Committee referred to in Article 109c has been consulted, the Council may, acting by a qualified majority, decide that the State concerned shall amend, suspend or abolish the protective measures referred to above.

4. Subject to Article 109k(6), this Article shall cease to apply from the beginning of the third stage.

GENERAL NOTE

This Article is complementary to the preceding Art. 109h and gives the Member States a strictly guarded right to take autonomous measures to meet sudden crises in their balance of payments. The Council can amend or override the unilateral action of the Member State by qualified majority vote. Once again, this provision will continue to apply in the third stage only as regards Member States with a derogation.

Articles 109h and 109i are very similar to their predecessors, Arts. 108 and 109 E.E.C. Given the removal of any limitations on the free movement of capital during the second stage of economic and monetary union, it may well be that Arts. 109h and 109i will be resorted to by the Member States.

Article 109j

1. The Commission and the EMI shall report to the Council on the progress made in the fulfilment by the Member States of their obligations regarding the achievement of economic and monetary union.

These reports shall include an examination of the compatibility between each Member State's national legislation, including the statutes of its national central bank, and Articles 107 and 108 of this Treaty and the Statute of the ESCB. The reports shall also examine the achievement of a high degree of sustainable convergence by reference to the fulfilment by each Member State of the following criteria:
   — the achievement of a high degree of price stability; this will be apparent from a rate of inflation which is close to that of, at most, the three best performing Member States in terms of price stability;
   — the sustainability of the government financial position; this will be apparent from having achieved a government budgetary position without a deficit that is excessive as determined in accordance with Article 104c(6);
   — the observance of the normal fluctuation margins provided for by the Exchange Rate Mechanism of the European Monetary System, for at least two years, without devaluing against the currency of any other Member State;
   — the durability of convergence achieved by the Member State and of its participation in the Exchange Rate Mechanism of the European Monetary System being reflected in the long-term interest rate levels.

The four criteria mentioned in this paragraph and the relevant periods over which they are to be respected are developed further in a Protocol annexed to this Treaty. The reports of the Commission and the EMI shall also take account of the development of the ECU, the results of the integration of markets, the situation and development of the balances of payments on current account and an examination of the development of unit labour costs and other price indices.

2. On the basis of these reports, the Council, acting by a qualified majority on a recommendation from the Commission, shall assess:
   — for each Member State, whether it fulfils the necessary conditions for the adoption of a single currency;
   — whether a majority of the Member States fulfil the necessary conditions for the adoption of a single currency,

and recommend its findings to the Council, meeting in the composition of the Heads of State or of Government. The European Parliament shall be consulted and forward its opinion to the Council, meeting in the composition of the Heads of State or of Government.

3. Taking due account of the reports referred to in paragraph 1 and the opinion of the European Parliament referred to in paragraph 2, the Council, meeting in the composition of Heads of State or of Government, shall, acting by a qualified majority, not later than 31 December 1996:
   — decide, on the basis of the recommendations of the Council referred to in paragraph 2, whether a majority of the Member States fulfil the necessary conditions for the adoption of a single currency;
   — decide whether it is appropriate for the Community to enter the third stage,

and if so
   — set the date for the beginning of the third stage.

4. If by the end of 1997 the date for the beginning of the third stage has not been set, the third stage shall start on 1 January 1999. Before 1 July 1998, the Council, meeting in the composition of Heads of State or of Government, after a repetition of the procedure provided for in paragraphs 1 and 2, with the exception of the second indent of paragraph 2, taking into account the reports referred to in paragraph 1 and the opinion of the European Parliament, shall, acting by a qualified majority and on the basis of the recommendations of the Council referred to in paragraph 2, confirm which Member States fulfil the necessary conditions for the adoption of a single currency.

GENERAL NOTE

The date on which the transition to stage three will take place will depend upon a number of factors, but particularly on the degree of economic convergence. Article 109j, as elaborated by the Protocol on the convergence criteria, outlines the criteria by which the Member States will be judged. The Commission and the European Monetary Institute (see Art. 7 of the European Monetary Institute Statute) will have to report to the Council on the progress made by the Member States. In addition to the statistical analysis as regards the four economic criteria on which most commentators tend to concentrate, the report shall examine the compatibility of each Member State's national legislation, including the statute of the national central bank, with Arts. 107 and 108 of the Treaty and the Statute of the European System of Central Banks. Other matters to be considered are: the development of the ECU; the results of the integration of the markets; the situation and development of the balances of payments on current account; and an examination of the development of unit labour costs and other price indices. Thus, very little economic data will be excluded from consideration. This is quite in keeping with the consequences of moving to a single currency, which will have effects in all areas of economic life. Moreover, as the unification of Germany highlighted, the costs of unifying entities with divergent economic bases, even with enormous political will behind the venture, can be huge. For this reason, the Germans were very keen to ensure strict convergence criteria to keep the pain to a minimum.

The convergence criteria themselves are laid out in the four indents in this Article and developed, as mentioned previously, in the Protocol annexed to the Treaty. These convergence criteria will not be easy to achieve. At the beginning of 1992 only France and Luxembourg had fulfilled all the criteria (in relation to excessive government deficits see note on Art. 104c(2)). By 1993 only Luxembourg had met all the arithmetical targets. The huge financial strains imposed upon the ERM in August 1993 have led to the creation of new wide 15 per cent. bands in the ERM. In strictly legal terms, the opening up of this wider band means, paradoxically, that the convergence requirement is made much easier to achieve. Article 3 of the Protocol simply requires the Member State to have observed the normal fluctuation margins provided for by the ERM for at least two years without severe tensions. With a 15 per cent. "normal" banding, the Member States ought not to have any difficulty observing this condition. Unfortunately, in this field economics hold sway over legal provisions. If the Member States were to secure economic union with their currencies at widely different levels, the costs might be enormous. A number of the Member States have therefore made explicit calls for a swift return to the narrow ERM bandings. Whether or not this will take place is a matter for political determination. The U.K. Government will not return to the ERM for the foreseeable future and is sceptical about the timetable for economic and monetary union (see John Major's article in *The Economist*, September 24, 1993).

On the basis of the reports submitted to it, the Council, acting by a qualified majority on a recommendation from the Commission, shall assess, for each Member State, whether it has fulfilled the necessary conditions for the adoption of a single currency and whether or not a majority of the Member States fulfil the requisite conditions. The Council will then recommend its findings to the Council composed of the heads of state or government. This latter body, after having obtained the opinion of the European Parliament, will then decide by qualified majority vote whether a majority of the Member States fulfil the necessary conditions for the adoption of a single currency. This decision is to be taken no later than December 31, 1996. Even if there exists a majority of the Member States having fulfilled the necessary conditions, the Council is left with the discretion to "decide whether it is appropriate for the Community to enter the third stage". It is quite possible that this will take account of the composition of the States having fulfilled the conditions. If Germany is not one of the majority States that have fulfilled the criteria then it is very difficult to envisage any move to the third stage. If the decision is taken to move to the third stage the Council will then set the date for this occurrence.

Paragraph 4 is the fall-back provision in the event of no decision having been taken on the commencement of the third stage by the end of 1997. This is then set to take place regardless on

January 1, 1999. Before July 1, 1998, the Council, acting on the basis of the reports prepared under para. 1, will determine the Member States which fulfil the necessary conditions for the adoption of the single currency. There is no minimum number of States laid down in the Treaty for commencement of the third stage but practical considerations would have to be taken into account in the event of only two or three States meeting the standards. In particular, as already suggested, it would be unlikely for any such move to the third stage to take place without the participation of Germany, no matter how many imperatives as to the irrevocable nature of the process are included in the Treaty. This commitment to a single currency on January 1, 1999 may be amended at the inter-governmental conference in 1996.

Article 109k

1. If the decision has been taken to set the date in accordance with Article 109j(3), the Council shall, on the basis of its recommendations as referred to in Article 109j(2), acting by a qualified majority on a recommendation from the Commission, decide whether any, and if so which, Member States shall have a derogation as defined in paragraph 3 of this Article. Such Member States shall in this Treaty be referred to as 'Member States with a derogation'.

If the Council has confirmed which Member States fulfil the necessary conditions for the adoption of a single currency, in accordance with Article 109j(4), those Member States which do not fulfil the conditions shall have a derogation as defined in paragraph 3 of this Article. Such Member States shall in this Treaty be referred to as 'Member States with a derogation'.

2. At least once every two years, or at the request of a Member State with a derogation, the Commission and the ECB shall report to the Council in accordance with the procedure laid down in Article 109j(1). After consulting the European Parliament and after discussion in the Council, meeting in the composition of the Heads of State or of Government, the Council shall, acting by a qualified majority on a proposal from the Commission, decide which Member States with a derogation fulfil the necessary conditions on the basis of the criteria set out in Article 109j(1), and abrogate the derogations of the Member States concerned.

3. A derogation referred to in paragraph 1 shall entail that the following Articles do not apply to the Member State concerned: Article 104c(9) and (11), 105(1), (2), (3) and (5), 105a, 108a, 109, and 109a(2)(b). The exclusion of such a Member State and its national central bank from rights and obligations within the ESCB is laid down in Chapter IX of the Statute of the ESCB.

4. In Articles 105(1), (2) and (3), 105a, 108a, 109 and 109a(2)(b), 'Member States' shall be read as 'Member States without a derogation'.

5. The voting rights of the Member States with a derogation shall be suspended for the Council decisions referred to in the Articles of this Treaty mentioned in paragraph 3. In that case, by way of derogation from Articles 148 and 189a(1), a qualified majority shall be defined as two thirds of the votes of the representatives of the Member States without a derogation weighted in accordance with Article 148(2), and unanimity of those Member States shall be required for an act requiring unanimity.

6. Articles 109h and 109i shall continue to apply to a Member State with a derogation.

GENERAL NOTE

This Article makes provision for the "Member States with a derogation". The likely scenario of a two-speed Community when the third stage comes into being will lead to a great many questions being asked of the Treaty structure and the compatibility of actions of the derogating states with those States committed to the third stage. This Article attempts to tie up as many loose ends as possible in this respect. Nevertheless, it is possible that clashes will occur. In the economic sphere, Member States outwith the central core may see a substantial number of monetary and financial decisions taken against their interests. It is one of the key features of this Article that Member States with a derogation are excluded from the decision-making bodies of the third stage.

Para. (1)

This provides that, if a date has been set for the commencement of the third stage under Art. 109j(3), then those Member States which have not fulfilled the conditions for the move to a single currency, as determined by the Council on the basis of its recommendations under Art. 109j(2), will be classed as Member States with a derogation for the purposes of the present Article.

If the Council has confirmed under Art. 109j(4) which Member States fulfil the necessary conditions then the remainder shall constitute Member States with a derogation.

Para. (2)

At least once every two years, or at the request of a Member State with a derogation, the status of Member States with a derogation shall be reviewed. This envisages an identical procedure to Art. 109j(1), under which the Council, acting in the composition of the heads of state or government, may decide, by a qualified majority vote, on the suitability of the Member State concerned for the move to a single currency. If this decision is taken then the Member State shall enter forthwith into the third stage. This procedure is not applicable to the U.K. until its Government and Parliament decide to move to the third stage and request the Council to apply the Art. 109k(2) procedure to see if the U.K. fulfils the necessary economic conditions to join the single currency (see the preamble to, and paras. 1 and 10 of, the Protocol relating to the U.K., No.11 below).

Para. (3)

This paragraph makes reference to those Articles of the Treaty which will not apply to the Member States with derogations. These include: the punitive measures envisaged for non-compliance with Council recommendations on the reduction of excessive government deficits (Art. 104c(9) and (11)); the provisions on the European System of Central Banks in the field of monetary policy (Art. 105(1), (2), (3) and (5)); the issue of banknotes and coinage (Art. 105a); the promulgation of legislative measures by the European Central Bank (Art. 108); the setting of and amendment of the ECU rate in an exchange rate system with third countries (Art. 109); and the appointment of the Executive Board of the European Central Bank (Art. 109a(2)(b)).

Para. (4)

This merely gives further weight to the above paragraph. While para. 3 removed the application of certain Articles from Member States with a derogation, so this paragraph provides for a change of wording to emphasise that these Articles apply only to Member States without a derogation.

Para. (5)

The disapplication of the Articles specified above to Member States with a derogation is to be coupled, quite naturally, with the disapplication of the voting rights of those States in these same Articles. This paragraph then goes on to specify the means of calibrating a qualified majority vote in the event of derogating States. It is to be calculated as two-thirds of the votes of the Member States without a derogation, weighted in accordance with Art. 148(2). Unanimity of these Member States will be required for an act requiring unanimity. It is likely that, as provided under Art. 148(3) E.C., abstentions by Member States without a derogation, present in person or represented at the Council, shall not prevent the adoption of acts which require unanimity.

Para. (6)

Articles 109h and 109i, relating to balance of payments difficulties, continue to apply to all Member States with a derogation. They are, of course, inapplicable to States that have achieved the single currency.

Article 109l

1. Immediately after the decision on the date for the beginning of the third stage has been taken in accordance with Article 109j(3), or, as the case may be, immediately after 1 July 1998:

— the Council shall adopt the provisions referred to in Article 106(6);
— the governments of the Member States without a derogation shall appoint, in accordance with the procedure set out in Article 50 of the Statute of the ESCB, the President, the Vice-President and the other members of the Executive Board of the ECB.

If there are Member States with a derogation, the number of members of the Executive Board may be smaller than provided for in Article 11.1 of the Statute of the ESCB, but in no circumstances shall it be less than four.

As soon as the Executive Board is appointed, the ESCB and the ECB shall be established and shall prepare for their full operation as described in this Treaty and the Statute of the ESCB. The full exercise of their powers shall start from the first day of the third stage.

2. As soon as the ECB is established, it shall if necessary, take over functions of the EMI. The EMI shall go into liquidation upon the establishment of the ECB; the modalities of liquidation are laid down in the Statute of the EMI.

3. If and as long as there are Member States with a derogation, and without prejudice to Article 106(3) of this Treaty, the General Council of the ECB referred to in Article 45 of the Statute of the ESCB shall be constituted as a third decision-making body of the ECB.

4. At the starting date of the third stage, the Council shall, acting with the unanimity of the Member States without a derogation, on a proposal from the Commission and after consulting the ECB, adopt the conversion rates at which their currencies shall be irrevocably fixed and at which irrevocably fixed rate the ECU shall be substituted for these currencies, and the ECU will become a currency in its own right. This measure shall by itself not modify the external value of the ECU. The Council shall, acting according to the same procedure, also take the other measures necessary for the rapid introduction of the ECU as the single currency of those Member States.

5. If it is decided, according to the procedure set out in Article 109k(2), to abrogate a derogation, the Council shall, acting with the unanimity of the Member States without a derogation and the Member State concerned, on a proposal from the Commission and after consulting the ECB, adopt the rate at which the ECU shall be substituted for the currency of the Member State concerned, and take the other measures necessary for the introduction of the ECU as the single currency in the Member State concerned.

GENERAL NOTE

Immediately after the decision on the date for the beginning of the third stage has been taken in accordance with Art. 109j(3), or immediately after July 1, 1998; the provisions included in this Article must be implemented. Among these requirements is appointment of the President, Vice-President and other members of the Executive Board of the European Central Bank. This is to be carried out by the governments of the Member States without a derogation, acting by common accord. The recommendation is to come from the Council and the decision can only be taken at head of government or Head of State level and after the European Parliament and the Council of the European Monetary Institute have been consulted. While the President shall be appointed for eight years, the Vice-President is to have the shorter period of office of four years and other members of the Executive Board periods of between five and eight years. No term of office is renewable (see Art. 50 of the European System of Central Banks Statute). Such divergent terms of office in the appointments phase are designed to create staggered eight-year appointments in the future and avoid the whole Executive Board changing at the same time, thus creating serious problems of discontinuity. The membership of the Executive Board is governed by Art. 11.1 of the Statute on the European Central Bank which provides for a President, Vice-President and four other members. This is not a set figure, and the present Article provides that membership of the Executive Board shall on no account be less than four, presumably implying a President, Vice-President and two other members. It may be less than six if there are a number of Member States with a derogation. This is a somewhat curious provision in that, even if only one Member State were to make the transition to the third stage, the only nationality requirement is that the Board members must be nationals of a Member State. The Member State could, in theory, appoint four of its own nationals.

The Executive Board will take all the necessary steps to prepare for the full operation of the European Central Bank and European System of Central Banks. Their full powers shall not, however, take effect until the start of the third stage. Upon the coming into force of the European Central Bank and European System of Central Banks, the European Monetary Institute is to go into liquidation.

Para. (3)

This provision provides for the operation of the General Council of the European Central Bank as laid down in Art. 45 of the Statute on the European Central Bank. This body will consist of the President and the Vice-President of the European Central Bank and the governors of the national central banks. The other members of the Executive Board may participate, without having the right to vote, in meetings of the General Council. The General Council is to be the third decision-making body of the European Central Bank and will operate so long as there exist Member States with derogations. The General Council, by way of its makeup, permits these countries to have a say on matters crucial to the operation of the Community. This is achieved through the medium of the national central bank governors. The responsibilities of the General Council are laid down in Art. 47 of the Protocol on the Statute of the European Central Bank. They are mainly consultative and advisory, but they are to deal with a number of areas on the border of the second and third stages which are complicated by the existence of Member States with a derogation. Examples include the giving of advice in the preparation of the abrogation of the derogations provided for in Art. 109k, and, probably most importantly, the General Council is to contribute to the preparations necessary for irrevocably fixing the exchange rates of the currencies of the Member States with a derogation against the single currency (Art. 109l(5) E.C. and Art. 47.3 of the Statute of the European System of Central Banks). The General Council is to adopt its own rules of procedure.

Para. (4)

This paragraph deals with one of the fundamental elements of the move to the third stage. The Council, acting with the unanimity of the Member States without a derogation, on a proposal from the Commission and after having consulted the European Central Bank, shall adopt the conversion rates at which their currencies shall be irrevocably fixed and at which rate the ECU shall be substituted. As the provision makes clear; "the ECU will become a currency in its own right". The Council is then required to take, by the same procedure, other measures necessary for the rapid introduction of the ECU as the single currency of those Member States. Paragraph 5 then deals with the application of the single currency to Member States previously with a derogation. The procedure is essentially similar to para. 4. Paragraphs 4 and 5 do not apply to the U.K. while it is exercising its right to opt-out from the single currency (para. 5 of the U.K. opt-out Protocol).

Article 109m

1. Until the beginning of the third stage, each Member State shall treat its exchange rate policy as a matter of common interest. In so doing, Member States shall take account of the experience acquired in co-operation within the framework of the European Monetary System (EMS) and in developing the ECU, and shall respect existing powers in this field.

2. From the beginning of the third stage and for as long as a Member State has a derogation, paragraph 1 shall apply by analogy to the exchange rate policy of that Member State.

GENERAL NOTE

This Article deals with the exchange rate policies of the Member States during the second stage. They are to be treated as matters of common interest, and the desire to see some degree of convergence as laid down in Art. 109j must, therefore, be one of the primary issues here. Indeed, the present Article makes explicit reference to the "experience acquired in co-operation within the framework of the EMS".

While this Article will necessarily lapse as regards States moving to the single currency upon the coming into force of the third stage, it will continue in force in relation to Member States with a derogation. While not within the single currency system, they are not to be freed from the duty to ensure that they do not adopt exchange rate policies prejudicial to the Community. There is no mechanism for ensuring that a Member State with a derogation will treat its exchange rate policy as a matter of common interest. Member States without a single currency will be at liberty to engage in competitive devaluation if they so choose.

TITLE VII: Common Commercial Policy

GENERAL NOTE
   With the physical separation of the economic and monetary union provisions in the Treaty, Arts. 110 to 116 E.E.C. are removed from the economic policy title and appear now under the separate heading, "common commercial policy". The area itself is largely unchanged. The general principles of a common Community customs tariff and common commercial policy towards third countries remain; Art. 110 itself is unamended. The repeal of Art. 111 E.E.C. marks its falling into desuetude; it dealt solely with the operation of the common policies up to the end of the transitional period. The majority of the other amendments follow this trend of consequential amendments and the updating of out-of-date provisions.

Article 110

By establishing a customs union between themselves Member States aim to contribute, in the common interest, to the harmonious development of world trade, the progressive abolition of restrictions on international trade and the lowering of customs barriers.
   The common commercial policy shall take into account the favourable effect which the abolition of customs duties between Member States may have on the increase in the competitive strength of undertakings in those States.

Article 111

(Repealed at Maastricht)

Article 112

1. Without prejudice to obligations undertaken by them within the framework of other international organisations, Member States shall, before the end of the transitional period, progressively harmonise the systems whereby they grant aid for exports to third countries, to the extent necessary to ensure that competition between undertakings of the Community is not distorted.
   On a proposal from the Commission, the Council, shall, acting unanimously until the end of the second stage and by a qualified majority thereafter, issue any directives needed for this purpose.
2. The preceding provisions shall not apply to such drawback of customs duties or charges having equivalent effect nor to such repayment of indirect taxation including turnover taxes, excise duties and other indirect taxes as is allowed when goods are exported from a Member State to a third country, in so far as such drawback or repayment does not exceed the amount imposed, directly or indirectly, on the products exported.

Article 113

1. The common commercial policy shall be based on uniform principles, particularly in regard to changes in tariff rates, the conclusion of tariff and trade agreements, the achievement of uniformity in measures of liberalisation, export policy and measures to protect trade such as those to be taken in case of dumping or subsidies.
2. The Commission shall submit proposals to the Council for implementing the common commercial policy.
3. Where agreements with one or more States or international organisations need to be negotiated, the Commission shall make recommendations to the Council, which shall authorise the Commission to open the necessary negotiations.

The Commission shall conduct these negotiations in consultation with a special committee appointed by the Council to assist the Commission in this task and within the framework of such directives as the Council may issue to it.

The relevant provisions of Article 228 shall apply.

4. In exercising the powers conferred upon it by this Article, the Council shall act by a qualified majority.

GENERAL NOTE

The wording which previously opened this Article, "After the transitional period has ended", is removed as it is redundant. In para. 3, the reference to "agreements with third States" is replaced by reference to "one or more States or international organisations".

The Community represents the Member States in such negotiations. The means of negotiating agreements in this sphere will remain the same post-Maastricht. The Commission makes the recommendations to the Council, which then authorises the Commission to open the necessary negotiations. The Commission then conducts these negotiations in consultation with a special committee, appointed by the Council to assist the Commission in this task. This procedure, unamended by the TEU, must now be carried out in the light of the amended Art. 228 E.C.

There is no requirement to consult the European Parliament about agreements concluded under Art. 113(3), see Art. 228(3). This is a serious weakness in the powers of the Parliament. The Council may choose to consult the European Parliament in relation to some commercial policy agreements, but it is not obliged to do so (see Bradley, (1989) 9 YEL 235, 246). One reason for not giving the Parliament a right to be consulted is the short deadlines which often operate if a commercial agreement is to be satisfactorily concluded. The position could be overcome if the Parliament were required to give its opinion within the deadlines that operate for that particular agreement.

The Commission has considerable discretion in negotiating agreements in the commercial policy field because it is only required to persuade a qualified majority of the Council (para. 4) to vote for the agreement. In that regard the position is the same as it was before the Maastricht Treaty came into force.

Article 114

GENERAL NOTE

This Article is repealed because it was of purely historical interest, specifying the use of unanimity in the Council in relation to Art. 113 during the transitional period.

Article 115

In order to ensure that the execution of measures of commercial policy taken in accordance with this Treaty by any Member State is not obstructed by deflection of trade, or where differences between such measures lead to economic difficulties in one or more Member States, the Commission shall recommend the methods for the requisite co-operation between Member States. Failing this, the Commission may authorise Member States to take the necessary protective measures, the conditions and details of which it shall determine.

In case of urgency, Member States shall request authorisation to take the necessary measures themselves from the Commission, which shall take a decision as soon as possible; the Member States concerned shall then notify the measures to the other Member States. The Commission may decide at any time that the Member States concerned shall amend or abolish the measures in question. In the selection of such measures, priority shall be given to those which cause the least disturbance to the functioning of the common market.

GENERAL NOTE

Article 115 provides a procedure whereby the Member States may request authorisation to control the importation of third country goods from other Member States, where deflection of trade occurs or economic difficulties arise. The reason for the existence of this Article is the incomplete nature of the common commercial policy. The external boundaries of the Community are not identical State by State; while the external Community competence in commercial policy is, in theory, exclusive to the Community in order to achieve uniformity, it remains the case that different Member States may be permitted or empowered by the Community to impose different quotas on the importation of goods from particular third countries. There would be a risk that such concessions would be subverted if third country goods could freely enter a State which had been permitted to impose a quota, via another Member State. Therefore, the Member States have Art. 115 E.C. under which they may request authorisation to control the importation of such goods from another Member State. External disunity has thus created internal disunity. If the commercial policy was operating as envisaged, then Art. 115 E.C. would be unnecessary. The demise of Art. 115 is dependent on the establishment of a comprehensive and uniform common commercial policy. That this has not taken place is highlighted by the retention of Art. 115 by the Maastricht amendments. While it has been altered slightly, its essential basis remains. The major change concerns the adoption of urgent measures. Under the E.E.C. Treaty, the Member States were permitted, during the transitional period, to take the necessary measures and only then notify them to the Commission and to the other Member States. This power for Member States to act unilaterally expired at the end of the transitional period. The amended Art. 115 E.C. provides for the adoption of urgent measures only after express authorisation from the Commission. As before, the Commission is free to decide at any time that the Member State concerned shall amend or abolish the measure in question.

Another difference from Art. 115 E.E.C. is that, in the last sentence of para. 1, the Commission is no longer obliged to authorise Member States to take the necessary protective measures but it "may" do so.

The last sentence of the amended Art. 115, carried over from Art. 115 E.E.C., maintains an analogous principle to that of proportionality; priority will be given to the measure which will cause the least disturbance to the functioning of the common market. The sentence no longer makes reference to the need to expedite the introduction of the common customs tariff, because this has long since been introduced.

Article 116
(repealed at Maastricht)

GENERAL NOTE

The repeal of Art. 116 E.E.C. has removed the obligation on the Member States to proceed only by common action, in respect of all matters of particular interest to the common market, within the framework of international organisations of an economic character. This was greeted with approval by the U.K. Government who saw this obligation as an unnecessary fetter on national competences. Mr Garel-Jones asserted that "we shall continue to act together, because in most cases it is in our best interests to do so" (*Hansard*, H.C. Vol. 217, col. 61). The effects on the pursuit of a common commercial policy of this injection of national discretion will remain to be seen.

TITLE VIII: Social Policy, Education, Vocational Training and Youth

Chapter 1 (Social Provisions)

GENERAL NOTE

The European Community has always had a social dimension, encompassed primarily within Arts. 117–122 E.E.C. Through these provisions, a large raft of social measures have been enunciated in a wide variety of fields. Nevertheless, in recent years, pressure has grown from a number of Member States and Community institutions for the process to be made more dynamic and far-reaching. The meetings of the European Council at Hanover and Madrid (June 1988 and 1989, respectively) called for the "same importance to be given to social aspects as to economic aspects and for their development in a balanced fashion". The U.K. on the other hand has consistently argued that the development of the social arena implies increased expense for industry and thus diminished international competitiveness. The proposals put forward for the strengthening of the social provisions of the Treaty, with wider areas of Community competence and increased scope for qualified majority voting, were found acceptable by 11 of the 12 Member States at Maastricht but not, therefore, by the U.K. The result is the novel approach in which the 11 Member States, refusing to permit the watering down of the already modest developments proposed in the field simply to satisfy one Member State, have annexed a Protocol to the E.C. Treaty containing an "Agreement on Social Policy concluded between the Member States of the E.C. with the exception of the United Kingdom". The Protocol notes that the 11 Member States (excluding the U.K.) "wish to continue along the path laid down in the 1989 Social Charter". All 12 Member States have authorised the 11 to have recourse to the "institutions, procedures and mechanisms of the Treaty for the purpose of taking and implementing decisions based on the agreement". All 12 have also agreed that the U.K. "shall not take part in the deliberations and the adoption by the Council of Commission proposals" made under the agreement and that attendant "financial consequences other than administrative costs entailed for the institutions" shall not apply to the U.K.

The result of this approach is that the social provisions of the E.C. Treaty are largely unamended, although the Social Protocol annexed to the Treaty had originally been envisaged as taking the place of the Treaty provisions. Indeed, Art. 1 of the Social Policy Agreement substantially reiterates Art. 117 E.C. in laying down the policy of the 11 in this field. The greatest difference between the Treaty provisions and the Social Policy Agreement is in the scope of qualified majority voting. Under the E.C. Treaty the only area covered by qualified majority voting is that of health and safety (Art. 118a E.C.). Under the Social Policy Agreement, this is expanded to cover: working conditions; the information and consultation of workers; equality between men and women with regard to labour market opportunities and treatment at work; the integration of persons excluded from the labour market, without prejudice to Art. 127 E.C. and improvement of the working environment to protect workers' health and safety (Art. 2(1) of the Agreement). It is arguable that the Community already has the powers to legislate in the majority of these fields, but the potential for effective action is opened up by the application of qualified majority voting under the Agreement. Under Art. 118a E.E.C., the Community passed the Council Directives of June 12, 1989 on the introduction of measures to encourage improvements in the health and safety of workers at work (Dir. 89/391/E.E.C., [1989] O.J. L183/1).

The agreement adopted between the 11 Member States is declared to be "without prejudice to the provisions of this Treaty, particularly those relating to social policy" (see the preamble to the Protocol). The legal implications of the U.K. opt-out from the Social Policy Agreement are, however, somewhat unclear. The existence of two distinct sets of provisions on social policy operating side by side undoubtedly opens up the potential of legislative confusion or even conflict. One of the possible scenarios following the coming into force of the TEU is the Commission withdrawing some proposals on directives which the U.K. is currently blocking and re-presenting them under the Social Policy Agreement. There are a number of prime candidates for such a transfer, including the draft directive on European Works Councils (4466/91, COM (90) 581 final) which, having been introduced under Art. 100 E.E.C., at present requires unanimity for adoption. Although unanimous agreement as to its adoption among the 11 is possible; it would only require a qualified majority to secure its coming into force among the 11 Member States under the Social Policy Agreement. It would seem that any attempt to put this Directive before the Council using a legal basis under the E.C. Treaty that requires only qualified majority voting would mean the U.K. exercising their "veto" under the Luxembourg compromise, and if a legal basis requiring unanimity is retained then the U.K. would be able to block its passage by voting against it (see the *Financial Times*, June 5, 1993). This Directive may be the first to be transferred into the sphere of the Social Policy Agreement ("Works Council go-ahead likely", *Financial Times*, July 8, 1993). Other candidates for such transfers include the draft Directives on part-time and temporary workers (three were published in COM(90) 228 8072/90). It is also possible that some of the provisions dropped in Directives recently adopted, to take account of the U.K. could be resurrected. The recent Directive on the protection at work of pregnant women or women who have recently given birth (Dir. 92/85/E.E.C., [1992] O.J. L348) was adopted without the originally mooted principle that maternity leave be on full pay, thanks to U.K. opposition (see E.C. Commission, Background Report, E.C. B3/93, 11/1/93). A proposed Directive covering parental leave from work was being considered within the framework of the E.C. Treaty in November 1993 (see "Britain to oppose increased time off for parents", *The Times*, November 24, 1993). While many of the Member States already have more advanced labour laws than the U.K., the Social Protocol increases the potential of a growing divergence between the 11 and the U.K. This could create a number of awkward legal consequences.

The first of these is a challenge before the E.C.J. claiming that the U.K.'s failure to participate in the Social Policy Agreement breaches the Community's competition or equal treatment laws. The second question is whether measures adopted under the Social Policy Agreement can take supremacy over conflicting measures adopted under the E.C. Treaty. In this regard the provisions agreed under the E.C. Treaty must have supremacy in the U.K. The Protocol on Social Policy states that "this protocol and the said Agreement are without prejudice to the provisions of this Treaty, particularly those relating to social policy which constitute an integral part of the *acquis communautaire*". The issue, however, remains open in the other 11 Member States. Thirdly, if the U.K. were to sign up to the Social Policy Agreement at some later date, would it then become bound by the decisions reached by the 11 during its period of non-involvement? The answers to the latter two questions will depend on the attitude which the E.C.J. takes to the status of measures enacted under the Social Policy Agreement. It is unlikely that the E.C.J. will confront the issue head on. The only guarantee is that the area will provide a fertile ground for litigation (see A Social Policy for Europe: Politicians 1: Lawyers 0, International Journal of Comparative Labour Law and Industrial Relations (1992), 15). The potential of challenges on the ground of the anti-competitive nature of the U.K. opt-out raise equally difficult questions. It can be argued that the U.K.'s ability to maintain a less regulated labour market due to its non-participation in the Social Policy Agreement enables firms in the U.K. to gain a competitive advantage over firms in other Member States. On the other hand, in an era of minimum harmonisation, the Community does not attempt to create a uniform level of regulation throughout the Member States but rather a minimum floor of regulation which will be built upon in varying ways in the Member States (*cf.* Art. 118a(3) E.C., allowing Member States to introduce more stringent measures to protect working conditions than those agreed in a Community Directive). The fact that the Member States have all agreed to the Social Protocol is significant. The E.C.J.'s opinion on the proposed European Economic Area Agreement signalled that it would not shy away from contentious constitutional matters (Opinion 1/91 [1992] 1 C.M.L.R. 245). Whether it would take a similarly radical stance where its own competences are not threatened and where it would be calling into question the provisions of primary Community law (a Protocol annexed to the E.C. Treaty is an integral part of that Treaty) is very doubtful. In Opinion 1/91 the Court regarded the E.C. Treaty as the "constitutional charter" of the Community (see p. 269).

Article 117

Member States agree upon the need to promote improved working conditions and an improved standard of living for workers, so as to make possible their harmonisation while the improvement is being maintained.

They believe that such a development will ensue not only from the functioning of the common market, which will favour the harmonisation of social systems, but also from the procedures provided for in this Treaty and from the approximation of provisions laid down by law, regulation or administrative action.

Article 118

Without prejudice to the other provisions of this Treaty and in conformity with its general objectives, the Commission shall have the task of promoting close co-operation between Member States in the social field, particularly in matters relating to:
— employment;
— labour law and working conditions;
— basic and advanced vocational training;
— social security;
— prevention of occupational accidents and diseases;
— occupational hygiene;
— the right of association, and collective bargaining between employers and workers.

To this end, the Commission shall act in close contact with Member States by making studies, delivering opinions and arranging consultations both on problems arising at national levels and on those of concern to international organisations.

Before delivering the opinions provided for in this Article, the Commission shall consult the Economic and Social Committee.

Article 118a

1. Member States shall pay particular attention to encouraging improvements, especially in the working environment, as regards the health and safety of workers, and shall set as their objective the harmonisation of conditions in this area, while maintaining the improvements made.

2. In order to help achieve the objective laid down in the first paragraph, the Council, acting in accordance with the procedure referred to in Article 189c and after consulting the Economic and Social Committee, shall adopt, by means of directives, minimum requirements for gradual implementation, having regard to the conditions and technical rules obtaining in each of the Member States.

Such directives shall avoid imposing administrative, financial and legal constraints in a way which would hold back the creation and development of small and medium-sized undertakings.

3. The provisions adopted pursuant to this Article shall not prevent any Member State from maintaining or introducing more stringent measures for the protection of working conditions compatible with this Treaty.

GENERAL NOTE

This Article, inserted by the SEA, provides for the adoption of measures aimed at the protection of the health and safety of workers. A number of directives have been passed in this field. One example is the Directive on the protection at work of pregnant women or women who have recently given birth (Dir. 92/85/E.E.C., [1992] O.J. L348). The E.C. Directive on Working Time was adopted on November 23, 1993 under this Article, despite U.K. opposition. David Hunt, the U.K. Employment Secretary, stated that the U.K. would seek the annulment of the Directive in an action under Art. 173 E.C. before the E.C.J. (see *The Times*, November 24, 1993).

The danger is that Art. 118a is used as the legal basis for measures which have only a limited connection with "health and safety" because it is the only one of the social provisions under the E.C. Treaty which allows for qualified majority voting in the Council.

The amendment to this Article simply alters the name of the co-operation procedure to the "procedure referred to in Art. 189c". No substantive amendments are made to the Article itself. On the position on health and safety implementing measures, see E.C. Commission Background Report, E.C. B3/93, November 1, 1993.

Article 118b

The Commission shall endeavour to develop the dialogue between management and labour at European level which could, if the two sides consider it desirable, lead to relations based on agreement.

Article 119

Each Member State shall during the first stage ensure and subsequently maintain the application of the principle that men and women should receive equal pay for equal work.

For the purpose of this Article, 'pay' means the ordinary basic or minimum wage or salary and any other consideration, whether in cash or in kind, which the worker receives, directly or indirectly, in respect of his employment from his employer.

Equal pay without discrimination based on sex means:
(a) that pay for the same work at piece rates shall be calculated on the basis of the same unit of measurement;
(b) that pay for work at time rates shall be the same for the same job.

Article 120

Member States shall endeavour to maintain the existing equivalence between paid holiday schemes.

Article 121

The Council may, acting unanimously and after consulting the Economic and Social Committee, assign to the Commission tasks in connection with the implementation of common measures, particularly as regards social security for the migrant workers referred to in Articles 48 to 51.

Article 122

The Commission shall include a separate chapter on social developments within the Community in its annual report to the European Parliament.

The European Parliament may invite the Commission to draw up reports on any particular problems concerning social conditions.

Chapter 2 (The European Social Fund)

Article 123

In order to improve employment opportunities for workers in the internal market and to contribute thereby to raising the standard of living, a European Social Fund is hereby established in accordance with the provisions set out below; it shall aim to render the employment of workers easier and to increase their geographical and occupational mobility within the Community, and to facilitate their adaptation to industrial changes and to changes in production systems in particular through vocational training and retraining.

GENERAL NOTE
The provisions relating to the European Social Fund are amended by enlarging the Fund's stated aims to include helping workers adapt to industrial changes and to changes in production systems, in particular through vocational training and retraining. These changes have been incorporated into the new regulations governing the operation of the structural funds as a whole from January 1, 1994 to the end of 1999 (see Reg. 2052/88 [1988] O.J. L185/9 as amended by Regs. 2081/93 and 2082/93, [1993] O.J. L193/5 and L193/20); see note on Art. 125. The administration of the Fund by the Commission, assisted by a Social Fund Committee is retained (Art. 124 E.C.).

Article 124

The Fund shall be administered by the Commission.

The Commission shall be assisted in this task by a Committee presided over by a member of the Commission and composed of representatives of Governments, trade unions and employers' organisations.

Article 125

The Council, acting in accordance with the procedure referred to in Article 189c and after consulting the Economic and Social Committee, shall adopt implementing decisions relating to the European Social Fund.

GENERAL NOTE
The detailed provisions governing the application of the Social Fund, found in Art. 125 E.E.C., have been replaced by a brief provision that the Council is to adopt implementing decisions in this field, using the co-operation procedure. Articles 126, 127, and 128 E.E.C., previously encompassing supplementary provisions as to the Social Fund and general provisions on vocational training, are removed. The repeal of these Articles does not leave a void as to the application process for the Social Fund. Since the adoption of the SEA, the three structural funds have been aimed at the achievement of common "priority objectives" laid down in detailed secondary legislation adopted under Art. 130d E.E.C. (see Art. 1, Reg. 2052/88, on the task of the structural funds and on co-ordination of their activities ([1988] O.J. L185/9 as amended by Reg. 2081/93, *supra*)). Regulation 2052/88 lays down the framework for these three funds: the European Social Fund (see specifically Reg. 4255/88 as amended by Reg. 2084/93 [1993] O.J. L193/39); the European Regional Development Fund (see specifically Reg. 4254/88 as amended by Reg. 2083/93 [1993] O.J. L193/34); the European Agricultural Guidance and Guarantee Fund (see specifically Reg. 4256/88 as amended by Reg. 2085/93 [1993] O.J. L193/44; all three regulations in [1988] O.J. L374/1–25). Of the five objectives originally envisaged for these funds, only the European Social Fund was specifically geared to the achievement of all

five. Objective one is the top priority of the funds and aims "to promote the development and adjustment of the regions whose development is lagging behind (less than 75 per cent. of the Community average)".

At the Edinburgh European Council, agreement was reached in principle as to the application of the structural funds in the period January 1, 1994 to the end of 1999. These amendments provided primarily for the creation of the Cohesion Fund (see Art. 130d and the Protocol on Economic and Social Cohesion). This new fund, aimed exclusively at the four cohesion countries (Spain, Portugal, Ireland and Greece) will set out to alleviate the regional disparities between the Community countries, particularly evident in these four "poorer" States. Thus, the cohesion fund can be seen to be aimed at "objective one", (see Reg. 2052/88 above) which will continue to be the top priority, accounting for some 70 per cent. of the total funds. This leaves the Social Fund with the primary duty of addressing what were objectives three and four of Regulation 2052/88: "the combating of long-term unemployment and facilitating the integration into working life of young people and those socially excluded from the labour market". This is in line with the TEU amendment to the objectives of the European Social Fund laid out in Art. 123 E.C. which increases the fund's stated aims to cover vocational training and retraining to facilitate adaptation to structural change in industry. The governing provisions in this field are now Arts. 1–9 of Reg. 2084/93 ([1993] O.J. L193/39) replacing Arts. 1–9 of Reg. 4255/88.

Any requests for financial assistance under the Fund must be submitted as operational programmes, global grant schemes or projects (Art. 5, Reg. 2084/93). This information must include specific data particular to each proposed project, as laid down in Art. 14(2) of Reg. 4253/88 and Art. 5 of Reg. 2084/93. This will include the groups targeted by the project, the number of persons and the duration of the operations. Requests for financial assistance under the Social Fund are put forward by Member States or by bodies governed by public law and the acceptance of such requests by the Commission and the Social Fund Committee can mean a reimbursement of a percentage of the expenditure incurred by the State or public sector body. Article 1 of Reg. 2084/93 lays down the type of programmes qualifying for financial assistance. These include vocational training measures designed to help the long-term unemployed, measures promoting equal opportunities for men and women, and programmes designed to facilitate the adaptation of workers to industrial change. Article 2 then sets out the expenditure eligible for reimbursement from the Social Fund.

The revised structural funds for the period 1993–1999, agreed provisionally at the Edinburgh European Council, provide for a two-fold increase in the amount of funds available compared to the previous period. From 21,277 million ECU in 1993, the funds will progressively increase to 30,000 million ECU in 1999. The figures for the cohesion fund itself are 1,500 million ECU in 1993 rising to 2,600 million ECU in 1999. This increase is primarily aimed at the cohesion needed by the time of the envisaged achievement of the third stage of economic and monetary union (see conclusions of the Presidency, S.N. 456/92, pp. 8–11).

On the Social Fund and structural funds in general see Mathijsen, *A Guide to European Community Law*, pp. 234–242 and 256–257 and E.C. Commission, Background Report, B16/93, 28/5/93.

The removal of the detailed Treaty provisions on the application of the European Social Fund has provided a convenient slot for the Articles on education and culture.

Chapter 3 (Education, Vocational Training and Youth)

GENERAL NOTE

While these are, at first glance, new Community competences (save as respects vocational training, see Art. 127), the powers made available to the Community through the Council are very limited and the thrust of the new material is towards declaring Community aims while reiterating that these areas essentially remain the responsibility of the Member States.

Article 126

1. The Community shall contribute to the development of quality education by encouraging co-operation between Member States and, if necessary, by supporting and supplementing their action, while fully respecting the responsibility of the Member States for the content of teaching and the organisation of education systems and their cultural and linguistic diversity.

2. Community action shall be aimed at:

— developing the European dimension in education, particularly through the teaching and dissemination of the languages of the Member States;
— encouraging mobility of students and teachers, *inter alia* by encouraging the academic recognition of diplomas and periods of study;
— promoting co-operation between educational establishments;
— developing exchanges of information and experience on issues common to the education systems of the Member States;
— encouraging the development of youth exchanges and of exchanges of socio-educational instructors;
— encouraging the development of distance education.

3. The Community and the Member States shall foster co-operation with third countries and the competent international organisations in the sphere of education, in particular the Council of Europe.

4. In order to contribute to the achievement of the objectives referred to in this Article, the Council:
— acting in accordance with the procedure referred to in Article 189b, after consulting the Economic and Social Committee and the Committee of the Regions, shall adopt incentive measures, excluding any harmonisation of the laws and regulations of the Member States;
— acting by qualified majority on a proposal from the Commission, shall adopt recommendations.

GENERAL NOTE

This Article incorporates into the Community Treaties for the first time an explicit legal base for the adoption of measures in the educational field. Prior to the conclusion of the TEU, intergovernmental co-operation in this field through exchanges of information, pilot studies and non-binding resolutions were backed up by the Community's own education programmes. These programmes came about partly under the old Art. 128 E.E.C. and partly under the Action Programme on Education agreed in 1986 (O.J. 1986 C33). ERASMUS, LINGUA and COMMETT have been adopted under Arts. 128 and 235 E.E.C. and provide for links between universities and industry (COMMETT, Decision 86/365, [1986] O.J. L222 and Decision 89/271, [1989] O.J. L13), the promotion of foreign language teaching (LINGUA, Decision 89/489, [1989] O.J. L239) and Community university exchange programmes (ERASMUS, Decision 87/327, [1987] O.J. L166). The new education Article puts this co-operation between Member States on a firmer footing.

The rôle of the Community in this field will be restricted to the adoption of incentive measures; with the express proviso that these shall exclude "any harmonisation of the laws and regulations of the Member States" (Art. 126(4) E.C.). Mr Garel-Jones, in committee, stated that this would be an effective barrier to what he referred to as "creeping competences" (*Hansard*, H.C. Vol. 217, col. 63). These measures are to be adopted under the conciliation and veto procedure in Art. 189b E.C., and only after consultation of the Economic and Social Committee and the Committee of the Regions has taken place. This amounts to the most convoluted process for the adoption of legislation under the whole Treaty. The Council is also empowered to enact non-binding recommendations, acting by a qualified majority on a proposal from the Commission.

The principle of subsidiarity is implicit throughout this Article; phrases such as "fully respecting the responsibility of the Member States for the content of teaching and the organisation of education systems and their cultural and educational diversity" making quite clear where the balance of power is to lie. This reflects the sensitive national feelings towards any standardisation of the school curriculum, etc., which is explicitly excluded by the provisions of the Article.

The U.K. was quite happy to see this formalisation of the Community's educational rôle for two reasons. Firstly, it operates to prevent "the Commission inserting itself into education through the training Article (Art. 128 E.E.C., repealed) in an inappropriate manner" (*Hansard*, H.C. Vol. 217, col. 395): the areas of Community competence are expressly delimited under Art. 126(2) E.C. Secondly, the new process removes the scope of application of simple majority voting previously available under Art. 128 E.E.C. and which the U.K. Government denigrated as not permitting sufficient control by Member States over Council decisions. Simple majority voting had the effect of allowing Government ministers representing the large majority of the population of the E.C. to be outvoted, not a defensible position when substantive decisions are being made. The more normal procedures of qualified majority voting and unanimity in Council will now apply.

Article 127

1. The Community shall implement a vocational training policy which shall support and supplement the action of the Member States, while fully respecting the responsibility of the Member States for the content and organisation of vocational training.

2. Community action shall aim to:
— facilitate adaptation to industrial changes, in particular through vocational training and retraining;
— improve initial and continuing vocational training in order to facilitate vocational integration and reintegration into the labour market;
— facilitate access to vocational training and encourage mobility of instructors and trainees and particularly young people;
— stimulate co-operation on training between educational or training establishments and firms;
— develop exchanges of information and experience on issues common to the training systems of the Member States.

3. The Community and the Member States shall foster co-operation with third countries and the competent international organisations in the sphere of vocational training.

4. The Council, acting in accordance with the procedure referred to in Article 189c and after consulting the Economic and Social Committee, shall adopt measures to contribute to the achievement of the objectives referred to in this Article, excluding any harmonisation of the laws and regulations of the Member States.

GENERAL NOTE

This Article lays down the scope of the Community vocational training policy; previously enunciated by Art. 128 E.E.C. In common with the provision on education above, the Community is only empowered to implement a vocational training policy in support of Member State action (Art. 127(1) E.C.). The aims of the Community action are listed under para. 2. The only rôle for the Council is to adopt measures under the co-operation procedure with the goal of achieving these objectives. The influence of the principle of subsidiarity is felt, with the express exclusion of "any harmonisation of the laws and regulations of the Member States" and the requirement to "fully respect the responsibility of the Member States for the content and organisation of vocational training" (*Hansard*, H.C. Vol. 217, col. 64).

The repeal of Art. 128 E.E.C. removes the application of simple majority voting in Council and replaces it with qualified majority and unanimity, depending on the way the European Parliament votes in the second reading under the co-operation procedure (Art. 189c E.C.). The U.K. Government welcomed this change as allowing the Member States to wield much greater control over the training budget. Whether or not this will be the case remains to be seen.

While this Article bears a number of similarities to the preceding provision on education, it seems to permit greater scope for Community action. In the first place it is built upon an explicit pre-existing Community competence and an established process for the reimbursement of Member States for expenditure incurred in training programmes. Secondly, unlike the education provisions, the scope for Community measures in the training field is not restricted to incentive measures but to measures "contributing to the achievement of the objectives referred to in the Article". Thirdly, the E.C.J. in *Gravier* v. *City of Liège* (Case 293/83 [1985] E.C.R. 593), in the context of Art. 128 E.E.C., observed that access to vocational training is a means of bringing about the key objective of free movement of persons throughout the Community. Thus Community nationals could rely on Art. 7 E.E.C./6 E.C., to claim equality with nationals of the Member State providing the training, in qualifying for access to the course. The E.C.J. in *Gravier* envisaged a very wide notion of vocational training covering "any form of education which prepares for a qualification for a particular profession, trade or employment or which provides the necessary skills and training for such a profession, trade or employment . . . even if the training programme includes an element of general education" (para. 30). The E.C.J. confirmed the breadth of this principle in *Blaizot* v. *University of Liège* (Case 24/86 [1988] E.C.R. 379) where it stated that "only certain courses of study . . . intended for persons wishing to improve their general knowledge rather than prepare themselves for an occupation" fall outside the scope of vocational training (para. 20). The whole of Art. 127 E.C. must be read in the light of the above case law. The duty of the Community to facilitate access to vocational training (Art. 127(2) E.C., third indent) would seem to have been achieved to a large extent by the E.C.J. Financial assist-ance of non-nationals attending vocational training in another Member State is however wholly at the discretion of the Member State concerned (*Brown* v. *Secretary of State for Scotland* (Case 197/86, [1988] E.C.R. 3205)). Financial matters will be a major consideration in any develop-ment of the Community vocational training policy under Art. 127 E.C. In this respect see the annotations on the European Social Fund under Arts. 123–125 E.C.

TITLE IX: Culture

Article 128

1. The Community shall contribute to the flowering of the cultures of the Member States, while respecting their national and regional diversity and at the same time bringing the common cultural heritage to the fore.

2. Action by the Community shall be aimed at encouraging co-operation between Member States and, if necessary, supporting and supplementing their action in the following areas:
— improvement of the knowledge and dissemination of the culture and history of the European peoples;
— conservation and safeguarding of cultural heritage of European significance;
— non-commercial cultural exchanges;
— artistic and literary creation, including in the audiovisual sector.

3. The Community and the Member States shall foster co-operation with third countries and the competent international organisations in the sphere of culture, in particular the Council of Europe.

4. The Community shall take cultural aspects into account in its action under other provisions of this Treaty.

5. In order to contribute to the achievement of the objectives referred to in this Article, the Council:
— acting in accordance with the procedure referred to in Article 189b and after consulting the Committee of the Regions, shall adopt incen-tive measures, excluding any harmonisation of the laws and regu-lations of the Member States.
    The Council shall act unanimously throughout the procedures referred to in Article 189b;
— acting unanimously on a proposal from the Commission, shall adopt recommendations.

GENERAL NOTE
In line with Community competences in the field of education, the incorporation of culture into the Community sphere is subject to an array of provisos restricting the scope of Community action in this field. In this area, where national diversity is manifest, the Community is to play only a small rôle because the culture provisions are by far the most restrictive of Community action. Article 128 roughly follows the pattern of the preceding Articles. The Community is under a duty to "contribute to the flowering of the cultures of the Member States" and to bring "the common cultural heritage to the fore". The Community is empowered, in pursuit of the objectives laid down in Art. 128(2) E.C., to adopt incentive measures, but excluding any har-monisation of the laws and regulations of the Member States, and to adopt recommendations on the subject. The adoption of the incentive measures is to take place under the conciliation and veto procedure but with the added requirement that the Council act by unanimity throughout. This effectively renders the Art. 189b process otiose, the conciliation element is much less likely to work effectively given the unanimity requirement in Council (see note on Art. 189b E.C.). The adoption of recommendations, which are non-binding, is similarly tied to a position of una-nimity in Council. The promulgation of even the limited measures envisaged under this Article is thus made very difficult. The adoption of measures in the field of "culture" in the past was achieved under Art. 235 and thus similarly required unanimity. Cultural matters have also been evident in European legislation enacted under different Community headings. The "Television Without Frontiers" Directive enacted in 1989, has, as one of its aims, the encouragement of European production of television material. In pursuit of this goal, it lays down guidelines speci-fying that a majority of transmission time ought, "wherever practicable", to be devoted to European works. This is then backed up by complicated statistics regarding the status of

sporting, news and teletext programmes. Thus, a directive aimed at the free movement of television programmes has an inescapably cultural backdrop. The Commission has recently challenged the U.K. to justify the Independent Television Council's decision to grant a licence to a satellite station to broadcast cartoons 24 hours a day. The reason for this was the almost exclusively non-European origin of the cartoons. The E.C. Commissioner for Cultural Affairs based his challenge on cultural as well as free movement grounds (The Week in Europe, E.C. Commission, September 16, 1993). This would seem to infer the inclusion of cultural affairs in the Treaty long before the Maastricht amendments came into being; moreover, the adoption of cultural measures under existing treaty provisions, Art. 100a in particular, will remain more tempting to the Commission in future given the limited scope for action under the cultural heading itself.

Usher asserts that the Community had developed a new Community policy in the culture field as early as 1988 and did so without even making reference to Art. 235. In a Resolution passed on May 27, 1988, the Council set out the future plan of action for work in this area. They called for, *inter alia*, the setting up of a committee on cultural affairs and for the Commission to implement decisions of the Council at the Community level ([1988], O.J. C197/1; from *Current Issues in European and International Law* (in memoriam, Frank Dowrick), eds. White and Smythe, at p. 18).

Article 128(4) states that "the Community shall take cultural matters into account in its actions under other provisions of the Treaty". While this is not as imperative a requirement as that enunciated under the analogous environmental provision, it ought to give cultural arguments greater weight. Venables has asserted that cultural considerations could well surface in many initiatives for the completion of the internal market in relation to copyright, and other measures to protect intellectual property, approximation of VAT and other indirect taxes and levies (Venables, *The Amendment of the Treaties*, Butterworths (1992) at p. 58).

The provision under the educational title that the Committee of the Regions be consulted (Art. 127) is not duplicated here. It is arguable that co-operation among the Member States in the cultural field would have a strong regional element. The conclusion that consultation of the Committee of the Regions has been appended to a variety of Articles on an ad hoc basis is hard to avoid.

TITLE X: Public Health

Article 129

1. The Community shall contribute towards ensuring a high level of human health protection by encouraging co-operation between the Member States and, if necessary, lending support to their action. Community action shall be directed towards the prevention of diseases, in particular the major health scourges, including drug dependence, by promoting research into their causes and their transmissions, as well as health information and education.

Health protection requirements shall form a constituent part of the Community's other policies.

2. Member States shall, in liaison with the Commission, co-ordinate among themselves their policies and programmes in the areas referred to in paragraph 1. The Commission may, in close contact with the Member States, take any useful initiative to promote such co-ordination.

3. The Community and the Member States shall foster co-operation with third countries and the competent international organisations in the sphere of public health.

4. In order to contribute to the achievement of the objectives referred to in this Article, the Council:

— acting in accordance with the procedure referred to in Article 189b, after consulting the Economic and Social Committee and the Committee of the Regions, shall adopt incentive measures, excluding any harmonisation of the laws and regulations of the Member States;

— acting by a qualified majority on a proposal from the Commission, shall adopt recommendations.

GENERAL NOTE

This provision aims to ensure a high level of health protection in the Community. This is to be achieved through the promotion of research and the sharing of information and education. In common with the rest of these "new" competences, this marks a formalisation of the Community's rôle in this area. The Article reflects the principle of subsidiarity both in general and in the more specific exclusion of any harmonisation of the laws and regulations of the Member States. Article 129(1) follows the pattern of the preceding Articles by laying down the rôle of the Community as one of encouraging co-operation between the Member States. The addition of the proviso that "if necessary", the Community may "lend support to their action" does not appear to alter the underlying balance of power in any substantial fashion. Any such "necessary" action would still have to be read in the light of Art. 129(4), explicitly excluding any harmonisation of national law.

The Commission is given the task of liaising with the Member States to co-ordinate their actions in the fields of disease prevention, drug dependence, and research into their causes and transmissions. The Council is empowered to adopt incentive measures under the conciliation and veto procedure, avoiding any harmonisation of national laws, or to enact non-binding recommendations on the basis of a Commission proposal. The latter measures are to be adopted by qualified majority, but bypass any European Parliamentary consideration.

Community measures in the field of health protection have been promulgated under a variety of different legal bases in the past; in particular Arts. 100a and 235 E.E.C. Council Directive 89/622 on the approximation of the laws of the Member States concerning the labelling of tobacco products was passed under Art. 100a E.E.C., with the preamble citing the Directive's goal as "a vital factor in the protection of public health" (see recently on this Directive *R.* v. *Secretary of State for Health*, Case C-11/92, judgment of June 22, 1993, unreported, E.C.J. found the U.K. acted legally in demanding warnings 50 per cent. bigger than stipulated by the directive, as minimum harmonisation applied). (See also Council Resolution on future action in the field of public health, [1993] O.J. C174/1).

TITLE XI: Consumer Protection

Article 129a

1. The Community shall contribute to the attainment of a high level of consumer protection through:

   (a) measures adopted pursuant to Article 100a in the context of the completion of the internal market;

   (b) specific action which supports and supplements the policy pursued by the Member States to protect the health, safety and economic interests of consumers and to provide adequate information to consumers.

2. The Council, acting in accordance with the procedure referred to in Article 189b and after consulting the Economic and Social Committee, shall adopt the specific action referred to in paragraph 1(b).

3. Action adopted pursuant to paragraph 2 shall not prevent any Member State from maintaining or introducing more stringent protective measures. Such measures must be compatible with this Treaty. The Commission shall be notified of them.

GENERAL NOTE

This Article would seem to afford a rather strong legislative base for the adoption of measures in the field of consumer protection. The restrictions on the subject matter and the form that Community action should take which are found in the headings on culture and health are not found in this Article. This could well be due to the fact that consumer protection has been explicitly recognised in the Community Treaties since the SEA, and dealt with under a variety of headings since early on in the development of the single European market. In 1975 the Council adopted a Resolution concerning a preliminary programme for a consumer protection and information policy, [1975] O.J. C92/1. This dealt with the protection of the consumers' health and safety, misleading advertising, consumer information, etc. A number of legislative enactments were promulgated under these headings. In 1986, the Council adopted a Resolution setting out its policy of integration of consumer policy into other common policies of the Community, [1987] O.J. C3/1. Then Art. 100a(3) E.E.C., inserted by the SEA, empowered the Commission to make proposals for the establishment of the Single Market "concerning health, safety, environmental protection and consumer protection" to "take as a base a high level of protection". While there was still no express Community competence in this field, consumer protection legislation continued to be passed, especially under both Arts. 100 and 100a E.E.C. The legislation passed in this field has often had consumer protection as a by-product of some form of internal market harmonisation but there have also been some measures exclusively

aimed at consumer protection. A prime example is Council Directive 88/378 on the approximation of laws of the Member States concerning the safety of toys (on consumer safety measures
in general see E.C. Commission Background Report E.C. B2/93 and Weatherill, Consumer
Safety Legislation in the U.K. and Article 30 E.E.C. (1988) 13 E.L.Rev. 87. Measures recently
passed in the consumer protection field include the Directive on unfair terms in consumer contracts ([1993] O.J. L95; see Brander and Ulmer, The Community Directive on Unfair terms in
Consumer Contracts: Some Critical Comments on the proposal submitted by the E.C. Commission (1991) 28 C.M.L.Rev. 647–662) and the General Product Safety Directive (Dir. 92/59,
[1992] O.J. L228/24).

Consumer protection legislation has now got its own legal base under Art. 129a. The Community is empowered, as before, to attempt to secure a high degree of consumer protection
through the adoption of Art. 100a measures. Secondly, and more importantly, the Community is
to take specific action which supports and supplements the policy of the Member States to protect the health, safety and economic interests of consumers. This suggests a very broad scope,
without the proviso common to the preceding Articles that the measures shall exclude any harmonisation of national laws and regulations. This power must however be exercised in accordance with the principle of subsidiarity. The general product safety Directive mentioned above
contains more than an element of this principle in its operative provisions. This is in line with the
three year action plan of consumer policy in the E.E.C. adopted in 1990, which made explicit
reference to the subsidiarity principle and to its enunciation in the consumer protection field
(COM (90) 98 at p. 3). Measures adopted under this heading will be by the conciliation and veto
procedure. Expressly provided for in this Article is the notion of minimum harmonisation,
whereby Member States can maintain or introduce more stringent measures than laid down in
the secondary legislation, subject to their notifying the Commission of their existence. This is
quite in keeping with the idea of subsidiarity, as well as avoiding the situation under which the
pursuit of Community policies could lead to a lowering of standards in the more advanced Member States (see Goyens, Consumer Protection in a Single European Market: What Challenge for
the E.C. Agenda?, (1992) 29 C.M.L.Rev. 71–92).

Finally, the Community is also given the power to provide adequate information to consumers
(one of the measures dropped by the Commission at the Edinburgh European Council in the
name of subsidiarity concerned the compulsory nutritional labelling of foodstuffs previously
proposed in [1988] O.J. C 282).

TITLE XII: Trans-European Networks

GENERAL NOTE

These Articles mark something of a new departure for the internal market. The aim is to
permit the citizens of the union to "derive full benefit from the setting up of an area without any
internal frontiers". This is to be achieved through Community contribution to the establishment
and development of trans-European networks in the areas of transport, telecommunications,
and energy infrastructures. This contribution is to be aimed at the achievement of the "objectives referred to in Arts. 7a and 130a"; in other words, the completion of the internal market and
economic and social cohesion.

The scope for Community action under this heading is large. The Community, in aiming to
achieve the interconnection and inter-operability of the national networks and access to such
networks, is to establish guidelines on the subject, as well as implementing measures aimed at
the inter-operability of the networks. The second indent of Art. 129c alludes to the adoption of
measures necessary for the inter-operability of the networks, especially through the field of
technical harmonisation. The adoption of the guidelines envisaged under the first indent of Art.
129c(1) is by the conciliation and veto procedure following the consultation of the Economic and
Social Committee and the Committee of the Regions. The implementation of measures under
the second indent is to be on the basis of the co-operation procedure. The third indent of Art.
129c is one of the more interesting provisions of the Treaty. It permits the Community to support
the financial efforts made by the Member States in common projects, identified under the guidelines referred to previously. The Community is to assist the Member States in these projects
through feasibility studies, loan guarantees or interest rate subsidies. Alternatively, the Community may utilise the Cohesion Fund (Art. 130d E.C.) to finance projects relating to the transport infrastructure. In the adoption of guidelines or projects of common interest which relate to
the territory of a Member State then the approval of that Member State shall be required (Art.
129d).

The Commission has made it clear that, although the Community will support projects of
European interest, and is supporting less prosperous regions through its Regional Development

Fund and the new Cohesion Fund, in view of its limited resources, it does not see itself as the major provider of finance for transport infrastructure programmes and is keen to encourage private sector investment (E.C. Commission, E.C. B10/93 at p.3). Tristan Garel-Jones was keen to emphasise in the House of Commons that the funding for such projects would not come (directly) from the national purse but from the European structural funds and, as the Commission has asserted, from the private sector.

This Article also provides that "the Community may decide to co-operate with third countries to promote objects of mutual interest and to ensure the inter-operability of networks (Art. 129c (3)). No provision is, however, made as to the procedure to be utilised in deciding to go ahead with such co-operation, nor is any mention made of the source of funding, if required.

Article 129b

1. To help achieve the objectives referred to in Articles 7a and 130a and to enable citizens of the Union, economic operators and regional and local communities to derive full benefit from the setting up of an area without internal frontiers, the Community shall contribute to the establishment and development of trans-European networks in the areas of transport, telecommunications and energy infrastructures.

2. Within the framework of a system of open and competitive markets, action by the Community shall aim at promoting the interconnection and inter-operability of national networks as well as access to such networks. It shall take account in particular of the need to link island, landlocked and peripheral regions with the central regions of the Community.

Article 129c

1. In order to achieve the objectives referred to in Article 129b, the Community:
— shall establish a series of guidelines covering the objectives, priorities and broad lines of measures envisaged in the sphere of trans-European networks; these guidelines shall identify projects of common interest;
— shall implement any measures that may prove necessary to ensure the inter-operability of the networks, in particular in the field of technical standardisation;
— may support the financial efforts made by the Member States for projects of common interest financed by Member States, which are identified in the framework of the guidelines referred to in the first indent, particularly through feasibility studies, loan guarantees or interest rate subsidies; the Community may also contribute, through the Cohesion Fund to be set up no later than 31 December 1993 pursuant to Article 130d, to the financing of specific projects in Member States in the area of transport infrastructure.
The Community's activities shall take into account the potential economic viability of the projects.

2. Member States shall, in liaison with the Commission, co-ordinate among themselves the policies pursued at national level which may have a significant impact on the achievement of the objectives referred to in Article 129b. The Commission may, in close co-operation with the Member States, take any useful initiative to promote such co-ordination.

3. The Community may decide to co-operate with third countries to promote projects of mutual interest and to ensure the inter-operability of networks.

Article 129d

The guidelines referred to in Article 129c(1) shall be adopted by the Council, acting in accordance with the procedure referred to in Article 189b and after consulting the Economic and Social Committee and the Committee of the Regions.

Guidelines and projects of common interest which relate to the territory of a Member State shall require the approval of the Member State concerned.

The Council, acting in accordance with the procedure referred to in Article 189c and after consulting the Economic and Social Committee and the Committee of the Regions, shall adopt the other measures provided for in Article 129c(1).

TITLE XIII: Industry

Article 130

1. The Community and the Member States shall ensure that the conditions necessary for the competitiveness of the Community's industry exist.

For that purpose, in accordance with a system of open and competitive markets, their action shall be aimed at:

— speeding up the adjustment of industry to structural changes;
— encouraging an environment favourable to initiative and to the development of undertakings throughout the Community, particularly small and medium-sized undertakings;
— encouraging an environment favourable to co-operation between undertakings;
— fostering better exploitation of the industrial potential of policies of innovation, research and technological development.

2. The Member States shall consult each other in liaison with the Commission and, where necessary, shall co-ordinate their action. The Commission may take any useful initiative to promote such co-ordination.

3. The Community shall contribute to the achievement of the objectives set out in paragraph 1 through the policies and activities it pursues under other provisions of this Treaty. The Council, acting unanimously on a proposal from the Commission, after consulting the European Parliament and the Economic and Social Committee, may decide on specific measures in support of action taken in the Member States to achieve the objectives set out in paragraph 1.

This Title shall not provide a basis for the introduction by the Community of any measure which could lead to a distortion of competition.

GENERAL NOTE

Opinions on the likely effect of this Article vary markedly. It has been argued that it will provide a basis for substantial Community expenditure on matters currently financed by the Member States (Select Committee on European Legislation, (1991–1992), 24, xlvi). The opposite view is that it marks no real change from the pre-Maastricht position. The latter view appears the most cogent. Mr Garel-Jones asserted in the House of Commons that "the key change for which Britain pressed was the last sentence on the need to preserve 'open and competitive markets'" (a reference to Art. 130(1) second sentence; see *Hansard*, H.C. Vol. 217, col. 141). Advocates of an integrationist industrial policy are, however, more likely to be thwarted by the requirement of unanimity in Council for the adoption of any measures to support Member State action under this heading than by any restraints imposed by the wording of the Article (on reputed French desire for strongly interventionist industrial policy, at least prior to the election of a centre-right government, see Maillet, Le double visage de Maastricht: Achevement et nouveau depart, (1992) RMC, 209). Any other Community action aimed at the achievement of the objectives laid down in para. 1 will be carried out under other provisions of the Treaty. (See also Bangemann, Pour une politique industrielle europeenne, (1992), RMC, 367). The last sentence of Art. 130(3) gives priority to Community competition policy over its industrial policy.

Despite the tenor of this Article, which seems to be aimed at the avoidance of an interventionist industrial policy, the Delors II package on the future financing of the Community (S.N. 456/92) adopted at the Edinburgh European Council of December 1993 places some emphasis on industrial policy, but, significantly, not in the context of the present Article. Rather, it envisages the use of an increased social fund to protect employees in industries under threat from competitors both within and outwith the Community (see Venables, *The Amendment of the Treaties*, Butterworths, 1992, p. 62 and annotations on Arts. 123–125 E.C.).

TITLE XIV: Economic and Social Cohesion

GENERAL NOTE
This title, inserted by the SEA with the express purpose of securing the goals laid down under Art. 130a E.E.C., is re-enacted with considerable extension. The overall aim remains the strengthening of economic and social cohesion and the reduction of disparities between the levels of development of the various regions (Art. 130a E.C., which makes only very small amendments to the wording of the second paragraph). The formal provisions of this title must be read in the light of an appended Protocol laying down various policy goals (Protocol No. 15 on Economic and Social Cohesion). The major substantive amendment to this Title is the provision for the creation of a new "Cohesion Fund" to stand alongside the three existing structural funds. Article 130d, second indent, provides that "the Council shall, before December 31, 1993, set up a Cohesion Fund to provide a financial contribution to projects in the fields of the environment and trans-European networks in the area of transport infrastructure". This fund will be open to the four "cohesion countries" defined as those, at the pertinent time, whose Gross National Product per capita is below 90 per cent. of the Community average. The four countries who will qualify in this category are Spain, Portugal, Ireland and Greece. Other amendments relate to the procedures to be applied in the adoption and amendment of the funds themselves.

Article 130a

In order to promote its overall harmonious development, the Community shall develop and pursue its actions leading to the strengthening of its economic and social cohesion.

In particular the Community shall aim at reducing disparities between the levels of development of the various regions and the backwardness of the least-favoured regions, including rural areas.

GENERAL NOTE
Paragraph 1 of the Article is unamended by the TEU. Paragraph 2 is amended to make explicit reference to "rural areas" being included among the "least favoured regions". The appended Protocol further elaborates the goals set out in Art. 130a E.C.

Article 130b

Member States shall conduct their economic policies and shall co-ordinate them in such a way as, in addition, to attain the objectives set out in Article 130a. The formulation and implementation of the Community's policies and actions and the implementation of the internal market shall take into account the objectives set out in Article 130a and shall contribute to their achievement. The Community shall also support the achievement of these objectives by the action it takes through the Structural Funds (European Agricultural Guidance and Guarantee Fund, Guidance Section; European Social Fund; European Regional Development Fund), the European Investment Bank and the other existing financial instruments.

The Commission shall submit a report to the European Parliament, the Council, the Economic and Social Committee and the Committee of the Regions every three years on the progress made towards achieving economic and social cohesion and on the manner in which the various means provided for in this Article have contributed to it. This report shall, if necessary, be accompanied by appropriate proposals.

If specific actions prove necessary outside the Funds and without prejudice to the measures decided upon within the framework of the other Community policies, such actions may be adopted by the Council acting unanimously on a proposal from the Commission and after consulting the European Parliament, the Economic and Social Committee and the Committee of the Regions.

GENERAL NOTE

This Article continues to place responsibility for the achievement of the goals listed in Art. 130a on the Member States. They are to be assisted by Community action in the collection and distribution of the structural funds listed under this Article and the other financial institutions mentioned, specifically the European Investment Bank.

The second paragraph to this Article is new and requires the Commission, which exercises executive responsibilities in the administration of the structural funds, to submit a report every three years to the Council, European Parliament, Economic and Social Committee and the Committee of the Regions on the progress being made towards economic and social cohesion.

The third paragraph is another addition. This permits the adoption of specific actions necessary for the achievement of the goals of economic and social cohesion, in areas where the mechanism of Fund support is inappropriate or inapplicable. Such actions are to be adopted by the Council, acting by a unanimous vote on a Commission proposal. The European Parliament, Economic and Social Committee and the Committee of the Regions are all to be consulted.

Article 130c

The European Regional Development Fund is intended to help redress the main regional imbalances in the Community through participating in the development and structural adjustment of regions whose development is lagging behind and in the conversion of declining industrial regions.

GENERAL NOTE

This Article is unamended. On the European Regional Development Fund in general see Mathijsen, *A Guide to European Community Law* pp. 234–236 and Scott and Mansell, European Regional Development: Confusing Quantity with Quality?, (1993) 18 E.L.Rev. pp. 87–108).

Article 130d

Without prejudice to Article 130e, the Council, acting unanimously on a proposal from the Commission and after obtaining the assent of the European Parliament and consulting the Economic and Social Committee and the Committee of the Regions, shall define the tasks, priority objectives and the organisation of the Structural Funds, which may involve grouping the Funds. The Council, acting by the same procedure, shall also define the general rules applicable to them and the provisions necessary to ensure their effectiveness and the co-ordination of the Funds with one another and with the other existing financial instruments.

The Council, acting in accordance with the same procedure, shall before 31 December 1993 set up a Cohesion Fund to provide a financial contribution to projects in the fields of environment and trans-European networks in the area of transport infrastructure.

GENERAL NOTE

This Article contains the major alteration and innovation encompassed in this Title of the Treaty. From the date of the coming into force of the TEU, all decisions concerning the tasks, priority objectives and the organisation of the structural funds will have to be adopted in accordance with the procedure laid down in this Article. This provides for the unanimous agreement of the Council, acting on a Commission proposal. The European Parliament must then give its assent to any agreement so reached. The Committee of the Regions, with its special interest in such matters, is to be consulted, as is the Economic and Social Committee. This same procedure is also applicable for the adoption of the general rules governing the funds and the provisions necessary to ensure the effectiveness and the co-ordination of the funds with one another. In other words, effectively all subsequent decisions concerning the nature of the structural funds, rather than their implementation, will be passed in accordance with the procedure laid down in this Article. The latest alterations to the Fund regulations and, in particular, Regulation 2052/88 on the tasks of the structural funds and on the co-ordination of their activities, [1988] O.J. L185/9, were carried out under the old Art. 130d E.E.C. It also required unanimity in the Council and provided only for European Parliamentary consultation. The aim of these new regulations was partly to improve the effectiveness of the funds, and partly to prepare for the smooth transition to the new period of structural fund financing beginning in 1994 (see Regs. 2081/93, 2082/93, 2083/93, 2084/93, 2085/93, [1993] O.J. L193/5–47). Any subsequent decisions governing the Funds will take place under the amended procedures laid down in these regulations.

The second paragraph of this Article makes provision for the creation of a Cohesion Fund by the end of 1993: "to provide a financial contribution to projects in the fields of the environment and trans-European networks in the area of transport infrastructure". This fund came into being on April 1, 1993, before the coming into force of the TEU. Council Regulation 792/93 established a "temporary cohesion financial instrument" in advance of the formal Cohesion Fund which will come into existence once the TEU is in force, [1993] O.J. L79/44–48. The Edinburgh European Council meeting in December 1992 was substantially concerned with the issue of the amount of cohesion funding. The Spanish Prime Minister, Felipe Gonzalez, held out for a substantial increase in the funding applicable to his country under the new Cohesion Fund. This Fund is to apply in the areas mentioned above, *i.e.* transport infrastructure and environment, and is applicable to the four cohesion countries identified prior to the Maastricht summit as having a per capita Gross National Product of less than 90 per cent. of the Community average (Greece, Ireland, Portugal and Spain). The funding which was agreed to provisionally at Edinburgh and subsequently approved provides for the four cohesion countries to see their incomes from the Funds increase by over 100 per cent. in the period 1994 to 1999. The precondition of this funding, in the light of the overall pursuit of economic convergence, is that the Member States concerned must maintain a programme for the attainment of economic convergence in accordance with Art. 104c E.C. (this last obligation is substantially reiterated in Regulation 792/93 setting up the temporary cohesion funding instrument; see also the Protocol on Economic and Social Cohesion). The provision of funding in the areas specified, *viz*, environmental measures and trans-European networks, will be in the manner described under the Cohesion fund regulations and subject to the conditions laid down in the relevant Articles (on trans-European networks see Art. 129b(1) and environmental measures see Art. 130s(5)).

Article 130e

Implementing decisions relating to the European Regional Development Fund shall be taken by the Council, acting in accordance with the procedure referred to in Article 189c and after consulting the Economic and Social Committee and the Committee of the Regions.

With regard to the European Agricultural Guidance and Guarantee Fund, Guidance Section, and the European Social Fund, Articles 43, and 125 respectively shall continue to apply.

GENERAL NOTE

The implementing measures to be taken concerning the European Regional Development Fund are to continue to be taken on the basis of the co-operation procedure, but the Article is amended to give a right of consultation on such measures to the Economic and Social Committee and the Committee of the Regions.

The second paragraph of this Article is amended to remove the reference to Arts. 126 and 127 which are no longer relevant in the consideration of the structural fund provisions. As a result of the TEU amendments these Articles deal with education, vocational training and youth.

TITLE XV: Research and Technological Development

GENERAL NOTE

The provisions of the E.E.C. Treaty inserted by the SEA governing the research and technological development policy of the Community were long and complex (Arts. 130f–q E.E.C.). The amendments made at Maastricht primarily aim to redefine and extend the powers of the Community in this area. The final result is little more than a tidying up exercise. While the legislative procedures relevant to this Title have been altered, the overall régime familiar after the SEA amendments to the E.E.C. Treaty remains. This régime consists primarily of the adoption of a multiannual framework programme defining the objectives, priorities and extent of overall Community finance for the research and development programme (Art. 130i). The Council then, acting on the basis of a Commission proposal, passes specific programmes governing particular areas of research and technological development (Art. 130i (4)). These specific programmes must be geared to the achievement of the aims listed in Art. 130g, be in accordance with the multiannual framework programme, and lay down detailed rules for their implementation, duration and envisaged cost (Art. 130i(3)).

One of the most pertinent amendments made is to the procedure for the adoption of the multi-annual framework programme (Art. 130i E.C.). Under the Maastricht amendments, this is to be achieved through the conciliation and veto procedure under Art. 189b E.C. but tied to the achievement of unanimity in Council. The Commission had sought the application of qualified majority voting to this programme, and not only to the sectoral programmes adopted under it. This was provided for in both the Luxembourg and Dutch draft Treaties but removed at the Maastricht meeting itself. The Commission's support for the application of the qualified majority procedure was aimed at the alleviation of the delays caused trying to secure such unanimous agreement. The delay in the adoption of the four-year framework programme leads to related delays in the application of the sectoral programmes themselves and causes problems as to their continuity. If the Council is having difficulty securing the adoption of such measures with a Council of 12, it will find it more difficult with a Community of 15 or 20 Member States. Nevertheless, the adoption of the first multiannual framework programme; requiring a unanimous vote in the Council under the old Art. 130q E.E.C., proceeded relatively expeditiously (Council Decision 87/516, [1987] O.J. L302/1). The right to pass the implementing measures adopted under the multiannual framework programme had also been sought by the Commission, but this right remains with the Council (Art. 130o and see E.C. Bull. Supp. 2/91, p. 137). For the 1990–1994 multiannual framework programme see Decision 90/221 ([1990] O.J. L117/28) and for the Commission proposal to the Council for the 1994–1998 programme, see [1993] O.J. C230/4. Under the multiannual framework programme a vast number of specific programmes have appeared in diverse fields such as energy technology (THERMIE), telecommunications (RACE), agriculture and industry (ECLAIR), etc. For a detailed breakdown of these projects, see Commission DG XII Catalogue, 1992.

Another important amendment is made in Art. 130f on the goals of the Community research policy. The old Art. 130f advocated research solely for the purpose of increasing the competitiveness of European industry. This has now been qualified by an acceptance that research is to be encouraged where "it is deemed necessary by virtue of other chapters of the Treaty". In this respect it is likely that the research may well continue mainly along the lines of increasing the wealth-creation potential of Community industry, but it will also have regard to the environmental impact of such increased competitiveness, and other related factors such as the quality of life.

On the Community's research and development programmes in general see: Kapteyn, *supra*, pp. 645–650; Mathijsen, *supra*, pp. 249–252 and Peterson, Technology Policy in Europe: Explaining the Framework Programme and Eureka in Theory and Practice, 29 Journal of Common Market Studies, 269–290.

Article 130f

1. The Community shall have the objective of strengthening the scientific and technological bases of Community industry and encouraging it to become more competitive at international level, while promoting all the research activities deemed necessary by virtue of other Chapters of this Treaty.

2. For this purpose the Community shall, throughout the Community encourage undertakings, including small and medium-sized undertakings, research centres and universities in their research and technological development activities of high quality; it shall support their efforts to co-operate with one another, aiming, notably, at enabling undertakings to exploit the internal market potential to the full, in particular through the opening up of national public contracts, the definition of common standards and the removal of legal and fiscal obstacles to that co-operation.

3. All Community activities under this Treaty in the area of research and technological development, including demonstration projects, shall be decided on and implemented in accordance with the provisions of this Title.

GENERAL NOTE

The first paragraph of this Article is amended so that the Community's objective in the field of research and technological development shall also include the promotion of "all research activities deemed necessary by virtue of other chapters of the Treaty". Thus the promotion of research and development is not to be tied exclusively to the promotion of industrial competitiveness but is to be utilised for other goals. One likely area for promotion is the research and development necessary for the achievement of effective environmental protection under the strengthened Title XVI.

The third paragraph of this Article makes another important alteration to the existing provision. The new wording ties the achievement of all Community activities in the field of research and development to the procedures laid down in this title. This effectively means that action under Art. 100a E.C. or Art. 235 E.C. are effectively precluded. Both of these provisions have been used in the past to promulgate specific measures in this field (see Usher, The Development of Community Powers under the SEA, in *Current Issues in European and International Law* eds. White and Smythe, (1990)). It applies equally to the use of any other Treaty provision for the adoption of research and development measures, something which has been done before. The vocational training Article, Art. 128 E.E.C., has been used as the basis for COMETT decisions, the programme for co-operation between universities and industry regarding training in the field of technology (Council Decision 89/27, [1989] O.J. L13/28). This decision was taken under Art. 128 E.E.C., despite the explicit inclusion in Art. 130g E.E.C., as one of the goals of the research and development title, of "the stimulation of the training and mobility of researchers in the Community". While research and development programmes are now to be aimed at the achievement of other Treaty goals (Art. 130f(1)), it will not be possible to base them on any other Treaty provision. Thus, any attempt to secure a more "favourable" legal base (such as the simple majority vote which originally applied under Art. 128 E.E.C.) will be readily susceptible to challenge under the new Art. 130f.

Article 130g

In pursuing these objectives the Community shall carry out the following activities, complementing the activities carried out in the Member States:

- (a) implementation of research, technological development and demonstration programmes, by promoting co-operation with and between undertakings, research centres and universities;
- (b) promotion of co-operation in the field of Community research, technological development, and demonstration with third countries and international organisations;
- (c) dissemination and optimisation of the results of activities in Community research, technological development, and demonstration;
- (d) stimulation of the training and mobility of researchers in the Community.

GENERAL NOTE
The activities of the Community laid out in this Article are unamended. They must, however, be read in the light of the extended Community rôle laid out in Art. 130h.

Article 130h

1. The Community and the Member States shall co-ordinate their research and technological development activities so as to ensure that national policies and Community policy are mutually consistent.

2. In close co-operation with the Member States, the Commission may take any useful initiative to promote the co-ordination referred to in paragraph 1.

GENERAL NOTE
Under the old Art. 130h, the Member States were to "co-ordinate among themselves the policies and programmes carried out at national level". The Commission were to have a liaison rôle in this process. The amended Article shifts the onus of action towards the Community by providing that the Community and the Member States are to co-ordinate their research so as to ensure that "national policies and Community policy are mutually consistent". This marks a significant expansion of the Community's rôle in this area. Moreover, the Commission is empowered to "take any useful initiative to promote such co-operation". This will permit it to act in a much broader area than was the case when it was simply a liaison body for the Member States, ensuring merely the co-ordination of national measures rather than Community and national actions.

Article 130i

1. A multiannual framework programme, setting out all the activities of the Community, shall be adopted by the Council, acting in accordance with

the procedure referred to in Article 189b after consulting the Economic and Social Committee. The Council shall act unanimously throughout the procedures referred to in Article 189b.

The framework programme shall:

— establish the scientific and technological objectives to be achieved by the activities provided for in Article 130g and fix the relevant priorities;

— indicate the broad lines of such activities;

— fix the maximum overall amount and the detailed rules for Community financial participation in the framework programme and the respective shares in each of the activities provided for.

2. The framework programme shall be adapted or supplemented as the situation changes.

3. The framework programme shall be implemented through specific programmes developed within each activity. Each specific programme shall define the detailed rules for implementing it, fix its duration and provide for the means deemed necessary. The sum of the amounts deemed necessary, fixed in the specific programmes, may not exceed the overall maximum amount fixed for the framework programme and each activity.

4. The Council, acting by a qualified majority on a proposal from the Commission and after consulting the European Parliament and the Economic and Social Committee, shall adopt the specific programmes.

GENERAL NOTE

This Article lays down the means by which the measures to be adopted under this title will come about. The two-tier approach of multiannual framework and subordinate specific programmes remains, but the procedures for their adoption are altered. Article 130i(1) dictates that the conciliation and veto procedure shall apply to the adoption of the multiannual framework programmes. This is to be tied to the requirement of unanimity in Council. The old procedure, that of unanimity in Council and the consultation of the European Parliament at least had the advantage of being relatively simple, procedurally. The conciliation and veto procedure, where it is tied to a requirement of unanimity in Council, amounts to a very significant procedural challenge to the adoption of any measures. Moreover, the procedure can last upwards of nine months. While the adoption of the multiannual framework programme is made more difficult, so the adoption of the specific programmes is simplified. The old procedure called for the adoption of such measures under the co-operation procedure, the new Art. 130i(4) simply provides for a qualified majority vote in the Council and the consultation of the European Parliament. Thus while the procedure is simplified, it also marks a downgrading of the rôle of the European Parliament.

In the light of the Community drive for financial efficiency, the amended Art. 130i(3) provides that the "sum of the amounts deemed necessary, fixed in the specific programmes, may not exceed the overall maximum amount fixed for the framework programme and each activity". This places a more stringent duty on the Community and Member States to keep within budget than was the case under the similarly worded Art. 130p E.E.C.

Article 130j

For the implementation of the multiannual framework programme the Council shall:

— determine the rules for the participation of undertakings, research centres and universities;

— lay down the rules governing the dissemination of research results.

GENERAL NOTE

While this Article is new, the matters contained therein have already been dealt with in the implementation of previous multiannual framework programmes. The Council adopted a specific programme for the dissemination and utilisation of research results (Value) (XXIII General Report of the E.E.C. (1989), p. 164). University involvement in the research development process of the Communities has also been long recognised (Commission, DG XIII, Report on University and Research Interfaces in Europe, 1992). The Article merely formalises existing practice.

Article 130k

In implementing the multiannual framework programme, supplementary programmes may be decided on involving the participation of certain Member States only, which shall finance them subject to possible Community participation.

The Council shall adopt the rules applicable to supplementary programmes, particularly as regards the dissemination of knowledge and access by other Member States.

GENERAL NOTE

This, and the following Articles, simply reiterate the existing provisions of the Title, but with some consequential amendments to take account of the amended legislative procedures applicable in this field. Article 130p is the only new addition among the remaining Articles. Some reallocation of the content of the provisions in this Title has led to Art. 130q being repealed.

Article 130l

In implementing the multiannual framework programme the Community may make provision, in agreement with the Member States concerned, for participation in research and development programmes undertaken by several Member States, including participation in the structures created for the execution of those programmes.

Article 130m

In implementing the multiannual framework programme the Community may make provision for co-operation in Community research, technological development and demonstration with third countries or international organisations.

The detailed arrangements for such co-operation may be the subject of agreements between the Community and the third parties concerned, which shall be negotiated and concluded in accordance with Article 228.

Article 130n

The Community may set up joint undertakings or any other structure necessary for the efficient execution of Community research, technological development and demonstration programmes.

Article 130o

The Council, acting unanimously on a proposal from the Commission and after consulting the European Parliament and the Economic and Social Committee, shall adopt the provisions referred to in Article 130n.

The Council, acting in accordance with the procedure referred to in Article 189c and after consulting the Economic and Social Committee, shall adopt the provisions referred to in Articles 130j to 130l. Adoption of the supplementary programmes shall require the agreement of the Member States concerned.

Article 130p

At the beginning of each year the Commission shall send a report to the European Parliament and the Council. The report shall include information on research and technological development activities and the dissemination of results during the previous year, and the work programme for the current year.

GENERAL NOTE

This Article, added by the TEU, provides for the Commission to send a report to the European Parliament and the Council on the research and development programme.

Article 130q

(*repealed at Maastricht*)

TITLE XVI: Environment

GENERAL NOTE

Articles 130r to 130t E.C. on the environment are substantially amended. The environment, from being an area of Community action, is promoted to a Community policy. While the objectives of this policy remain substantially unaltered, attempts are made to include environmental considerations into other areas of Community competence (Art. 130r(2)). The principle of minimum harmonisation, applicable to the environment since its inclusion in the Treaties by the SEA, continues to be applicable. This principle dictates that the measures laid down by the Community with the aim of securing the goals under this heading shall not preclude the Member States from maintaining or introducing more stringent protective measures (Art. 130t E.C.). Such a provision is especially relevant as regards the environment, where levels of protection are manifestly different throughout the Member States and yet the most effective protection available is the common goal. A strict harmonising approach to the subject would lead to unattainable targets being set in certain Member States, while the more "developed" Member States would be forced to reduce the level of environmental protection previously enjoyed. Therefore, environmental protection measures were made subject to the doctrine of minimum harmonisation. The adverse effects which such an approach has on market uniformity are tempered somewhat by the requirements laid down, under Art. 130t, of Commission notification and compliance with the fundamental norms of the Community system. The necessity of such minimum harmonisation should be somewhat mitigated by the introduction of the Cohesion Fund to assist those countries to whom the fund is applicable, by enabling them to draw on the funds therein for environmental projects which would otherwise require them to incur disproportionate expenditure (Art. 130s(5) E.C.).

The existing environmental protection legislation enacted by the Community covers a vast range of areas and there is an ever growing corpus of Community law dealing with such matters. The Community is now active in the fields of aquatic environment, air pollution, noise abatement, control of chemicals, industrial hazards and biotechnology, conservation of the natural heritage, etc., (see Mathijsen, *supra*, p. 277). The Treaty amendments introduce the goal of securing the future sustainable growth of industry et al. (Art. 2 E.C.). The concept of sustainable growth seems to be used almost interchangeably with the notion of sustainable development as espoused in the Commission document "Towards Sustainability", E.C. Commission, Luxembourg, Office for Official Publications of the E.C. (1993). Sustainable development has been approved by the Heads of government and of State of the Community in a Declaration of June 26, 1990, and underlays the Treaty which emerged from the United Nations Conference on Environment and Development (UNCED) in Rio de Janeiro on June 3–14, 1992. Whatever approach the Community is to take, the vast majority of the legislative enactments in this field are in the form of directives, and the supervision of their implementation is one of the most demanding tasks placed upon the Commission. For an excellent analysis of the rate of national compliance with Community law in this sector see Macrory, The Enforcement of Community Environmental Laws: Some Critical Issues (1992) 29 C.M.L.Rev. 364 (see also House of Lords, Select Committee on the E.C., Implementation and enforcement of environmental legislation, 9th Report, Session 1991–1992). It is quite likely that the new principle of state responsibility enunciated in *Francovich and Boniface* v. *Italy* (Cases C–6/90 and 9/90, [1991] E.C.R. 5359 will prove most influential in this field. (See Murgatroyd, State Liability and the European Environment: Francovich, Maastricht and the question of compensation (1993) *Environmental Liability*, Vol. 1, pp. 11–15 and Crocket and Schultz, The Integration of environmental policy and the E.C.: Recent Problems of implementation and enforcement, 29 *Columbia Journal of Transnational Law*, 169–192).

Article 130r

1. Community policy on the environment shall contribute to pursuit of the following objectives:
   — preserving, protecting and improving the quality of the environment;
   — protecting human health;
   — prudent and rational utilisation of natural resources;

— promoting measures at international level to deal with regional or worldwide environmental problems.

2. Community policy on the environment shall aim at a high level of protection taking into account the diversity of situations in the various regions of the Community. It shall be based on the precautionary principle and on the principles that preventive action should be taken, that environmental damage should as a priority be rectified at source and that the polluter should pay. Environmental protection requirements must be integrated into the definition and implementation of other Community policies.

In this context, harmonisation measures answering these requirements shall include, where appropriate, a safeguard clause allowing Member States to take provisional measures, for non-economic environmental reasons, subject to a Community inspection procedure.

3. In preparing its policy on the environment, the Community shall take account of:

— available scientific and technical data;
— environmental conditions in the various regions of the Community;
— the potential benefits and costs of action or lack of action;
— the economic and social development of the Community as a whole and the balanced development of its regions.

4. Within their respective spheres of competence, the Community and the Member States shall co-operate with third countries and with the competent international organisations.

The arrangements for Community co-operation may be the subject of agreements between the Community and the third parties concerned, which shall be negotiated and concluded in accordance with Article 228.

The previous subparagraph shall be without prejudice to Member States' competence to negotiate in international bodies and to conclude international agreements.

GENERAL NOTE

The fourth indent of this Article is a new addition to the list of Community objectives in the field of the environment. It, however, does little more than entrench existing practice, with the express duty imposed on the Community to promote "measures at international level to deal with regional or world-wide environmental problems". This is quite in keeping with policies adopted by the Community in the numerous environmental measures promulgated both prior to and subsequent to the SEA. The Community has long recognised that environmental policy must take account of such trans-boundary problems as global warming, tropical deforestation, acid rain, etc. The Community has been a party to the majority of the international initiatives in these fields, *e.g.* the Convention on International Trade in Endangered Species of Wild Flora and Fauna ([1982] O.J. L384/1, modified [1989] O.J. L66/24); see also Art. 130r(4) E.C.

Para. (2)

Added to the first paragraph of this Article is the obligation that environmental protection requirements be integrated into the definition and implementation of other Community policies. This marks a realisation that environmental matters cannot be considered in isolation and signals a more dynamic integrative approach than that included in the old Art. 130r(2) E.E.C., which stated that "environmental protection requirements shall be a component of the Community's other policies". The new approach is evident in the recent Commission strategy on the common transport policy. Mirroring the current environmental buzz-words "sustainable growth", the common transport strategy is to be based on "sustainable mobility", whereby the new transport policy will aim to enhance the economic and social benefits of all means of transport whilst reducing their environmental impact (see COM (92) 48 final).

Para. (3)

This Article is unamended but, in the light of the new commitment to cohesion funding for the less developed regions of the Community, to assist with environmental projects, the second and fourth indents of this Article are given a new relevance.

Para. (4)

The old Art. 130r(4) E.E.C. is replaced by what was the old Art. 130r(5) E.E.C. The repealed provision contained an implicit reference to the principle of subsidiarity, stating that "the Community shall take action relating to the environment to the extent to which objectives referred to in para. 1 can be attained better at Community level". This Article has been replaced by the general notion of subsidiarity encompassed in Art. 3b E.C. Nevertheless, the principle included in the old Art. 130r(4) E.E.C. seems to have been worded in a manner more conducive to Community action. This Article presented the first bite of the legislative cherry to the Community, subject to the proviso that it should renounce its competence if it were proved that the action could be better achieved by the Member States. Under the new Art. 3b E.C., the burden is subtly altered with the insertion of the condition that the Community shall act, but only if and in so far as the objectives of the proposed action cannot be sufficiently achieved by the Member States. The words "only in so far as" and "sufficiently achieved" would seem to shift the presumption towards Member State action.

Article 130s

1. The Council, acting in accordance with the procedure referred to in Article 189c and after consulting the Economic and Social Committee, shall decide what action is to be taken by the Community in order to achieve the objectives referred to in Article 130r.

2. By way of derogation from the decision-making procedure provided for in paragraph 1 and without prejudice to Article 100a, the Council, acting unanimously on a proposal from the Commission and after consulting the European Parliament and the Economic and Social Committee, shall adopt:

— provisions primarily of a fiscal nature;

— measures concerning town and country planning, land use with the exception of waste management and measures of a general nature, and management of water resources;

— measures significantly affecting a Member State's choice between different energy sources and the general structure of its energy supply.

The Council may, under the conditions laid down in the preceding subparagraph, define those matters referred to in this paragraph on which decisions are to be taken by a qualified majority.

3. In other areas, general action programmes setting out priority objectives to be attained shall be adopted by the Council, acting in accordance with the procedure referred to in Article 189b and after consulting the Economic and Social Committee.

The Council, acting under the terms of paragraph 1 or paragraph 2 according to the case, shall adopt the measures necessary for the implementation of these programmes.

4. Without prejudice to certain measures of a Community nature, the Member States shall finance and implement the environment policy.

5. Without prejudice to the principle that the polluter should pay, if a measure based on the provisions of paragraph 1 involves costs deemed disproportionate for the public authorities of a Member State, the Council shall, in the act adopting that measure, lay down appropriate provisions in the form of:

— temporary derogations and/or

— financial support from the Cohesion Fund to be set up no later than 31 December 1993 pursuant to Article 130d.

GENERAL NOTE

This Article lays down the applicable legislative procedures for the adoption of Community measures in the field of environmental protection. The applicable procedure will depend on the specific type of measure envisaged. This Article, taken as a whole, is often given as an example of the convoluted legislative pattern introduced by the TEU amendments, with the existence of widely varying legislative procedures. In Art. 130s alone, there are three different legislative procedures available. This state of affairs will no doubt lead to challenges to the legal base, especially with all too predictable divergent interpretations. When the difference between procedures is the difference between being outvoted in Council or not, or alternatively in the case of the European Parliament, the difference between mere consultation and an actual say in the legislative measure, the stakes are undeniably raised.

Para. (1)
   This Article lays down the basic legislative procedure envisaged by the Treaty for the adoption of measures aimed at the securing of the objectives in Art. 130r. Such measures are to be adopted under the co-operation procedure, which opens up this area of environmental policy to the scope of qualified majority voting (previously unanimity under Art. 130s E.E.C.). This type of voting will apply to a wide variety of legislation, given the broad legislative base of Art. 130r.

Para. (2)
   This Article marks a significant broadening of the future scope of Community environmental action. The Community is to have the power to adopt measures under the three new headings listed. The most hotly debated heading was the first one, permitting the adoption of "provisions primarily of a fiscal nature". This refers to the potential imposition of so-called "energy taxes" aimed at the economic enforcement of prudent energy policies (see House of Lords, Select Committee on the E.C., Carbon/Energy Tax, 8th Report, Session 1991–1992). It has long been accepted that the most efficient means of securing alternative consumer and industry compliance with environmental guidelines is through the imposition of punitive taxation on harmful and less environmentally friendly practices. This view has been supported by the experience of a higher level of taxation on leaded petrol in the U.K., with the aim of transferring motorists to the more environmentally friendly lead free variety. The first indent of this Article makes provision for the imposition of such taxes on a Community scale and in a wide variety of areas.
   The inclusion of this provision marks the recognition that the achievement of the goal of "sustainability" cannot be done simply through the setting of limits on pollutants. The scope for financial legislation and broadened competences is necessary to achieve such a goal. Nevertheless, the sensitivity of this, and the other two areas under this heading, has led to their being made exceptions to the general qualified majority voting rule applicable to the other areas of environmental protection. The relevant procedure regarding the adoption of measures under these headings is unanimity in the Council following a Commission proposal; the European Parliament and the Economic and Social Committee are to be consulted on any such actions. Nevertheless, provision is made for the alteration to the qualified majority procedure for whichever of these headings the Council selects without the necessity of a further inter-governmental conference. The decision to make such a transferral is to be taken by unanimity under the procedure laid down for the adoption of measures in this field.

Para. (3)
   This Article makes provision for the adoption of general action programmes which will set out the priority objectives of the environmental policy. This is to be achieved under the conciliation and veto procedure. The specific action programmes to be adopted under this heading will be the subject of the procedures applicable by reference to paras. 1 and 2; therefore, if the measure concerns a fiscal provision then this will be dealt with by unanimity under para. 2, etc.

Article 130t

The protective measures adopted in common pursuant to Article 130s shall not prevent any Member State from maintaining or introducing more stringent protective measures. Such measures must be compatible with this Treaty. They shall be notified to the Commission.

GENERAL NOTE
   This Article lays down the notion of minimum harmonisation whereby the existence of Community protective measures shall not prevent any Member State from maintaining or introducing more stringent protective measures. While such provisions detract from the notion of uniformity in the common market, they do reflect the notion of subsidiarity, in that they envisage the development of different levels of regulatory competence in the Community (see Bieber, (1988) 13 E.L.Rev. 147). The measures taken by the Member States must however be compatible with the Treaty itself. This inevitably involves a balancing of the relative weights of the arguments on either side. This was highlighted in the "Danish bottle" case (Case 302/86) *E.C. Commission (supported by U.K., intervener)* v. *Denmark* [1988] E.C.R. 4607. See Sexton, Enacting national environmental laws more stringent than other States' laws in the European Community: Re Disposable Beer cans: *Commission* v. *Denmark, 24 Cornell Int. Law J.* 563–593.
   As with the pre-existing provision under the E.E.C. Treaty, each Member State is under an obligation to notify the Commission of national protective measures more stringent than the

underlying Community rule. This gives the Commission, the body which exercises the majority of executive responsibilities in this field, the opportunity to assess the compliance of such measures with the Treaties and advise the Member State accordingly.

TITLE XVII: Development Co-operation

GENERAL NOTE

Articles 130u–130y provide a specific legal base for policies currently carried out in various ad hoc ways. The object of such policies is laid down in Art. 130u(1) and it is provided that any actions by the Community in other policy areas must always take account of these factors and the effect its actions will have on the developing countries (Art. 130v). The primary means of achieving the goals set out is the negotiation of international agreements with the third countries concerned. Article 130y provides for a link with the amended Art. 228 E.C.

Article 130u

1. Community policy in the sphere of development co-operation which shall be complementary to the policies pursued by the Member States, shall foster:
   — the sustainable economic and social development of the developing countries, and more particularly the most disadvantaged among them;
   — the smooth and gradual integration of the developing countries into the world economy;
   — the campaign against poverty in the developing countries.
2. The Community policy in this area shall contribute to the general objective of developing and consolidating democracy and the rule of law, and to that of respecting human rights and fundamental freedoms.
3. The Community and the Member States shall comply with the commitments and take account of the objectives they have approved in the context of the United Nations and other competent international organisations.

GENERAL NOTE

Paragraph 1 of this Article provides that the action of the Community in this field is to be complementary to that of the Member States. The goals at which Community policy is to aim are then set out. Paragraph 2 lays out the political motivation for the achievement of these goals, such as the consolidation of democracy and respect for human rights. The pursuit of development co-operation prior to the completion of the TEU, in the main carried out under the Afro-Caribbean-Pacific conventions (see note on Art. 130y), always had the realisation of these goals set out in the relevant Treaties. In a joint declaration contained in Annex I to the final Act in the signature of the Third Lomé convention, the contracting parties reiterated their obligations in the field of human rights. As Kapteyn notes, in the absence of any sanction procedure (now incidentally provided by Art. 228a in the field of the common foreign and security policy), the inclusion of such duties will remain of purely verbal significance; certain of the contracting states have less than perfect human rights records (see Kapteyn, *supra*, pp. 833–835).

Article 130v

The Community shall take account of the objectives referred to in Article 130u in the policies that it implements which are likely to affect developing countries.

Article 130w

1. Without prejudice to the other provisions of this Treaty the Council, acting in accordance with the procedure referred to in Article 189c, shall adopt the measures necessary to further the objectives referred to in Article 130u. Such measures may take the form of multiannual programmes.
2. The European Investment Bank shall contribute, under the terms laid down in its Statute, to the implementation of the measures referred to in paragraph 1.
3. The provisions of this Article shall not affect co-operation with the African, Caribbean and Pacific countries in the framework of the ACP-EEC Convention.

GENERAL NOTE
The adoption of the measures to further the objectives of this title is to be by the co-operation procedure. Unusually, the Community is given the discretion as to whether or not the adoption of multi-annual programmes is the best means of achieving these goals. It is more than likely that some form of general programme will be laid down in this field. Paragraph 3 of this Article makes clear that the established Afro-Caribbean-Pacific–E.E.C. agreements will continue to be applicable.

Article 130x

1. The Community and the Member States shall co-ordinate their policies on development co-operation and shall consult each other on their aid programmes, including in international organisations and during international conferences. They may undertake joint action. Member States shall contribute if necessary to the implementation of Community aid programmes.

2. The Commission may take any useful initiative to promote the co-ordination referred to in paragraph 1.

GENERAL NOTE
This Article marks, arguably, the most important part of this title. It provides that the Member States will be obliged to co-ordinate their actions with each other and with the Community, as well as consulting each other on their aid programmes. Thus some form of "Community" action is ensured in all areas, irrespective of whether or not the Community has an agreement up and running in the area. Thus the Member States will be in a position to respond rapidly to any urgent situation without formal co-operation and this will serve to co-ordinate their actions and thus alleviate waste and unnecessary expense. The Member States are similarly required to co-ordinate their actions and consult each other in international bodies and negotiations. The Commission will exercise a general co-ordination rôle in this respect, the second paragraph empowering it to take any useful initiative in this field.

Article 130y

Within their respective spheres of competence, the Community and the Member States shall co-operate with third countries and with the competent international organisations. The arrangements for Community co-operation may be the subject of agreements between the Community and the third parties concerned, which shall be negotiated and concluded in accordance with Article 228.

The previous paragraph shall be without prejudice to Member States' competence to negotiate in international bodies and to conclude international agreements.

GENERAL NOTE
This Article primarily provides for the adoption of international agreements, with the purpose of securing the goals laid out in Art. 130u(1). This has been the most popular means of securing development co-operation prior to the inclusion of an explicit legal base in the Treaty. The best known of such international agreements are the three Lomé conventions which set the ground for the co-operation between the Community and the Afro-Caribbean-Pacific countries. The essential basis of these conventions is their provision for trade and commodities co-operation. The fourth Lomé convention took effect on March 1, 1990 and will continue in existence for double the period common to its predecessors, expiring in the year 2000 (first Lomé convention, [1976] O.J. L25/1; second, [1980] O.J. L347/1; third [1986] O.J. L 86/3; fourth, [1990] O.J. L84/4; see on these conventions, Simmonds, The Lomé Convention and the new international economic order, (1976) 13 C.M.L.Rev. 315–334; The Second Lomé Convention; the innovative features, (1980) 17 C.M.L.Rev. 99–120; The Third Lomé Convention, (1985) 22 C.M.L.Rev. 389–420; The Fourth Lomé Convention, (1991) 28 C.M.L.Rev., 521–547). Any renegotiation of this convention in the meantime will take place under the new Art. 228 procedure, which is explicitly referred to under this heading. The same procedure is applicable for any other development agreements entered into after the coming into force of the TEU.

PART FOUR (ASSOCIATION OF THE OVERSEAS COUNTRIES AND TERRITORIES)

Article 131

The Member States agree to associate with the Community the non-European countries and territories which have special relations with Belgium, Denmark, France, Italy, the Netherlands and the United Kingdom. These countries and territories (hereinafter called the 'countries and territories') are listed in Annex IV to this Treaty.

The purpose of association shall be to promote the economic and social development of the countries and territories and to establish close economic relations between them and the Community as a whole.

In accordance with the principles set out in the Preamble to this Treaty, association shall serve primarily to further the interests and prosperity of the inhabitants of these countries and territories in order to lead them to the economic, social and cultural development to which they aspire.

Article 132

Association shall have the following objectives:

1. Member States shall apply to their trade with the countries and territories the same treatment as they accord each other pursuant to this Treaty.

2. Each country or territory shall apply to its trade with Member States and with the other countries and territories the same treatment as that which it applies to the European State with which it has special relations.

3. The Member States shall contribute to the investments required for the progressive development of these countries and territories.

4. For investments financed by the Community, participation in tenders and supplies shall be open on equal terms to all natural and legal persons who are nationals of a Member State or of one of the countries and territories.

5. In relations between Member States and the countries and territories the right of establishment of nationals and companies or firms shall be regulated in accordance with the provisions and procedures laid down in the Chapter relating to the right of establishment and on a non-discriminatory basis, subject to any special provisions laid down pursuant to Article 136.

Article 133

1. Customs duties on imports into the Member States of goods originating in the countries and territories shall be completely abolished in conformity with the progressive abolition of customs duties between Member States in accordance with the provisions of this Treaty.

2. Customs duties on imports into each country or territory from Member States or from the other countries or territories shall be progressively abolished in accordance with the provisions of Articles 12, 13, 14, 15 and 17.

3. The countries and territories may, however, levy customs duties which meet the needs of their development and industrialisation or produce revenue for their budgets.

The duties referred to in the preceding subparagraph shall nevertheless be progressively reduced to the level of those imposed on imports of products from the Member State with which each country or territory has special relations. The percentages and the timetable of the reductions provided for under this Treaty shall apply to the difference between the duty imposed on a product coming from the Member State which has special relations with the country or territory concerned and the duty imposed on the same product coming from within the Community on entry into the importing country or territory.

4. Paragraph 2 shall not apply to countries and territories which, by reason of the particular international obligations by which they are bound, already apply a non-discriminatory customs tariff when this Treaty enters into force.

5. The introduction of or any change in customs duties imposed on goods imported into the countries and territories shall not, either in law or in fact, give rise to any direct or indirect discrimination between imports from the various Member States.

Article 134

If the level of the duties applicable to goods from a third country on entry into a country or territory is liable, when the provisions of Article 133(1) have been applied, to cause deflections of trade to the detriment of any Member State, the latter may request the Commission to propose to the other Member States the measures needed to remedy the situation.

Article 135

Subject to the provisions relating to public health, public security or public policy, freedom of movement within Member States for workers from the countries and territories, and within the countries and territories for workers from Member States, shall be governed by agreements to be concluded subsequently with the unanimous approval of Member States.

Article 136

For an initial period of five years after the entry into force of this Treaty, the details of and procedure for the association of the countries and territories with the Community shall be determined by an Implementing Convention annexed to this Treaty.

Before the Convention referred to in the preceding paragraph expires, the Council shall, acting unanimously, lay down provisions for a further period, on the basis of the experience acquired and of the principles set out in this Treaty.

Article 136a

The provisions of Articles 131 to 136 shall apply to Greenland, subject to the specific provisions for Greenland set out in the Protocol on special arrangements for Greenland, annexed to this Treaty.

PART FIVE (INSTITUTIONS OF THE COMMUNITY)

TITLE I: Provisions Governing the Institutions

Chapter 1 (The Institutions)

SECTION 1: The European Parliament

Article 137

The European Parliament, which shall consist of representatives of the peoples of the States brought together in the Community, shall exercise the powers conferred upon it by this Treaty.

GENERAL NOTE

The amendment to this Article marks an acknowledgement of the developing powers of the European Parliament. The introduction of the conciliation and veto procedure (Art. 189b E.C.), while far from perfect, marks the first time that the European Parliament has had the opportunity to veto legislation approved by the Council. The Maastricht Treaty has also strengthened or formalised the rôle of the Parliament in other areas, such as the appointment of the Commission. There is still, however, some distance to go before the democratic deficit in the Community is addressed: in other words, powers transferred from national parliaments to the European level are not yet subject to adequate control by a democratically elected body in the European legislative process (see European Parliament Report on the Democratic Deficit in the E.C., rapporteur M. Toussaint, European Parliament Document A2–276/87 and Lodge, *The Democratic Deficit and the European Parliament*, Fabian Society, 1991). The Maastricht amendments do however mark the greatest single increase in the powers of the European Parliament since the establishment of the Community. In this respect, the wording of the old Art. 137 E.E.C. alluding to the "advisory and supervisory powers" of the European Parliament was somewhat out of date. The new article reflects the broader scope of European Parliament influence, making reference simply to the "powers conferred upon it by this Treaty" (see Bradley, Better Rusty than Missin': The Institutional Reforms of the Maastricht Treaty and the European Parliament, in *Legal Issues of the Maastricht Treaty*, eds. O'Keefe and Twomey (1993)).

Article 138

(Paras. 1 and 2 as replaced by Direct Elections Act, Arts. 1 and 2)
1. The representatives in the European Parliament of the peoples of the States brought together in the Community shall be elected by direct universal suffrage.
2. The number of representatives elected in each Member State is as follows:

Belgium	24
Denmark	16
Germany	81
Greece	24
Spain	60
France	81
Ireland	15
Italy	81
Luxembourg	6
Netherlands	25
Portugal	24
United Kingdom	81

3. The European Parliament shall draw up proposals for elections by direct universal suffrage in accordance with a uniform procedure in all Member States.

The Council shall, acting unanimously after obtaining the assent of the European Parliament, which shall act by a majority of its component members, lay down the appropriate provisions, which it shall recommend to Member States for adoption in accordance with their respective constitutional requirements.

GENERAL NOTE
One amendment to this Article is made not by the TEU but by the decision taken at the Edinburgh European Council to increase the number of MEP's, primarily to take account of German reunification. Article 138(2) has been amended accordingly. The number of seats is now as follows (pre-Edinburgh summit figures in brackets): Belgium 25 (24); Denmark 16 (16); Germany 99 (81); Greece 25 (24); Spain 64 (60); France 87 (81); Ireland 15 (15); Italy 87 (81); Luxembourg 6 (6); Netherlands 31 (25); Portugal 25 (24) and U.K. 87 (81). (Conclusions of the Presidency point 26 and Decision of February 1, 1993, [1993] O.J. L33/15). A bill was introduced in the House of Lords on June 11, 1993 to give effect to the changes to the U.K. allocation of European Parliament seats. The European Parliamentary Elections Act 1993 received the Royal Assent on November 5, 1993. These changes have helped to give better representation to the more populous Member States. The smaller Member States are still significantly over-represented, on the ratio of MEP's to head of population. One significant aspect of the new allocation of MEP's is that Germany now has more of them than the other major states (France, Italy and U.K.). This reflects the fact that East Germany has been absorbed into Germany and needed to be represented in the European Parliament without diminishing West German

representation, and that unification had given Germany a population significantly larger than the three next largest Member States.

Para. (3)
The first sentence of para. (3) remains unchanged. The basic principle still remains that the European Parliament is to draw up proposals for elections by direct universal suffrage, in accordance with a uniform electoral procedure in all Member States. This is the sole Article in the Treaty giving the Parliament the right to propose legislative measures, a power otherwise almost exclusively vested in the Commission (however, see also Art. 138e(4) E.C. which provides that the European Parliament is to propose the detailed rules governing the ombudsman's duties).

The European Parliament has been attempting for years to put forward proposals acceptable in all Member States, but without success. The primary obstacle has been the U.K.'s refusal to accept any form of proportional representation. The latest development in the saga was the European Parliament Resolution on draft electoral procedure for the election of MEP's ([1993] O.J. C115/121). These proposals, put forward by the Dutch MEP, Karel de Gucht, call for the introduction into the U.K. (and similarly for all other Member States) of a limited form of proportional representation prior to the forthcoming European Parliament elections. The resolution simply adopts certain principles about the electoral procedure, rather than proposing a particular electoral system. This is justified as respecting the principle of subsidiarity. The two core features of the European Parliament's principles are proportional representation and some use, at least, of a list system. It is highly unlikely that any new electoral procedure will be adopted in time for the 1994 European Parliament elections.

The procedure for the eventual adoption of the electoral procedure was amended at Maastricht. Unanimity in the Council has been preserved, as well as the requirement that the Member States adopt the measure in accordance with their respective constitutional requirements. Under Art. 138(3) E.E.C., the European Parliament was given no formal rôle in the adoption of the measure; this has now been upgraded to a power of veto. The European Parliament must give its assent, acting by a majority of its component Members, to the procedure agreed by the Council.

Article 138a

Political parties at European level are important as a factor for integration within the Union. They contribute to forming a European awareness and to expressing the political will of the citizens of the Union.

GENERAL NOTE
This Article is a political declaration of intent more suited to inclusion in the preamble than in the body of the Treaty. The formation of truly European political parties standing on a uniform ticket throughout the Community in the European Parliament elections is seen as a major factor in increasing European awareness. The situation at present, with groupings of like-minded national parties coming together in the European Parliament is one step towards such an occurrence, but still represents the European Parliament as a place where national interests are vented as opposed to European ones.

Article 138b

In so far as provided in this Treaty, the European Parliament shall participate in the process leading up to the adoption of Community acts by exercising its powers under the procedures laid down in Articles 189b and 189c and by giving its assent or delivering advisory opinions.

The European Parliament may, acting by a majority of its members, request the Commission to submit any appropriate proposal on matters on which it considers that a Community act is required for the purpose of implementing this Treaty.

GENERAL NOTE
As with all of Arts. 138a–e E.C., this Article was added by the TEU, and marks a further limited improvement of the European Parliament's position in the legislative process. The first paragraph simply emphasises the new diverse rôle which the European Parliament is to play in the varying legislative procedures now available for the adoption of Community legislation.

The second paragraph is only comprehensible if one looks at the reasoning behind its inclusion in the Treaty. In the run-up to the inter-governmental conference, the European Parliament had called for a limited right of legislative initiative. One of the fundamental principles of the Community is that the Commission holds the monopoly of legislative initiative: the idea is that the Commission will act in accordance with the spirit of the Treaty in developing the Community in the interests of all the Member States, not just the larger ones. The European Parliament accepted this basic principle but asked for "the right to initiate legislative proposals in cases where the Commission fails to respond within a specified deadline to a specific request adopted by a majority of MEPs" ("Martin II" report, [1990] O.J. C231/97). This was strenuously opposed by the Commission, who saw it as the thin end of the wedge as regards its monopoly in this field. Thus, the present Article was drafted, whereby the European Parliament may request the Commission to submit a legislative proposal, but the European Parliament has no right to act should the Commission fail to take up the European Parliament's request. This gives the European Parliament a very similar right to that which the Council has always had under Art. 152 E.E.C./E.C., but marks little more than an entrenchment of the previously utilised mechanism of "own initiative reports" drawn up by the European Parliament. Nevertheless, these reports were generally aimed at publicity for a particular issue rather than any real push for legislative influence and were treated as such by the Commission. The more direct legislative power encompassed in this Article ought to focus the European Parliament more towards its legislative function, in keeping with its development under Maastricht. Rule 36B of the European Parliament's Rules of Procedure (as amended subsequent to the TEU, see [1993] O.J. C268/51) states that any resolution requesting the Commission to submit a legislative proposal must be based on an own-initiative report, state the legal basis for the measure and give detailed recommendations as to the content of the proposal. The Commission and the European Parliament have generally enjoyed a cordial relationship in the past; since March 1988 they have agreed upon the annual legislative timetable at the beginning of each year. The European Parliament thus has a degree of influence over the legislative proposals to be passed in that period. This influence will only have increased with the greater involvement of the European Parliament in the legislative process post-Maastricht. The threat of European Parliament rejection, or at least the delay, of certain proposals in what is always a full legislative calendar has never been measured but is likely to be substantial.

Article 138c

In the course of its duties, the European Parliament may, at the request of a quarter of its members, set up a temporary Committee of Inquiry to investigate, without prejudice to the powers conferred by this Treaty on other institutions or bodies, alleged contraventions or maladministration in the implementation of Community law, except where the alleged facts are being examined before a court and while the case is still subject to legal proceedings.

The temporary Committee of Inquiry shall cease to exist on the submission of its report.

The detailed provisions governing the exercise of the right of inquiry shall be determined by common accord of the European Parliament, the Council and the Commission.

GENERAL NOTE

This provision marks the formalisation of a pre-existing European Parliament power. Since the advent of direct elections the European Parliament has increasingly used such committees as a means of highlighting issues of political concern and bringing them into the spotlight for public scrutiny (*e.g.*, Report by the Committee of Inquiry into Racism and Xenophobia A3–0195/90 which led to a number of Council and Commission initiatives on the subject).

At present there is no obligation upon the members of national governments, the Council or Commission to appear before such committees. For the latter two bodies, attendance is the norm. Whether or not such attendance is to be made compulsory is important as regards the democratic scrutiny of the whole Union structure. Should the European Parliament acquire the right to require the members of, for example, the Political Committee under the justice and home affairs pillar to appear before its committees, this would be a major coup for parliamentary democracy at the European level. Whether or not this will take place is to be the subject of an inter-institutional agreement under Art. 138c, third indent, whereby the detailed rules governing the exercise of the right of inquiry are to be determined by the common accord of the institutions. (For the text of the Draft Act establishing the Procedures for Exercising the Right of Inquiry adopted by Common Accord of the Institutions see [1993] O.J. C21/147–151).

As was the case prior to the Maastricht Treaty, such a committee will be set up if requested by one-quarter of the members of the European Parliament (pre-Maastricht, see Rule 109/3 of the European Parliament Rules of Procedure). The avoidance of matters which are *sub judice*, respected tacitly prior to Maastricht, is now formalised. Subsequent to the coming into force of the TEU, a new Rule of Procedure, Rule 109A, regulates a temporary committee of inquiry, see [1993] O.J. C268/51.

Article 138d

Any citizen of the Union, and any natural or legal person residing or having its registered office in a Member State, shall have the right to address, individually or in association with other citizens or persons, a petition to the European Parliament on a matter which comes within the Community's fields of activity and which affects him, her or it directly.

GENERAL NOTE

The addition of the right of Union citizens and other natural or legal persons resident in a Member State to petition the European Parliament adds very little to current practice. This right has been available since 1953 (Rule 128 of European Parliament Rules of Procedure). Its constitutionalisation may well lead to greater use being made of a procedure that is becoming an increasingly popular means of redress by disaffected citizens (fewer than 100 in 1979 to approximately 800 by 1989, see Jacobs and Corbett, *The European Parliament*, p. 242). The increased popularity of this process led to the creation in 1987 of an European Parliament Committee with exclusive competence to hear petitions. The Petitions Committee prepares an annual report on its work which is submitted to the European Parliament for debate in plenary session.

The Treaty does not specify any remedy for cases found by the European Parliament to merit some form of consideration. Thus, the satisfaction of the individual's claim depends on the existence of pre-existing remedies under the Treaty. It has therefore been observed that: "as is the experience of petition committees in national parliaments, or ombudsmen, little can be done to help the petitioner" (Jacobs and Corbett, *supra*, p. 243). If the matter concerns a failure to implement Community law in a Member State, then the European Parliament may notify the Commission, or it can similarly communicate its findings to the relevant body. In one important respect, the right of petition can be seen to be having somewhat of an effect. As a direct result of petitions to the European Parliament, and the subsequent notification of the Commission, a relatively large number of Art. 169 E.E.C. proceedings have been initiated for failure of a Member State to comply with Community law. In session 1989–90 alone, eight Art. 169 proceedings were initiated as a result of petitions to the European Parliament (see Bradley (1990) 10 YEL 367, 384). The right of petition has also been supplemented by an inter-institutional agreement reached between the European Parliament, Council and Commission which encourages "Member States to give as clear and swift replies as possible to those questions which the Commission might decide, after due examination, to forward to the Member States concerned" (see Bradley (1989) 9 YEL 235, 251).

This right is given express enunciation under the new citizenship heading in the Treaty at Art. 8d E.C. This is somewhat deceptive, in that the right is available to a much broader group than Union citizens *per se*, including resident natural persons and legal persons with a statutory seat in a Member State. Any petition must come from a person with the requisite *locus standi*; the case must involve "matters affecting him, her or it directly".

The right to petition would seem to have been intentionally circumscribed to exclude petitions concerning the new inter-governmental pillars of the Union. Article 138d restricts the area of competence of petitions to "matters within the Community's fields of activity" (Closa, The Concept of Citizenship in the Treaty on European Union (1992) 29 C.M.L.Rev. 1137, at p. 1164).

Article 138e

1. The European Parliament shall appoint an Ombudsman empowered to receive complaints from any citizen of the Union or any natural or legal person residing or having its registered office in a Member State concerning instances of maladministration in the activities of the Community institutions or bodies, with the exception of the Court of Justice and the Court of First Instance acting in their judicial rôle.

In accordance with his duties, the Ombudsman shall conduct inquiries for which he finds grounds, either on his own initiative or on the basis of complaints submitted to him direct or through a member of the European Parliament, except where the alleged facts are or have been the subject of legal proceedings. Where the Ombudsman establishes an instance of maladministration, he shall refer the matter to the institution concerned, which shall have a period of three months in which to inform him of its views.

The Ombudsman shall then forward a report to the European Parliament and the institution concerned. The person lodging the complaint shall be informed of the outcome of such inquiries.

The Ombudsman shall submit an annual report to the European Parliament on the outcome of his inquiries.

2. The Ombudsman shall be appointed after each election of the European Parliament for the duration of its term of office. The Ombudsman shall be eligible for reappointment.

The Ombudsman may be dismissed by the Court of Justice at the request of the European Parliament if he no longer fulfils the conditions required for the performance of his duties or if he is guilty of serious misconduct.

3. The Ombudsman shall be completely independent in the performance of his duties. In the performance of those duties he shall neither seek nor take instructions from any body.

The Ombudsman may not, during his term of office, engage in any other occupation, whether gainful or not.

4. The European Parliament shall, after seeking an opinion from the Commission and with the approval of the Council acting by a qualified majority, lay down the regulations and general conditions governing the performance of the Ombudsman's duties.

GENERAL NOTE

This Article gives voice to the decision at Maastricht to set up the office of Community Ombudsman to investigate instances of maladministration within the Community bodies. This is included in the section on the European Parliament because the independent Ombudsman is to be appointed by the European Parliament. The Ombudsman has the power to act on his own initiative or at the instance of a direct complaint from a Union citizen or a legal entity or person resident in one of the Member States. Complaints may also be directed through an MEP. The Ombudsman will then conduct inquiries into the matter and, should any instance of maladministration be discovered, the institution concerned will be informed of the decision; the institution has a period of three months to inform the Ombudsman of its views. The Ombudsman then forwards a report to the European Parliament and to the institution concerned. The person lodging the complaint is to be informed of the outcome of these inquiries, but nowhere in the procedure is there any sanction envisaged for the discovery of an instance of maladministration. The only recourse will take place as a result of the institution concerned deciding to remedy the problem itself.

The Ombudsman lacks any punitive sanctioning power and any influence exercised will be based on extra-legal considerations, such as the institution's desire to avoid any adverse publicity on the matter, or its respect for the fairness of the Ombudsman's adjudication. Whether the office of Ombudsman will amount to a useful addition to the Community remains to be seen. The European Parliament itself is not confident; its committee on petitions views the move as "an unwarranted and unnecessary increase in bureaucracy in an area where various mechanisms for complaint are already in existence" European Parliament News, June 10–14, 1991. Its existence alongside the pre-existing right to address petitions to the European Parliament would appear to be somewhat of a duplication of effort, unless the complaint is against the European Parliament, which causes confusion to citizens wanting to make a valid complaint about some aspect of the Community.

The underlying basis of the Community Ombudsman appears very similar to U.K. practice in this sphere. Indeed, the U.K. championed the inclusion of the Community Ombudsman at the Maastricht summit; something requested by neither the European Parliament nor the Commission. Whether or not this amounts to a smoke screen to obscure the relatively marginal increases in the powers of the European Parliament to scrutinise and control the other Community institutions agreed to at Maastricht is open to question.

The detailed rules governing the performance of the Ombudsman's duties are to be proposed by the European Parliament. This it has done, in the Draft European Parliament Decision on the Regulations and General Conditions governing the Performance of the Ombudsman's Duties ([1993] O.J. C21/142–147). This dictates that, *inter alia*, the Community institutions shall be obliged to supply the Ombudsman with the information requested and give him access to the files concerned; refusal on the grounds of confidentiality is precluded (Art. 3(2)). A similar duty is applied to the Member States, and officials and servants of the Community are to appear before the Ombudsman at his request (Art. 3(3)). Other provisions provide for a close relationship between the Ombudsman and the European Parliament Petitions Committee, as well as co-operation with the national ombudsmen (Arts. 2 and 5 respectively). While no firm decision has been taken on the actual procedures to govern the Ombudsman (an inter-institutional agreement being required to lay down the definitive set of governing rules) recent developments are not promising as regards the powers of scrutiny sought by the European Parliament. It appears that the Council is opposed to the Ombudsman having access to confidential papers sent by the Member State governments to the Commission (Report of European Parliament/Council/Commission meeting of June 7, 1993, see E.C. Ministers insist on a Veil of Secrecy, *The Guardian*, June 10, 1993 and EP Resolution B3–1347/93, [1993] O.J. C268/165). The procedures for the appointment and dismissal of the Ombudsman are set out in Rules 130A and 130B of the European Parliament's Rules of Procedure, as amended subsequent to the TEU, [1993] O.J. C268/51. Rule 130c provides that the detailed powers of the Ombudsman are to be laid down in a special annex to the Parliament's Rules of Procedure. This will take place after an interinstitutional agreement has been reached.

Article 139

The European Parliament shall hold an annual session. It shall meet, without requiring to be convened, on the second Tuesday in March.

The European Parliament may meet in extraordinary session at the request of a majority of its members or at the request of the Council or of the Commission.

Article 140

The European Parliament shall elect its President and its officers from among its members.

Members of the Commission may attend all meetings and shall, at their request, be heard on behalf of the Commission.

The Commission shall reply orally or in writing to questions put to it by the European Parliament or by its members.

The Council shall be heard by the European Parliament in accordance with the conditions laid down by the Council in its rules of procedure.

Article 141

Save as otherwise provided in this Treaty, the European Parliament shall act by an absolute majority of the votes cast.

The rules of procedure shall determine the quorum.

Article 142

The European Parliament shall adopt its rules of procedure, acting by a majority of its members.

The proceedings of the European Parliament shall be published in the manner laid down in its rules of procedure.

Article 143

The European Parliament shall discuss in open session the annual general report submitted to it by the Commission.

Article 144

If a motion of censure on the activities of the Commission is tabled before it, the European Parliament shall not vote thereon until at least three days after the motion has been tabled and only by open vote.

If the motion of censure is carried by a two-third majority of the votes cast, representing a majority of the members of the European Parliament, the members of the Commission shall resign as a body. They shall continue to deal with current business until they are replaced in accordance with Article

158. In this case, the term of office of the members of the Commission appointed to replace them shall expire on the date on which the term of office of the members of the Commission obliged to resign as a body would have expired.

GENERAL NOTE

The power of the European Parliament to dismiss the whole Commission, by a vote of censure carried by a two-thirds majority, is retained under the Maastricht amendments. This power has never been used, although its use has been threatened on a number of occasions in the last year (an excellent example was the motion on the Commission's handling of the GATT negotiations with the U.S. on agricultural matters (B3–1676/92; for vote see O.J. [1993] C21/124)). As with all such motions in the past, it failed to secure the requisite majority; see Weatherill and Beaumont, *EC Law*, p. 85. Its non-use has a great deal to do with the fact that it amounts to a very blunt instrument; the European Parliament can only remove the whole Commission rather than individual Commissioners. The generally cordial nature of the relationship between these two bodies, both of which pursue essentially similar pro-European goals, means that the European Parliament is very rarely sufficiently dissatisfied with the Commission to prompt recourse to such a draconian sanction. Moreover, such an action would not make for such cordiality between the bodies in future. Another reason for the non-utilisation of this procedure may have been that there was nothing to stop the Member States appointing a new Commission with views equally opposed to the European Parliament's, or even consisting of the same, recently sacked, members; the only remedy would then be the dismissal of this "new" Commission and so on. It was highly unlikely that the Member States would have risked sparking such a prolonged period of appointment and dismissal of the Commission for fear of leaving the running of the Community in effective limbo. After the Maastricht amendments the European Parliament does have a rôle in the appointment process (see Art. 158(2) E.C.) but still lacks the key power to block the appointment of individual Commissioners.

The TEU adds a new last sentence to the second paragraph of this Article. This simply clarifies the position should the European Parliament actually successfully censure the Commission. It provides that the new Commission appointed to replace the Commission sacked by the European Parliament is appointed only for the remainder of the latter's term of office (see Art. 158 E.C.). This was also made necessary by the novel two year period to be served by the Commission appointed in 1993. It is to cease operation in 1995 to make way for the utilisation of a new investiture process. Any censure of the short-term Commission could not have been allowed to postpone the taking of office of the new Commission in 1995, as this date was selected specifically to ensure the tying together of the periods of office of the European Parliament and the Commission (see Art. 158 E.C.).

A Dutch proposal prior to the inter-governmental conference was that the European Parliament should be empowered to remove individual Commissioners, as opposed to the removal of the whole body (Letter from the Dutch Prime Minister, Mr Lubbers, to the Rome European Council meeting of December 12, 1990, see Laursen and Finn, *The Intergovernmental Conference on Political Union*, (1992), at p. 315). The aim of such a process would be to strengthen the accountability of the Commission to the European Parliament, a form of ministerial responsibility. It could, however, undermine the collegiate nature of the Commission and its commitment to collective responsibility. Interestingly, this proposal originated with the man who is a possible successor to Mr Delors as the next President of the Commission (*Financial Times*, November 5, 1992, p. 2). The proposal was nevertheless not taken up by the inter-governmental conference which chose instead to concentrate on the process of appointment of the Commission.

SECTION 2: The Council

Article 145

To ensure that the objectives set out in the Treaty are attained, the Council shall, in accordance with the provisions of this Treaty:
— ensure co-ordination of the general economic policies of the Member States;
— have power to take decisions;
— confer on the Commission, in the acts which the Council adopts, powers for the implementation of the rules which the Council lays down. The Council may impose certain requirements in respect of the exercise of these powers. The Council may also reserve the right, in specific

cases, to exercise directly implementing powers itself. The procedures referred to above must be consonant with principles and rules to be laid down in advance by the Council, acting unanimously on a proposal from the Commission and after obtaining the Opinion of the European Parliament.

Article 146

The Council shall consist of a representative of each Member State at ministerial level, authorised to commit the government of that Member State.

The office of President shall be held in turn by each Member State in the Council for a term of six months, in the following order of Member States:
— for a first cycle of six years: Belgium, Denmark, Germany, Greece, Spain, France, Ireland, Italy, Luxembourg, Netherlands, Portugal, United Kingdom,
— for the following cycle of six years: Denmark, Belgium, Greece, Germany, France, Spain, Italy, Ireland, Netherlands, Luxembourg, United Kingdom, Portugal.

GENERAL NOTE

The original Art. 146 E.E.C. was repealed by the Merger Treaty of April 8, 1965, which laid down similar rules with respect to the institutions existing separately at that time under the three Community Treaties. The newly added Art. 146 E.C. is essentially a reworded Art. 2 of the Merger Treaty.

The first paragraph of the new Article has caused something of a debate. Article 2 of the Merger Treaty provided that "The Council shall consist of representatives of the Member States. Each government shall delegate to it one of its members". The second sentence of Art. 2 of the Merger Treaty left it open to the Member States to send a member of the government. This implied a member of the national rather than the regional government but did not specify that the person was at ministerial level nor that he or she must be authorised to commit the national government of that State. It has been suggested that the broadened reference in the new Art. 146 to "a representative of each Member State at ministerial level" indicates that the Member States are not obliged to be represented at the national level. It has thus been interpreted as meaning that regional ministers could attend as a matter of course.

The second paragraph is also a reiteration of Art. 2 of the Merger Treaty, setting down the order in which the six-month Presidency is to rotate between the different Member States. Article 146, like its predecessor, lays down a slightly different order, running in two six-year cycles. This ensures that the same procession of Presidencies doesn't occur for at least 12 years. The change of Presidencies takes place on January 1 and July 1 every year.

Article 147

The Council shall meet when convened by its President on his own initiative or at the request of one of its members or of the Commission.

GENERAL NOTE

This Article replicates Art. 3 of the Merger Treaty and, as with several of the other Articles relating to the Council and to the Commission, reintegrates the material into the E.C. Treaty. On the Council in general see 51 Halsbury's Laws of England (4th ed.), paras. 1.78–1.83; Kapteyn, *The Law of European Communities*, pp. 103–141 and Weatherill and Beaumont, *EC Law*, Chap. 3.

Article 148

1. Save as otherwise provided in this Treaty, the Council shall act by a majority of its members.
2. Where the Council is required to act by a qualified majority, the votes of its members shall be weighted as follows:

Belgium	5
Denmark	3
Germany	10
Greece	5
Spain	8

France	10
Ireland	3
Italy	10
Luxembourg	2
Netherlands	5
Portugal	5
United Kingdom	10

For their adoption, acts of the Council shall require at least:
— 54 votes in favour where this Treaty requires them to be adopted on a proposal from the Commission,
— 54 votes in favour, cast by at least eight members, in other cases.

3. Abstentions by members present in person or represented shall not prevent the adoption by the Council of acts which require unanimity.

Article 149

(repealed at Maastricht)

Article 150

Where a vote is taken, any member of the Council may also act on behalf of not more than one other member.

Article 151

1. A committee consisting of the Permanent Representatives of the Member States shall be responsible for preparing the work of the Council and for carrying out the tasks assigned to it by the council.

2. The Council shall be assisted by a General Secretariat, under the direction of a Secretary-General. The Secretary-General shall be appointed by the Council acting unanimously.

The Council shall decide on the organisation of the General Secretariat.

3. The Council shall adopt its rules of procedure.

GENERAL NOTE

The original Art. 151 E.E.C. was repealed by the Merger Treaty of April 8, 1965; Art. 4 of which had formalised the rôle of COREPER in the Community set-up. Article 151 E.C. adds nothing new to current practice; para. 1 of the present Article is an exact replica of the existing Art. 4 of the Merger Treaty. Paragraph 2, on the other hand, gives Treaty status to the General Secretariat, the body of Community civil servants with the task of assisting the Council in its day to day work and providing a permanent service to the rotating presidency and the working groups thereunder. The provision in the present Article that the Secretary-General shall be appointed by the Council acting unanimously was in the Council's Rules of Procedure (see [1979] O.J. L268, as amended by [1987] O.J. L291, Art. 17(1)) as was the power of the Council to decide on the organisation of the General Secretariat (Art. 17(2)). The General Secretariat must be distinguished from COREPER, which consists of national civil servants/diplomats and operates in a manner analogous to the Council itself. It prepares the ground for Council meetings; a positive decision on a matter in the preceding COREPER meeting usually leads to its adoption at full Council without debate (see Weatherill and Beaumont, *supra*, pp. 72–73). The General Secretariat on the other hand, composed of Community civil servants, is not attributed such widespread powers. On COREPER and the General Secretariat generally see 51 Halsbury's Laws of England (4th ed.), para 1.82.

The Council adopted new Rules of Procedure by a Decision of December 6, 1993, [1993] O.J. L304/1, which entered into force on December 7, 1993. The Council styles itself the "Council of the European Union" (see Art. 13 of the Rules of Procedure). Article 6 specifies that the policy debates on the Presidency's six-month work programme will be televised, but that other debates will be televised only if unanimity is obtained in the Council. Another important development is that Art. 7(5) of the Rules prescribes in detail when the record of the votes in the Council will be made public.

Article 152

The Council may request the Commission to undertake any studies the Council considers desirable for the attainment of the common objectives, and to submit to it any appropriate proposals.

Article 153

The Council shall, after receiving an opinion from the Commission, determine the rules governing the committees provided for in this Treaty.

Article 154

The Council shall, acting by a qualified majority, determine the salaries, allowances and pensions of the President and members of the Commission, and of the President, Judges, Advocates General and Registrar of the Court of Justice. It shall also, again by a qualified majority, determine any payment to be made instead of remuneration.

GENERAL NOTE
This Article is a carbon copy of its predecessor, Art. 6 of the Merger Treaty. It is now restored to its proper place within the E.C. Treaty.

SECTION 3: The Commission

The Commission
The relevant Articles with regard to the Commission were in great need of attention, having been substantially altered by the provisions of the Merger Treaty. Articles 156 to 163 E.E.C., repealed by the Merger Treaty, are re-enacted with some modifications, although the rôle of the Commission post-Maastricht remains relatively unchanged. The primary amendment in the institutional sphere relates to its appointment (Art. 158 E.C.). On the Commission in general, see Weatherill and Beaumont, *supra*, Chap. 2 and, pre-Maastricht, Kapteyn, *supra*, Chap. 4.

Article 155

In order to ensure the proper functioning and development of the common market, the Commission shall:
— ensure that the provisions of this Treaty and the measures taken by the institutions pursuant thereto are applied;
— formulate recommendations or deliver opinions on matters dealt with in this Treaty, if it expressly so provides or if the Commission considers it necessary;
— have its own power of decision and participate in the shaping of measures taken by the Council and by the European Parliament in the manner provided for in this Treaty;
— exercise the powers conferred on it by the Council for the implementation of the rules laid down by the latter.

Article 156

The Commission shall publish annually, not later than one month before the opening of the session of the European Parliament, a general report on the activities of the Community.

GENERAL NOTE
Articles 156 to 163 E.E.C. were repealed by the Merger Treaty of 1965 and replaced by the detailed provisions enclosed in the latter document. The re-enactment of these Articles by the TEU marks an attempt at greater clarity in the provisions governing the operation of the Commission. This has been achieved to a great extent by the movement of the pertinent provisions of the Merger Treaty back into the body of the E.C. Treaty.
   The present Art. 156 E.C. is an example of this; simply inserting Art. 18 of the Merger Treaty into the new E.C. Treaty. Its insertion thus has no effect upon current practice; the Commission is required to publish an annual general report on the activities of the Community, at least one month before the opening session of the European Parliament.

Article 157

1. The Commission shall consist of 17 members, who shall be chosen on the grounds of their general competence and whose independence is beyond doubt.

The number of members of the Commission may be altered by the Council, acting unanimously.

Only nationals of Member States may be members of the Commission.

The Commission must include at least one national of each of the Member States, but may not include more than two members having the nationality of the same State.

2. The members of the Commission shall, in the general interest of the Community, be completely independent in the performance of their duties.

In the performance of these duties, they shall neither seek nor take instructions from any government or from any other body. They shall refrain from any action incompatible with their duties. Each Member State undertakes to respect this principle and not to seek to influence the members of the Commission in the performance of their tasks.

The members of the Commission may not, during their term of office, engage in any other occupation, whether gainful or not. When entering upon their duties they shall give a solemn undertaking that, both during and after their term of office, they will respect the obligations arising therefrom and in particular their duty to behave with integrity and discretion as regards the acceptance, after they have ceased to hold office, of certain appointments or benefits. In the event of any breach of these obligations, the Court of Justice may, on application by the Council or the Commission, rule that the member concerned be, according to the circumstances, either compulsorily retired in accordance with Article 160 or deprived of his right to a pension or other benefits in its stead.

GENERAL NOTE

This Article essentially reiterates Art. 10 of the Merger Treaty. The Commission is declared to consist of 17 members, chosen on the grounds of general competence rather than specialist expertise. The number of Commissioners may be altered by the Council, acting unanimously. The issue of the number of Commissioners has surfaced recently, particularly in the debates over the enlargement of the Community. A proposal to the inter-governmental conference that the number of Commissioners be reduced from 17 to 12 (*i.e.* one per Member State) was postponed but will no doubt have to be addressed again in the near future in the negotiation of accession agreements with new Member States. The Treaty still includes the proviso that the Commission "must include at least one national of each of the Member States" and not more than two from one Member State, but a declaration appended to the TEU states that a review of the number of Commissioners (and of MEPs) will begin "no later than the end of 1992" and be completed prior to the 1994 elections (Declaration No.15). The U.K. has long supported the principle of one Commissioner per Member State; also advocated by Jacques Delors, but the U.K. would seem to be alone among the larger Member States in adopting this stance (Economist Intelligence Unit, European Trends No. 4 1991, at pp. 84–85). It is quite possible that even one Commissioner per Member State will become untenable by around the end of the decade. Two waves of new members are envisaged; the European Free Trade Association states in the second half of the decade and the Central European States after the year 2000. After the latter have joined, membership will rise to around 20 and this excludes other potential applicants, such as the Baltic States, and some of the existing applicants, like Malta, Cyprus and Turkey. The effects throughout the institutional structure of the Community will be manifest; a prime difficulty is the number of working languages which would be necessitated, given the expense at present of maintaining the existing official languages. It is possible that the situation will eventually be reached where the Commissioner chairs are passed in rotation between the Member States, perhaps with the larger states having a guaranteed appointee and the smaller states figuring in the rotation (as in the appointment of Advocates General to the E.C.J.). This could be looked at by the next inter-governmental conference in 1996. (On the problem in general see; Ungerer, Institutional Consequences of Broadening and Deepening the Community, (1993) 30 C.M.L.Rev. 71–83).

The remainder of Art. 157(1) lays down the conditions for the post of Commissioner. These are not based on any professional qualification, but simply on a nationality criteria. The notion of Union citizenship does not seem to have percolated into the institutional provisions; the simple requirement that the Commissioners be nationals of a Member State is retained.

Article 157(2) lays down the principles enjoining the Commissioners' independence in the performance of their duties. The Member States are to undertake to respect this principle. To further ensure their independence, the Commissioners are prohibited from engaging in any other occupation during their period of office. The duties continue after their term ends, with the obligation that they "behave with integrity and discretion". Any breach of these duties could lead to compulsory retirement or, alternatively, the suspension of any pension or other post-employment rights. The former sanction is to be carried out in accordance with the procedure enunciated in Art. 160 E.C. (previously Art. 13 of the Merger Treaty). It is highly likely that the decision to suspend the pension rights of an ex-Commissioner would be similarly carried out under the "serious misconduct" procedure of Art. 160 E.C. There has not yet been an example of such an action.

Article 158

1. The members of the Commission shall be appointed, in accordance with the procedure referred to in paragraph 2, for a period of five years, subject, if need be, to Article 144.

Their term of office shall be renewable.

2. The governments of the Member States shall nominate by common accord, after consulting the European Parliament, the person they intend to appoint as President of the Commission.

The governments of the Member States shall, in consultation with the nominee for President, nominate the other persons whom they intend to appoint as members of the Commission.

The President and the other members of the Commission thus nominated shall be subject as a body to a vote of approval by the European Parliament. After approval by the European Parliament, the President and the other members of the Commission shall be appointed by common accord of the governments of the Member States.

3. Paragraphs 1 and 2 shall be applied for the first time to the President and the other members of the Commission whose term of office begins on 7 January 1995.

The President and the other members of the Commission whose term of office begins on 7 January 1993 shall be appointed by common accord of the governments of the Member States. Their term of office shall expire on 6 January 1995.

GENERAL NOTE

Prior to the Maastricht inter-governmental conference, the European Parliament had called for a rôle in the appointment of the Commission, something which was lacking in the existing Treaties. The Martin report to the inter-governmental conference requested that the European Parliament have the power to elect the President of the European Commission, acting on a proposal of the European Council (European Parliament Doc A3–166/90; [1990] O.J. C231 p.97). Such an election would come about immediately after the European Parliamentary elections, allowing the electorate to see a direct result of their vote in the composition of the executive. In order to make this feasible, it was proposed that the term of office of the Commission be increased from four to five years and chronologically linked to the parliamentary term.

The agreement reached at Maastricht followed the European Parliament's wishes, in that the Commission's term of office is to be altered to five years to link with that of the European Parliament. This means that the Commission appointed in January 1993 will serve only a two-year period of office (Art. 158(3) E.C.). The new procedure will come into force after the European elections in the summer of 1994. The new Commission will then take office from January 7, 1995. The delay between the European Parliament elections and the investiture of the new Commission has advantages and drawbacks. In practical terms, it permits the use of the autumn months to go through the new procedures. On the other hand, it distances the vote in the European elections from the appointment of the Commission. Whether or not this was an intention of the Member States negotiating at Maastricht is unclear. The slightly increased democratic legitimisation of the Commission weakens the claim that the Commission is the unaccountable bureaucracy of the Communities.

Instead of the right to elect the President of the Commission, the European Parliament has gained the right to be consulted on his/her appointment. However, Corbett, among others, takes the view that such "consultation" is, in effect, tantamount to an election. Any person nominated by the Member States would be very reluctant to take up office in the face of rejection by an elected body with which he or she would have to work closely (Corbett, The Inter-governmental Conference on Political Union, (1992) *Journal of Common Market Studies* XXX, at p. 294). In practice, the Enlarged Bureau of the European Parliament has been consulted on the appointment of a new Commission President (see Weatherill and Beaumont, *supra*, p. 82). The European Parliament has amended its Rules of Procedure subsequent to the TEU (see [1993] O.J. C268/51). The Enlarged Bureau has been replaced by the Conference of Presidents (Rule 23), *i.e.* the President of the Parliament and the chairmen of the political groups. Rule 29 now governs the procedure for the appointment of the Commission President. The nominee will be invited to make a statement to the Parliament, and this will be followed by a vote where a single majority of the votes cast is sufficient. It is difficult to imagine the Governments appointing the nominee, or that person continuing to seek appointment, in the face of an adverse vote in the European Parliament.

The other proposal of the European Parliament which was taken up at Maastricht was the formalisation of the vote of confidence in the Commission as a whole after its appointment by the common accord of the Member States (Art. 158(2), third indent). Since 1982, the European Parliament has held a debate and a vote of confidence on the incoming Commission when it presents itself to the European Parliament with its legislative programme. This was recognised by the national governments in the Stuttgart Solemn Declaration on European Union of 1983 (see [1983] 6 E.C. Bull. 26, pt. 2.3.5) and the Delors Commissions have waited until they received this vote of confidence before taking their oath of office before the E.C.J. This is an important gesture on the part of the Commission and strengthens the public perception of the European Parliament. The result of a "no" vote in the European Parliament is not explicitly laid out but the wording of Art. 158(3) makes it apparent that the appointment of the President and other members of the Commission may only take place after such a positive vote is forthcoming. Rule 29A of the Parliament's Rules of Procedure (see [1993] O.J. C268/51) provides that the persons nominated to serve on the Commission will be invited to appear before the "appropriate committees according to their prospective fields of responsibility". The committees of Parliament involved in this process would report to the Parliament before it votes on whether to approve the Commission as a whole by a majority of the votes cast. It will be interesting to see whether Commission nominees subject themselves to scrutiny by the appropriate committees of Parliament. They are not obliged to do so, but the implied threat of the Rules of Procedure is that the Commission as a whole will not be approved if nominees do not submit to a hearing before the relevant committee. Another element of this system is that it presupposes that the portfolios of the new members of the Commission will be agreed while they are still simply the nominees of their governments. The European Parliament cannot compel the nascent Commission to do this unless it is prepared to vote against approving the Commission over this issue.

This new two-tier investiture process thus marks both a formalisation and a strengthening of the rôle of the European Parliament in the appointment of the Commission. Nevertheless, the Member States were reluctant to allow the Commission's appointment to be drawn any further from their influence. This could be seen in the rejection of the European Parliament's proposal that the President-elect of the Commission be engaged in a joint decision-making process with the Member States as to the selection of the other members of the Commission. Instead, the President-elect will be consulted on the incoming Commissioners, but no more (this merely confirms existing practice, Weatherill and Beaumont, *supra*, p. 42, and Van Miert, (1973) 10 C.M.L.Rev. 257). This shows that, despite Treaty declarations as to the obligation on the Member States not to seek to influence the members of the Commission in the performance of their duties (Merger Treaty Art. 10(2), now Art. 157(2), second indent), these Member States are reluctant to lessen their hold over the appointment of individual Commissioners. While opinions as to their independence varies, there can be little doubt that Commissioners' ideologies play a very large part in their appointment and reappointment, as each Member State can identify its own criteria of selection. The ability of Member States to reappoint Commissioners (retained in Art. 158(1), second indent) entails the risk that the Member States will fail to reappoint Commissioners who are no longer in favour, as opposed to exercising this discretion on more satisfactory grounds, such as diminished administrative ability (the refusal of Mrs Thatcher to reappoint Lord Cockfield as one of the U.K. Commissioners is the most oft-cited example of the potential for misuse of this provision, see Lodge, The European Parliament, *The Parliamentarian*, Vol. 70, at p. 74 and George, *An Awkward Partner: Britain in the European Community* (1990, Clarendon Press), p. 197). The non-renewable term of employment of the European Central Bank executive board signals the direction which perhaps ought to have been followed. On the other side of the coin, this would entail the enforced loss of valuable and skilled Commissioners after a certain period, regardless of their ability. (See Kapteyn, *supra*, p. 111 and Weatherill and Beaumont, *supra*, pp. 38–39).

Article 159

Apart from normal replacement, or death, the duties of a member of the Commission shall end when he resigns or is compulsorily retired.

The vacancy thus caused shall be filled for the remainder of the member's term of office by a new member appointed by common accord of the governments of the Member States. The Council may, acting unanimously, decide that such a vacancy need not be filled.

In the event of resignation, compulsory retirement or death, the President shall be replaced for the remainder of his term of office. The procedure laid down in Article 158(2) shall be applicable for the replacement of the President.

Save in the case of compulsory retirement under the provisions of Article 160, members of the Commission shall remain in office until they have been replaced.

GENERAL NOTE

Previously Art. 12 of the Merger Treaty, Art. 159 E.C. lays down the procedure should any of the Commissioners die, resign or be dismissed (compulsorily retired). The vacancy thus created shall be filled for the remainder of the member's term of office by a new member, appointed by the common accord of the Member States. The Council could, if agreed to unanimously, decide not to fill the vacancy. In the absence of a subsequent unanimous decision that the number of Commissioners remain permanently reduced, this vacancy would have to be filled when the new Commission took office.

Article 160

If any member of the Commission no longer fulfils the conditions required for the performance of his duties or if he has been guilty of serious misconduct, the Court of Justice may, on application by the Council or the Commission, compulsorily retire him.

GENERAL NOTE

This Article was previously Art. 13 of the Merger Treaty and its substance is unchanged. In order to ensure the independence of the Commission, there are only two means of removing Commissioners against their will. The first is through an European Parliament motion of censure under Art. 144 E.C. The other is provided for in the present Article, and is the only means by which an individual Commissioner may be removed. The Court of Justice, acting on an application by the Commission or the Council, may decide to remove a Commissioner "if he no longer fulfils the conditions required for the performance of his duties or if he has been guilty of serious misconduct". This provision has been utilised only once, to replace a critically and terminally ill Commissioner (see Decision 76/619 [1976] O.J. L201/31). The phrase "serious misconduct" has yet to be tested.

Article 161

The Commission may appoint a Vice-President or two Vice-Presidents from among its members.

GENERAL NOTE

This Article marks an alteration to the Merger Treaty provision, which required the appointment of six vice-presidents of the Commission (Art. 14 as amended by the Act of Accession (1985), which provided that the Council could, acting by a unanimous vote, amend the number of vice-presidents). The present Article alludes simply to the potential appointment of up to two Commission vice-presidents. Notwithstanding this provision, the Council has recently appointed six vice-presidents under Art. 14 of the Merger Treaty, with the proviso that they serve until the TEU enters into force or until January 5, 1995 at the latest (Council Decision 93/382 [1993] O.J. L164/11). The provision agreed at Maastricht recognised the reality of the situation that no more than two people are needed to deputise for the President in chairing Commission meetings.

Article 162

1. The Council and the Commission shall consult each other and shall settle by common accord their methods of co-operation.

2. The Commission shall adopt its rules of procedure so as to ensure that both it and its departments operate in accordance with the provisions of this Treaty. It shall ensure that these rules are published.

GENERAL NOTE

This Article simply reiterates the provisions of Arts. 15 and 16 of the Merger Treaty in paras. one and two of the present Article respectively.

In common with the other major political institutions of the Community (the European Parliament and the Council), the Commission is empowered to adopt its own rules of procedure. This is a major power and permits the adoption of the most favourable conditions possible under the leeway afforded by the Treaty itself. The European Parliament has proven most adept at manipulating this restricted freedom to its best effect. The Commission's current rules of procedure are published as the Provisional Rules of Procedure of July 6, 1967 ([1967] O.J. Spec. ed. 2nd. Ser. (VII) 14), subsequently much amended, see Toth, *The Oxford Encyclopaedia of Community Law*, 67–68. These rules of procedure must be adhered to. In *BASF AG* v. *Commission*, Art. 12 of the Rules of Procedure, which requires the original text of Commission measures to be annexed to the minutes in which their adoption was recorded, was not complied with in adopting Commission Decision 89/190. The Commission was unable to produce an authenticated version of the decision, which was then declared non-existent by the Court of First Instance (joined cases T–79/89, T–84–6/89, T89/89, T91/2–89, T94/89, T96/89, T98/89, T102/89 and T104/89, judgment of February 27, 1992, *The Times*, March 25, 1992). The Commission has appealed to the E.C.J. and Advocate General Van Gerven has recommended to the Court that the Court of First Instance decision should be overturned (case C–137/92, proceedings of the E.C.J., No.21/93).

Article 163

The Commission shall act by a majority of the number of members provided for in Article 157.

A meeting of the Commission shall be valid only if the number of members laid down in its rules of procedure is present.

GENERAL NOTE

This Article relates to the normal working procedures of the Commission (repeating identical Art. 17 of the Merger Treaty). The Commission acts collectively by simple majority vote. This is the case whatever function it is exercising, be it executive or legislative. All Commissioners have an equal standing and weight in the voting process (see 51 *Halsbury's Laws of England* (4th ed.), para 1.91).

SECTION 4: The Court of Justice

Amendments to the institutional structure of the E.C.J. are relatively minimal. The greatest alteration arises under Art. 171(2) E.C. whereby the E.C.J. acquires the right to impose fines on Member States who fail to fulfil their obligations under the Treaty. This is a fundamental innovation and gives the E.C.J. unlimited discretion to apply penalties for non-compliance. Another major change is a widening of the category of case that the Council can decide to transfer from the jurisdiction of the E.C.J. to the Court of First Instance (Art. 168a E.C.). Other alterations to the rôle of the E.C.J. may well result from the coming into force of the TEU. These will not be factors directly aimed at the E.C.J. but which will arise out of its interpretative jurisdiction. Sooner or later the E.C.J. will have to rule on subsidiarity challenges. It will probably also have to deal with the thorny implications of the U.K. opt-out from the Social Policy Agreement appended to the Treaty. That the E.C.J. will accept such an overtly constitutional rôle was made all the more likely by its 1991 Opinion on the E.C./European Free Trade Association Agreement on the European Economic Area. The E.C.J. found this agreement incompatible with the existing Community legal system, and thereby unconstitutional (see Opinion 1/91 [1992] 1 C.M.L.R. 245). The result of this decision was the revision and postponement of the European Economic Area agreement (see (1992) 29 C.M.L.Rev. 991–1009).

Article 164

The Court of Justice shall ensure that in the interpretation and application of this Treaty the law is observed.

Article 165

The Court of Justice shall consist of 13 Judges.

The Court of Justice shall sit in plenary session. It may, however, form chambers, each consisting of three or five Judges, either to undertake certain preparatory inquiries or to adjudicate on particular categories of cases in accordance with rules laid down for these purposes. The Court of Justice shall sit in plenary session when a Member State or a Community institution that is a party to the proceedings so requests. Should the Court of Justice so request, the Council may, acting unanimously, increase the number of Judges and make the necessary adjustments to the second and third paragraphs of this Article and to the second paragraph of Article 167.

GENERAL NOTE

The amendment to the third indent of this Article marks a "watering down" of the mandatory requirement that the E.C.J. should meet in plenary session in cases brought by a Member State or a Community institution. The new Art. 165 E.C. provides that seven to 13 judges need only convene in such cases if so requested by the Member State or Community institution concerned. This power to request a plenary session is, however, extended by Art. 165 E.C. to instances where the case is against a Member State or Community institution. This is a regrettable decrease in the ability of the E.C.J. to reduce its backlog of cases by using a Chamber rather than a plenary session. The aim should be to prevent the time wasted in an already crowded schedule when seven to 13 judges are called upon to sit in, for example, a case against a Member State for failure to comply with its Community law obligations, where no defence of substance is lodged. Such cases are better dealt with by a chamber of three or five judges, as more than one chamber can then sit at a time. Unfortunately, Art. 95(2) of the revised E.C.J. Rules of Procedure ([1991] O.J. L176/7) permits a Member State or Community institution to insist on a plenary session of the E.C.J. even where they are only intervening in the case or making written observations in a preliminary ruling.

Article 166

The Court of Justice shall be assisted by six Advocates General.

It shall be the duty of the Advocate-General, acting with complete impartiality and independence, to make, in open court, reasoned submissions on cases brought before the Court of Justice, in order to assist the Court in the performance of the task assigned to it in Article 164.

Should the Court of Justice so request, the Council may, acting unanimously, increase the number of Advocates General and make the necessary adjustments to the third paragraph of Article 167.

Article 167

The Judges and Advocates General shall be chosen from persons whose independence is beyond doubt and who possess the qualifications required for appointment to the highest judicial offices in their respective countries or who are jurisconsults of recognised competence; they shall be appointed by common accord of the Governments of the Member States for a term of six years.

Every three years there shall be a partial replacement of the Judges. Seven and six Judges shall be replaced alternately.

Every three years there shall be a partial replacement of the Advocates General. Three Advocates General shall be replaced on each occasion.

Retiring Judges and Advocates General shall be eligible for reappointment.

The Judges shall elect the President of the Court of Justice from among their number for a term of three years. He may be re-elected.

Article 168

The Court of Justice shall appoint its Registrar and lay down the rules governing his service.

Article 168a

1. A Court of First Instance shall be attached to the Court of Justice with jurisdiction to hear and determine at first instance, subject to a right of appeal

to the Court of Justice on points of law only and in accordance with the conditions laid down by the Statute, certain classes of action or proceeding defined in accordance with the conditions laid down in paragraph 2. The Court of First Instance shall not be competent to hear and determine questions referred for a preliminary ruling under Article 177.

2. At the request of the Court of Justice and after consulting the European Parliament and the Commission, the Council, acting unanimously, shall determine the classes of action or proceeding referred to in paragraph 1 and the composition of the Court of First Instance and shall adopt the necessary adjustments and additional provisions to the Statute of the Court of Justice. Unless the Council decides otherwise, the provisions of this Treaty relating to the Court of Justice, in particular the provisions of the Protocol on the Statute of the Court of Justice, shall apply to the Court of First Instance.

3. The members of the Court of First Instance shall be chosen from persons whose independence is beyond doubt and who possess the ability required for appointment to judicial office; they shall be appointed by common accord of the governments of the Member States for a term of six years. The membership shall be partially renewed every three years. Retiring members shall be eligible for reappointment.

4. The Court of First Instance shall establish its rules of procedure in agreement with the Court of Justice. Those rules shall require the unanimous approval of the Council.

GENERAL NOTE

This Article, inserted by the SEA, provides for the creation and subsequent operation of the new Court of First Instance attached to the E.C.J. The Council, acting on the basis of this Article, made provision for the setting up of the Court of First Instance on October 24, 1988 (see Decision 88/591, [1988] O.J. L319/1 and [1989] O.J. C215/1 (corrected version)).

In the original Art. 168a E.E.C., the jurisdiction of the Court of First Instance was to be determined by the Council, but specifically excluded actions brought by Member States or Community institutions, and questions referred for preliminary rulings under Art. 177. Such cases account for about two-thirds of the E.C.J.'s case-load. Within the limited area of the E.C.J.'s jurisdiction which could be transferred to the Court of First Instance, the Council decided not to transfer jurisdiction in cases brought by legal entities or persons under Arts. 173 and 175 relating to measures to protect trade within the meaning of Art. 113 of the Treaty in the case of dumping and subsidies. The E.C.J. had requested that the Court of First Instance be given such jurisdiction, but the Council merely promised to re-examine the E.C.J.'s proposal after two years of operation of the Court of First Instance (Decision 88/591, Art. 3(3)). The Council did confer jurisdiction upon the Court of First Instance in relation to staff cases (*i.e.* disputes between servants of the Community and its institutions under Art. 179) and in actions brought against a Community institution by natural or legal persons under Arts. 173 and 175 E.E.C. relating to the implementation of competition rules as regards undertakings.

In the run-up to the Maastricht inter-governmental conference, the Court of First Instance suggested that "a point has been reached beyond which, unless care is taken, the law's delays will be such as to discourage those who seek the law's protection" (see Reflections on the Future Development of the Community Judicial System (1991) 16 E.L.Rev. 175). The Court of First Instance, set up to alleviate some of the burden on the E.C.J., had not had sufficient effect; the average length of proceedings before the E.C.J. in preliminary rulings was 17.5 months in 1988 and 18.5 months in 1991. In direct actions, the figures were even worse: 23.7 months in 1988 and 24.2 months in 1991. It was therefore agreed at Maastricht to amend Art. 168a E.C., whereby the Council, acting unanimously on a request from the European Court and after consulting the Commission and the European Parliament, can transfer any area of the E.C.J.'s jurisdiction to the Court of First Instance, except for preliminary rulings under Art. 177. The E.C.J. attaches a great deal of importance to Art. 177, because it is the mechanism by which it can ensure the uniform application of Community law. In Council Decision 93/350 (amending 88/591), the Council has conferred jurisdiction on the Court of First Instance in all direct actions concerning legal entities or persons (Art. 1 of the Decision; [1993] O.J. L144/21 to take effect from August 1, 1993) except that the jurisdiction in anti-dumping and subsidy cases shall remain with the E.C.J., subject to a future unanimous vote to transfer such competences. On September 27, 1993, 515 cases were transferred from the E.C.J. to the Court of First Instance as a consequence of Decision 93/350. The vast majority of the cases relate to the non-contractual liability of the Community arising from, and/or the illegality of, Community measures concerning milk quotas.

On the Court of First Instance in general see: Weatherill and Beaumont, *EC Law*, pp. 158–164; Due, The Court of First Instance (1987) 7 YEL 1; Kennedy, The Essential Minimum: The Establishment of the Court of First Instance, (1989) 14 E.L.Rev. 7; Vesterdorf, The Court of First Instance of the E.C. after Two Full Years in Operation, (1992) 29 C.M.L.Rev. 897 and Millett, *The Court of First Instance*, Butterworths, 1990.

Article 169

If the Commission considers that a Member State has failed to fulfil an obligation under this Treaty, it shall deliver a reasoned opinion on the matter after giving the State concerned the opportunity to submit its observations.

If the State concerned does not comply with the opinion within the period laid down by the Commission, the latter may bring the matter before the Court of Justice.

Article 170

A Member State which considers that another Member State has failed to fulfil an obligation under this Treaty may bring the matter before the Court of Justice.

Before a Member State brings an action against another Member State for an alleged infringement of an obligation under this Treaty, it shall bring the matter before the Commission.

The Commission shall deliver a reasoned opinion after each of the States concerned has been given the opportunity to submit its own case and its observations on the other party's case both orally and in writing.

If the Commission has not delivered an opinion within three months of the date on which the matter was brought before it, the absence of such opinion shall not prevent the matter from being brought before the Court of Justice.

Article 171

1. If the Court of Justice finds that a Member State has failed to fulfil an obligation under this Treaty, the State shall be required to take the necessary measures to comply with the judgment of the Court of Justice.

2. If the Commission considers that the Member State concerned has not taken such measures it shall, after giving that State the opportunity to submit its observations, issue a reasoned opinion specifying the points on which the Member State concerned has not complied with the judgment of the Court of Justice. If the Member State concerned fails to take the necessary measures to comply with the Court's judgment within the time-limit laid down by the Commission, the latter may bring the case before the Court of Justice. In so doing it shall specify the amount of the lump sum or penalty payment to be paid by the Member State concerned which it considers appropriate in the circumstances. If the Court of Justice finds that the Member State concerned has not complied with its judgment it may impose a lump sum or penalty payment on it. This procedure shall be without prejudice to Article 170.

GENERAL NOTE

The amendment to this Article marks a fundamental shift in the means available for securing the effective implementation of Community law. The E.E.C. Treaty provided only for weak remedies should the Member States fail to fulfil their obligations under that Treaty. While the E.C.J. had jurisdiction under Arts. 169 and 170 E.E.C. to rule on the Member States' failures, the only subsequent remedy relied on the state taking "the necessary measures to comply with the Court's judgments" (Art. 171 E.E.C.). The Court's judgments in infringement proceedings were declaratory and, though they are binding on the Member State concerned, the E.C.J. had no further powers. The result was that some Member States were slow to comply with the Court's judgments. Indeed, by the end of 1992, 90 of the Court's judgments had not been complied with, including six regarding the U.K. Considering that 244 cases of infringement of Community law by the Member States were decided by the E.C.J. between 1988 and the end of 1992, non-compliance in 90 cases is an unacceptably high proportion (see the *Tenth Annual Report on Commission Monitoring of the Application of Community Law*, [1993] O.J. C233/68 and 207). The only remedy, prior to the Maastricht Treaty, was for the Commission to initiate new infringement proceedings against the Member State. This required the whole of the Art. 169 process to be gone through again, a very cumbersome procedure with an uncertain outcome (see further Weatherill and Beaumont, *supra*, pp. 180–182). Indeed, by the end of 1992, the E.C.J. had been forced to give a second decision against a Member State on a repeat infringement proceeding on 12 occasions (see *Tenth Annual Report, supra*, at Annex 5).

This problem has been addressed by the Maastricht inter-governmental conference. Following a proposal from the U.K. Government, which initially received a lukewarm reception from the Commission (see E.C. Bull. Supp. 2/91, pp. 81 and 151–152), Art. 171 was amended to provide that the E.C.J. may impose penalties on Member States which fail to comply with its judgments under Arts. 169 and 170 E.C. This is a very important step in the enforcement of Community law, but will not be without difficulties in its application. One major problem seems to be that the process leading up to the imposition of the sanction will be very lengthy. The procedure under either Arts. 169 or 170 must first be satisfied before Art. 171 itself comes into play. Under the latter Article, it will fall to the Commission to determine whether or not the Member State has taken measures to alleviate its breach. It will then request the Member State concerned to give its observations, and issue a reasoned opinion specifying the nature of the State's non-compliance with the Court's judgment and giving a time-limit for compliance. The Commission will then, if it considers that the State has failed to take the necessary measures to comply with the Court's judgment within the time-limit, bring the case before the E.C.J. with a recommendation as to the level of fine that should be imposed. At all stages of the proceedings, the Commission has a discretion whether or not to proceed with the case (see Weatherill and Beaumont, *supra*, p. 172). The full process requires two references to the E.C.J. and two reasoned opinions from the Commission, followed by responses from the Member State concerned. This could take upwards of three years from the outset of the proceedings! One other factor mitigating against its effective application is the absence of any proviso providing for the retention of Community funds due to the Member State concerned. This would make for a very effective sanction, as the Member State would not have to be pursued for the amount of the fine because it is simply docked from its allocation. Under Art. 88 of the European Coal and Steel Community Treaty, the Commission, with the assent of the Council acting by a two-thirds majority, may suspend the payment of any sums which the Community may be liable to pay to the state in question. It would appear that this procedure has never been used.

Another potential problem arises from the failure of Art. 171 E.C. to permit the tailoring of the sanction to fit the breach, for example, the imposition of an injunction on a Member State. The scope of the phrase "lump sum or penalty payment" is unclear. Could it mean that the court has to choose between these alternative penalties, as a literal interpretation would suggest, or could it apply a penalty payment for every day that a Member State fails to pay the lump sum ordered by the Court (see Curtin, The Constitutional Structure of the Union: A Europe of Bits and Pieces, (1993) 30 C.M.L.Rev., 17, 32–34). There is always the chance that a state will fail to pay a lump sum or penalty payment. What the Community could do in that situation is far from clear, but would no doubt rest on extra-legal considerations.

Nevertheless, the new procedure under Art. 171, while far from perfect does mark a significant departure for the European Community. Empowering a Community institution to adopt a penal sanction on a Member State is a significant surrender of national sovereignty. Ironically, the loss of sovereignty caused by this centralising "federal" measure was proposed by the same U.K. Government which so strongly resisted the inclusion of the "f" word in the TEU and trumpeted its opt-outs from the third stage of economic and monetary union and from the Social Policy Agreement. The U.K. has a comparatively good record of compliance with judgments of the E.C.J. and was doubtless motivated by a desire to improve the rate of compliance in the Member States with a comparatively poor record (*e.g.* Belgium, Greece and Italy). The U.K. wanted to protect the rule of law and in this context, unlike Social and Monetary Policy, to ensure a level playing field in the Community.

There are, of course, other mechanisms for enforcing Community law, that have been developed by the E.C.J. With the lack of formal sanctions in the E.E.C. Treaty for non-compliance with Community law, it fell on the E.C.J. to secure its uniform application. This was evident from the development of the principles of direct effect (see Case 26/62 *Van Gend en Loos* v. *Nederlandse Belastingadministratie* [1963] E.C.R. 1) and supremacy of Community law (see Case 6/64 *Costa* v. *Ente Nazionale per l'Energia Elettrica* (ENEL) [1964] E.C.R. 585). These principles were to be embellished and built upon throughout the subsequent decades, in particular to secure the effective application (*effet utile*) of Directives throughout the Member States. Firstly, by giving vertical direct effect to directives in *Van Duyn* v. *Home Office* (Case 41/74 [1975] Ch. 358) and in the *Ratti* case (*Pubblico Ministero* v. *Ratti* (Case 148/78) [1979] E.C.R. 1629). Secondly, by developing the Art. 5 obligation to encompass the national courts in the interpretation of national law in accordance with Community obligations (indirect effects) (see Case 14/83,

Von Colson and Kamann v. *Land Nordrhein-Westfahlen* [1984] E.C.R. 1891 and Case C-106/89, *Marleasing SA* v. *La Comercial Internacional de Alimentation SA* [1990] E.C.R. 4135). (See generally: Curtin, The Effectiveness of Judicial Protection of Individual Rights (1990) 27 C.M.L.Rev. 709; Steiner, From Direct Effects to Francovich: Shifting the Means of Enforcement of Community Law, (1993) 18 E.L.Rev. 2; and de Burca, Giving Effect to European Community Directives (1992) 55 M.L.R. 215).

The jurisprudence reached its zenith with the now famous *Francovich and Boniface* v. *Italy* case (Cases C-6, C-9/90 [1991] E.C.R. 5359, noted by Bebr (1992) 29 C.M.L.Rev. 57 and Duffy (1992) 17 E.L.Rev. 133). This laid down the principle of state liability, whereby a Member State is, in certain circumstances, obliged to make good damage to individuals arising from non-implementation of a directive. The application of the principle in this case arose in a clear and blatant case of non-implementation. Francovich and Boniface were employees of an undertaking that became insolvent, leaving substantial arrears of salary unpaid. They brought proceedings in the Italian courts for the recovery of the compensation provided for by Dir. 80/987 on the protection of employees in the event of the insolvency of their employer, or, in the alternative, damages. Italy had, however, failed to implement this Directive by the envisaged date of October 23, 1983 and had even been found guilty of this breach before the E.C.J. in *Commission* v. *Italian Republic* (Case 22/87, [1989] E.C.R. 143). The Italian courts sought a preliminary reference from the E.C.J. The Court first considered whether the relevant provisions of Directive 80/987 were directly effective. The Court applied the usual test for establishing direct effect: whether or not the provisions were unconditional and sufficiently precise. The Directives provided guarantees for the payment of unpaid remuneration in the case of the insolvency of the employer. These guarantees were sufficiently precise and unconditional in relation to their content and the persons entitled to them, but not in relation to the person or persons obliged to pay the guaranteed sums. Thus the applicants could not rely on the direct effect of the Directive against the state, even though the time-limit had run out.

Given that Directive 80/987 was not sufficiently precise in establishing who was liable to pay the guarantees contained in it, Community law, prior to the *Francovich* case, would have been of no avail to the applicants. The Court, however, decided that the principle of liability of a Member State for damage caused to individuals by infringements of Community law for which it was responsible was inherent in the scheme of the E.E.C. Treaty. In particular, the obligation stemmed from Art. 5 of the Treaty which provides that "Member States shall take all appropriate measures, whether general or particular, to ensure fulfilment of the obligations arising out of the Treaty". The Court also argued that the "full effectiveness" of Community rules might be called into question and the protection of the rights that they conferred would be weakened if individuals could not obtain compensation where their rights were infringed by a breach of Community law imputable to a Member State. It is a matter for each Member State to determine the competent courts and appropriate procedures for legal actions intended to enable individuals to obtain damages from the state. The European Court has indicated that these procedures must be no less favourable to applicants than those relating to similar claims under internal law, and must not be so organised as to make it practically impossible or excessively difficult to obtain damages from the state.

The result of this principle is that Member States will find themselves subject to potentially unlimited damages payments for non-implementation of Directives, restricted only by the number of applicants. Moreover, rather than the centralised enforcement procedure envisaged by Art. 171, the Member State will find it almost impossible to ignore a judgment from a domestic court. The E.C.J. was well aware of this when it enunciated this principle (on what are admittedly shaky foundations: see Weatherill and Beaumont, *EC Law*, 301–304). The result is a very powerful tool in the hands of the E.C.J. and domestic courts to secure the implementation of Community directives. It puts the onus for securing the effective implementation of Community law onto interested parties rather than relying on absolute Commission discretion (see Evans, The Enforcement Procedure of Article 169: Commission Discretion, (1979) 4 E.L.Rev. 442 and Weatherill and Beaumont, *supra*, 171–172). There is still some doubt as to the scope of the *Francovich* principle. The breach of Community law in that case was blatant, having been the subject of an infringement proceeding before the E.C.J. Cases concerning less clearcut breaches of Community law, where the State's "fault" is not so palpable, will determine just how far reaching the *Francovich* principle is, but it has been argued that it "gives claws and teeth far sharper and more incisive than those concocted by the authors of the Maastricht Treaty" (Mancini and Keeling, From CILFIT to ERT: The Constitutional Challenge Facing the E.C.J., (1992) 12 YEL). However, this remedy will not be available in relation to all violations of Community law by Member States. The conditions laid down in *Francovich* will not be met in all cases, the conditions being: (a) the result laid down in the Directive must involve the attribution of rights attached to individuals; (b) the content of the rights must be capable of being identified from the provisions of the Directive; and (c) there must be a causal link between the failure by the Member State to fulfil its obligations and the damage suffered by the individual. Where *Francovich* does not apply Art. 171 might well be used as an effective back-stop.

Article 172

Regulations adopted jointly by the European Parliament and the Council, and by the Council, pursuant to the provisions of this Treaty, may give the Court of Justice unlimited jurisdiction with regard to the penalties provided for in such regulations.

GENERAL NOTE

This Article is consequentially amended to take account of the fact that under the new conciliation and veto procedure, legislative measures are adopted jointly by the Council and the European Parliament. The substantive content of the Article is unaltered.

Article 173

The Court of Justice shall review the legality of acts adopted jointly by the European Parliament and the Council, of acts of the Council, of the Commission and of the ECB, other than recommendations and opinions, and of acts of the European Parliament intended to produce legal effects *vis-à-vis* third parties.

It shall for this purpose have jurisdiction in actions brought by a Member State, the Council or the Commission on grounds of lack of competence, infringement of an essential procedural requirement, infringement of this Treaty or of any rule of law relating to its application, or misuse of powers.

The Court shall have jurisdiction under the same conditions in actions brought by the European Parliament and by the ECB for the purpose of protecting their prerogatives.

Any natural or legal person may, under the same conditions, institute proceedings against a decision addressed to that person or against a decision which, although in the form of a regulation or a decision addressed to another person, is of direct and individual concern to the former.

The proceedings provided for in this Article shall be instituted within two months of the publication of the measure, or of its notification to the plaintiff, or, in the absence thereof, of the day on which it came to the knowledge of the latter, as the case may be.

GENERAL NOTE

The first paragraph of this Article was amended at Maastricht to permit the review by the E.C.J. of acts "adopted jointly by the European Parliament and the Council . . . and of acts of the European Parliament intended to produce legal effects vis-à-vis third parties". The former provision applies to measures adopted under the conciliation and veto procedure laid down in Art. 189b E.C., while the latter provision is merely a recognition of existing E.C.J. case law on the interpretation of Art. 173 E.E.C. (Case 294/83, *Les Verts* v. *European Parliament* [1986] E.C.R. 1339).

The second paragraph is amended, partly to formalise the E.C.J.'s decision that the European Parliament ought to be permitted to take actions under this Article "for the purposes of protecting its own prerogatives" (Case C-70/88 *European Parliament* v. *Council* [1990] E.C.R. I-2041 (the *Chernobyl* case)) and partly to attribute a similar right of action to the European Central Bank.

This Article thus gives Treaty status to the European Parliament's ability to bring actions for annulment. This was a matter on which some debate had been raised, thanks to two divergent decisions of the E.C.J. on the matter. In Case 302/87, *European Parliament* v. *E.C. Council* [1988] E.C.R. 5615 (the *Comitology* case), the E.C.J., sitting with 13 judges, took a literal approach to the interpretation of Art. 173 E.E.C. and refused the European Parliament any *locus standi* under this provision. A nine judge Court, however, in Case C-70/88, *supra*, was prepared to grant the limited *locus standi* now recognised by Art. 173 E.C. (See Bebr, The Standing of the European Parliament in the Community System of Legal Remedies, (1990) 10 YEL 171 and Weatherill and Beaumont, *E.C. Law*, (1993), Penguin, 89–90 and on Art. 173 in general see: Weatherill and Beaumont, *EC Law*, Ch. 8; Brown and Jacobs, *The Court of Justice*, 95–125 and Schermers and Waelbroeck, *Judicial Protection*, 139–221.

Article 174

If the action is well founded, the Court of Justice shall declare the act concerned to be void.

In the case of a regulation, however, the Court of Justice shall, if it considers this necessary, state which of the effects of the regulation which it has declared void shall be considered as definitive.

Article 175

Should the European Parliament, the Council or the Commission, in infringement of this Treaty, fail to act, the Member States and the other institutions of the Community may bring an action before the Court of Justice to have the infringement established.

The action shall be admissible only if the institution concerned has first been called upon to act. If, within two months of being so called upon, the institution concerned has not defined its position, the action may be brought within a further period of two months.

Any natural or legal person may, under the conditions laid down in the preceding paragraphs, complain to the Court of Justice that an institution of the Community has failed to address to that person any act other than a recommendation or an opinion.

The Court of Justice shall have jurisdiction, under the same conditions, in actions or proceedings brought by the ECB in the areas falling within the latter's field of competence and in actions or proceedings brought against the latter.

GENERAL NOTE

This Article is amended, as with Art. 173 to which it is closely related, to take account of existing E.C.J. case law on the status of the European Parliament and to attribute analogous rights to the European Central Bank on its coming into operation. It has always been clear from Art. 175 E.E.C. that the European Parliament has *locus standi* to bring actions for failure to act against the Council or the Commission (utilised for the first time in Case 13/83, *European Parliament* v. *E.C. Council* [1985] E.C.R. 1513). The amendment of the Article recognises the right of the other institutions to challenge the European Parliament over its failure to act. The last paragraph of Art. 175 E.C. has been inserted to enable actions for failure to act to be brought against the European Central Bank. The Bank can bring an action for failure to act against the Commission, Council and European Parliament but only in areas falling within the Bank's "field of competence".

Article 176

The institution or institutions whose act has been declared void or whose failure to act has been declared contrary to this Treaty shall be required to take the necessary measures to comply with the judgment of the Court of Justice.

This obligation shall not affect any obligation which may result from the application of the second paragraph of Article 215.

This Article shall also apply to the ECB.

GENERAL NOTE

The amendment to this Article simply consists of the addition of the third paragraph to take account of the legislative rôle envisaged for the European Central Bank in the third stage of economic and monetary union. Substantively, the Article is unaltered.

Article 177

The Court of Justice shall have jurisdiction to give preliminary rulings concerning:

(a) the interpretation of this Treaty;
(b) the validity and interpretation of acts of the institutions of the Community and of the ECB;

   (c) the interpretation of the statutes of bodies established by an act of the Council, where those statutes so provide.

Where such a question is raised before any court or tribunal of a Member State, that court or tribunal may, if it considers that a decision on the question is necessary to enable it to give judgment, request the Court of Justice to give a ruling thereon.

Where any such question is raised in a case pending before a court or tribunal of a Member State against whose decisions there is no judicial remedy under national law, that court or tribunal shall bring the matter before the Court of Justice.

GENERAL NOTE

The new Art. 177 is amended consequentially to take account of the coming into being of the European Central Bank in the third stage of economic and monetary union. A reference to the European Central Bank is appended to para. (b).

Article 178

The Court of Justice shall have jurisdiction in disputes relating to compensation for damage provided for in the second paragraph of Article 215.

Article 179

The Court of Justice shall have jurisdiction in any dispute between the Community and its servants within the limits and under the conditions laid down in the Staff Regulations or the Conditions of Employment.

Article 180

The Court of Justice shall, within the limits hereinafter laid down, have jurisdiction in disputes concerning:

   (a) the fulfilment by Member States of obligations under the Statute of the European Investment Bank. In this connection, the Board of Directors of the Bank shall enjoy the powers conferred upon the Commission by Article 169;

   (b) measures adopted by the Board of Governors of the European Investment Bank. In this connection, any Member State, the Commission or the Board of Directors of the Bank may institute proceedings under the conditions laid down in Article 173;

   (c) measures adopted by the Board of Directors of the European Investment Bank. Proceedings against such measures may be instituted only by Member States or by the Commission, under the conditions laid down in Article 173, and solely on the grounds of non-compliance with the procedure provided for in Article 21(2), (5), (6) and (7) of the Statute of the Bank.

   (d) the fulfilment by national central banks of obligations under this Treaty and the Statute of the ESCB. In this connection the powers of the Council of the ECB in respect of national central banks shall be the same as those conferred upon the Commission in respect of Member States by Article 169. If the Court of Justice finds that a national central bank has failed to fulfil an obligation under this Treaty, that bank shall be required to take the necessary measures to comply with the judgment of the Court of Justice.

GENERAL NOTE

Paragraph (d) is added to this Article to give the E.C.J. jurisdiction in cases where the fulfilment by the national central banks of their obligations under the Treaty or under the Statute of the European System of Central Banks is in question. The Council of the European Central Bank is declared to have the same powers as the Commission under Art. 169 E.C. where the actions of the national central banks are concerned (see also Art. 35.6 of the Statute of the European System of Central Banks). The wording of Art. 180 does not seem to preclude the

Commission from also taking steps under Art. 169 regarding the national central banks. Thus, in this area there are two entities given the task of ensuring compliance with the E.C. Treaty, a rôle previously carried out by the Commission. In paras. (b) and (c) the words "European Investment" have been added, to indicate that the Bank referred to is not the European Central Bank.

Article 181

The Court of Justice shall have jurisdiction to give judgment pursuant to any arbitration clause contained in a contract concluded by or on behalf of the Community, whether that contract be governed by public or private law.

Article 182

The Court of Justice shall have jurisdiction in any dispute between Member States which relates to the subject matter of this Treaty if the dispute is submitted to it under a special agreement between the parties.

Article 183

Save where jurisdiction is conferred on the Court of Justice by this Treaty, disputes to which the Community is a party shall not on that ground be excluded from the jurisdiction of the courts or tribunals of the Member States.

Article 184

Notwithstanding the expiry of the period laid down in the fifth paragraph of Article 173, any party may, in proceedings in which a regulation adopted jointly by the European Parliament and the Council, or a regulation of the Council, of the Commission or of the ECB is at issue, plead the grounds specified in the second paragraph of Article 173 in order to invoke before the Court of Justice the inapplicability of that regulation.

GENERAL NOTE
This Article is amended simply to take account of alterations made in Arts. 173 and 189b of the Treaty. The references to the relevant paras. of Art. 173 are updated to take account of the additions made thereto, while the potential of legislative measures being adopted jointly by the Council and the European Parliament (Art. 189b E.C.) is also accounted for.

Article 185

Actions brought before the Court of Justice shall not have suspensory effect. The Court of Justice may, however, if it considers that circumstances so require, order that application of the contested act be suspended.

Article 186

The Court of Justice may in any cases before it prescribe any necessary interim measures.

Article 187

The judgments of the Court of Justice shall be enforceable under the conditions laid down in Article 192.

Article 188

The Statute of the Court of Justice is laid down in a separate Protocol.
The Council may, acting unanimously at the request of the Court of Justice and after consulting the Commission and the European Parliament, amend the provisions of Title III of the Statute.
The Court of Justice shall adopt its rules of procedure. These shall require the unanimous approval of the Council.

SECTION 5: The Court of Auditors

GENERAL NOTE
With the Court of Auditors being attributed the status of an institution by the Maastricht Treaty amendments (see Art. 4 E.C.), the substantive provisions governing this body have been moved from Arts. 206 and 206a E.E.C., into the institutional chapter of the E.C. Treaty. Thus, a new section 5 is appended to the institutional heading and the material from the old Articles is substantially reiterated in Arts. 188a–188c E.C.

Article 188a

The Court of Auditors shall carry out the audit.

GENERAL NOTE
This is a new provision stating in simple terms the Court of Auditors' main task, that of carrying out the audit of the Community's finances.

Article 188b

1. The Court of Auditors shall consist of 12 members.

2. The members of the Court of Auditors shall be chosen from among persons who belong or have belonged in their respective countries to external audit bodies or who are especially qualified for this office. Their independence must be beyond doubt.

3. The members of the Court of Auditors shall be appointed for a term of six years by the Council, acting unanimously after consulting the European Parliament.

However, when the first appointments are made, four members of the Court of Auditors, chosen by lot, shall be appointed for a term of office of four years only.

The members of the Court of Auditors shall be eligible for reappointment.

They shall elect the President of the Court of Auditors from among their number for a term of three years.

The President may be re-elected.

4. The members of the Court of Auditors shall, in the general interest of the Community, be completely independent in the performance of their duties.

In the performance of these duties, they shall neither seek nor take instructions from any government or from any other body. They shall refrain from any action incompatible with their duties.

5. The members of the Court of Auditors may not, during their term of office, engage in any other occupation, whether gainful or not. When entering upon their duties they shall give a solemn undertaking that, both during and after their term of office, they will respect the obligations arising therefrom and in particular their duty to behave with integrity and discretion as regards the acceptance, after they have ceased to hold office, of certain appointments or benefits.

6. Apart from normal replacement, or death, the duties of a member of the Court of Auditors shall end when he resigns, or is compulsorily retired by a ruling of the Court of Justice pursuant to paragraph 7. The vacancy thus caused shall be filled for the remainder of the member's term of office.

Save in the case of compulsory retirement, members of the Court of Auditors shall remain in office until they have been replaced.

7. A member of the Court of Auditors may be deprived of his office or of his right to a pension or other benefits in its stead only if the Court of Justice, at the request of the Court of Auditors, finds that he no longer fulfils the requisite conditions or meets the obligations arising from his office.

8. The Council, acting by a qualified majority, shall determine the conditions of employment of the President and the members of the Court of Auditors and in particular their salaries, allowances and pensions. It shall

also, by the same majority, determine any payment to be made instead of remuneration.

9. The provisions of the Protocol on the Privileges and Immunities of the European Communities applicable to the Judges of the Court of Justice shall also apply to the members of the Court of Auditors.

GENERAL NOTE
    This Article duplicates the provisions previously enclosed in Art. 206(2) to (10) E.E.C. No substantive amendments are made to any of these paragraphs but they are renumbered as (1) to (9). The appointment of members of the Court and the conditions surrounding their period of office is thereby unaltered. The old para. (1) is deleted because it referred to the establishment of the Court of Auditors.

Article 188c

1. The Court of Auditors shall examine the accounts of all revenue and expenditure of the Community. It shall also examine the accounts of all revenue and expenditure of all bodies set up by the Community in so far as the relevant constituent instrument does not preclude such examination.
    The Court of Auditors shall provide the European Parliament and the Council with a statement of assurance as to the reliability of the accounts and the legality and regularity of the underlying transactions.
2. The Court of Auditors shall examine whether all revenue has been received and all expenditure incurred in a lawful and regular manner and whether the financial management has been sound.
    The audit of revenue shall be carried out on the basis of the amounts established as due and the amounts actually paid to the Community.
    The audit of expenditure shall be carried out on the basis both of commitments undertaken and payments made.
    These audits may be carried out before the closure of accounts for the financial year in question.
3. The audit shall be based on records and, if necessary, performed on the spot in the other institutions of the Community and in the Member States. In the Member States the audit shall be carried out in liaison with the national audit bodies or, if these do not have the necessary powers, with the competent national departments. These bodies or departments shall inform the Court of Auditors whether they intend to take part in the audit.
    The other institutions of the Community and the national audit bodies or, if these do not have the necessary powers, the competent national departments, shall forward to the Court of Auditors, at its request, any document or information necessary to carry out its task.
4. The Court of Auditors shall draw up an annual report after the close of each financial year. It shall be forwarded to the other institutions of the Community and shall be published, together with the replies of these institutions to the observations of the Court of Auditors, in the Official Journal of the European Communities.
    The Court of Auditors may also, at any time, submit observations, particularly in the form of special reports, on specific questions and deliver opinions at the request of one of the other institutions of the Community.
    It shall adopt in its annual report, special reports or opinions by a majority of its members.
    It shall assist the European Parliament and the Council in exercising their powers of control over the implementation of the budget.

GENERAL NOTE
    As with the preceding Articles on the Court of Auditors, the present Article is largely unaltered from the old Art. 206a E.E.C. One alteration is the addition of a new second indent to para. 1. The assertion contained therein must be read in the light of the new Art. 209a E.C., which provides that the Member States are to take "the same measures to counter fraud affecting the financial interests of the Community as they take to counter fraud affecting their own

financial interests". The U.K. was keen to see the inclusion of this Article as well as the bolster-ing of the standing of the Court of Auditors. In paras. (3) and (4) the word "other" is inserted before "institutions", because the Court of Auditors was elevated to institutional status in Art. 4 E.C. Paragraph (4) empowers the Court of Auditors to prepare "special reports" when asked to do so by any of the other institutions of the Community.

Chapter 2 (Provisions Common to Several Institutions)

Article 189

In order to carry out their task and in accordance with the provisions of this Treaty, the European Parliament acting jointly with the Council, the Council and the Commission shall make regulations and issue directives, take decisions, make recommendations or deliver opinions.

A regulation shall have general application. It shall be binding in its entirety and directly applicable in all Member States.

A directive shall be binding, as to the result to be achieved, upon each Member State to which it is addressed, but shall leave to the national author-ities the choice of form and methods.

A decision shall be binding in its entirety upon those to whom it is addressed.

Recommendations and opinions shall have no binding force.

GENERAL NOTE

This Article is amended to take account of the new decision-making process under Art. 189b E.C. whereby some Community acts are to be adopted jointly by the European Parliament and the Council. This apart, the Article is unaltered.

Article 189a

1. Where in pursuance of this Treaty, the Council acts on a proposal from the Commission, unanimity shall be required for an act constituting an amendment to that proposal, subject to Article 189b(4) and (5).

2. As long as the Council has not acted, the Commission may alter its proposal at any time during the procedures leading to the adoption of a Community act.

GENERAL NOTE

This Article, previously Art. 149(1) and (2) E.E.C., is amended to account for the new concili-ation and veto procedure under Art. 189b E.C. The first of the basic principles previously encompassed in Art. 149(1) E.E.C., that the Council, acting on the basis of a Commission pro-posal must act by unanimity if they wish to adopt an act constituting an amendment to the Com-mission proposal, is watered down with regard to the conciliation stage under Art. 189b E.C. During this part of the procedure, the Commission is relegated to the rôle of honest broker, and the Council and the European Parliament members, meeting in the conciliation committee, may adopt an act different from the original Commission proposal. In certain legislative areas this will be done by qualified majority voting in Council (for example, the adoption of legislation under Art. 100a E.C.). Whether or not this will amount to a significant diminution of power for the Commission is uncertain. It is likely that the rôle of the Commission in taking "all the necess-ary initiatives with a view to reconciling the positions of the European Parliament and the Coun-cil" will be significant, but all will depend on subsequent practice. The Commission's powers are only diluted if a conciliation committee is convened under Art. 189b(4) and (5) E.C. The normal rule continues to apply to amendments to the Commission proposal prior to this. Thus, the Council must act by unanimity to accept any amendments of the European Parliament on which the Commission has expressed a negative opinion or to put forward its own amendments (Art. 189b(3) E.C.). Nevertheless, as soon as a conciliation committee is convened, the Council may adopt amendments to the Commission proposal by qualified majority vote. Hartley suggests that the Council may well simply wait for the three-month period under Art. 189b(3) E.C. to elapse, without approving any European Parliament amendments, and when the conciliation committee is thereby convened, adopt any amendments it desires by qualified majority vote. The Commission's loss is thereby the European Parliament's gain; for the first time it can have its amendments, opposed by the Commission, adopted by qualified majority vote (Hartley, Constitutional and Institutional Aspects of the Maastricht Agreement, (1993) 42 I.C.L.Q. 213–237, 225).

One factor justifying the amendment to this Article is that the usefulness of the conciliation process under Art. 189b E.C. would be prejudiced by the necessity of unanimity, its purpose being the securing of compromises between the European Parliament and the Council. Such compromises are much more unlikely where one body is required to take certain of its decisions by unanimity (see note on Art. 189b E.C.).

The second paragraph of Art. 189a is unaltered from its original form under Art. 149(2) E.E.C.

Article 189b

1. Where reference is made in this Treaty to this Article for the adoption of an act, the following procedure shall apply.

2. The Commission shall submit a proposal to the European Parliament and the Council.

The Council, acting by a qualified majority after obtaining the Opinion of the European Parliament, shall adopt a common position. The common position shall be communicated to the European Parliament. The Council shall inform the European Parliament fully of the reasons which led it to adopt its common position. The Commission shall inform the European Parliament fully of its position.

If, within three months of such communication, the European Parliament:

(a) approves the common position, the Council shall definitively adopt the act in question in accordance with that common position;

(b) has not taken a decision, the Council shall adopt the act in question in accordance with its common position;

(c) indicates, by an absolute majority of its component members, that it intends to reject the common position, it shall immediately inform the Council. The Council may convene a meeting of the Conciliation Committee referred to in paragraph 3 to explain further its position. The European Parliament shall thereafter either confirm, by an absolute majority of its component members, its rejection of the common position, in which event the proposed act shall be deemed not to have been adopted, or propose amendments in accordance with sub-paragraph (d) of this paragraph;

(d) proposes amendments to the common position by an absolute majority of its component members, the amended text shall be forwarded to the Council and to the Commission, which shall deliver an opinion on those amendments.

3. If, within three months of the matter being referred to it, the Council, acting by a qualified majority, approves all the amendments of the European Parliament, it shall amend its common position accordingly and adopt the act in question; however, the Council shall act unanimously on the amendments on which the Commission has delivered a negative opinion. If the Council does not approve the act in question, the President of the Council, in agreement with the President of the European Parliament, shall forthwith convene a meeting of the Conciliation Committee.

4. The Conciliation Committee, which shall be composed of the members of the Council or their representatives and an equal number of representatives of the European Parliament, shall have the task of reaching agreement on a joint text, by a qualified majority of the members of the Council or their representatives and by a majority of the representatives of the European Parliament. The Commission shall take part in the Conciliation Committee's proceedings and shall take all the necessary initiatives with a view to reconciling the positions of the European Parliament and the Council.

5. If, within six weeks of its being convened, the Conciliation Committee approves a joint text, the European Parliament, acting by an absolute majority of the votes cast, and the Council, acting by a qualified majority, shall have a period of six weeks from that approval in which to adopt the act in question

in accordance with the joint text. If one of the two institutions fails to approve the proposed act, it shall be deemed not to have been adopted.

6. Where the Conciliation Committee does not approve a joint text, the proposed act shall be deemed not to have been adopted unless the Council, acting by a qualified majority within six weeks of expiry of the period granted to the Conciliation Committee, confirms the common position to which it agreed before the conciliation procedure was initiated, possibly with amendments proposed by the European Parliament. In this case, the act in question shall be finally adopted unless the European Parliament, within six weeks of the date of confirmation by the Council, rejects the text by an absolute majority of its component members, in which case the proposed act shall be deemed not to have been adopted.

7. The periods of three months and six weeks referred to in this Article may be extended by a maximum of one month and two weeks respectively by common accord of the European Parliament and the Council. The period of three months referred to in paragraph 2 shall be automatically extended by two months where paragraph 2(c) applies.

8. The scope of the procedure under this Article may be widened, in accordance with the procedure provided for in Article N(2) of the Treaty on European Union, on the basis of a report to be submitted to the Council by the Commission by 1996 at the latest.

GENERAL NOTE

This Article sets out the new conciliation and veto procedure hammered out at Maastricht. The procedure is simply referred to throughout the E.C. Treaty as "the procedure referred to in Art. 189b", the U.K. being unable to accept the sovereignty implications of the term "co-decision". This would, in any event, have been somewhat of a misnomer, in so far as the procedure does not confer a true right of co-decision on the European Parliament in the adoption of Community legislation. Rather, it provides for the convening of a conciliation committee of equal numbers of MEP's and Council members, or their representatives, to meet and attempt to resolve their differences if divergences in their positions exist (the conciliation facet). If the conciliation committee reaches agreement, the resulting text has to be approved by the appropriate majorities in both the Council and the European Parliament. If, however, no agreement is reached in the conciliation committee, the two institutions are not in an equal position. The Council can adopt its common position, perhaps with some of the European Parliament's amendments if it so desires, and the European Parliament only has the options of accepting it or vetoing it. Nonetheless, for the first time the European Parliament enjoys the right to block legislation upon which the Council has expressed a positive opinion.

This procedure is some distance from the right of co-decision requested by the European Parliament in the run-up to the inter-governmental conference, [1990] O.J. C231/97 at point 31. The European Parliament took the view that it was only through such a process that the democratic deficit in the Community could be properly addressed. Despite the fact that a majority of the Member States were in favour of conferring such positive powers upon the European Parliament a vocal minority ensured that such a sea change in the Community balance of powers was not going to be achieved at Maastricht (see Laursen and Finn (eds.), *The Inter-governmental conference on Political Union*, at Chap. 2 – Germany, Holland, Belgium, Italy, Greece, Spain and France expressed support for full co-decision). The procedure which was agreed at Maastricht therefore, unsurprisingly, bears the scars of compromise, not just as regards its name.

Rather than describe the complex process in segments relating to the individual paragraphs of Art. 189b, it will be easier to follow in one overall assessment, with references to the corresponding paragraphs of the Article.

The process commences, as with the majority of Community legislation, with a Commission proposal (Art. 189b(2)). As with the co-operation procedure introduced by the SEA (Art. 149(2) E.E.C./Art. 189c E.C.), this is forwarded to the European Parliament and the Council. The Council then, acting by a qualified majority, adopts a common position on the proposal, after receiving the opinion of the European Parliament. The Council and the Commission must then inform the European Parliament of their positions on the matter, in the Council's case this amounts to a statement of reasons underlying its common position. This again is similar to the co-operation procedure.

The next stage of the process involves the European Parliament's reaction to the common position. This amounts to the second reading by the European Parliament, but it is constrained by a three month time-limit in which to operate (although this may be extended in accordance with Art. 189b(7) on the common accord of the Council and the European Parliament). The European Parliament has four alternative courses of action. It can approve the common position, in which case the Council will adopt the act as it stands (Art. 189b(2)(a)). Secondly, if the European Parliament fails to act within the requisite time period, the Council can again adopt the act in accordance with the common position (Art. 189b(2)(b)). Thus far, the procedure is very similar to that under the existing co-operation procedure, the differences become manifest only where the European Parliament signals its intention to reject the common position or proposes amendments of its own. With regard to the former scenario, the decision of the European Parliament, by an absolute majority of its members (as opposed to a majority of votes cast), to reject the common position, is not determinative (Art. 189b(2)(c)). The last sentence of Art. 189b(7) provides that, in the event of the European Parliament giving notification of its intention to reject, the three month time period will be automatically extended by two months. Such a motion is taken as a notice of intention to the Council. The Council may then convene a meeting of the conciliation committee, provided for in Art. 189b(4), to further explain its position. Once this has taken place, the European Parliament may confirm its rejection, again acting by an absolute majority of its members, or it may propose amendments to the common position. If the European Parliament rejects the measure a second time then the act is deemed not to have been adopted. This is not quite as simple as may at first sight appear. The mustering of an absolute majority of MEP's is no mean feat, and this is even more difficult to achieve twice. The European Parliament, in its resolution on the procedure, indicated the difficulties it would face in this respect but also that it would not permit such procedural difficulties from preventing it rejecting "unacceptable" legislative proposals ([1992] O.J. C21/138–141, 139).

Should the European Parliament propose amendments to the common position either at second reading or subsequent to a notification of intent to reject, Art. 189b(2)(d) applies. According to this procedure, the European Parliament, by an absolute majority of its members, may propose amendments to the common position; these are then forwarded to the Commission and the Council. The Council acts by qualified majority in relation to the amendments on which the Commission has not expressed a negative opinion, but by unanimity in relation to those amendments where the Commission has expressed such an opinion (see note on Art. 189a(1)). In the likely event that the Council does not adopt all Parliament's amendments, the President of the Council, must, in agreement with the President of the European Parliament, convene a meeting of the conciliation committee (Art. 189b(3)).

This committee is to consist of an equal number of members of the European Parliament and the Council or its representatives and its aim is to reach agreement on a joint text. It would seem to be unlikely that government ministers will attend many, if any, conciliation committees. The Council will probably be represented by the Member States' Permanent Representatives and Deputy Permanent Representatives who sit in COREPER. The composition of Parliament's delegation to the conciliation committee is regulated by Rule 52B of the Rules of Procedure (as amended subsequent to the TEU, see [1993] O.J. C268/51). For the first 12 months of the operation of Art. 189b, Parliament's delegation will include three Vice Presidents as permanent members. The President of the Parliament, or one of the three permanent members, will lead the delegation. Other members of the delegation will include the chairman and rapporteur of the Parliamentary committee responsible for handling the legislative proposal under discussion. The choice of the remaining MEP's to attend the conciliation committee will be made by the political groups under the direction of the Conference of Presidents (*i.e.* the President of the Parliament and the chairmen of the political groups). Most, if not all, of those selected will be members of the committee responsible for dealing with the piece of legislation in issue during its first and second reading. By ensuring that three or four of Parliament's leaders attend all the conciliation committees during the first year of their operation, Parliament is indicating the high level of commitment that it is making to this process. The Commission is not attributed its usual rights under Art. 189a(1) E.C., but instead will "take all necessary initiatives with a view to reconciling the positions of the European Parliament and the Council" (Art. 189b(4)). The European Parliament supports the Commission's involvement because the European Parliament and the Council may come together in the conciliation committee with widely divergent positions. The Commission has vast experience in such inter-institutional matters. As Curtin states, the Council has little experience of a direct institutional dialogue with the European Parliament as envisaged by the conciliation committee procedure (Curtin, *supra*, at p.37). The Commission will still have the power to alter the proposed act where this may assist the process of conciliation (Art. 189a(2) E.C.). The European Parliament has also highlighted that it wishes as much as possible of the negotiating to take place either prior to the commencement of the procedure, or during the first reading, when all of the institutions may interact in accordance with their normal prerogatives. In other words, the stated aim of the European Parliament is to reach agreement on legislative provisions as soon as possible and to avoid having to go through the stages of what is a very complicated and potentially time consuming legislative process, [1992] O.J. C21 138–

141, 139. The prospect of increased inter-institutional discussion may well be one positive and necessary result of this complicated procedure.

Returning to the question of amendments in the conciliation committee. If, within a period of six weeks following the convening of the committee, a joint text is approved, the European Parliament and the Council have a further six weeks in which to approve it (once more subject to extension in accordance with Art. 189b(7)). In general, the Council acts by qualified majority, while the European Parliament acts by a majority of votes cast. This is, however, not always the case. In two specific areas, the Council is bound to act by unanimity. These are measures under Art. 128(5) in the field of culture and Art. 130i on research and technological development. Articles 128(5) and 130i E.C. state that "the Council shall act unanimously throughout the procedures referred to in Article 189b". This will make the achievement of workable compromises very difficult, given that the Council side can have their progress halted by one dissenting voice.

One area of the procedure which has caused real controversy is the final stage of the process, should the European Parliament or the Council fail to reach agreement in the conciliation committee. Article 189b(6) provides that the Council may, acting by a qualified majority, adopt its own common position, possibly with amendments approved by the European Parliament. The onus then falls upon the European Parliament to positively reject such a text within six weeks; failure to achieve the requisite absolute majority of members within this time leads to the act coming into force. The risk inherent in this procedure is that the Council may simply go through the motions of the conciliation committee without reaching agreement, and then adopt its common position thereafter. The European Parliament must then muster an absolute majority of its members, not just a majority of votes cast, to veto the Council's text. Moreover, it leads to the European Parliament taking full blame for the long drawn out legislative process coming to an end without any result. It would appear that unsuccessful attempts were made by Chancellor Kohl of Germany to alter this stage of the procedure during the Maastricht negotiations. While the Art. 189b E.C. procedure gives the impression of co-decision between the European Parliament and the Council (for example the act is jointly signed into being by the Presidents of the Council and the European Parliament (Art. 191 E.C.)), the reality is that the balance of power is still with the Council. Nevertheless, for the first time the European Parliament is given the right to veto legislation approved by the Council, albeit within a very complex procedure.

One very important factor concerns the scope of the new procedure. It will at first apply to 13 different legislative bases; these are Art. 49 on legislation on the free movement of workers, Art. 54(2) on directives on the freedom of establishment, Art. 56(2) on the co-ordination of Member State constraints on the freedom of establishment, Art. 57(1) and (2) on the mutual recognition of diplomas and co-ordination of Member State provisions on the taking up of activities by self-employed persons respectively, Art. 100a on the adoption of internal market harmonisation measures, Art. 126(4) on the adoption of incentive measures in the field of education, Art. 128 (5) for incentive measures in the field of culture, Art. 129(4) on the adoption of incentive measures in the field of public health, Art. 129a(2) on consumer protection measures, Art. 129d(1) on guidelines in the field of trans-European networks, Art. 130i(1) on the multi-annual framework programmes for research and technological development and Art. 130s(3) on general action programmes regarding environmental policy.

This coverage is far from what the European Parliament had sought in the run-up to the inter-governmental conference and, as a rule, avoids the vast majority of nationally sensitive areas as well as all constitutional matters. It does, however, cover a wider number of legislative bases than the co-operation procedure did when introduced by the SEA. The co-operation procedure, with a more limited scope, had a significant impact on the rôle of the European Parliament in the legislative process, and the conciliation and veto procedure should have an even greater impact. Thanks to pressure from states not happy with the range of bases to which the conciliation and veto procedure applies, Art. 189b(8) provides that the next inter-governmental conference is to look at the widening of this procedure's scope.

In conclusion, the new process marks an important development in the legislative powers of the European Parliament and thus in its democratic legitimacy. Unfortunately, the process is very complicated, and thus will make the adoption of legislation both time-consuming and lacking in transparency to an outside observer. This is to be regretted on both counts. Whether or not the more dramatic predictions that its complexity could paralyse the Community's decision-making structure will be borne out is a matter of some doubt, but actual practice in its application will prove very important; not least the degree to which the institutions can adapt to the new tri-partite system and achieve meaningful three-way dialogues.

Article 189c

Where reference is made in this Treaty to this Article for the adoption of an act, the following procedure shall apply:

(a) The Council, acting by a qualified majority on a proposal from the Commission and after obtaining the Opinion of the European Parliament, shall adopt a common position.

(b) The Council's common position shall be communicated to the European Parliament. The Council and the Commission shall inform the European Parliament fully of the reasons which led the Council to adopt its common position and also of the Commission's position.

If, within three months of such communication, the European Parliament approves this common position or has not taken a decision within that period, the Council shall definitively adopt the act in question in accordance with the common position.

(c) The European Parliament may, within the period of three months referred to in point (b), by an absolute majority of its component members, propose amendments to the Council's common position. The European Parliament may also, by the same majority, reject the Council's common position. The result of the proceedings shall be transmitted to the Council and the Commission.

If the European Parliament has rejected the Council's common position, unanimity shall be required for the Council to act on a second reading.

(d) The Commission shall, within a period of one month, re-examine the proposal on the basis of which the Council adopted its common position, by taking into account the amendments proposed by the European Parliament.

The Commission shall forward to the Council, at the same time as its re-examined proposal, the amendments of the European Parliament which it has not accepted, and shall express its opinion on them. The Council may adopt these amendments unanimously.

(e) The Council, acting by a qualified majority, shall adopt the proposals as re-examined by the Commission.

Unanimity shall be required for the Council to amend the proposal as re-examined by the Commission.

(f) In the cases referred to in points (c), (d) and (e), the Council shall be required to act within a period of three months. If no decision is taken within this period, the Commission proposal shall be deemed not to have been adopted.

(g) The periods referred to in points (b) and (f) may be extended by a maximum of one month by common accord between the Council and the European Parliament.

GENERAL NOTE

This Article, previously Art. 149(2) E.E.C. contains the co-operation procedure introduced by the SEA. The procedure itself remains unchanged, but the scope of application of the procedure, which has been widely used, is somewhat increased, despite the majority of the internal market provisions being promoted to the conciliation and veto procedure. For further details on which Treaty provisions the co-operation procedure applies to (before and after the TEU amendments) and how it has worked in the first few years of operation, see Weatherill and Beaumont, *supra*, at pp. 97–102.

Article 190

Regulations, directives and decisions adopted jointly by the European Parliament and the Council, and such acts adopted by the Council or the Commission, shall state the reasons on which they are based and shall refer to any proposals or opinions which were required to be obtained pursuant to this Treaty.

GENERAL NOTE

This Article has been amended in a way that recognises that some Community legislation will be adopted jointly by the European Parliament and the Council under the new conciliation and veto procedure (Art. 189b). The Article continues to make the stating of reasons essential for all binding Community legislation. For a brief analysis of Art. 190 see Weatherill and Beaumont, *E.C. Law*, 122–123 and 215–216.

Article 191

1. Regulations, directives and decisions adopted in accordance with the procedure referred to in Article 189b shall be signed by the President of the European Parliament and by the President of the Council and published in the Official Journal of the Community. They shall enter into force on the date specified in them or, in the absence thereof, on the 20th day following that of their publication.

2. Regulations of the Council and of the Commission, as well as directives of those institutions which are addressed to all Member States, shall be published in the Official Journal of the Community. They shall enter into force on the date specified in them or, in the absence thereof, on the 20th day following that of their publication.

3. Other directives, and decisions, shall be notified to those to whom they are addressed and shall take effect upon such notification.

GENERAL NOTE

The first paragraph was added by the TEU as it applies to binding legislative measures adopted under the new conciliation and veto procedure provided for in Art. 189b E.C. All such measures must be published in the Official Journal. Given their binding nature they will in practice be published in the "L" series of the Official Journal. The paragraph adopts the traditional time for regulations to come into force, i.e. when stated in the regulation or, if no date is specified, 20 days after publication (see Art. 191(1) E.E.C.), but extends its application to directives and decisions.

Paragraph two is an amended version of Art. 191(1) E.E.C. The requirement of publication in the Official Journal has been extended to apply to directives which are applicable to all Member States.

Paragraph three replicates the old Art. 191(2) E.E.C. with the insertion of "Other" at the beginning. This change is necessitated by the fact that directives and decisions adopted under the Art. 189b procedure, and directives addressed to all Member States, are for the first time subject to a requirement to be published in the Official Journal. It is unfortunate that all decisions which are addressed to all the Member States are not subject to the same publication requirement. Such decisions are binding and could have direct effect (see Weatherill and Beaumont, *supra*, pp.306–307), so they should be readily available to lawyers and the general public. In practice, it is likely that such decisions will be published in the Official Journal, but a Treaty requirement would have been more satisfactory.

Article 192

Decisions of the Council or of the Commission which impose a pecuniary obligation on persons other than States, shall be enforceable.

Enforcement shall be governed by the rules of civil procedure in force in the State in the territory of which it is carried out. The order for its enforcement shall be appended to the decision, without other formality than verification of the authenticity of the decision, by the national authority which the Government of each Member State shall designate for this purpose and shall make known to the Commission and to the Court of Justice.

When these formalities have been completed on application by the party concerned, the latter may proceed to enforcement in accordance with the national law, by bringing the matter directly before the competent authority.

Enforcement may be suspended only by a decision of the Court of Justice. However, the courts of the country concerned shall have jurisdiction over complaints that enforcement is being carried out in an irregular manner.

Chapter 3 (The Economic and Social Committee)

Article 193

An Economic and Social Committee is hereby established. It shall have advisory status.

The Committee shall consist of representatives of the various categories of economic and social activity, in particular, representatives of producers, farmers, carriers, workers, dealers, craftsmen, professional occupations and representatives of the general public.

Article 194

The number of members of the Committee shall be as follows:

Belgium	12
Denmark	9
Germany	24
Greece	12
Spain	21
France	24
Ireland	9
Italy	24
Luxembourg	6
Netherlands	12
Portugal	12
United Kingdom	24

The members of the Committee shall be appointed by the Council, acting unanimously, for four years. Their appointments shall be renewable.

The members of the Committee may not be bound by any mandatory instructions. They shall be completely independent in the performance of their duties, in the general interest of the Community.

The Council, acting by a qualified majority, shall determine the allowances of members of the Committee.

GENERAL NOTE

The last two sentences of this Article have been inserted by the Treaty on European Union. They reinforce the independence of members of the Economic and Social Committee. Previously they could not be bound by any mandatory instructions but now they must also be "completely independent" like members of the Commission (Art. 157(2)) and of the Committee of the Regions (Art. 198a). The symmetry with the new provisions on the Committee of the Regions is reflected in a common size (compare Arts. 194 and 198a) and common support staff in Brussels (see Protocol No. 16 below). However, the provisions governing the two Committees are not identical. Curiously enough the Maastricht Treaty has amended Art. 194 so that the Council, by qualified majority, can decide what allowances Economic and Social Committee members will get, but there is no express provision on the point for the new Committee of the Regions.

Article 195

1. For the appointment of the members of the Committee, each Member State shall provide the Council with a list containing twice as many candidates as there are seats allocated to its nationals.

The composition of the Committee shall take account of the need to ensure adequate representation of the various categories of economic and social activity.

2. The Council shall consult the Commission. It may obtain the opinion of European bodies which are representative of the various economic and social sectors to which the activities of the Community are of concern.

Article 196

The Committee shall elect its chairman and officers from among its members for a term of two years.

It shall adopt its rules of procedure.

The Committee shall be convened by its chairman at the request of the Council or of the Commission. It may also meet on its own initiative.

GENERAL NOTE

The only change to this Article is the addition of the last sentence. The Economic and Social Committee can now meet on its own initiative, not just when requested by the Council or Commission. This mirrors the right given to the Committee of the Regions in Art. 198b. This may well lead to more meetings held at the Community taxpayer's expense. As the Committee has an unconstrained power to adopt its own rules of procedure, it could make it possible for its meetings to be called by relatively few members. Since the Committee is purely advisory and is made up of members appointed by the Council there is a good case for its elimination rather than giving it an expanded rôle (see Weatherill and Beaumont, *supra*, p.129 but contrast Gordon Smith (1989) Stat. L. Rev. 56, 68). The European Parliament has been elected since 1979 and its powers have been gradually increased to give it a real say in the Community legislative process. Appointed Committees lack democratic legitimacy and expend scarce resources to little or no good purpose. Sufficient mechanisms for careful scrutiny by "experts" is provided by the Commission and by Council working groups.

Article 197

The Committee shall include specialised sections for the principal fields covered by this Treaty.

In particular, it shall contain an agricultural section and a transport section, which are the subject of special provisions in the Titles relating to agriculture and transport.

These specialised sections shall operate within the general terms of reference of the Committee. They may not be consulted independently of the Committee.

Sub-committees may also be established within the Committee to prepare on specific questions or in specific fields, draft opinions to be submitted to the Committee for its consideration.

The rules of procedure shall lay down the methods of composition and the terms of reference of the specialised sections and of the sub-committees.

Article 198

The Committee must be consulted by the Council or by the Commission where this Treaty so provides. The Committee may be consulted by these institutions in all cases in which they consider it appropriate. It may [take the initiative of issuing an opinion] in cases in which it considers such action appropriate.

The Council or the Commission shall, if it considers it necessary, set the Committee, for the submission of its opinion, a time limit which may not be less than one month from the date on which the chairman receives notification to this effect. Upon expiry of the time limit, the absence of an opinion shall not prevent further action.

The opinion of the Committee and that of the specialised section, together with a record of the proceedings, shall be forwarded to the Council and to the Commission.

GENERAL NOTE

In some versions of the treaty the words in brackets read "issue an opinion on its own initiative".

The last sentence of the first paragraph is an amendment introduced by the TEU. It gives the Economic and Social Committee the power to give an opinion on its own initiative whenever it wishes to do so. The same right is given to the Committee of the Regions in Art. 198c. In both cases this is a recipe for the Committee pontificating about all aspects of Community policy and doing so by proliferating their meetings (see note on Art. 196 above). It is questionable whether these own initiative opinions will prove to be helpful in the development of the Community.

In para. two the Economic and Social Committee's delaying power has been increased from 10 days to one month. This change avoids the necessity of the Committee having to meet more than once a month and is therefore to be welcomed.

Chapter 4 (The Committee of the Regions)

GENERAL NOTE
For an overview of the rôle of this committee see the Introduction and General Note above and the criticism of its creation by Weatherill and Beaumont, *supra*, pp. 129–130.

Article 198a

A Committee consisting of representatives of regional and local bodies, hereinafter referred to as the 'Committee of the Regions,' is hereby established with advisory status.

The number of members of the Committee of the Regions shall be as follows:

Belgium	12
Denmark	9
Germany	24
Greece	12
Spain	21
France	24
Ireland	9
Italy	24
Luxembourg	6
Netherlands	12
Portugal	12
United Kingdom	24

The members of the Committee and an equal number of alternate members shall be appointed for four years by the Council acting unanimously on proposals from the respective Member States. Their term of office shall be renewable.

The members of the Committee may not be bound by any mandatory instructions. They shall be completely independent in the performance of their duties, in the general interest of the Community.

GENERAL NOTE
The provision is very similar to Art. 194 concerning the Economic and Social Committee. One difference between the two Articles is mentioned in the note on Art. 194. In addition, the Council is required to appoint alternate members to the Committee of the Regions but not to the Economic and Social Committee.

Article 198b

The Committee of the Regions shall elect its chairman and officers from among its members for a term of two years.

It shall adopt its rules of procedure and shall submit them for approval to the Council, acting unanimously.

The Committee shall be convened by its chairman at the request of the Council or of the Commission. It may also meet on its own initiative.

GENERAL NOTE
This provision is identical to Art. 196 concerning the Economic and Social Committee, except that the Committee of the Regions cannot control its own rules of procedure but must have them approved unanimously by the Council.

Article 198c

The Committee of the Regions shall be consulted by the Council or by the Commission where this Treaty so provides and in all other cases in which one of these two institutions considers it appropriate.

The Council or the Commission shall, if it considers it necessary, set the Committee, for the submission of its opinion, a time-limit which may not be less than one month from the date on which the chairman receives notification to this effect. Upon expiry of the time-limit, the absence of an opinion shall not prevent further action.

Where the Economic and Social Committee is consulted pursuant to Article 198, the Committee of the Regions shall be informed by the Council or the Commission of the request for an opinion. Where it considers that specific regional interests are involved, the Committee of the Regions may issue an opinion on the matter.

It may [take the initiative of issuing an opinion] in cases in which it considers such action appropriate.

The opinion of the Committee, together with a record of the proceedings, shall be forwarded to the Council and to the Commission.

GENERAL NOTE

In some versions of the Treaty the words in brackets read "issue an opinion on its own initiative".

The substance of this Article is very similar to Art. 198 concerning the Economic and Social Committee. Many more Treaty Articles require mandatory consultation of that body than require consultation of the Committee of the Regions (Arts. 49, 54, 63, 75, 79, 84, 99, 100, 100a, 118a, 121, 126, 127, 129, 129a, 129d, 130, 130b, 130d, 130e, 130i, 130o and 130s compared with Arts. 126, 128, 129, 129d, 130b, 130d and 130e). Paragraph two requires the Committee of the Regions to be informed whenever the Economic and Social Committee is asked for an opinion (whether mandatory or optional). The Committee of the Regions can then choose to give its own opinion on the proposed legislation.

It is likely that any failure to consult the Committee of the Regions (or the Economic and Social Committee) in cases where the Treaty requires such consultation would mean that if an action was competently brought before the European Court under Art. 173, the legislation would be annulled (*cf.* the analogous requirement to consult the European Parliament in Case 139/79 *Roquette Frères* v. *Council* [1980] E.C.R. 3333).

Chapter 5 (European Investment Bank)

Article 198d

The European Investment Bank shall have legal personality.

The members of the European Investment Bank shall be the Member States.

The Statute of the European Investment Bank is laid down in a Protocol annexed to this Treaty.

GENERAL NOTE

This Article repeats what was formerly in Art. 129 E.E.C. with the exclusion of any reference to the establishing of the European Investment Bank, as it has been established since the founding of the Community.

Article 198e

The task of the European Investment Bank shall be to contribute, by having recourse to the capital market and utilising its own resources, to the balanced and steady development of the common market in the interest of the Community. For this purpose the Bank shall, operating on a non-profit-making basis, grant loans and give guarantees which facilitate the financing of the following projects in all sectors of the economy:

(a) projects for developing less-developed regions;

(b) projects for modernising or converting undertakings or for developing fresh activities called for by the progressive establishment of the common market, where these projects are of such a size or nature that they cannot be entirely financed by the various means available in the individual Member States;

(c) projects of common interest to several Member States which are of such a size or nature that they cannot be entirely financed by the various means available in the individual Member States.

In carrying out its task, the Bank shall facilitate the financing of investment programmes in conjunction with assistance from the structural funds and other Community financial instruments.

GENERAL NOTE

This provision is identical to its predecessor, Art. 130 E.E.C., except for the addition of the last paragraph. This explicit reference to the work of the European Investment Bank in the context of the structural funds, ties in with the reference to the Bank in Art. 130b (introduced by the SEA) as a means by which the Community can take action to support the objectives associated with economic and social cohesion set out in Art. 130a (see note on that Article). In the Protocol on Economic and Social Cohesion the Member States reaffirmed their conviction that the European Investment Bank should "continue to devote the majority of its resources to the promotion of economic and social cohesion, and declare their willingness to review the capital needs of the European Investment Bank as soon as this is necessary for that purpose".

TITLE II: Financial Provisions

Article 199

All items of revenue and expenditure of the Community, including those relating to the European Social Fund, shall be included in estimates to be drawn up for each financial year and shall be shown in the budget.

The administrative expenditure occasioned for the institutions by the provisions of the Treaty on European Union relating to common foreign and security policy and to co-operation in the [spheres] of justice and home affairs shall be charged to the budget. The operational expenditure occasioned by the implementation of the said provisions may, under the conditions referred to therein, be charged to the budget.

The revenue and expenditure shown in the budget shall be in balance.

GENERAL NOTE

In some versions of the text the word in square brackets is fields.

The second paragraph was added by the TEU. The administrative expenditure relating to the common foreign and security policy and justice and home affairs pillars is to be charged to the E.C. budget. This gives the European Parliament a significant financial rôle in constraining the cash allocated to the administration of the two inter-governmental pillars, even though it has a very limited rôle in the decision-making process as regards the substantive issues under those pillars. The degree of influence the European Parliament will have will depend on whether the expenditure is categorised as compulsory or non-compulsory. Articles J.11(2) and K.8(2) of the TEU lay down the procedure whereby the Council charges the operating expenditure of the common foreign and security policy and justice and home affairs either to the E.C. budget or to the Member States. It requires a unanimous decision for the Council to charge operational expenditure to the E.C. budget. It is not as clear as to which voting procedure applies in relation to a decision to charge the Member States. Logically, it should be less than unanimity because some mechanism for paying operational expenditure must be agreed, and if it has to be done unanimously there is a danger that no mechanism will be agreed. On the other hand, Arts. J.8(2) and K.4(3) of the TEU provide that in these pillars the Council is to act unanimously "except on matters of procedure . . .". Therefore unanimity will be required unless the Council regards the question as to who must pay for operational expenditure as a procedural matter.

Article 200

GENERAL NOTE

This Article has been repealed. It was long overdue for repeal, as it related to the financial contributions of the six original Member States to the Community budget revenue. Article 201 E.E.C. had envisaged the replacement of Art. 200 by a Community measure laying down a system of the Community's own resources. This was done first of all in the Council Decision on the Replacement of Financial Contributions from Member States by the Community's own Resources (Dec. 70/243 of April 21, [1970] J.O. [1970] L 94/19; O.J. Dec. [1970] (I) 224). Later, it was replaced by Council Decision 85/257 ([1985] O.J. L128/15). This in turn was replaced by Council Decision 88/376 of June 24, 1988 ([1988] O.J. L185/24).

Article 201

Without prejudice to other revenue, the budget shall be financed wholly from own resources. The Council, acting unanimously on a proposal from the Commission and after consulting the European Parliament, shall lay down provisions relating to the system of own resources of the Community, which it shall recommend to the Member States for adoption in accordance with their respective constitutional requirements.

GENERAL NOTE
The procedure whereby decisions about the Community's own resources can be taken, is the same as that provided in Art. 201 E.E.C. The change that has been made is the removal of references to the possibility of moving from Member States financing the Community by contributions, to the system of own resources. The latter is, of course, an accepted fact of Community life and the new Art. 201 is able to declare that the budget shall be financed wholly from own resources. The old Art. 201 explicitly referred to revenue from the common customs tariff as a possible own resource. The new Article does not specify what the constituent elements of the own resource are or should be. The last major change to the system of own resources, first established by Decision 70/243 (see note on Art. 200 above), was taken following the European Council meeting in Brussels in February 1988 (Bull 2–1988, 13 *et seq.* and Bull 3–1988, 105). Council Decision 88/376 added a fourth source of revenue, based on a Gross National Product scale, to the three sources first established in the 1970 Decision (agricultural levies, common customs tariff and a percentage of VAT). For a quick guide to the Community's own resources see Mathijsen, *A Guide to European Community Law* (1990, 5th ed.) pp. 104–107. For a slightly fuller analysis see Kapteyn and Van Themaat, *Introduction to the Law of the European Communities* (2nd ed. 1990, by Gormley), pp. 215–219.

Article 201a

With a view to maintaining budgetary discipline, the Commission shall not make any proposal for a Community act, or alter its proposals, or adopt any implementing measure which is likely to have appreciable implications for the budget without providing the assurance that that proposal or that measure is capable of being financed within the limit of the Community's own resources arising under provisions laid down by the Council pursuant to Article 201.

GENERAL NOTE
This is a new Article, inserted into the Treaty. For the first time, the idea of maintaining budgetary discipline has been embedded in the Treaty. The three political institutions, Commission, Council and Parliament, had earlier entered into an inter-institutional agreement on budgetary discipline and improvement of the budgetary procedure (see [1988] O.J. L185) and P. Zangl, The Inter-institutional Agreement on Budgetary Discipline and Improvement of the Budgetary Procedure (1989) 26 C.M.L.Rev. 675–685. The new Article places the onus on the Commission not to make proposals which would have the effect of breaching the limit of finances available from own resources. In the agreement on own resources in 1988, an overall ceiling on own resources was set at 1.2 per cent. of total Community Gross National Product for payments. The inter-institutional agreement attempts to ensure that the own resources ceilings are not overstepped, but it does not have binding legal force. A new Interinstitutional Agreement on budgetary discipline and improvement of the budgetary procedure was adopted on October 29, 1993 (see [1993] O.J. C333/1). It covers the 1993 to 1999 financial perspective agreed at the Edinburgh European Council in December 1992.

Article 202

The expenditure shown in the budget shall be authorised for one financial year, unless the regulations made pursuant to Article 209 provide otherwise.

In accordance with conditions to be laid down pursuant to Article 209, any appropriations, other than those relating to staff expenditure, that are unexpended at the end of the financial year may be carried forward to the next financial year only.

Appropriations shall be classified under different chapters grouping items of expenditure according to their nature or purpose and subdivided, as far as may be necessary, in accordance with the regulations made pursuant to Article 209.

The expenditure of the European Parliament, the Council, the Commission and the Court of Justice shall be set out in separate parts of the budget, without prejudice to special arrangements for certain common items of expenditure.

Article 203

1. The financial year shall run from 1 January to 31 December.

2. Each institution of the Community shall, before 1 July, draw up estimates of its expenditure. The Commission shall consolidate these estimates in a preliminary draft budget. It shall attach thereto an opinion which may contain different estimates.

The preliminary draft budget shall contain an estimate of revenue and an estimate of expenditure.

3. The Commission shall place the preliminary draft budget before the Council not later than 1 September of the year preceding that in which the budget is to be implemented.

The Council shall consult the Commission and, where appropriate, the other institutions concerned whenever it intends to depart from the preliminary draft budget.

The Council, acting by a qualified majority, shall establish the draft budget and forward it to the European Parliament.

4. The draft budget shall be placed before the European Parliament not later than 5 October of the year preceding that in which the budget is to be implemented.

The European Parliament shall have the right to amend the draft budget, acting by a majority of its members, and to propose to the Council, acting by an absolute majority of the votes cast, modifications to the draft budget relating to expenditure necessarily resulting from this Treaty or from acts adopted in accordance therewith.

If, within 45 days of the draft budget being placed before it, the European Parliament has given its approval, the budget shall stand as finally adopted. If within the period the European Parliament has not amended the draft budget nor proposed any modifications thereto, the budget shall be deemed to be finally adopted.

If within this period the European Parliament has adopted amendments or proposed modifications, the draft budget together with the amendments or proposed modifications shall be forwarded to the Council.

5. After discussing the draft budget with the Commission and, where appropriate, with the other institutions concerned, the Council shall act under the following conditions:

    (a) The Council may, acting by a qualified majority, modify any of the amendments adopted by the European Parliament;

    (b) With regard to the proposed modifications:

    — where a modification proposed by the European Parliament does not have the effect of increasing the total amount of the expenditure of an institution, owing in particular to the fact that the increase in expenditure which it would involve would be expressly compensated by one or more proposed modifications correspondingly reducing expenditure, the Council may, acting by a qualified majority, reject the proposed modification. In the absence of a decision to reject it, the proposed modification shall stand as accepted;

— where a modification proposed by the European Parliament has the effect of increasing the total amount of the expenditure of an institution, the Council may, acting by a qualified majority, accept this proposed modification. In the absence of a decision to accept it, the proposed modification shall stand as rejected;

— where, in pursuance of one of the two preceding subparagraphs, the Council has rejected a proposed modification, it may, acting by a qualified majority, either retain the amount shown in the draft budget or fix another amount.

The draft budget shall be modified on the basis of the proposed modifications accepted by the Council.

If, within 15 days of the draft being placed before it, the Council has not modified any of the amendments adopted by the European Parliament and if the modifications proposed by the latter have been accepted, the budget shall be deemed to be finally adopted. The Council shall inform the European Parliament that it has not modified any of the amendments and that the proposed modifications have been accepted.

If within the period the Council has modified one or more of the amendments adopted by the European Parliament or if the modifications proposed by the latter have been rejected or modified, the modified draft budget shall again be forwarded to the European Parliament. The Council shall inform the European Parliament of the results of its deliberations.

6. Within 15 days of the draft budget being placed before it, the European Parliament, which shall have been notified of the action taken on its proposed modifications, may, acting by a majority of its members and three-fifths of the votes cast, amend or reject the modifications to its amendments made by the Council and shall adopt the budget accordingly. If within this period the European Parliament has not acted, the budget shall be deemed to be finally adopted.

7. When the procedure provided for in this Article has been completed, the President of the European Parliament shall declare that the budget has been finally adopted.

8. However, the European Parliament, acting by a majority of its members and two-thirds of the votes cast, may, if there are important reasons, reject the draft budget and ask for a new draft to be submitted to it.

9. A maximum rate of increase in relation to the expenditure of the same type to be incurred during the current year shall be fixed annually for the total expenditure other than that necessarily resulting from this Treaty or from acts adopted in accordance therewith.

The Commission shall, after consulting the Economic Policy Committee, declare what this maximum rate is as it results from:

— the trend, in terms of volume, of the gross national product within the Community;

— the average variation in the budgets of the Member States;
and

— the trend of the cost of living during the preceding financial year.

The maximum rate shall be communicated, before 1 May, to all the institutions of the Community. The latter shall be required to conform to this during the budgetary procedure, subject to the provisions of the fourth and fifth subparagraphs of this paragraph.

If, in respect of expenditure other than that necessarily resulting from this Treaty or from acts adopted in accordance therewith, the actual rate of increase in the draft budget, established by the Council is over half the maximum rate, the European Parliament may, exercising its right of amendment, further increase the total amount of that expenditure to a limit not exceeding half the maximum rate.

Where the European Parliament, the Council or the Commission consider that the activities of the Communities require that the rate determined according to the procedure laid down in this paragraph should be exceeded, another rate may be fixed by agreement between the Council, acting by a qualified majority, and the European Parliament, acting by a majority of its members and three-fifths of the votes cast.

10. Each institution shall exercise the powers conferred upon it by this Article, with due regard for the provisions of the Treaty and for acts adopted in accordance therewith, in particular those relating to the Communities' own resources and to the balance between revenue and expenditure.

Article 204

If at the beginning of a financial year, the budget has not yet been voted, a sum equivalent to not more than one-twelfth of the budget appropriations for the preceding financial year may be spent each month in respect of any chapter or other subdivision of the budget in accordance with the provisions of the Regulations made pursuant to Article 209; this arrangement shall not, however, have the effect of placing at the disposal of the Commission appropriations in excess of one-twelfth of those provided for in the draft budget in course of preparation.

The Council may, acting by a qualified majority, provided that the other conditions laid down in the first subparagraph are observed, authorise expenditure in excess of one-twelfth.

If the decision relates to expenditure which does not necessarily result from this Treaty or from acts adopted in accordance therewith, the Council shall forward it immediately to the European Parliament; within 30 days the European Parliament, acting by a majority of its members and three-fifths of the votes cast, may adopt a different decision on the expenditure in excess of the one-twelfth referred to in the first subparagraph. This part of the decision of the Council shall be suspended until the European Parliament has taken its decision. If within the said period the European Parliament has not taken a decision which differs from the decision of the Council, the latter shall be deemed to be finally adopted.

The decisions referred to in the second and third subparagraphs shall lay down the necessary measures relating to resources to ensure application of this Article.

Article 205

The Commission shall implement the budget, in accordance with the provisions of the regulations made pursuant to Article 209, on its own responsibility and within the limits of the appropriations, having regard to the principles of sound financial management.

The regulations shall lay down detailed rules for each institution concerning its part in effecting its own expenditure.

Within the budget, the Commission may, subject to the limits and conditions laid down in the regulations made pursuant to Article 209, transfer appropriations from one chapter to another or from one sub-division to another.

GENERAL NOTE

The last clause of the first paragraph: "having regard to the principles of sound financial management" has been added by the TEU. This is a very minor change that acts as a reminder to the Commission to implement the budget in a financially prudent way. It is difficult to see how this clause might successfully be invoked against the Commission in any claim that it had imprudently implemented the budget. The Commission merely has to have regard to the principles referred to, and it is not at all clear what these principles are.

Article 205a

The Commission shall submit annually to the Council and to the European Parliament the accounts of the preceding financial year relating to the implementation of the budget. The Commission shall also forward to them a financial statement of the assets and liabilities of the Community.

Article 206

1. The European Parliament, acting on a recommendation from the Council which shall act by a qualified majority, shall give a discharge to the Commission in respect of the implementation of the budget. To this end, the Council and the European Parliament in turn shall examine the accounts and the financial statement referred to in Article 205a, the annual report by the Court of Auditors together with the replies of the institutions under audit to the observations of the Court of Auditors and any relevant special reports by the Court of Auditors.

2. Before giving a discharge to the Commission, or for any other purpose in connection with the exercise of its powers over the implementation of the budget, the European Parliament may ask to hear the Commission give evidence with regard to the execution of expenditure or the operation of financial control systems. The Commission shall submit any necessary information to the European Parliament at the latter's request.

3. The Commission shall take all appropriate steps to act on the observations in the decisions giving discharge and on other observations by the European Parliament relating to the execution of expenditure, as well as on comments accompanying the recommendations on discharge adopted by the Council.

At the request of the European Parliament or the Council, the Commission shall report on the measures taken in the light of these observations and comments and in particular on the instructions given to the departments which are responsible for the implementation of the budget. These reports shall also be forwarded to the Court of Auditors.

GENERAL NOTE

The first paragraph of Art. 206 is derived from Art. 206b E.E.C. with the addition of the last clause: "and any relevant special reports by the Court of Auditors".

Paragraphs 2 and 3 are new material added by the TEU. Paragraph 2 gives the Parliament explicit, Treaty based, power to glean any necessary information from the Commission on its execution of expenditure or the operation of financial control systems. Paragraph 3 requires the Commission to "take all appropriate steps" to carry out the observations of the European Parliament and Council in relation to the discharge. This does not seem to require the Commission to do what the other institutions say, but does require it to do what it regards as "appropriate" to comply with the wishes of the other institutions. The Commission has to report on the actions it takes to the other institutions and the Court of Auditors. It is difficult to see how the Commission can be compelled to take the steps that the Parliament and Council want.

These two paragraphs were part of the attempt at Maastricht to bring the Commission under even closer scrutiny by the Parliament and to tighten up the financial discipline and prudence in the Community.

Article 206a

(repealed at Maastricht)

Article 206b

(repealed at Maastricht)

GENERAL NOTE

These Articles were repealed by the TEU. Article 206a E.E.C. concerned the Court of Auditors and an amended version can now be found in Art. 188c E.C. Article 206b E.E.C. has been absorbed into Art. 206 E.C. (see note on that article).

Article 207

The budget shall be drawn up in the unit of account determined in accordance with the provisions of the regulations made pursuant to Article 209.

The financial contributions provided for in Article 200(1) shall be placed at the disposal of the Community by the Member States in their national currencies.

The available balances of these contributions shall be deposited with the Treasuries of Member States or with bodies designated by them. While on deposit, such funds shall retain the value corresponding to the parity, at the date of deposit, in relation to the unit of account referred to in the first paragraph.

The balances may be invested on terms to be agreed between the Commission and the Member State concerned.

The regulations made pursuant to Article 209 shall lay down the technical conditions under which financial operations relating to the European Social Fund shall be carried out.

GENERAL NOTE

This Article is not amended by the TEU. This is unfortunate given that the second sentence contains a reference to Art. 200 which was repealed by the TEU. Hopefully, this discrepancy will be removed at the next inter-governmental conference in 1996.

Article 208

The Commission may, provided it notifies the competent authorities of the Member States concerned, transfer into the currency of one of the Member States its holdings in the currency of another Member State, to the extent necessary to enable them to be used for purposes which come within the scope of this Treaty. The Commission shall as far as possible avoid making such transfers if it possesses cash or liquid assets in the currencies which it needs.

The Commission shall deal with each Member State through the authority designated by the State concerned. In carrying out financial operations the Commission shall employ the services of the bank of issue of the Member State concerned or of any other financial institution approved by that State.

Article 209

The Council, acting unanimously on a proposal from the Commission and after consulting the European Parliament and obtaining the opinion of the Court of Auditors, shall:

(a) make Financial Regulations specifying in particular the procedure to be adopted for establishing and implementing the budget and for presenting and auditing accounts;

(b) determine the methods and procedure whereby the budget revenue provided under the arrangements relating to the Community's own resources shall be made available to the Commission, and determine the measures to be applied, if need be, to meet cash requirements;

(c) lay down rules concerning the responsibility of financial controllers, authorising officers and accounting officers, and concerning appropriate arrangements for inspection.

GENERAL NOTE

Only para. (c) has been amended, by the insertion of the words "financial controllers" before "authorising officers". This is a very minor amendment.

Article 209a

Member States shall take the same measures to counter fraud affecting the financial interests of the Community as they take to counter fraud affecting their own financial interests.

Without prejudice to other provisions of this Treaty, Member States shall co-ordinate their action aimed at protecting the financial interests of the Community against fraud. To this end they shall organise, with the help of the

Commission, close and regular co-operation between the competent departments of their administrations.

<small>GENERAL NOTE</small>

This is a new practice designed to help the fight against fraudulent use of Community finances. The obligation in the first paragraph is one of parallelism; the Member States are to be just as vigilant in countering fraud against Community finances as they are in dealing with fraud affecting their own interests. The symbolism of this paragraph is positive, but how can it be enforced?

The second paragraph imposes on Member States a requirement to co-ordinate their anti-fraud activities. This may be of some help in the battle against fraud, but it is questionable whether such co-ordination is sufficient.

PART SIX (GENERAL AND FINAL PROVISIONS)

Article 210

The Community shall have legal personality.

Article 211

In each of the Member States, the Community shall enjoy the most extensive legal capacity accorded to legal persons under their laws; it may, in particular, acquire or dispose of movable and immovable property and may be a party to legal proceedings. To this end, the Community shall be represented by the Commission.

Article 212

(*as replaced by Merger Treaty, Art. 24(1)*)

24(1). The officials and other servants of the European Coal and Steel Community, the European Economic Community and the European Atomic Energy Community shall, at the date of entry into force of this Treaty, become officials and other servants of the European Communities and form part of the single administration of those Communities.

The Council shall, acting by a qualified majority on a proposal from the Commission and after consulting the other institutions concerned, lay down the Staff Regulations of officials of the European Communities and the Conditions of Employment of other servants of those Communities.

Article 213

The Commission may, within the limits and under conditions laid down by the Council in accordance with the provisions of this Treaty, collect any information and carry out any checks required for the performance of the tasks entrusted to it.

Article 214

The members of the institutions of the Community, the members of committees, and the officials and other servants of the Community shall be required, even after their duties have ceased, not to disclose information of the kind covered by the obligation of professional secrecy, in particular information about undertakings, their business relations or their cost components.

Article 215

The contractual liability of the Community shall be governed by the law applicable to the contract in question.

In the case of non-contractual liability, the Community shall, in accordance with the general principles common to the laws of the Member States, make good any damage caused by its institutions or by its servants in the performance of their duties.

The preceding paragraph shall apply under the same conditions to damage caused by the ECB or by its servants in the performance of their duties.

The personal liability of its servants towards the Community shall be governed by the provisions laid down in their Staff Regulations or in the Conditions of Employment applicable to them.

GENERAL NOTE

Paragraph two concerning the non-contractual liability of the Community has been extended by para. three to cover damage caused by the European Central Bank or by its servants, in the performance of their duties. For a brief summary of the Court's jurisdiction in relation to Art. 215(2), provided for by Art. 178, see Weatherill and Beaumont, *supra*, pp. 269–273 and for further reading see the references on p. 807 of that book.

Article 216

The seat of the institutions of the Community shall be determined by common accord of the Governments of the Member States.

Article 217

The rules governing the languages of the institutions of the Community shall, without prejudice to the provisions contained in the rules of procedure of the Court of Justice, be determined by the Council, acting unanimously.

Article 218

(as replaced by Merger Treaty, Art. 28(1))

28(1). The European Communities shall enjoy in the territories of the Member States such privileges and immunities as are necessary for the performance of their tasks, under the conditions laid down in the Protocol annexed to this Treaty. The same shall apply to the European Investment Bank.

Article 219

Member States undertake not to submit a dispute concerning the interpretation or application of this Treaty to any method of settlement other than those provided for therein.

Article 220

Member States shall, so far as is necessary, enter into negotiations with each other with a view to securing for the benefit of their nationals:

— the protection of persons and the enjoyment and protection of rights under the same conditions as those accorded by each State to its own nationals;

— the abolition of double taxation within the Community;

— the mutual recognition of companies or firms within the meaning of the second paragraph of Article 48, the retention of legal personality in the event of transfer of their seat from one country to another, and the possibility of mergers between companies or firms governed by the laws of different countries;

— the simplification of formalities governing the reciprocal recognition and enforcement of judgments of courts or tribunals and of arbitration awards.

Article 221

Within three years of the entry into force of this Treaty, Member States shall accord nationals of the other Member States the same treatment as their own nationals as regards participation in the capital of companies or firms within the meaning of Article 58, without prejudice of the other provisions of this Treaty.

Article 222

This Treaty shall in no way prejudice the rules in Member States governing the system of property ownership.

Article 223

1. The provisions of this Treaty shall not preclude the application of the following rules:
  (a) No Member State shall be obliged to supply information the disclosure of which it considers contrary to the essential interests of its security;
  (b) Any Member State may take such measures as it considers necessary for the protection of the essential interests of its security which are connected with the production of or trade in arms, munitions and war material; such measures shall not adversely affect the conditions of competition in the common market regarding products which are not intended for specifically military purposes.
2. During the first year after the entry into force of this Treaty, the Council shall, acting unanimously, draw up a list of products to which the provisions of paragraph 1(b) shall apply.
3. The Council may, acting unanimously on a proposal from the Commission, make changes in this list.

Article 224

Member States shall consult each other with a view to taking together the steps needed to prevent the functioning of the common market being affected by measures which a Member State may be called upon to take in the event of serious internal disturbances affecting the maintenance of law and order, in the event of war, serious international tension constituting a threat of war, or in order to carry out obligations it has accepted for the purpose of maintaining peace and international security.

Article 225

If measures taken in the circumstances referred to in Articles 223 and 224 have the effect of distorting the conditions of competition in the common market, the Commission shall, together with the State concerned, examine how these measures can be adjusted to the rules laid down in this Treaty.

By way of derogation from the procedure laid down in Articles 169 and 170, the Commission or any Member State may bring the matter directly before the Court of Justice if it considers that another Member State is making improper use of the powers provided for in Articles 223 and 224. The Court of Justice shall give its ruling *in camera*.

Article 226

1. If, during the transitional period, difficulties arise which are serious and liable to persist in any sector of the economy or which could bring about serious deterioration in the economic situation of a given area, a Member State may apply for authorisation to take protective measures in order to rectify the situation and adjust the sector concerned to the economy of the common market.
2. On application by the State concerned, the Commission shall, by emergency procedure, determine without delay the protective measures which it considers necessary, specifying the circumstances and the manner in which they are to be put into effect.
3. The measures authorised under paragraph 2 may involve derogations from the rules of this Treaty, to such an extent and for such periods as are strictly necessary in order to attain the objectives referred to in paragraph 1.

Priority shall be given to such measures as will least disturb the functioning of the common market.

Article 227

1. This Treaty shall apply to the Kingdom of Belgium, the Kingdom of Denmark, the Federal Republic of Germany, the Hellenic Republic, the Kingdom of Spain, the French Republic, Ireland, the Italian Republic, the Grand Duchy of Luxembourg, the Kingdom of the Netherlands, the Portuguese Republic and the United Kingdom of Great Britain and Northern Ireland.

2. With regard to the French overseas departments, the general and particular provisions of this Treaty relating to:
— the free movement of goods;
— agriculture, save for Article 40(4);
— the liberalisation of services;
— the rules on competition;
— the protective measures provided for in Articles 109h, 109i and 226;
— the institutions,
shall apply as soon as this Treaty enters into force.

The conditions under which the other provisions of this Treaty are to apply shall be determined, within two years of the entry into force of this Treaty, by decisions of the Council, acting unanimously on a proposal from the Commission.

The institutions of the Community will, within the framework of the procedures provided for in this Treaty, in particular Article 226, take care that the economic and social development of these areas is made possible.

3. The special arrangements for association set out in Part Four of this Treaty shall apply to the overseas countries and territories listed in Annex IV to this Treaty.

This Treaty shall not apply to those overseas countries and territories having special relations with the United Kingdom of Great Britain and Northern Ireland which are not included in the aforementioned list.

4. The provisions of this Treaty shall apply to the European territories for whose external relations a Member State is responsible.

5. Notwithstanding the preceding paragraphs:
(a) This Treaty shall not apply to the Faeroe Islands.
(b) This Treaty shall not apply to the Sovereign Base Areas of the United Kingdom of Great Britain and Northern Ireland in Cyprus.
(c) This Treaty shall apply to the Channel Islands and the Isle of Man only to the extent necessary to ensure the implementation of the arrangements for those islands set out in the Treaty concerning the accession of new Member States to the European Economic Community and to the European Atomic Energy Community signed on 22 January 1972.

GENERAL NOTE
Only two amendments have been made to this Article. Paragraph two no longer applies to Algeria, and para. 5 now simply declares that the Treaty does not apply to the Faeroe Islands. Article 227(5) of the E.E.C. Treaty had given Denmark the power to declare that the Treaty would apply to the Faeroe Islands, but this option expired on December 31, 1975. Thus, the amendment simply removes some dead wood from the Treaty.

Article 228

1. Where this Treaty provides for the conclusion of agreements between the Community and one or more States or international organisations, the Commission shall make recommendations to the Council, which shall authorise the Commission to open the necessary negotiations. The Commission shall conduct these negotiations in consultation with special committees

appointed by the Council to assist it in this task and within the framework of such directives as the Council may issue to it.

In exercising the powers conferred upon it by this paragraph, the Council shall act by a qualified majority, except in the cases provided for in the second sentence of paragraph 2, for which it shall act unanimously.

2. Subject to the powers vested in the Commission in this field, the agreements shall be concluded by the Council, acting by a qualified majority on a proposal from the Commission. The Council shall act unanimously when the agreement covers a field for which unanimity is required for the adoption of internal rules, and for the agreements referred to in Article 238.

3. The Council shall conclude agreements after consulting the European Parliament, except for the agreements referred to in Article 113(3), including cases where the agreement covers a field for which the procedure referred to in Article 189b or that referred to in Article 189c is required for the adoption of internal rules. The European Parliament shall deliver its Opinion within a time limit which the Council may lay down according to the urgency of the matter. In the absence of an Opinion within that time limit, the Council may act.

By way of derogation from the previous subparagraph, agreements referred to in Article 238, other agreements establishing a specific institutional framework by organising co-operation procedures, agreements having important budgetary implications for the Community and agreements entailing amendment of an act adopted under the procedure referred to in Article 189b shall be concluded after the assent of the European Parliament has been obtained.

The Council and the European Parliament may, in an urgent situation, agree upon a time limit for the assent.

4. When concluding an agreement, the Council may, by way of derogation from paragraph 2, empower the Commission to approve modifications on behalf of the Community where the agreement provides for them to be adopted by a simplified procedure or by a body set up by the agreement; it may attach specific conditions to such empowerment.

5. When the Council envisages concluding an agreement which calls for amendments to this Treaty, the amendments must first be adopted in accordance with the procedure laid down in Article N of the Treaty on European Union.

6. The Council, the Commission or a Member State may obtain the opinion of the Court of Justice as to whether an agreement envisaged is compatible with the provisions of this Treaty. Where the opinion of the Court of Justice is adverse, the agreement may enter into force only in accordance with Article N of the Treaty on European Union.

7. Agreements concluded under the conditions set out in this Article shall be binding on the institutions of the Community and on Member States.

GENERAL NOTE

The procedure whereby the Community can enter into different international agreements is set out in this, greatly extended, version of Art. 228. Previously, the procedure whereby agreements under the common commercial policy and association agreements were arrived at was set out under Arts. 113 and 238 E.E.C., respectively.

Para. (1)

This has adopted the procedure prescribed by Art. 113 E.E.C. for concluding international agreements in the context of the common commercial policy, and extended it to all international agreements. Previously, these other international agreements were required to be negotiated by the Commission (Art. 228(1) E.E.C.), but no provision was made for the Council to set up Committees which the Commission has to consult during the negotiations. More importantly, the Council was not explicitly authorised to constrain the negotiating mandate of the Commission within the framework of Council directives.

Para. (2)

This clarifies the voting procedure in the Council in relation to all international agreements. Agreements under the common commercial policy will continue to be reached by qualified majority (*cf.* Art. 113(4) E.E.C.) and association agreements will still require unanimity (*cf.* Art. 238 E.E.C.). Since the landmark decision of the European Court in the *ERTA* case (Case 22/70 *Commission* v. *Council* [1971] E.C.R. 263) the Community has had implied powers to enter into international agreements in any area where it has power to legislate internally (see also Opinion 1/78 *Rubber Agreement Opinion* [1979] E.C.R. 2871). Article 228 E.E.C. was silent on the voting procedure to be adopted in the Council, therefore it was unclear what voting requirements applied to international agreements falling within the Community's implied powers. It was at least arguable that the silence of Art. 228 E.E.C. in regard to how the Council is to conclude such agreements implied that a simple majority was sufficient (see Art. 148(1) E.E.C./E.C. which states that: "Save as otherwise provided in this Treaty, the Council shall act by a majority of its members"). Paragraph 2 of Art. 228 E.C. should remove any doubt. International agreements require at least a qualified majority vote in the Council, and where internal rules can be adopted only by unanimity, then international agreements must be adopted on the same basis.

Para. (3)

This clarifies the rôle of the European Parliament in relation to international agreements. The Parliament is still given no formal rôle in relation to international agreements under the common commercial policy (see the note on Art. 113 above). As previously required by Art. 238 E.E.C., the Parliament must give its assent to an association agreement, but that paragraph does not lay down any requirement as to the majority needed in Parliament. Under Art. 238 E.E.C. an absolute majority of Parliament's component members was required, but now under Rule 33(7) of the European Parliament's Rules of Procedure (as amended subsequent to the TEU, see [1993] O.J. C268/51) assent can be given by a majority of votes cast. In relation to other international agreements, the Parliament has now been given a comprehensive right to be consulted. This is advantageous for the Parliament in relation to agreements where internal Community rules could be adopted without any consultation of the European Parliament (see Weatherill and Beaumont, *supra*, pp. 796–7). Article 228 E.E.C. gave a right to Parliament to be consulted about the adoption of an international agreement only "where required by this Treaty". However, in the context of matters adopted internally under the co-operation procedure (Art. 189c) or the conciliation and veto procedure (Art. 189b), consulting the Parliament gives it much less influence and power in external agreements than it has been granted over internal rules. This is a potential means to circumvent Parliament's internal veto under Art. 189b. Where the international agreement requires an amendment to an act adopted under the conciliation and veto procedure, the Parliament must give its assent.

In two other areas the Parliament has been given, for the first time, the power to block an international agreement. Firstly, where the agreement has important budgetary implications for the Community. That is an appropriate, if somewhat belated, change reflecting the fact that the Community's budget has been adopted jointly by the Council and Parliament since the Budgetary Treaties of the 1970's. Secondly, where the agreement establishes a specific institutional framework by organising co-operation procedures. It is not at all clear what is meant by "co-operation procedures".

Where the Parliament has a right to be consulted, the Council is given a new right to set a time-limit, within which Parliament must give its Opinion. If the Opinion is not given within the time-limit, then the Council is free to act. This is a sensible provision to prevent the Parliament turning a right to be consulted into a veto, by indefinitely failing to give an Opinion. The only danger is that the Council may set an unrealistically short deadline. In such circumstances the Court might declare the Agreement void, due to failure to give Parliament sufficient time to give its Opinion. Where the Parliament's assent is required then the Council cannot unilaterally impose a time-limit on the Parliament. The two institutions may agree a time-limit. Parliament may delay giving its assent in order to try to force concessions from the Council (see Bradley, (1988) 8 YEL 189, 198–199).

Para. (4)

This is a new provision authorising the Council to delegate to the Commission the power to modify an international agreement, without having to go through the full procedure. This would remove the Parliament's right to be consulted or to give its assent and the Council's right to vote on its adoption by qualified majority or unanimity. This new power to delegate in the field of international agreements echoes the long-standing power of the Council to delegate internal legislative power to the Commission (see Art. 145 indent 3 E.E.C./E.C.). In the internal context the Council has delegated a lot of legislative power to the Commission in terms of quantity but very little in terms of quality. The Council has developed an elaborate committee structure to monitor the Commission's delegated powers (see Weatherill and Beaumont, *supra*, pp. 51–54 and Council Decision 87/373 [1987] O.J. L197/33). It will be interesting to see if the Council makes use of this power to delegate to the Commission in the context of international agreements, and if it sets up management or regulatory committees to monitor the delegated power, relying on its discretion to "attach specific conditions to such authorisation".

Para. (5)

The substance of this provision was formerly in Art. 238(3) E.E.C. (see note on that Article). Paragraph 5 has a much wider scope than its predecessor, in that it applies to all international agreements and not just association agreements. The paragraph effectively bars any attempt to amend the E.C. Treaty by the devious route of concluding an international agreement with another State. Such agreements can be adopted by qualified majority in the Council and do not necessarily require the assent of the Parliament: these are much lower requirements than those provided for by Art. N TEU on treaty amendments.

Para. (6)

This provision replicates its predecessor in Art. 228 E.E.C., except that the reference to Art. 236 E.E.C. has been replaced by a reference to Art. N TEU. The former has been repealed and the latter now regulates the treaty amendment procedure (see the note on the repeal of Art. 236). For a brief treatment of the Court's power to give opinions under Art. 228 see Weatherill and Beaumont, *supra*, pp. 275–277.

Para. (7)

This provision is carried over from Art. 228 E.E.C. It impliedly makes international agreements entered into by the Community a higher source of law than any legislation adopted by the Community.

Article 228a

Where it is provided, in a common position or in a joint action adopted according to the provisions of the Treaty on European Union relating to the common foreign and security policy, for an action by the Community to interrupt or to reduce, in part or completely, economic relations with one or more third countries, the Council shall take the necessary urgent measures. The Council shall act by a qualified majority on a proposal from the Commission.

GENERAL NOTE

This provision provides an intersection between the E.C. Treaty and the common foreign and security policy pillar established by the TEU. If a foreign policy decision is taken to impose economic sanctions on a third State, then this requires to be followed up by a measure under the E.C. Treaty. Clearly any severance, or reduction, of trade with a non-Member State represents a change in the Community's common commercial policy, and thus E.C. legislation is called for. Article 228a for the first time creates a specific mechanism to deal with the problem. The Commission makes a proposal, which the Council passes by qualified majority vote. The European Parliament is not given any rôle in the legislative process, presumably because these measures often require to be passed very quickly.

Article 228a is a new solution but the problem is not a new one. Under European Political Co-operation, the predecessor of common foreign and security policy, formalised in the SEA, it was recognised that there needed to be consistency between "The external policies of the European Community and the policies agreed in European Political Co-operation" (Art. 30(5) SEA). Often the problem is further complicated by the fact that the economic sanctions are imposed by the United Nations and then specific Community legislation is needed to implement the sanctions. This legislation may permit exceptions to the sanctions which may be taken up in some Member States and not in others. For the problems this can cause see the sanctions imposed on Serbia and Montenegro by E.E.C. Regulation 1432/92 discussed in *R.* v. *H.M. Treasury,* ex p. *Centro-Com Sarl., The Times,* October 7, 1993.

Almost as soon as the TEU entered into force, Art. 228a was used as the legal basis for Regs. 3274/93 and 3275/93 concerning sanctions in relation to Libya, following various UN Security Council Resolutions (see [1993] O.J. L295).

Article 229

It shall be for the Commission to ensure the maintenance of all appropriate relations with the organs of the United Nations, of its specialised agencies and of the General Agreement on Tariffs and Trade.

The Commission shall also maintain such relations as are appropriate with all international organisations.

Article 230

The Community shall establish all appropriate forms of co-operation with the Council of Europe.

Article 231

The Community shall establish close co-operation with the Organisation for Economic Co-operation and Development, the details of which shall be determined by common accord.

GENERAL NOTE

This Article was long overdue for amendment. The version in the E.E.C. Treaty referred to the Community establishing "close co-operation with the Organisation for European Economic Co-operation". That body was a relatively weak inter-governmental institution set up after the Second World War to disburse the very substantial amount of money given by the United States for the development of Europe in the Marshall Plan. By 1961 the Organisation for European Economic Co-operation had evolved into the Organisation for Economic Co-operation and Development. The latter is based in Paris but is not a European international institution. It is concerned with monitoring economic performance in its member countries, and with helping to improve the economies of developing countries.

Article 232

1. The provisions of this Treaty shall not affect the provisions of the Treaty establishing the European Coal and Steel Community, in particular as regards the rights and obligations of Member States, the powers of the institutions of that Community and the rules laid down by that Treaty for the functioning of the common market in coal and steel.

2. The provisions of this Treaty shall not derogate from those of the Treaty establishing the European Atomic Energy Community.

Article 233

The provisions of this Treaty shall not preclude the existence or completion of regional unions between Belgium and Luxembourg, or between Belgium, Luxembourg and the Netherlands, to the extent that the objectives of these regional unions are not attained by application of this Treaty.

Article 234

The rights and obligations arising from agreements concluded before the entry into force of this Treaty between one or more Member States on the one hand, and one or more third countries on the other, shall not be affected by the provisions of this Treaty.

To the extent that such agreements are not compatible with this Treaty, the Member State or States concerned shall take all appropriate steps to eliminate the incompatibilities established. Member States shall, where necessary, assist each other to this end and shall, where appropriate, adopt a common attitude.

In applying the agreements referred to in the first paragraph, Member States shall take into account the fact that the advantages accorded under this Treaty by each Member State form an integral part of the establishment of the Community and are thereby inseparably linked with the creation of common institutions, the conferring of powers upon them and the granting of the same advantages by all the other Member States.

Article 235

If action by the Community should prove necessary to attain, in the course of the operation of the common market, one of the objectives of the Community and this Treaty has not provided the necessary powers, the Council shall, acting unanimously on a proposal from the Commission and after consulting the European Parliament, take the appropriate measures.

Article 236

(*repealed at Maastricht*)

Article 237

(*repealed at Maastricht*)

GENERAL NOTE

Article 236 E.E.C. was the provision which outlined the mechanism by which the Treaty could be amended. It has been replaced by Art. N of the TEU. The latter is very similar to the former. Article N of the TEU provides a common method for amending all the Treaties on which the Union is founded (*i.e.* the European Coal and Steel Community, E.C. and Euratom Treaties, as well as the TEU). The one substantive change in the procedure for Treaty amendment, introduced by Art. N TEU is that the European Central Bank is to be "consulted in the case of institutional changes in the monetary area".

Paragraph 2 of Art. N TEU provides that an inter-governmental conference shall be convened in 1996 to examine those provisions of the Treaties for which revision is provided. Article 189b(8) E.C. provides that the scope of the procedure laid down under that Article – conciliation and veto – may be widened at the 1996 inter-governmental conference. The Commission is to submit a report to the Council on this matter by 1996. Article J(4) TEU, concerning security and defence policy, is to be considered for revision at the 1996 inter-governmental conference. The Council is to submit a report to the European Council concerning Art. J(4) by 1996. Doubtless the 1996 inter-governmental conference will consider other Treaty amendments, including the possibility of establishing an appropriate hierarchy between the different categories of Community acts (see Declaration No. 16 below).

Article 237 E.E.C. dealt with the procedure by which a State could become a member of the Community. Article O TEU applies to the method by which a State becomes a member of the European Union. The substance of the two Articles is identical, except that by becoming a member of the Union a State becomes a member of the three Communities which form part of the Union, including the E.C., as well as the two inter-governmental pillars of the common foreign and security policy and co-operation in the fields of justice and home affairs.

Article 238

The Community may conclude with one or more States or international organisations agreements establishing an association involving reciprocal rights and obligations, common action and special procedures.

GENERAL NOTE

Paragraphs 2 and 3 of Art. 238 E.E.C. have been repealed. The substance of para. 2 is now found in Art. 228(3) E.C. The Council still requires unanimity and the Parliament still has to give its assent to any agreement adopted under Art. 238. Two minor reforms to the old para. 2 have been made. Firstly, it is no longer specified that an absolute majority of the component members of the Parliament must vote for the agreement for Parliament's assent to be given. Secondly, the Council and the European Parliament may, in an urgent situation, agree upon a time-limit for the latter's assent. A revised version of para. 3 of Art. 238 E.E.C. is now found in Art. 228(5) E.C. No substantive change has been made. If the agreement calls for amendments to the E.C. Treaty, then the amendments must first be adopted in accordance with the procedure laid down for amending the Treaty in Art. N TEU.

The first paragraph of Art. 238 E.C. still refers to the adoption of association agreements. The wording is altered only marginally from para. 1 of Art. 238 E.E.C. The words "conclude with a third state, a union of states or an international organisation" have been replaced with "conclude with one or more states or international organisations". The key change here is that an association agreement may be entered into with more than one State or international organisation.

Article 239

The Protocols annexed to this Treaty by common accord of the Member States shall form an integral part thereof.

Article 240

This Treaty is concluded for an unlimited period.

SETTING UP OF THE INSTITUTIONS

Article 241

The Council shall meet within one month of the entry into force of this Treaty.

Article 242

The Council shall, within three months of its first meeting, take all appropriate measures to constitute the Economic and Social Committee.

Article 243

The Assembly shall meet within two months of the first meeting of the Council, having been convened by the President of the Council, in order to elect its officers and draw up its rules of procedure. Pending the election of its officers, the oldest member shall take the chair.

Article 244

The Court of Justice shall take up its duties as soon as its members have been appointed. Its first President shall be appointed for three years in the same manner as its members.

The Court of Justice shall adopt its rules of procedure within three months of taking up its duties.

No matter may be brought before the Court of Justice until its rules of procedure have been published. The time within which an action must be brought shall run only from the date of this publication.

Upon his appointment, the President of the Court of Justice shall exercise the powers conferred upon him by this Treaty.

Article 245

The Commission shall take up its duties and assume the responsibilities conferred upon it by this Treaty as soon as its members have been appointed.

Upon taking up its duties, the Commission shall undertake the studies and arrange the contacts needed for making an overall survey of the economic situation of the Community.

Article 246

1. The first financial year shall run from the date on which this Treaty enters into force until 31 December following. Should this Treaty, however, enter into force during the second half of the year, the first financial year shall run until 31 December of the following year.

2. Until the budget for the first financial year has been established, Member States shall make the Community interest-free advances which shall be deducted from their financial contributions to the implementation of the budget.

3. Until the Staff Regulations of officials and the Conditions of Employment of other servants of the Community provided for in Article 212 have been laid down, each institution shall recruit the Staff it needs and to this end conclude contracts of limited duration.

Each institution shall examine together with the Council any question concerning the number, remuneration and distribution of posts.

FINAL PROVISIONS

Article 247

This Treaty shall be ratified by the High Contracting Parties in accordance with their respective constitutional requirements. The instruments of ratification shall be deposited with the Government of the Italian Republic.

This Treaty shall enter into force on the first day of the month following the deposit of the instrument of ratification by the last signatory State to take this step. If, however, such deposit is made less than 15 days before the beginning of the following month, this Treaty shall not enter into force until the first day of the second month after the date of such deposit.

Article 248

This Treaty, drawn up in a single original in the Dutch, French, German and Italian languages, all four texts being equally authentic, shall be deposited in the archives of the Government of the Italian Republic, which shall transmit a certified copy to each of the Governments of the other signatory States.

APPENDICES

APPENDIX 1

TREATY ON EUROPEAN UNION

ADOPTED BY THE E.C. MEMBER STATES

(Done at Maastricht)   7 February 1992
Entry into force: 1 November 1993
Territorial application: E.C. Member States

TABLE OF CONTENTS

Arrangement of Articles

ARTICLE

TITLE I—*Common Provisions*

A   Establishment of European Union.
B   Objectives of Union.
C   Consistency and continuity of Union activities.
D   European Council.
E   Institutions governed by provisions in E.C. Treaty etc.
F   Respect for national identities of Member States and for fundamental rights.

TITLE II—*Provisions amending the EEC Treaty with a view to establishing the European Community*

G   Amendments to EEC Treaty, including change of name to E.C. Treaty [for content of amendments see E.C. Treaty above]

TITLE III—*Provisions amending the ECSC Treaty*

H   Amendments to ECSC Treaty [not included here]

TITLE IV—*Provisions amending the Euratom Treaty*

I   Amendments to Euratom Treaty [not included here]

TITLE V—*Provisions on a Common Foreign and Security Policy*

J   Establishment of a common foreign and security policy.
    J.1   Objectives; support by Member States.
    J.2   Co-ordination of Member States' action.
    J.3   Procedure for joint action.
    J.4   Defence; involvement of WEU.
    J.5   Representation of Union by the Presidency; responsibilities of Member States in international organisations of which only some Member States are members.
    J.6   Co-operation by diplomatic and consular missions.
    J.7   Consultation of European Parliament.
    J.8   Role of European Council.
    J.9   Involvement of E.C. Commission.
    J.10   Review of security provisions.
    J.11   Application of E.C. Treaty provisions on Parliament, Council & Commission; budget.

TITLE VI—*Provisions on Co-operation in the Fields of Justice and Home Affairs*

K   Introduction of co-operation in administration of civil, criminal & administrative justice and police.

TITLE VII—*Final Provisions*

PROTOCOLS

CHAPTER I: *Constitution of the ECSB*

CHAPTER II: *Objectives and Tasks of the ECSB*

CHAPTER III: *Organisation of the ECSB*

[16]   Economic & Social Committee and Committee of the Regions to have common organisational structure.

[17]   Saving of Article 40.3.3. (anti-abortion amendment) of the Irish Constitution.

DECLARATIONS

(1)   Civil protection, energy and tourism.

(2)   Nationality of a Member State.

(3)   Part 3, Titles III & VI of the E.C. Treaty (meeting of Finance Council).

(4)   Part 3, Title VI of the E.C. Treaty (attendance of Finance Ministers at meetings of European Council when discussing EMU matters).

(5)   Monetary co-operation with non-Community countries.

(6)   Monetary relations with San Marino, Vatican City & Monaco.

(7)   Art. 73d E.C. Treaty: standstill for certain national tax laws.

(8)   Art. 109 E.C. Treaty: use of term 'formal agreements.'

(9)   Part 3, Title XVI of the E.C. Treaty (nature conservation).

(10) Arts. 109, 130r & 130y E.C. Treaty: saving of the rules laid down by the European Court in the ERTA case.

(11) Maintenance of derogations to Spain & Portugal under the Emissions Directive 88/609.

(12) Financing of European Development Fund.

(13) Role of national Parliaments in the European Union.

(14) Conference of the Parliaments.

(15) The number of members of the Commission and European Parliament.

(16) Hierarchy of Community acts.

(17) Right of access to information.

(18) Estimated costs to be included in Commission proposals.

(19) Implementation of Community law by Member States.

(20) Environmental impact assessment statement to be included in Commission proposals.

(21) Court of Auditors.

(22) Economic & Social Committee budget and staff management.

(23) Co-operation with charitable associations.

(24) Protection of animals.

(25) Representation of the interests of overseas countries & territories.

(26) The outermost regions of the Community (French overseas departments, Azores, Madeira, Canary Is.).

(27) Voting in the field of the common foreign & security policy.

(28) Practical arrangements in the field of the common foreign & security policy.

(29) Use of languages in the field of the common foreign & security policy.

(30) Western European Union I & II.

(31) Asylum.

(32) Police co-operation.

(33) Disputes between the ECB & the EMI and their servants.

THE TREATY

[The Heads of State of Belgium, Denmark, Germany, Greece, Spain, France, Ireland, Italy, Luxembourg, the Netherlands, Portugal and the United Kingdom]

RESOLVED to mark a new stage in the process of European integration undertaken with the establishment of the European Communities,

RECALLING the historic importance of the ending of the division of the European continent and the need to create firm bases for the construction of the future Europe,

CONFIRMING their attachment to the principles of liberty, democracy and respect for human rights and fundamental freedoms and of the rule of law,

DESIRING to deepen the solidarity between their peoples while respecting their history, their culture and their traditions,

DESIRING to enhance further the democratic and efficient functioning of the institutions so as to enable them better to carry out, within a single institutional framework, the tasks entrusted to them,

RESOLVED to achieve the strengthening and the convergence of their economies and to establish an economic and monetary union including, in accordance with the provisions of this Treaty, a single and stable currency,

DETERMINED to promote economic and social progress for their peoples, within the context of the accomplishment of the internal market and of reinforced cohesion and environmental protection, and to implement policies ensuring that advances in economic integration are accompanied by parallel progress in other fields,

RESOLVED to establish a citizenship common to nationals of their countries,

RESOLVED to implement a common foreign and security policy including the eventual framing of a common defence policy, which might in time lead to a common defence, thereby reinforcing the European identity and its independence in order to promote peace, security and progress in Europe and in the world,

REAFFIRMING their objective to facilitate the free movement of persons, while ensuring the safety and security of their peoples, by including provisions on justice and home affairs in this Treaty,

RESOLVED to continue the process of creating an ever closer union among the peoples of Europe, in which decisions are taken as closely as possible to the citizen in accordance with the principle of subsidiarity,

IN VIEW of further steps to be taken in order to advance European integration,

HAVE DECIDED to establish a European Union and to this end have designated [their plenipotentiaries]

WHO, having exchanged their full powers, found in good and due form, have agreed as follows:

TITLE I

Common Provisions

Article A

By this Treaty, the High Contracting Parties establish among themselves a European Union, hereinafter called 'the Union.'

This Treaty marks a new stage in the process of creating an ever closer union among the peoples of Europe, in which decisions are taken as closely as possible to the citizen.

The Union shall be founded on the European Communities, supplemented by the policies and forms of co-operation established by this Treaty. Its task shall be to organise, in a manner demonstrating consistency and solidarity, relations between the Member States and between their peoples.

Article B

The Union shall set itself the following objectives:

— to promote economic and social progress which is balanced and sustainable, in particular through the creation of an area without internal frontiers, through the strengthening of economic and social cohesion and through the establishment of economic and monetary union,

ultimately including a single currency in accordance with the provisions of this Treaty;
— to assert its identity on the international scene, in particular through
the implementation of a common foreign and security policy including
the eventual framing of a common defence policy, which might in time
lead to a common defence;
— to strengthen the protection of the rights and interests of the nationals
of its Member States through the introduction of a citizenship of the
Union;
— to develop close co-operation on justice and home affairs;
— to maintain in full the '*acquis communautaire*' and build on it with a
view to considering, through the procedure referred to in Article N(2),
to what extent the policies and forms of co-operation introduced by
this Treaty may need to be revised with the aim of ensuring the effectiveness of the mechanisms and the institutions of the Community.

The objectives of the Union shall be achieved as provided in this Treaty
and in accordance with the conditions and the timetable set out therein while
respecting the principle of subsidiarity as defined in Article 3b of the Treaty
establishing the European Community.

Article C

The Union shall be served by a single institutional framework which shall
ensure the consistency and the continuity of the activities carried out in order
to attain its objectives while respecting and building upon the '*acquis
communautaire.*'

The Union shall in particular ensure the consistency of its external activities as a whole in the context of its external relations, security, economic and
development policies. The Council and the Commission shall be responsible
for ensuring such consistency. They shall ensure the implementation of these
policies, each in accordance with its respective powers.

Article D

The European Council shall provide the Union with the necessary impetus
for its development and shall define the general political guidelines thereof.

The European Council shall bring together the Heads of State or of
Government of the Member States and the President of the Commission.

They shall be assisted by the Ministers for Foreign Affairs of the Member
States and by a Member of the Commission. The European Council shall
meet at least twice a year, under the chairmanship of the Head of State or of
Government of the Member State which holds the Presidency of the Council.

The European Council shall submit to the European Parliament a report
after each of its meetings and a yearly written report on the progress achieved
by the Union.

Article E

The European Parliament, the Council, the Commission and the Court of
Justice shall exercise their powers under the conditions and for the purposes
provided for, on the one hand, by the provisions of the Treaties establishing
the European Communities and of the subsequent Treaties and Acts modifying and supplementing them and, on the other hand, by the other provisions of this Treaty.

Article F

1. The Union shall respect the national identities of its Member States,
whose systems of government are founded on the principles of democracy.

2. The Union shall respect fundamental rights, as guaranteed by the European Convention for the Protection of Human Rights and Fundamental

Freedoms signed in Rome on 4 November 1950 and as they result from the constitutional traditions common to the Member States, as general principles of Community law.

3. The Union shall provide itself with the means necessary to attain its objectives and carry through its policies.

TITLE II

Provisions Amending the Treaty Establishing the European Economic Community with a View to Establishing The European Community

Article G

The Treaty establishing the European Economic Community shall be amended in accordance with the provisions of this Article, in order to establish a European Community.

GENERAL NOTE
The amendments to the E.E.C. Treaty transforming it into the E.C. Treaty are incorporated into the text of the E.C. Treaty or set out above and are explained in the annotations.

TITLE III

Provisions Amending the Treaty Establishing The European Coal and Steel Community

Article H

The Treaty establishing the European Coal and Steel Community shall be amended in accordance with the provisions of this Article.

GENERAL NOTE
The amendments to this Treaty are not reproduced or commented upon here due to the relatively narrow scope of their applicability.

TITLE IV

Provisions Amending the Treaty Establishing The European Atomic Energy Community

Article I

The Treaty establishing the European Atomic Energy Community shall be amended in accordance with the provisions of this Article.

GENERAL NOTE
The amendments to this Treaty are not reproduced or commented upon here due to the relatively narrow scope of their applicability.

TITLE V

Provisions on a Common Foreign and Security Policy

Article J

A common foreign and security policy is hereby established which shall be governed by the following provisions.

Article J.1

1. The Union and its Member States shall define and implement a common foreign and security policy, governed by the provisions of this Title and covering all areas of foreign and security policy.

2. The objectives of the common foreign and security policy shall be:
— to safeguard the common values, fundamental interests and independence of the Union;
— to strengthen the security of the Union and its Member States in all
ways;
— to preserve peace and strengthen international security, in accordance
with the principles of the United Nations Charter as well as the principles of the Helsinki Final Act and the objectives of the Paris Charter;
— to promote international co-operation;
— to develop and consolidate democracy and the rule of law, and respect
for human rights and fundamental freedoms.
3. The Union shall pursue these objectives:
— by establishing systematic co-operation between Member States in
the conduct of policy, in accordance with Article J.2;
— by gradually implementing, in accordance with Article J.3, joint action
in the areas in which the Member States have important interests in
common.
4. The Member States shall support the Union's external and security policy actively and unreservedly in a spirit of loyalty and mutual solidarity. They
shall refrain from any action which is contrary to the interests of the Union or
likely to impair its effectiveness as a cohesive force in international relations.
The Council shall ensure that these principles are complied with.

Article J.2

1. Member States shall inform and consult one another within the Council
on any matter of foreign and security policy of general interest in order to
ensure that their combined influence is exerted as effectively as possible by
means of concerted and convergent action.
2. Whenever it deems it necessary, the Council shall define a common
position.
Member States shall ensure that their national policies conform to the
common positions.
3. Member States shall co-ordinate their action in international organisations and at international conferences. They shall uphold the common positions in such fora.
In international organisations and at international conferences where not
all the Member States participate, those which do take part shall uphold the
common positions.

Article J.3

The procedure for adopting joint action in matters covered by the foreign
and security policy shall be the following:
1. The Council shall decide, on the basis of general guidelines from the
European Council, that a matter should be the subject of joint action.
Whenever the Council decides on the principle of joint action, it
shall lay down the specific scope, the Union's general and specific
objectives in carrying out such action, if necessary its duration, and the
means, procedures and conditions for its implementation.
2. The Council shall, when adopting the joint action and at any stage
during its development, define those matters on which decisions are to
be taken by a qualified majority.
Where the Council is required to act by a qualified majority pursuant to the preceding subparagraph, the votes of its members shall be
weighted in accordance with Article 148(2) of the Treaty establishing

the European Community, and for their adoption, acts of the Council shall require at least 54 votes in favour, cast by at least eight members.

3. If there is a change in circumstances having a substantial effect on a question subject to joint action, the Council shall review the principles and objectives of that action and take the necessary decisions. As long as the Council has not acted, the joint action shall stand.

4. Joint actions shall commit the Member States in the positions they adopt and in the conduct of their activity.

5. Whenever there is any plan to adopt a national position or take national action pursuant to a joint action, information shall be provided in time to allow, if necessary, for prior consultations within the Council. The obligation to provide prior information shall not apply to measures which are merely a national transposition of Council decisions.

6. In cases of imperative need arising from changes in the situation and failing a Council decision, Member States may take the necessary measures as a matter of urgency having regard to the general objectives of the joint action. The Member State concerned shall inform the Council immediately of any such measures.

7. Should there be any major difficulties in implementing a joint action, a Member State shall refer them to the Council which shall discuss them and seek appropriate solutions. Such solutions shall not run counter to the objectives of the joint action or impair its effectiveness.

Article J.4

1. The common foreign and security policy shall include all questions related to the security of the Union, including the eventual framing of a common defence policy, which might in time lead to a common defence.

2. The Union requests the Western European Union (WEU), which is an integral part of the development of the Union, to elaborate and implement decisions and actions of the Union which have defence implications. The Council shall, in agreement with the institutions of the WEU, adopt the necessary practical arrangements.

3. Issues having defence implications dealt with under this Article shall not be subject to the procedures set out in Article J.3.

4. The policy of the Union in accordance with this Article shall not prejudice the specific character of the security and defence policy of certain Member States and shall respect the obligations of certain Member States under the North Atlantic Treaty and be compatible with the common security and defence policy established within that framework.

5. The provisions of this Article shall not prevent the development of closer co-operation between two or more Member States on a bilateral level, in the framework of the WEU and the Atlantic Alliance, provided such co-operation does not run counter to or impede that provided for in this Title.

6. With a view to furthering the objective of this Treaty, and having in view the date of 1998 in the context of Article XII of the Brussels Treaty, the provisions of this Article may be revised as provided for in Article N(2) on the basis of a report to be presented in 1996 by the Council to the European Council, which shall include an evaluation of the progress made and the experience gained until then.

Article J.5

1. The Presidency shall represent the Union in matters coming within the common foreign and security policy.

2. The Presidency shall be responsible for the implementation of common measures; in that capacity it shall in principle express the position of the Union in international organisations and international conferences.

3. In the tasks referred to in paragraphs 1 and 2, the Presidency shall be assisted if need be by the previous and next Member States to hold the Presidency. The Commission shall be fully associated in these tasks.

4. Without prejudice to Article J.2(3) and Article J.3(4), Member States represented in international organisations or international conferences where not all the Member States participate shall keep the latter informed of any matter of common interest.

Member States which are also members of the United Nations Security Council will concert and keep the other Member States fully informed. Member States which are permanent members of the Security Council will, in the execution of their functions, ensure the defence of the positions and the interests of the Union, without prejudice to their responsibilities under the provisions of the United Nations Charter.

Article J.6

The diplomatic and consular missions of the Member States and the Commission Delegations in third countries and international conferences, and their representations to international organisations, shall co-operate in ensuring that the common positions and common measures adopted by the Council are complied with and implemented.

They shall step up co-operation by exchanging information, carrying out joint assessments and contributing to the implementation of the provisions referred to in Article 8c of the Treaty establishing the European Community.

Article J.7

The Presidency shall consult the European Parliament on the main aspects and the basic choices of the common foreign and security policy and shall ensure that the views of the European Parliament are duly taken into consideration. The European Parliament shall be kept regularly informed by the Presidency and the Commission of the development of the Union's foreign and security policy.

The European Parliament may ask questions of the Council or make recommendations to it. It shall hold an annual debate on progress in implementing the common foreign and security policy.

Article J.8

1. The European Council shall define the principles of and general guidelines for the common foreign and security policy.

2. The Council shall take the decisions necessary for defining and implementing the common foreign and security policy on the basis of the general guidelines adopted by the European Council. It shall ensure the unity, consistency and effectiveness of action by the Union.

The Council shall act unanimously, except for procedural questions and in the case referred to in Article J.3(2).

3. Any Member State or the Commission may refer to the Council any question relating to the common foreign and security policy and may submit proposals to the Council.

4. In cases requiring a rapid decision, the Presidency, of its own motion, or at the request of the Commission or a Member State, shall convene an extraordinary council meeting within 48 hours or, in an emergency, within a shorter period.

5. Without prejudice to Article 151 of the Treaty establishing the European Community, a Political Committee consisting of Political Directors

shall monitor the international situation in the areas covered by common foreign and security policy and contribute to the definition of policies by delivering opinions to the Council at the request of the Council or on its own initiative. It shall also monitor the implementation of agreed policies, without prejudice to the responsibility of the Presidency and the Commission.

Article J.9

The Commission shall be fully associated with the work carried out in the common foreign and security policy field.

Article J.10

On the occasion of any review of the security provisions under Article J.4, the conference which is convened to that effect shall also examine whether any other amendments need to be made to provisions relating to the common foreign and security policy.

Article J.11

1. The provisions referred to in Articles 137, 138, 139 to 142, 146, 147, 150 to 153, 157 to 163 and 217 of the Treaty establishing the European Community shall apply to the provisions relating to the areas referred to in this Title.

2. Administrative expenditure which the provisions relating to the areas referred to in this Title entail for the institutions shall be charged to the budget of the European Communities.

The Council may also:

— either decide unanimously that operating expenditure to which the implementation of those provisions gives rise is to be charged to the budget of the European Communities; in that event, the budgetary procedure laid down in the Treaty establishing the European Community shall be applicable;

— or determine that such expenditure shall be charged to the Member States, where appropriate in accordance with a scale to be decided.

TITLE VI

Provisions on Co-operation in the Fields of Justice and Home Affairs

Article K

Co-operation in the fields of justice and home affairs shall be governed by the following provisions.

Article K.1

For the purposes of achieving the objectives of the Union, in particular the free movement of persons, and without prejudice to the powers of the European Community, Member States shall regard the following areas as matters of common interest:

1. asylum policy;
2. rules governing the crossing by persons of the external borders of the Member States and the exercise of controls thereon;
3. immigration policy and policy regarding nationals of third countries:
   (a) conditions of entry and movement by nationals of third countries to the territory of Member States;
   (b) conditions of residence by nationals of third countries on the territory of Member States, including family reunion and access to employment;

> (c) combating unauthorised immigration, residence and work by nationals of third countries on the territory of Member States;
> 4. combating drug addiction in so far as this is not covered by 7 to 9.
> 5. combating fraud on an international scale in so far as this is not covered by 7 to 9;
> 6. judicial co-operation in civil matters;
> 7. judicial co-operation in criminal matters;
> 8. customs co-operation;
> 9. police co-operation for the purposes of preventing and combating terrorism, unlawful drug trafficking and other serious forms of international crime, including if necessary certain aspects of customs co-operation, in connection with the organisation of a Union-wide system for exchanging information within a European Police Office (Europol).

Article K.2

1. The matters referred to in Article K.1 shall be dealt with in compliance with the European Convention for the Protection of Human Rights and Fundamental Freedoms of 4 November 1950 and the Convention relating to the Status of Refugees of 28 July 1951 and having regard to the protection afforded by Member States to persons persecuted on political grounds.

2. This Title shall not affect the exercise of the responsibilities incumbent upon Member States with regard to the maintenance of law and order and the safeguarding of internal security.

Article K.3

1. In the areas referred to in Article K.1, Member States shall inform and consult one another within the Council with a view to co-ordinating their action. To that end, they shall establish collaboration between the relevant departments of their administrations.

2. The Council may:
— on the initiative of any Member State or of the Commission, in the areas referred to in Article K.1(1) to (6);
— on the initiative of any Member State, in the areas referred to in Article K.1(7) to (9):

> (a) adopt joint positions and promote, using the appropriate form and procedures, any co-operation contributing to the pursuit of the objectives of the Union;
> (b) adopt joint action in so far as the objectives of the Union can be attained better by joint action than by the Member States acting individually on account of the scale or effects of the action envisaged; it may decide that measures implementing joint action are to be adopted by a qualified majority;
> (c) without prejudice to Article 220 of the Treaty establishing the European Community, draw up conventions which it shall recommend to the Member States for adoption in accordance with their respective constitutional requirements.
>
> Unless otherwise provided by such conventions, measures implementing them shall be adopted within the Council by a majority of two-thirds of the High Contracting Parties.
>
> Such conventions may stipulate that the Court of Justice shall have jurisdiction to interpret their provisions and to rule on any disputes regarding their application, in accordance with such arrangements as they may lay down.

Article K.4

1. A Co-ordinating Committee shall be set up consisting of senior officials. In addition to its co-ordinating role, it shall be the task of the Committee to:
— give opinions for the attention of the Council, either at the Council's request or on its own initiative;
— contribute, without prejudice to Article 151 of the Treaty establishing the European Community, to the preparation of the Council's discussions in the areas referred to in Article K.1 and, in accordance with the conditions laid down in Article 100d of the Treaty establishing the European Community, in the areas referred to in Article 100c of that Treaty.

2. The Commission shall be fully associated with the work in the areas referred to in this Title.

3. The Council shall act unanimously, except on matters of procedure and in cases where Article K.3 expressly provides for other voting rules.

Where the Council is required to act by a qualified majority, the votes of its members shall be weighted as laid down in Article 148(2) of the Treaty establishing the European Community, and for their adoption, acts of the Council shall require at least 54 votes in favour, cast by at least eight members.

Article K.5

Within international organisations and at international conferences in which they take part, Member States shall defend the common positions adopted under the provisions of this Title.

Article K.6

The Presidency and the Commission shall regularly inform the European Parliament of discussions in the areas covered by this Title.

The Presidency shall consult the European Parliament on the principal aspects of activities in the areas referred to in this Title and shall ensure that the views of the European Parliament are duly taken into consideration.

The European Parliament may ask questions of the Council or make recommendations to it. Each year, it shall hold a debate on the progress made in implementation of the areas referred to in this Title.

Article K.7

The provisions of this Title shall not prevent the establishment or development of closer co-operation between two or more Member States in so far as such co-operation does not conflict with, or impede, that provided for in this Title.

Article K.8

1. The provisions referred to in Articles 137, 138, 139 to 142, 146, 147, 150 to 153, 157 to 163 and 217 of the Treaty establishing the European Community shall apply to the provisions relating to the areas referred to in this Title.

2. Administrative expenditure which the provisions relating to the areas referred to in this Title entail for the institutions shall be charged to the budget of the European Communities.

The Council may also:
— either decide unanimously that operating expenditure to which the implementation of those provisions gives rise is to be charged to the budget of the European Communities; in that event, the budgetary procedure laid down in the Treaty establishing the European Community shall be applicable;
— or determine that such expenditure shall be charged to the Member States, where appropriate in accordance with a scale to be decided.

Article K.9

The Council, acting unanimously on the initiative of the Commission or a Member State, may decide to apply Article 100c of the Treaty establishing the European Community to action in areas referred to in Article K.1(1) to (6), and at the same time determine the relevant voting conditions relating to it. It shall recommend the Member States to adopt that decision in accordance with their respective constitutional requirements.

TITLE VII

Final Provisions

Article L

The provisions of the Treaty establishing the European Community, the Treaty establishing the European Coal and Steel Community and the Treaty establishing the European Atomic Energy Community concerning the powers of the Court of Justice of the European Communities and the exercise of those powers shall apply only to the following provisions of this Treaty:
  (a) provisions amending the Treaty establishing the European Economic Community with a view to establishing the European Community, the Treaty establishing the European Coal and Steel Community and the Treaty establishing the European Atomic Energy Community;
  (b) the third subparagraph of Article K.3(2)(c);
  (c) Articles L to S.

Article M

Subject to the provisions amending the Treaty establishing the European Economic Community with a view to establishing the European Community, the Treaty establishing the European Coal and Steel Community and the Treaty establishing the European Atomic Energy Community, and to these final provisions, nothing in this Treaty shall affect the Treaties establishing the European Communities or the subsequent Treaties and Acts modifying or supplementing them.

Article N

1. The government of any Member State or the Commission may submit to the Council proposals for the amendment of the Treaties on which the Union is founded.

If the Council, after consulting the European Parliament and, where appropriate, the Commission, delivers an opinion in favour of calling a conference of representatives of the governments of the Member States, the conference shall be convened by the President of the Council for the purpose of determining by common accord the amendments to be made to those Treaties. The European Central Bank shall also be consulted in the case of institutional changes in the monetary area.

The amendments shall enter into force after being ratified by all the Member States in accordance with their respective constitutional requirements.

2. A conference of representatives of the governments of the Member States shall be convened in 1996 to examine those provisions of this Treaty for which revision is provided, in accordance with the objectives set out in Articles A and B.

Article O

Any European State may apply to become a Member of the Union. It shall address its application to the Council, which shall act unanimously after consulting the Commission and after receiving the assent of the European Parliament, which shall act by an absolute majority of its component members.

The conditions of admission and the adjustments to the Treaties on which the Union is founded which such admission entails shall be the subject of an agreement between the Member States and the applicant State. This agreement shall be submitted for ratification by all the Contracting States in accordance with their respective constitutional requirements.

GENERAL NOTE
  Articles N and O of the TEU are considered above in the General Note on the repealed Arts. 236 and 237 of the E.E.C. Treaty.

Article P

1. Articles 2 to 7 and 10 to 19 of the Treaty establishing a single Council and a single Commission of the European Communities, signed in Brussels on 8 April 1965, are hereby repealed.
2. Article 2, Article 3(2) and Title III of the Single European Act signed in Luxembourg on 17 February 1986 and in The Hague on 28 February 1986 are hereby repealed.

Article Q

This Treaty is concluded for an unlimited period.

Article R

1. This Treaty shall be ratified by the High Contracting Parties in accordance with their respective constitutional requirements. The instruments of ratification shall be deposited with the government of the Italian Republic.
2. This Treaty shall enter into force on 1 January 1993, provided that all the instruments of ratification have been deposited, or, failing that, on the first day of the month following the deposit of the instrument of ratification by the last signatory State to take this step.

Article S

This Treaty, drawn up in a single original in the Danish, Dutch, English, French, German, Greek, Irish, Italian, Portuguese and Spanish languages, the texts in each of these languages being equally authentic, shall be deposited in the archives of the government of the Italian Republic, which will transmit a certified copy to each of the governments of the other signatory States.

PROTOCOLS[1]

PROTOCOL ON THE ACQUISITION OF PROPERTY IN DENMARK

(Annexed to E.C. Treaty)

Notwithstanding the provisions of this Treaty, Denmark may maintain the existing legislation on the acquisition of second homes.

PROTOCOL CONCERNING ARTICLE 119 OF THE TREATY ESTABLISHING THE EUROPEAN COMMUNITY

(Annexed to E.C. Treaty)

For the purposes of Article 119 of this Treaty, benefits under occupational social security schemes shall not be considered as remuneration if and in so far as they are attributable to periods of employment prior to 17 May 1990, except in the case of workers or those claiming under them who have before

---

[1] The preambles to most of the Protocols have been omitted.

that date initiated legal proceedings or introduced an equivalent claim under the applicable national law.

PROTOCOL ON THE STATUTE OF THE EUROPEAN SYSTEM OF CENTRAL BANKS AND OF THE EUROPEAN CENTRAL BANK

(Annexed to E.C. Treaty (Article 4a))

CHAPTER I: Constitution of the ESCB

Article 1 (The European System of Central Banks)

1.1. The European System of Central Banks (ESCB) and the European Central Bank (ECB) shall be established in accordance with Article 4a of this Treaty; they shall perform their tasks and carry on their activities in accordance with the provisions of this Treaty and of this Statute.

1.2. In accordance with Article 106(1) of this Treaty, the ESCB shall be composed of the ECB and of the central banks of the Member States ('national central banks'). The Institut Monétaire Luxembourgeois will be the central bank of Luxembourg.

CHAPTER II: Objectives and Tasks of the ESCB

Article 2 (Objectives)

In accordance with Article 105(1) of this Treaty, the primary objective of the ESCB shall be to maintain price stability.

Without prejudice to the objective of price stability, it shall support the general economic policies in the Community with a view to contributing to the achievement of the objectives of the Community as laid down in Article 2 of this Treaty.

The ESCB shall act in accordance with the principle of an open market economy with free competition, favouring an efficient allocation of resources, and in compliance with the principles set out in Article 3a of this Treaty.

Article 3 (Tasks)

3.1. In accordance with Article 105(2) of this Treaty, the basic tasks to be carried out through the ESCB shall be:
— to define and implement the monetary policy of the Community;
— to conduct foreign exchange operations consistent with the provisions of Article 109 of this Treaty;
— to hold and manage the official foreign reserves of the Member States;
— to promote the smooth operation of payment systems.

3.2. In accordance with Article 105(3) of this Treaty, the third indent of Article 3.1 shall be without prejudice to the holding and management by the governments of Member States of foreign exchange working balances.

3.3. In accordance with Article 105(5) of this Treaty, the ESCB shall contribute to the smooth conduct of policies pursued by the competent authorities relating to the prudential supervision of credit institutions and the stability of the financial system.

Article 4 (Advisory functions)

In accordance with Article 105(4) of this Treaty:
(a) the ECB shall be consulted:
— on any proposed Community act in its fields of competence;
— by national authorities regarding any draft legislative provision in its fields of competence, but within the limits and under the con-

ditions set out by the Council in accordance with the procedure laid down in Article 42;

(b) the ECB may submit opinions to the appropriate Community institutions or bodies or to national authorities on matters in its fields of competence.

Article 5 (Collection of statistical information)

5.1. In order to undertake the tasks of the ESCB, the ECB, assisted by the national central banks, shall collect the necessary statistical information either from the competent national authorities or directly from economic agents. For these purposes it shall co-operate with the Community institutions or bodies and with the competent authorities of the Member States or third countries and with international organisations.

5.2. The national central banks shall carry out, to the extent possible, the tasks described in Article 5.1.

5.3. The ECB shall contribute to the harmonisation, where necessary, of the rules and practices governing the collection, compilation and distribution of statistics in the areas within its fields of competence.

5.4. The Council, in accordance with the procedure laid down in Article 42, shall define the natural and legal persons subject to reporting requirements, the confidentiality regime and the appropriate provisions for enforcement.

Article 6 (International co-operation)

6.1. In the field of international co-operation involving the tasks entrusted to the ESCB, the ECB shall decide how the ESCB shall be represented.

6.2. The ECB and, subject to its approval, the national central banks may participate in international monetary institutions.

6.3. Articles 6.1 and 6.2 shall be without prejudice to Article 109(4) of this Treaty.

CHAPTER III: Organisation of the ESCB

Article 7 (Independence)

In accordance with Article 107 of this Treaty, when exercising the powers and carrying out the tasks and duties conferred upon them by this Treaty and this Statute, neither the ECB, nor a national central bank, nor any member of their decision-making bodies shall seek or take instructions from Community institutions or bodies, from any government of a Member State or from any other body. The Community institutions and bodies and the governments of the Member States undertake to respect this principle and not to seek to influence the members of the decision-making bodies of the ECB or of the national central banks in the performance of their tasks.

Article 8 (General principle)

The ESCB shall be governed by the decision-making bodies of the ECB.

Article 9 (The European Central Bank)

9.1. The ECB which, in accordance with Article 106(2) of this Treaty, shall have legal personality, shall enjoy in each of the Member States the most extensive legal capacity accorded to legal persons under its law; it may, in particular, acquire or dispose of movable and immovable property and may be a party to legal proceedings.

9.2. The ECB shall ensure that the tasks conferred upon the ESCB under Article 105(2), (3), and (5) of this Treaty are implemented either by its own activities pursuant to this Statute or through the national central banks pursuant to Articles 12.1 and 14.

9.3. In accordance with Article 106(3) of this Treaty, the decision-making bodies of the ECB shall be the Governing Council and the Executive Board.

Article 10 (The Governing Council)

10.1. In accordance with Article 109a(1) of this Treaty, the Governing Council shall comprise the members of the Executive Board of the ECB and the Governors of the national central banks.

10.2. Subject to Article 10.3, only members of the Governing Council present in person shall have the right to vote. By way of derogation from this rule, the Rules of Procedure referred to in Article 12.3 may lay down that members of the Governing Council may cast their vote by means of tele-conferencing. These rules shall also provide that a member of the Governing Council who is prevented from voting for a prolonged period may appoint an alternate as a member of the Governing Council.

Subject to Articles 10.3 and 11.3, each member of the Governing Council shall have one vote. Save as otherwise provided for in this Statute, the Governing Council shall act by a simple majority. In the event of a tie, the President shall have the casting vote.

In order for the Governing Council to vote, there shall be a quorum of two-thirds of the members. If the quorum is not met, the President may convene an extraordinary meeting at which decisions may be taken without regard to the quorum.

10.3. For any decisions to be taken under Articles 28, 29, 30, 32, 33 and 51, the votes in the Governing Council shall be weighted according to the national central banks' shares in the subscribed capital of the ECB. The weights of the votes of the members of the Executive Board shall be zero. A decision requiring a qualified majority shall be adopted if the votes cast in favour represent at least two thirds of the subscribed capital of the ECB and represent at least half of the shareholders. If a Governor is unable to be present, he may nominate an alternate to cast his weighted vote.

10.4. The proceedings of the meetings shall be confidential. The Governing Council may decide to make the outcome of its deliberations public.

10.5. The Governing Council shall meet at least ten times a year.

Article 11 (The Executive Board)

11.1. In accordance with Article 109a(2)(a) of this Treaty, the Executive Board shall comprise the President, the Vice-President and four other members.

The members shall perform their duties on a full-time basis. No member shall engage in any occupation, whether gainful or not, unless exemption is exceptionally granted by the Governing Council.

11.2. In accordance with Article 109a(2)(b) of this Treaty, the President, the Vice-President and the other Members of the Executive Board shall be appointed from among persons of recognised standing and professional experience in monetary or banking matters by common accord of the governments of the Member States at the level of the Heads of State or of Government, on a recommendation from the Council after it has consulted the European Parliament and the Governing Council.

Their term of office shall be eight years and shall not be renewable.

Only nationals of Member States may be members of the Executive Board.

11.3. The terms and conditions of employment of the members of the Executive Board, in particular their salaries, pensions and other social security benefits shall be the subject of contracts with the ECB and shall be fixed by the Governing Council on a proposal from a Committee comprising three members appointed by the Governing Council and three members appointed by the Council. The members of the Executive Board shall not have the right to vote on matters referred to in this paragraph.

11.4. If a member of the Executive Board no longer fulfils the conditions required for the performance of his duties or if he has been guilty of serious misconduct, the Court of Justice may, on application by the Governing Council or the Executive Board, compulsorily retire him.

11.5. Each member of the Executive Board present in person shall have the right to vote and shall have, for that purpose, one vote. Save as otherwise provided, the Executive Board shall act by a simple majority of the votes cast. In the event of a tie, the President shall have the casting vote. The voting arrangements shall be specified in the Rules of Procedure referred to in Article 12.3.

11.6. The Executive Board shall be responsible for the current business of the ECB.

11.7. Any vacancy on the Executive Board shall be filled by the appointment of a new member in accordance with Article 11.2.

Article 12 (Responsibilities of the decision-making bodies)

12.1. The Governing Council shall adopt the guidelines and take the decisions necessary to ensure the performance of the tasks entrusted to the ESCB under this Treaty and this Statute. The Governing Council shall formulate the monetary policy of the Community including, as appropriate, decisions relating to intermediate monetary objectives, key interest rates and the supply of reserves in the ESCB, and shall establish the necessary guidelines for their implementation.

The Executive Board shall implement monetary policy in accordance with the guidelines and decisions laid down by the Governing Council. In doing so the Executive Board shall give the necessary instructions to national central banks. In addition the Executive Board may have certain powers delegated to it where the Governing Council so decides.

To the extent deemed possible and appropriate and without prejudice to the provisions of this Article, the ECB shall have recourse to the national central banks to carry out operations which form part of the tasks of the ESCB.

12.2. The Executive Board shall have responsibility for the preparation of meetings of the Governing Council.

12.3. The Governing Council shall adopt Rules of Procedure which determine the internal organisation of the ECB and its decision-making bodies.

12.4. The Governing Council shall exercise the advisory functions referred to in Article 4.

12.5. The Governing Council shall take the decisions referred to in Article 6.

Article 13 (The President)

13.1. The President or, in his absence, the Vice-President shall chair the Governing Council and the Executive Board of the ECB.

13.2. Without prejudice to Article 39, the President or his nominee shall represent the ECB externally.

Article 14 (National central banks)

14.1. In accordance with Article 108 of this Treaty, each Member State shall ensure, at the latest at the date of the establishment of the ESCB, that its national legislation, including the statutes of its national central bank, is compatible with this Treaty and this Statute.

14.2. The statutes of the national central banks shall, in particular, provide that the term of office of a Governor of a national central bank shall be no less than five years.

A Governor may be relieved from office only if he no longer fulfils the conditions required for the performance of his duties or if he has been guilty of serious misconduct.

A decision to this effect may be referred to the Court of Justice by the Governor concerned or the Governing Council on grounds of infringement of this Treaty or of any rule of law relating to its application. Such proceedings shall be instituted within two months of the publication of the decision or of its notification to the plaintiff or, in the absence thereof, of the day on which it came to the knowledge of the latter, as the case may be.

14.3. The national central banks are an integral part of the ESCB and shall act in accordance with the guidelines and instructions of the ECB. The Governing Council shall take the necessary steps to ensure compliance with the guidelines and instructions of the ECB, and shall require that any necessary information be given to it.

14.4. National central banks may perform functions other than those specified in this Statute unless the Governing Council finds, by a majority of two thirds of the votes cast, that these interfere with the objectives and tasks of the ESCB. Such functions shall be performed on the responsibility and liability of national central banks and shall not be regarded as being part of the functions of the ESCB.

Article 15 (Reporting commitments)

15.1. The ECB shall draw up and publish reports on the activities of the ESCB at least quarterly.

15.2. A consolidated financial statement of the ESCB shall be published each week.

15.3. In accordance with Article 109b(3) of this Treaty, the ECB shall address an annual report on the activities of the ESCB and on the monetary policy of both the previous and the current year to the European Parliament, the Council and the Commission, and also to the European Council.

15.4. The reports and statements referred to in this Article shall be made available to interested parties free of charge.

Article 16 (Bank notes)

In accordance with Article 105a(1) of this Treaty, the Governing Council shall have the exclusive right to authorise the issue of bank notes within the Community.

The ECB and the national central banks may issue such notes. The bank notes issued by the ECB and the national central banks shall be the only such notes to have the status of legal tender within the Community.

The ECB shall respect as far as possible existing practices regarding the issue and design of bank notes.

CHAPTER IV: Monetary Functions and Operations of the ESCB

Article 17 (Accounts with the ECB and the national central banks)

In order to conduct their operations, the ECB and the national central banks may open accounts for credit institutions, public entities and other market participants and accept assets, including book-entry securities, as collateral.

Article 18 (Open market and credit operations)

18.1. In order to achieve the objectives of the ESCB and to carry out its tasks, the ECB and the national central banks may:
— operate in the financial markets by buying and selling outright (spot and forward) or under repurchase agreement and by lending or borrowing claims and marketable instruments, whether in Community or in non-Community currencies, as well as precious metals;
— conduct credit operations with credit institutions and other market participants, with lending being based on adequate collateral.

18.2. The ECB shall establish general principles for open market and credit operations carried out by itself or the national central banks, including for the announcement of conditions under which they stand ready to enter into such transactions.

Article 19 (Minimum reserves)

19.1. Subject to Article 2, the ECB may require credit institutions established in Member States to hold minimum reserves on accounts with the ECB and national central banks in pursuance of monetary policy objectives. Regulations concerning the calculation and determination of the required minimum reserves may be established by the Governing Council. In cases of non-compliance the ECB shall be entitled to levy penalty interest and to impose other sanctions with comparable effect.

19.2. For the application of this Article, the Council shall, in accordance with the procedure laid down in Article 42, define the basis for minimum reserves and the maximum permissible ratios between those reserves and their basis, as well as the appropriate sanctions in cases of non-compliance.

Article 20 (Other instruments of monetary control)

The Governing Council may, by a majority of two thirds of the votes cast, decide upon the use of such other operational methods of monetary control as it sees fit, respecting Article 2.

The Council shall, in accordance with the procedure laid down in Article 42, define the scope of such methods if they impose obligations on third parties.

Article 21 (Operations with public entities)

21.1. In accordance with Article 104 of this Treaty, overdrafts or any other type of credit facility with the ECB or with the national central banks in favour of Community institutions or bodies, central governments, regional, local or other public authorities, other bodies governed by public law or public undertakings of Member States shall be prohibited, as shall the purchase directly from them by the ECB or national central banks of debt instruments.

21.2. The ECB and national central banks may act as fiscal agents for the entities referred to in Article 21.1.

21.3. The provisions of this Article shall not apply to publicly-owned credit institutions which, in the context of the supply of reserves by central banks, shall be given the same treatment by national central banks and the ECB as private credit institutions.

Article 22 (Clearing and payment systems)

The ECB and national central banks may provide facilities, and the ECB may make regulations, to ensure efficient and sound clearing and payment systems within the Community and with other countries.

Article 23 (External operations)

The ECB and national central banks may:
— establish relations with central banks and financial institutions in other countries and, where appropriate, with international organisations;
— acquire and sell spot and forward all types of foreign exchange assets and precious metals; the term 'foreign exchange asset' shall include securities and all other assets in the currency of any country or units of account and in whatever form held;
— hold and manage the assets referred to in this Article;
— conduct all types of banking transactions in relations with third countries and international organisations, including borrowing and lending operations.

Article 24 (Other operations)

In addition to operations arising from their tasks, the ECB and national central banks may enter into operations for their administrative purposes or for their staff.

CHAPTER V: Prudential Supervision

Article 25 (Prudential supervision)

25.1. The ECB may offer advice to and be consulted by the Council, the Commission and the competent authorities of the Member States on the scope and implementation of Community legislation relating to the prudential supervision of credit institutions and to the stability of the financial system.
25.2. In accordance with any decision of the Council under Article 105(6) of this Treaty, the ECB may perform specific tasks concerning policies relating to the prudential supervision of credit institutions and other financial institutions with the exception of insurance undertakings.

CHAPTER VI: Financial Provisions of the ESCB

Article 26 (Financial accounts)

26.1. The financial year of the ECB and national central banks shall begin on the first day of January and end on the last day of December.
26.2. The annual accounts of the ECB shall be drawn up by the Executive Board, in accordance with the principles established by the Governing Council.
The accounts shall be approved by the Governing Council and shall thereafter be published.
26.3. For analytical and operational purposes, the Executive Board shall draw up a consolidated balance sheet of the ESCB, comprising those assets and liabilities of the national central banks that fall within the ESCB.
26.4. For the application of this Article, the Governing Council shall establish the necessary rules for standardising the accounting and reporting of operations undertaken by the national central banks.

Article 27 (Auditing)

27.1. The accounts of the ECB and national central banks shall be audited by independent external auditors recommended by the Governing Council and approved by the Council.
The auditors shall have full power to examine all books and accounts of the ECB and national central banks and obtain full information about their transactions.

27.2. The provisions of Article 188b of this Treaty shall only apply to an examination of the operational efficiency of the management of the ECB.

Article 28 (Capital of the ECB)

28.1. The capital of the ECB, which shall become operational upon its establishment, shall be 5,000 million ECUs.

The capital may be increased by such amounts as may be decided by the Governing Council acting by the qualified majority provided for in Article 10.3, within the limits and under the conditions set by the Council under the procedure laid down in Article 42.

28.2. The national central banks shall be the sole subscribers to and holders of the capital of the ECB. The subscription of capital shall be according to the key established in accordance with Article 29.

28.3. The Governing Council, acting by the qualified majority provided for in Article 10.3, shall determine the extent to which and the form in which the capital shall be paid up.

28.4. Subject to Article 28.5, the shares of the national central banks in the subscribed capital of the ECB may not be transferred, pledged or attached.

28.5. If the key referred to in Article 29 is adjusted, the national central banks shall transfer among themselves capital shares to the extent necessary to ensure that the distribution of capital shares corresponds to the adjusted key.

The Governing Council shall determine the terms and conditions of such transfers.

Article 29 (Key for capital subscription)

29.1. When in accordance with the procedure referred to in Article 109l(1) of this Treaty the ESCB and the ECB have been established, the key for subscription of the ECB's capital shall be established. Each national central bank shall be assigned a weighting in this key which shall be equal to the sum of:

— 50 per cent. of the share of its respective Member State in the population of the Community in the penultimate year preceding the establishment of the ESCB;

— 50 per cent. of the share of its respective Member State in the gross domestic product at market prices of the Community as recorded in the last five years preceding the penultimate year before the establishment of the ESCB;

The percentages shall be rounded up to the nearest multiple of 0·05 per cent. points.

29.2. The statistical data to be used for the application of this Article shall be provided by the Commission in accordance with the rules adopted by the Council under the procedure provided for in Article 42.

29.3. The weightings assigned to the national central banks shall be adjusted every five years after the establishment of the ESCB by analogy with the provisions laid down in Article 29.1.

The adjusted key shall apply with effect from the first day of the following year.

29.4. The Governing Council shall take all other measures necessary for the application of this Article.

Article 30 (Transfer of foreign reserve assets to the ECB)

30.1. Without prejudice to Article 28, the ECB shall be provided by the national central banks with foreign reserve assets, other than Member

States' currencies, ECUs, IMF reserve positions and SDRs, up to an amount equivalent to 50,000 million ECUs. The Governing Council shall decide upon the proportion to be called up by the ECB following its establishment and the amounts called up at later dates.

The ECB shall have the full right to hold and manage the foreign reserves that are transferred to it and to use them for the purposes set out in this Statute.

30.2. The contributions of each national central bank shall be fixed in proportion to its share in the subscribed capital of the ECB.

30.3. Each national central bank shall be credited by the ECB with a claim equivalent to its contribution.

The Governing Council shall determine the denomination and remuneration of such claims.

30.4. Further calls of foreign reserve assets beyond the limit set in Article 30.1 may be effected by the ECB, in accordance with Article 30.2, within the limits and under the conditions set by the Council in accordance with the procedure laid down in Article 42.

30.5. The ECB may hold and manage IMF reserve positions and SDRs and provide for the pooling of such assets.

30.6. The Governing Council shall take all other measures necessary for the application of this Article.

Article 31 (Foreign reserve assets held by national central banks)

31.1. The national central banks shall be allowed to perform transactions in fulfilment of their obligations towards international organisations in accordance with Article 23.

31.2. All other operations in foreign reserve assets remaining with the national central banks after the transfers referred to in Article 30, and Member States' transactions with their foreign exchange working balances shall, above a certain limit to be established within the framework of Article 31.3, be subject to approval by the ECB in order to ensure consistency with the exchange rate and monetary policies of the Community.

31.3. The Governing Council shall issue guidelines with a view to facilitating such operations.

Article 32 (Allocation of monetary income of national central banks)

32.1. The income accruing to the national central banks in the performance of the ESCB's monetary policy function (hereinafter referred to as 'monetary income') shall be allocated at the end of each financial year in accordance with the provisions of this Article.

32.2. Subject to Article 32.3, the amount of each national central bank's monetary income shall be equal to its annual income derived from its assets held against notes in circulation and deposit liabilities to credit institutions. These assets shall be earmarked by national central banks in accordance with guidelines to be established by the Governing Council.

32.3. If, after the start of the third stage, the balance sheet structure of the national central banks do not, in the judgment of the Governing Council, permit the application of Article 32.2, the Governing Council, acting by a qualified majority, may decide that, by way of derogation from Article 32.2, monetary income shall be measured according to an alternative method for a period of not more than five years.

32.4. The amount of each national central bank's monetary income shall be reduced by an amount equivalent to any interest paid by that central bank on its deposit liabilities to credit institutions in accordance with Article 19.

The Governing Council may decide that national central banks shall be indemnified against costs incurred in connection with the issue of bank notes or in exceptional circumstances for specific losses arising from monetary policy operations undertaken for the ESCB.

Indemnification shall be in a form deemed appropriate in the judgment of the Governing Council; these amounts may be offset against the national central banks' monetary income.

32.5. The sum of the national central banks' monetary income shall be allocated to the national central banks in proportion to their paid-up shares in the capital of the ECB, subject to any decision taken by the Governing Council pursuant to Article 33.2.

32.6. The clearing and settlement of the balances arising from the allocation of monetary income shall be carried out by the ECB in accordance with guidelines established by the Governing Council.

32.7. The Governing Council shall take all other measures necessary for the application of this Article.

Article 33 (Allocation of net profits and losses of the ECB)

33.1. The net profit of the ECB shall be transferred in the following order:
  (a) an amount to be determined by the Governing Council, which may not exceed 20 per cent. of the net profit, shall be transferred to the general reserve fund subject to a limit equal to 100 per cent. of the capital;
  (b) the remaining net profit shall be distributed to the shareholders of the ECB in proportion to their paid-up shares.

33.2. In the event of a loss incurred by the ECB, the shortfall may be offset against the general reserve fund of the ECB and, if necessary, following a decision by the Governing Council, against the monetary income of the relevant financial year in proportion and up to the amounts allocated to the national central banks in accordance with Article 32.5.

CHAPTER VII: General Provisions

Article 34 (Legal acts)

34.1. In accordance with Article 108a of this Treaty, the ECB shall:
— make regulations to the extent necessary to implement the tasks defined in Article 3.1, first indent, Articles 19.1, 22 or 25.2 and in cases which shall be laid down in the acts of the Council referred to in Article 42;
— take decisions necessary for carrying out the tasks entrusted to the ESCB under this Treaty and this Statute;
— make recommendations and deliver opinions.

34.2. A regulation shall have general application. It shall be binding in its entirety and directly applicable in all Member States.

Recommendations and opinions shall have no binding force.

A decision shall be binding in its entirety upon those to whom it is addressed.

Articles 190 and 192 of this Treaty shall apply to regulations and decisions adopted by the ECB.

The ECB may decide to publish its decisions, recommendations and opinions.

34.3. Within the limits and under the conditions adopted by the Council under the procedure laid down in Article 42, the ECB shall be entitled to impose fines or periodic penalty payments on undertakings for failure to comply with obligations under its regulations and decisions.

Article 35 (Judicial control and related matters)

35.1. The acts or omissions of the ECB shall be open to review or interpretation by the Court of Justice in the cases and under the conditions laid down in this Treaty.

The ECB may institute proceedings in the cases and under the conditions laid down in this Treaty.

35.2. Disputes between the ECB, on the one hand, and its creditors, debtors or any other person, on the other, shall be decided by the competent national courts, save where jurisdiction has been conferred upon the Court of Justice.

35.3. The ECB shall be subject to the liability regime provided for in Article 215 of this Treaty.

The national central banks shall be liable according to their respective national laws.

35.4. The Court of Justice shall have jurisdiction to give judgment pursuant to any arbitration clause contained in a contract concluded by or on behalf of the ECB, whether that contract be governed by public or private law.

35.5. A decision of the ECB to bring an action before the Court of Justice shall be taken by the Governing Council.

35.6. The Court of Justice shall have jurisdiction in disputes concerning the fulfilment by a national central bank of obligations under this Statute.

If the ECB considers that a national central bank has failed to fulfil an obligation under this Statute, it shall deliver a reasoned opinion on the matter after giving the national central bank concerned the opportunity to submit its observations.

If the national central bank concerned does not comply with the opinion within the period laid down by the ECB, the latter may bring the matter before the Court of Justice.

Article 36 (Staff)

36.1. The Governing Council, on a proposal from the Executive Board, shall lay down the conditions of employment of the staff of the ECB.

36.2. The Court of Justice shall have jurisdiction in any dispute between the ECB and its servants within the limits and under the conditions laid down in the conditions of employment.

Article 37 (Seat)

Before the end of 1992, the decision as to where the seat of the ECB will be established shall be taken by common accord of the governments of the Member States at the level of Heads of State or of Government.

Article 38 (Professional secrecy)

38.1. Members of the governing bodies and the staff of the ECB and the national central banks shall be required, even after their duties have ceased, not to disclose information of the kind covered by the obligation of professional secrecy.

38.2. Persons having access to data covered by Community legislation imposing an obligation of secrecy shall be subject to such legislation.

Article 39 (Signatories)

The ECB shall be legally committed to third parties by the President or by two members of the Executive Board or by the signatures of two members of the staff of the ECB who have been duly authorised by the President to sign on behalf of the ECB.

Article 40 (Privileges and immunities)

The ECB shall enjoy in the territories of the Member States such privileges and immunities as are necessary for the performance of its tasks, under the conditions laid down in the Protocol on the Privileges and Immunities of the European Communities annexed to the Treaty establishing a Single Council and a Single Commission of the European Communities.

CHAPTER VIII: Amendment of the Statute and Complementary Legislation

Article 41 (Simplified amendment procedure)

41.1. In accordance with Article 106(5) of this Treaty, Articles 5.1, 5.2, 5.3, 17, 18, 19.1, 22, 23, 24, 26, 32.2, 32.3, 32.4, 32.6, 33.1(a) and 36 of this Statute may be amended by the Council, acting either by a qualified majority on a recommendation from the ECB and after consulting the Commission, or unanimously on a proposal from the Commission and after consulting the ECB. In either case the assent of the European Parliament shall be required.

41.2. A recommendation made by the ECB under this Article shall require a unanimous decision by the Governing Council.

Article 42 (Complementary legislation)

In accordance with Article 106(6) of this Treaty, immediately after the decision on the date for the beginning of the third stage, the Council, acting by a qualified majority either on a proposal from the Commission and after consulting the European Parliament and the ECB, or on a recommendation from the ECB and after consulting the European Parliament and the Commission, shall adopt the provisions referred to in Articles 4, 5.4, 19.2, 20, 28.1, 29.2, 30.4 and 34.3 of this Statute.

CHAPTER IX: Transitional and Other Provisions for the ESCB

Article 43 (General Provisions)

43.1. A derogation as referred to in Article 109k(1) of this Treaty shall entail that the following Articles of this Statute shall not confer any rights or impose any obligations on the Member State concerned: 3, 6, 9.2, 12.1, 14.3, 16, 18, 19, 20, 22, 23, 26.2, 27, 30, 31, 32, 33, 34, 50 and 52.

43.2. The central banks of Member States with a derogation as specified in Article 109k(1) of this Treaty shall retain their powers in the field of monetary policy according to national law.

43.3. In accordance with Article 109k(4) of this Treaty, 'Member States' shall be read as 'Member States without a derogation' in the following Articles of this Statute: 3, 11.2, 19, 34.2 and 50.

43.4. 'National central banks' shall be read as 'central banks of Member States without a derogation' in the following Articles of this Statute: 9.2, 10.1, 10.3, 12.1, 16, 17, 18, 22, 23, 27, 30, 31, 32, 33.2 and 52.

43.5. 'Shareholders' shall be read as 'central banks of Member States without a derogation' in Articles 10.3 and 33.1.

43.6. 'Subscribed capital of the ECB' shall be read as 'capital of the ECB subscribed by the central banks of Member States without a derogation' in Articles 10.3 and 30.2.

Article 44 (Transitional tasks of the ECB)

The ECB shall take over those tasks of the EMI which, because of the derogations of one or more Member States, still have to be performed in the third stage.

The ECB shall give advice in the preparations for the abrogation of the derogations specified in Article 109l of this Treaty.

Article 45 (The General Council of the ECB)

45.1. Without prejudice to Article 106(3) of this Treaty, the General Council shall be constituted as a third decision-making body of the ECB.

45.2. The General Council shall comprise the President and Vice-President of the ECB and the Governors of the national central banks. The other members of the Executive Board may participate, without having the right to vote, in meetings of the General Council.

45.3. The responsibilities of the General Council are listed in full in Article 47 of this Statute.

Article 46 (Rules of procedure of the General Council)

46.1. The President or, in his absence, the Vice-President of the ECB shall chair the General Council of the ECB.

46.2. The President of the Council and a member of the Commission may participate, without having the right to vote, in meetings of the General Council.

46.3. The President shall prepare the meetings of the General Council.

46.4. By way of derogation from Article 12.3, the General Council shall adopt its Rules of Procedure.

46.5. The Secretariat of the General Council shall be provided by the ECB.

Article 47 (Responsibilities of the General Council)

47.1. The General Council shall:
— perform the tasks referred to in Article 44;
— contribute to the advisory functions referred to in Articles 4 and 25.1.

47.2. The General Council shall contribute to:
— the collection of statistical information as referred to in Article 5;
— the reporting activities of the ECB as referred to in Article 15;
— the establishment of the necessary rules for the application of Article 26 as referred to in Article 26.4;
— the taking of all other measures necessary for the application of Article 29 as referred to in Article 29.4;
— the laying down of the conditions of employment of the staff of the ECB as referred to in Article 36.

47.3. The General Council shall contribute to the necessary preparations for irrevocably fixing the exchange rates of the currencies of Member States with a derogation against the currencies, or the single currency, of the Member States without a derogation, as referred to in Article 109l(5) of this Treaty.

47.4. The General Council shall be informed by the President of the ECB of decisions of the Governing Council.

Article 48 (Transitional provisions for the capital of the ECB)

In accordance with Article 29.1 each national central bank shall be assigned a weighting in the key for subscription of the ECB's capital.

By way of derogation from Article 28.3, central banks of Member States with a derogation shall not pay up their subscribed capital unless the General Council, acting by a majority representing at least two thirds of the subscribed capital of the ECB and at least half of the shareholders, decides that a minimal percentage has to be paid up as a contribution to the operational costs of the ECB.

Article 49 (Deferred payment of capital, reserves and provisions of the ECB)

49.1. The central bank of a Member State whose derogation has been abrogated shall pay up its subscribed share of the capital of the ECB to the same extent as the central banks of other Member States without a derogation, and shall transfer to the ECB foreign reserve assets in accordance with Article 30.1. The sum to be transferred shall be determined by multiplying the ECU value at current exchange rates of the foreign reserve assets which have already been transferred to the ECB in accordance with Article 30.1, by the ratio between the number of shares subscribed by the national central bank concerned and the number of shares already paid up by the other national central banks.

49.2. In addition to the payment to be made in accordance with Article 49.1, the central bank concerned shall contribute to the reserves of the ECB, to those provisions equivalent to reserves, and to the amount still to be appropriated to the reserves and provisions corresponding to the balance of the profit and loss account as at 31 December of the year prior to the abrogation of the derogation. The sum to be contributed shall be determined by multiplying the amount of the reserves, as defined above and as stated in the approved balance sheet of the ECB, by the ratio between the number of shares subscribed by the central bank concerned and the number of shares already paid up by the other central banks.

Article 50 (Initial appointment of the members of the Executive Board)

When the Executive Board of the ECB is being established, the President, the Vice-President and the other members of the Executive Board shall be appointed by common accord of the governments of the Member States at the level of Heads of State or of Government, on a recommendation from the Council and after consulting the European Parliament and the Council of the EMI. The President of the Executive Board shall be appointed for eight years. By way of derogation from Article 11.2, the Vice-President shall be appointed for four years and the other members of the Executive Board for terms of office of between five and eight years. No term of office shall be renewable. The number of members of the Executive Board may be smaller than provided for in Article 11.1, but in no circumstance shall it be less than four.

Article 51 (Derogation from Article 32)

51.1. If, after the start of the third stage, the Governing Council decides that the application of Article 32 results in significant changes in national central banks' relative income positions, the amount of income to be allocated pursuant to Article 32 shall be reduced by a uniform percentage which shall not exceed 60 per cent. in the first financial year after the start of the third stage and which shall decrease by at least 12 percentage points in each subsequent financial year.

51.2. Article 51.1 shall be applicable for not more than five financial years after the start of the third stage.

Article 52 (Exchange of bank notes in Community currencies)

Following the irrevocable fixing of exchange rates, the Governing Council shall take the necessary measures to ensure that bank notes denominated in currencies with irrevocably fixed exchange rates are exchanged by the national central banks at their respective par values.

Article 53 (Applicability of the transitional provisions)

If and as long as there are Member States with a derogation Articles 43 to 48 shall be applicable.

PROTOCOL ON THE STATUTE OF THE EUROPEAN MONETARY INSTITUTE

(Annexed to the E.C. Treaty)

Article 1 (Constitution and name)

1.1 The European Monetary Institute (EMI) shall be established in accordance with Article 109f of this Treaty; it shall perform its functions and carry out its activities in accordance with the provisions of this Treaty and of this Statute.

1.2. The members of the EMI shall be the central banks of the Member States ('national central banks'). For the purposes of this Statute, the Institut Monétaire Luxembourgeois shall be regarded as the central bank of Luxembourg.

1.3. Pursuant to Article 109f of this Treaty, both the Committee of Governors and the European Monetary Co-operation Fund (EMCF) shall be dissolved. All assets and liabilities of the EMCF shall pass automatically to the EMI.

Article 2 (Objectives)

The EMI shall contribute to the realisation of the conditions necessary for the transition to the third stage of Economic and Monetary Union, in particular by:
— strengthening the co-ordination of monetary policies with a view to ensuring price stability;
— making the preparations required for the establishment of the European System of Central Banks (ESCB), and for the conduct of a single monetary policy and the creation of a single currency in the third stage;
— overseeing the development of the ECU.

Article 3 (General principles)

3.1. The EMI shall carry out the tasks and functions conferred upon it by this Treaty and this Statute without prejudice to the responsibility of the competent authorities for the conduct of the monetary policy within the respective Member States.

3.2. The EMI shall act in accordance with the objectives and principles stated in Article 2 of the Statute of the ESCB.

Article 4 (Primary tasks)

4.1. In accordance with Article 109f(2) of this Treaty, the EMI shall:
— strengthen co-operation between the national central banks;
— strengthen the co-ordination of the monetary polices of the Member States with the aim of ensuring price stability;
— monitor the functioning of the European Monetary System (EMS);
— hold consultations concerning issues falling within the competence of the national central banks and affecting the stability of financial institutions and markets;
— take over the tasks of the EMCF; in particular it shall perform the functions referred to in Articles 6.1, 6.2 and 6.3;
— facilitate the use of the ECU and oversee its development, including the smooth functioning of the ECU clearing system.
The EMI shall also:
— hold regular consultations concerning the course of monetary policies and the use of monetary policy instruments;
— normally be consulted by the national monetary authorities before they take decisions on the course of monetary policy in the context of the common framework for *ex ante* co-ordination.

4.2. At the latest by 31 December 1996, the EMI shall specify the regulatory, organisational and logistical framework necessary for the ESCB to perform its tasks in the third stage, in accordance with the principle of an open market economy with free competition. This framework shall be submitted by the Council of the EMI for decision to the ECB at the date of its establishment.

In accordance with Article 109f(3) of this Treaty, the EMI shall in particular:

— prepare the instruments and the procedures necessary for carrying out a single monetary policy in the third stage;
— promote the harmonisation, where necessary, of the rules and practices governing the collection, compilation and distribution of statistics in the areas within its field of competence;
— prepare the rules for operations to be undertaken by the national central banks in the framework of the ESCB;
— promote the efficiency of cross-border payments;
— supervise the technical preparation of ECU bank notes.

Article 5 (Advisory functions)

5.1. In accordance with Article 109f(4) of this Treaty, the Council of the EMI may formulate opinions or recommendations on the overall orientation of monetary policy and exchange rate policy as well as on related measures introduced in each Member State. The EMI may submit opinions or recommendations to governments and to the Council on policies which might affect the internal or external monetary situation in the Community and, in particular, the functioning of the EMS.

5.2. The Council of the EMI may also make recommendations to the monetary authorities of the Member States concerning the conduct of their monetary policy.

5.3. In accordance with Article 109f(6) of this Treaty, the EMI shall be consulted by the Council regarding any proposed Community act within its field of competence.

Within the limits and under the conditions set out by the Council acting by a qualified majority on a proposal from the Commission and after consulting the European Parliament and the EMI, the EMI shall be consulted by the authorities of the Member States on any draft legislative provision within its field of competence, in particular with regard to Article 4.2.

5.4. In accordance with Article 109f(5) of this Treaty, the EMI may publish its opinions and its recommendations.

Article 6 (Operational and technical functions)

6.1. The EMI shall:
— provide for the multilaterisation of positions resulting from interventions by the national central banks in Community currencies and the multilateralisation of intra-Community settlements;
— administer the very short-term financing mechanism provided for by the Agreement of 13 March 1979 between the central banks of the Member States of the European Community laying down the operating procedures for the European Monetary System (hereinafter referred to as 'EMS Agreement') and the short-term monetary support mechanism provided for in the Agreement between the central banks of the Member States of the European Economic Community of 9 February 1970, as amended;
— perform the functions referred to in Article 11 of Council Regulation 1969/88 of 24 June 1988 establishing a single facility providing medium-term financial assistance for Member States' balances of payments.

6.2. The EMI may receive monetary reserves from the national central banks and issue ECUs against such assets for the purpose of implementing the EMS Agreement. These ECUs may be used by the EMI and the national central banks as a means of settlement and for transactions between them and the EMI. The EMI shall take the necessary administrative measures for the implementation of this paragraph.

6.3. The EMI may grant to the monetary authorities of third countries and to international monetary institutions the status of 'Other Holders' of ECUs and fix the terms and conditions under which such ECUs may be acquired, held or used by Other Holders.

6.4. The EMI shall be entitled to hold and manage foreign exchange reserves as an agent for and at the request of national central banks. Profits and losses regarding these reserves shall be for the account of the national central bank depositing the reserves.

The EMI shall perform this function on the basis of bilateral contracts in accordance with rules laid down in a decision of the EMI.

These rules shall ensure that transactions with these reserves shall not interfere with the monetary policy and exchange rate policy of the competent monetary authority of any Member State and shall be consistent with the objectives of the EMI and the proper functioning of the Exchange Rate Mechanism of the EMS.

Article 7 (Other tasks)

7.1. Once a year the EMI shall address a report to the Council on the state of the preparations for the third stage. These reports shall include an assessment of the progress towards convergence in the Community, and cover in particular the adaptation of monetary policy instruments and the preparation of the procedures necessary for carrying out a single monetary policy in the third stage, as well as the statutory requirements to be fulfilled for national central banks to become an integral part of the ESCB.

7.2. In accordance with the Council decisions referred to in Article 109f(7) of this Treaty, the EMI may perform other tasks for the preparation of the third stage.

Article 8 (Independence)

The members of the Council of the EMI who are the representatives of their institutions shall, with respect to their activities, act according to their own responsibilities. In exercising the powers and performing the tasks and duties conferred upon them by this Treaty and this Statute, the Council of the EMI may not seek or take any instructions from Community institutions or bodies or governments of Member States.

The Community institutions and bodies as well as the governments of the Member States undertake to respect this principle and not to seek to influence the Council of the EMI in the performance of its tasks.

Article 9 (Administration)

9.1. In accordance with Article 109f(1) of this Treaty, the EMI shall be directed and managed by the Council of the EMI.

9.2. The Council of the EMI shall consist of a President and the Governors of the national central banks, one of whom shall be Vice-President. If a Governor is prevented from attending a meeting, he may nominate another representative of his institution.

9.3. The President shall be appointed by common accord of the governments of the Member States at the level of Heads of State or of Government, on a recommendation from, as the case may be, the Committee of Governors or the Council of the EMI, and after consulting the European Parliament and the Council.

The President shall be selected from among persons of recognised standing and professional experience in monetary or banking matters. Only nationals of Member States may be President of the EMI.

The Council of the EMI shall appoint the Vice-President. The President and Vice-President shall be appointed for a period of three years.

9.4. The President shall perform his duties on a full-time basis. He shall not engage in any occupation, whether gainful or not, unless exemption is exceptionally granted by the Council of the EMI.

9.5. The President shall:

— prepare and chair the meetings of the Council of the EMI;
— without prejudice to Article 22, present the views of the EMI externally;
— be responsible for the day-to-day management of the EMI.

In the absence of the President, his duties shall be performed by the Vice-President.

9.6. The terms and conditions of employment of the President, in particular his salary, pension and other social security benefits, shall be the subject of a contract with the EMI and shall be fixed by the Council of the EMI on a proposal from a Committee comprising three members appointed by the Committee of Governors or the Council of the EMI, as the case may be, and three members appointed by the Council. The President shall not have the right to vote on matters referred to in this paragraph.

9.7. If the President no longer fulfils the conditions required for the performance of his duties or if he has been guilty of serious misconduct, the Court of Justice may, on application by the Council of the EMI, compulsorily retire him.

9.8. The Rules of Procedure of the EMI shall be adopted by the Council of the EMI.

Article 10 (Meetings of the Council of the EMI and voting procedures)

10.1. The Council of the EMI shall meet at least ten times a year. The proceedings of Council meetings shall be confidential. The Council of the EMI may, acting unanimously, decide to make the outcome of its deliberations public.

10.2. Each member of the Council of the EMI or his nominee shall have one vote.

10.3. Save as otherwise provided for in this Statute, the Council of the EMI shall act by a simple majority of its members.

10.4. Decisions to be taken in the context of Articles 4.2, 5.4, 6.2 and 6.3. shall require unanimity of the members of the Council of the EMI.

The adoption of opinions and recommendations under Articles 5.1 and 5.2, the adoption of decisions under Articles 6.4, 16 and 23.6 and the adoption of guidelines under Article 15.3 shall require a qualified majority of two thirds of the members of the Council of the EMI.

Article 11 (Interinstitutional co-operation and reporting requirements)

11.1 The President of the Council and a member of the Commission may participate, without having the right to vote, in meetings of the Council of the EMI.

11.2. The President of the EMI shall be invited to participate in Council meetings when the Council is discussing matters relating to the objectives and tasks of the EMI.

11.3. At a date to be established in the Rules of Procedure, the EMI shall prepare an annual report on its activities and on monetary and financial conditions in the Community. The annual report, together with the annual accounts of the EMI, shall be addressed to the European Parliament, the Council and the Commission and also to the European Council.

The President of the EMI may, at the request of the European Parliament or on his own initiative, be heard by the competent Committees of the European Parliament.

11.4. Reports published by the EMI shall be made available to interested parties free of charge.

Article 12 (Currency denomination)

The operations of the EMI shall be expressed in ECUs.

Article 13 (Seat)

Before the end of 1992, the decision as to where the seat of the EMI will be established shall be taken by common accord of the governments of the Member States at the level of Heads of State or of Government.

Article 14 (Legal capacity)

The EMI, which in accordance with Article 109f(1) of this Treaty shall have legal personality, shall enjoy in each of the Member States the most extensive legal capacity accorded to legal persons under their law; it may, in particular, acquire or dispose of movable or immovable property and may be a party to legal proceedings.

Article 15 (Legal acts)

15.1. In the performance of its tasks, and under the conditions laid down in this Statute, the EMI shall:
— deliver opinions;
— make recommendations;
— adopt guidelines, and take decisions, which shall be addressed to the national central banks.

15.2. Opinions and recommendations of the EMI shall have no binding force.

15.3. The Council of the EMI may adopt guidelines laying down the methods for the implementation of the conditions necessary for the ESCB to perform its functions in the third stage. EMI guidelines shall have no binding force; they shall be submitted for decision to the ECB.

15.4. Without prejudice to Article 3.1, a decision of the EMI shall be binding in its entirety upon those to whom it is addressed. Articles 190 and 191 of this Treaty shall apply to these decisions.

Article 16 (Financial resources)

16.1. The EMI shall be endowed with its own resources. The size of the resources of the EMI shall be determined by the Council of the EMI with a view to ensuring the income deemed necessary to cover the administrative expenditure incurred in the performance of the tasks and functions of the EMI.

16.2. The resources of the EMI determined in accordance with Article 16.1 shall be provided out of contributions by the national central banks in accordance with the key referred to in Article 29.1 of the Statute of the ESCB and be paid up at the establishment of the EMI. For this purpose, the statistical data to be used for the determination of the key shall be provided by the Commission, in accordance with the rules adopted by the Council, acting by a qualified majority on a proposal from the Commission and after consulting the European Parliament, the Committee of Governors and the Committee referred to in Article 109c of this Treaty.

16.3. The Council of the EMI shall determine the form in which contributions shall be paid up.

Article 17 (Annual accounts and auditing)

17.1. The financial year of the EMI shall begin on the first day of January and end on the last day of December.

17.2. The Council of the EMI shall adopt an annual budget before the beginning of each financial year.

17.3. The annual accounts shall be drawn up in accordance with the principles established by the Council of the EMI. The annual accounts shall be approved by the Council of the EMI and shall thereafter be published.

17.4. The annual accounts shall be audited by independent external auditors approved by the Council of the EMI. The auditors shall have full power to examine all books and accounts of the EMI and to obtain full information about its transactions.

The provisions of Article 188b of this Treaty shall only apply to an examination of the operational efficiency of the management of the EMI.

17.5. Any surplus of the EMI shall be transferred in the following order:
- (a) an amount to be determined by the Council of the EMI shall be transferred to the general reserve fund of the EMI;
- (b) any remaining surplus shall be distributed to the national central banks in accordance with the key referred to in Article 16.2.

17.6. In the event of a loss incurred by the EMI, the shortfall shall be offset against the general reserve fund of the EMI. Any remaining shortfall shall be made good by contributions from the national central banks, in accordance with the key as referred to in Article 16.2.

Article 18 (Staff)

18.1. The Council of the EMI shall lay down the conditions of employment of the staff of the EMI.

18.2. The Court of Justice shall have jurisdiction in any dispute between the EMI and its servants within the limits and under the conditions laid down in the conditions of employment.

Article 19 (Judicial control and related matters)

19.1. The acts or omissions of the EMI shall be open to review or interpretation by the Court of Justice in the cases and under the conditions laid down in this Treaty. The EMI may institute proceedings in the cases and under the conditions laid down in this Treaty.

19.2. Disputes between the EMI, on the one hand, and its creditors, debtors or any other person, on the other, shall fall within the jurisdiction of the competent national courts, save where jurisdiction has been conferred upon the Court of Justice.

19.3. The EMI shall be subject to the liability regime provided for in Article 215 of this Treaty.

19.4. The Court of Justice shall have jurisdiction to give judgment pursuant to any arbitration clause contained in a contract concluded by or on behalf of the EMI, whether that contract be governed by public or private law.

19.5. A decision of the EMI to bring an action before the Court of Justice shall be taken by the Council of the EMI.

Article 20 (Professional secrecy)

20.1. Members of the Council of the EMI and the staff of the EMI shall be required, even after their duties have ceased, not to disclose information of the kind covered by the obligation of professional secrecy.

20.2. Persons having access to data covered by Community legislation imposing an obligation of secrecy shall be subject to such legislation.

Article 21 (Privileges and immunities)

The EMI shall enjoy in the territories of the Member States such privileges and immunities as are necessary for the performance of its tasks, under the conditions laid down in the Protocol on the Privileges and Immunities of the European Communities annexed to the Treaty establishing a Single Council and a Single Commission of the European Communities.

Article 22 (Signatories)

The EMI shall be legally committed to third parties by the President or the Vice-President or by the signatures of two members of the staff of the EMI who have been duly authorised by the President to sign on behalf of the EMI.

Article 23 (Liquidation of the EMI)

23.1. In accordance with Article 109l of this Treaty, the EMI shall go into liquidation on the establishment of the ECB.

All assets and liabilities of the EMI shall then pass automatically to the ECB.

The latter shall liquidate the EMI according to the provisions of this Article.

The liquidation shall be completed by the beginning of the third stage.

23.2. The mechanism for the creation of ECUs against gold and US dollars as provided for by Article 17 of the EMS Agreement shall be unwound by the first day of the third stage in accordance with Article 20 of the said Agreement.

23.3. All claims and liabilities arising from the very short-term financing mechanism and the short-term monetary support mechanism, under the Agreements referred to in Article 6.1, shall be settled by the first day of the third stage.

23.4. All remaining assets of the EMI shall be disposed of and all remaining liabilities of the EMI shall be settled.

23.5. The proceeds of the liquidation described in Article 23.4 shall be distributed to the national central banks in accordance with the key referred to in Article 16.2, 23.6.

The Council of the EMI may take the measures necessary for the application of Articles 23.4 and 23.5.

23.7. Upon the establishment of the ECB, the President of the EMI shall relinquish his office.

PROTOCOL ON THE EXCESSIVE DEFICIT PROCEDURE

(Annexed to E.C. Treaty (Article 104c))

Article 1

The reference values referred to in Article 104c(2) of this Treaty are:
— 3 per cent. for the ratio of the planned or actual government deficit to gross domestic product at market prices;

— 60 per cent. for the ratio of government debt to gross domestic product at market prices.

Article 2

In Article 104c of this Treaty and in this Protocol:
— government means general government, that is central government, regional or local government and social security funds, to the exclusion of commercial operations, as defined in the European System of Integrated Economic Accounts;
— deficit means net borrowing as defined in the European System of Integrated Economic Accounts;
— investment means gross fixed capital formation as defined in the European System of Integrated Economic Accounts;
— debt means total gross debt at nominal value outstanding at the end of the year and consolidated between and within the sectors of general government as defined in the first indent.

Article 3

In order to ensure the effectiveness of the excessive deficit procedure, the governments of the Member States shall be responsible under this procedure for the deficits of general government as defined in the first indent of Article 2. The Member States shall ensure that national procedures in the budgetary area enable them to meet their obligations in this area deriving from this Treaty. The Member States shall report their planned and actual deficits and the levels of their debt promptly and regularly to the Commission.

Article 4

The statistical data to be used for the application of this Protocol shall be provided by the Commission.

PROTOCOL ON THE CONVERGENCE CRITERIA REFERRED TO IN ARTICLE 109J
OF THE TREATY ESTABLISHING THE EUROPEAN COMMUNITY

(Annexed to E.C. Treaty (Article 109j))

Article 1

The criterion on price stability referred to in the first indent of Article 109j(1) of this Treaty shall mean that a Member State has a price performance that is sustainable and an average rate of inflation, observed over a period of one year before the examination, that does not exceed by more than 1½ percentage points that of, at most, the three best performing Member States in terms of price stability. Inflation shall be measured by means of the consumer price index (CPI) on a comparable basis, taking into account differences in national definitions.

Article 2

The criterion on the government budgetary position referred to in the second indent of Article 109j(1) of this Treaty shall mean that at the time of the examination the Member State is not the subject of a Council decision under Article 104c(6) of this Treaty that an excessive deficit exists.

Article 3

The criterion on participation in the Exchange Rate Mechanism of the European Monetary System referred to in the third indent of Article 109j(1) of this Treaty shall mean that a Member State has respected the normal fluctuation margins provided for by the Exchange Rate Mechanism of the European Monetary System without severe tensions for at least the last two years before the examination. In particular, the Member State shall not have devalued its currency's bilateral central rate against any other Member State's currency on its own initiative for the same period.

Article 4

The criterion on the convergence of interest rates referred to in the fourth indent of Article 109j(1) of this Treaty shall mean that, observed over a period of one year before the examination, a Member State has had an average nominal long-term interest rate that does not exceed by more than 2 percentage points that of, at most, the three best performing Member States in terms of price stability. Interest rates shall be measured on the basis of long term government bonds or comparable securities, taking into account differences in national definitions.

Article 5

The statistical data to be used for the application of this Protocol shall be provided by the Commission.

Article 6

The Council shall, acting unanimously on a proposal from the Commission and after consulting the European Parliament, the EMI or the ECB as the case may be, and the Committee referred to in Article 109c, adopt appropriate provisions to lay down the details of the convergence criteria referred to in Article 109j of this Treaty, which shall then replace this Protocol.

PROTOCOL AMENDING THE PROTOCOL ON THE PRIVILEGES AND IMMUNITIES OF THE EUROPEAN COMMUNITIES

(Annexed to E.C. Treaty)

Sole Article

The Protocol on the Privileges and Immunities of the European Communities, annexed to the Treaty establishing a Single Council and a Single Commission of the European Communities, shall be supplemented by the following provisions:

Article 23

This Protocol shall also apply to the European Central Bank, to the members of its organs and to its staff, without prejudice to the provisions of the Protocol on the Statute of the European System of Central Banks and the European Central Bank.

The European Central Bank shall, in addition, be exempt from any form of taxation or imposition of a like nature on the occasion of any increase in its capital and from the various formalities which may be connected therewith in the State where the bank has its seat. The activities of the Bank and of its organs carried on in accordance with the Statute of the European System of Central Banks and of the European Central Bank shall not be subject to any turnover tax.

The above provisions shall also apply to the European Monetary Institute. Its dissolution or liquidation shall not give rise to any imposition.

PROTOCOL ON DENMARK

(Annexed to E.C. Treaty)

The provisions of Article 14 of the Protocol on the Statute of the European System of Central Banks and of the European Central Bank shall not affect the right of the National Bank of Denmark to carry out its existing tasks concerning those parts of the Kingdom of Denmark which are not part of the Community.

PROTOCOL ON PORTUGAL

(Annexed to E.C. Treaty)

1. Portugal is hereby authorised to maintain the facility afforded to the Autonomous Regions of Azores and Madeira to benefit from an interest-free [credit] facility with the Banco de Portugal under the terms established by existing Portuguese law.

2. Portugal commits itself to pursue its best endeavours in order to put an end to the abovementioned facility as soon as possible.

PROTOCOL ON THE TRANSITION TO THE THIRD STAGE OF ECONOMIC AND MONETARY UNION

(Annexed to E.C. Treaty)

THE HIGH CONTRACTING PARTIES,

Declare the irreversible character of the Community's movement to the third stage of Economic and Monetary Union by signing the new Treaty provisions on Economic and Monetary Union.

Therefore all Member States shall, whether they fulfil the necessary conditions for the adoption of a single currency or not, respect the will for the Community to enter swiftly into the third stage, and therefore no Member State shall prevent the entering into the third stage.

If by the end of 1997 the date of the beginning of the third stage has not been set, the Member States concerned, the Community institutions and other bodies involved shall expedite all preparatory work during 1998, in order to enable the Community to enter the third stage irrevocably on 1 January 1999 and to enable the ECB and the ESCB to start their full functioning from this date.

PROTOCOL ON CERTAIN PROVISIONS RELATING TO THE UNITED KINGDOM OF GREAT BRITAIN AND NORTHERN IRELAND

(Annexed to E.C. Treaty)

THE HIGH CONTRACTING PARTIES,

RECOGNISING that the United Kingdom shall not be obliged or committed to move to the third stage of Economic and Monetary Union without a separate decision to do so by its government and Parliament,

NOTING the practice of the government of the United Kingdom to fund its borrowing requirement by the sale of debt to the private sector,

HAVE AGREED the following provisions,

1. The United Kingdom shall notify the Council whether it intends to move to the third stage before the Council makes its assessment under Article 109j (2) of this Treaty.

Unless the United Kingdom notifies the Council that it intends to move to the third stage, it shall be under no obligation to do so.

If no date is set for the beginning of the third stage under Article 109j(3) of this Treaty, the United Kingdom may notify its intention to move to the third stage before 1 January 1998.

2. Paragraphs 3 to 9 shall have effect if the United Kingdom notifies the Council that it does not intend to move to the third stage.

3. The United Kingdom shall not be included among the majority of Member States which fulfil the necessary conditions referred to in the second indent of Article 109j(2) and the first indent of Article 109j(3) of this Treaty.

4. The United Kingdom shall retain its powers in the field of monetary policy according to national law.

5. Articles 3a(2), 104c(1), (9) and (11), 105(1) to (5), 105a, 107, 108, 108a, 109, 109a(1) and (2)(b) and 109l(4) and (5) of this Treaty shall not apply to the United Kingdom. In these provisions references to the Community or the Member States shall not include the United Kingdom and references to national central banks shall not include the Bank of England.

6. Articles 109e(4) and 109h and i of this Treaty shall continue to apply to the United Kingdom. Articles 109c(4) and 109m shall apply to the United Kingdom as if it had a derogation.

7. The voting rights of the United Kingdom shall be suspended in respect of acts of the Council referred to in the Articles listed in paragraph 5. For this purpose the weighted votes of the United Kingdom shall be excluded from any calculation of a qualified majority under Article 109k(5) of this Treaty.

The United Kingdom shall also have no right to participate in the appointment of the President, the Vice-President and the other members of the Executive Board of the ECB under Articles 109a(2)(b) and 109l(1) of this Treaty.

8. Articles 3, 4, 6, 7, 9.2, 10.1, 10.3, 11.2, 12.1, 14, 16, 18 to 20, 22, 23, 26, 27, 30 to 34, 50 and 52 of the Protocol on the Statute of the European System of Central Banks and of the European Central Bank ('the Statute') shall not apply to the United Kingdom.

In those Articles, references to the Community or the Member States shall not include the United Kingdom and references to national central banks or shareholders shall not include the Bank of England.

References in Articles 10.3 and 30.2 of the Statute to 'subscribed capital of the ECB' shall not include capital subscribed by the Bank of England.

9. Article 109l(3) of this Treaty and Articles 44 to 48 of the Statute shall have effect, whether or not there is any Member State with a derogation, subject to the following amendments:

(a) References in Article 44 to the tasks of the ECB and the EMI shall include those tasks that still need to be performed in the third stage owing to any decision of the United Kingdom not to move to that stage.

(b) In addition to the tasks referred to in Article 47 the ECB shall also give advice in relation to and contribute to the preparation of any decision of the Council with regard to the United Kingdom taken in accordance with paragraphs 10(a) and 10(c).

(c) The Bank of England shall pay up its subscription to the capital of the ECB as a contribution to its operational costs on the same basis as national central banks of Member States with a derogation.

10. If the United Kingdom does not move to the third stage, it may change its notification at any time after the beginning of that stage. In that event:

(a) The United Kingdom shall have the right to move to the third stage provided only that it satisfies the necessary conditions. The Council, acting at the request of the United Kingdom and under the conditions and in accordance with the procedure laid down in Article 109k(2) of this Treaty, shall decide whether it fulfils the necessary conditions.

(b) The Bank of England shall pay up its subscribed capital, transfer to the ECB foreign reserve assets and contribute to its reserves on the same basis as the national central bank of a Member State whose derogation has been abrogated.

(c) The Council, acting under the conditions and in accordance with the procedure laid down in Article 109l(5) of this Treaty, shall take all other necessary decisions to enable the United Kingdom to move to the third stage.

If the United Kingdom moves to the third stage pursuant to the provisions of this protocol, paragraphs 3 to 9 shall cease to have effect.

11. Notwithstanding Articles 104 and 109e(3) of this Treaty and Article 21.1 of the Statute, the government of the United Kingdom may maintain its Ways and Means facility with the Bank of England if and so long as the United Kingdom does not move to the third stage.

PROTOCOL ON CERTAIN PROVISIONS RELATING TO DENMARK

(Annexed to E.C. Treaty)

THE HIGH CONTRACTING PARTIES,

TAKING INTO ACCOUNT that the Danish Constitution contains provisions which may imply a referendum in Denmark prior to Danish participation in the third stage of Economic and Monetary Union,
HAVE AGREED on the following provisions,

1. The Danish Government shall notify the Council of its position concerning participation in the third stage before the Council makes its assessment under Article 109j(2) of this Treaty.

2. In the event of a notification that Denmark will not participate in the third stage, Denmark shall have an exemption. The effect of the exemption shall be that all Articles and provisions of this Treaty and the Statute of the ESCB referring to a derogation shall be applicable to Denmark.

3. In such case, Denmark shall not be included among the majority of Member States which fulfil the necessary conditions referred to in the second indent of Article 109j(2) and the first indent of Article 109j(3) of this Treaty.

4. As for the abrogation of the exemption, the procedure referred to in Article 109k(2) shall only be initiated at the request of Denmark.

5. In the event of abrogation of the exemption status, the provisions of this Protocol shall cease to apply.

PROTOCOL ON FRANCE

(Annexed to E.C. Treaty)

France will keep the privilege of monetary emission in its overseas territories under the terms established by its national laws, and will be solely entitled to determine the parity of the CFP franc.

PROTOCOL ON SOCIAL POLICY

(Annexed to E.C. Treaty)

THE HIGH CONTRACTING PARTIES,

NOTING that 11 Member States, that is to say the Kingdom of Belgium, the Kingdom of Denmark, the Federal Republic of Germany, the Hellenic

Republic, the Kingdom of Spain, the French Republic, Ireland, the Italian Republic, the Grand Duchy of Luxembourg, the Kingdom of the Netherlands, the Portuguese Republic, wish to continue along the path laid down in the 1989 Social Charter; that they have adopted among themselves an Agreement to this end; that this Agreement is annexed to this Protocol; that this Protocol and the said Agreement are without prejudice to the provisions of this Treaty, particularly those which relate to social policy which constitute an integral part of the '*acquis communautaire*':

1. Agree to authorise those 11 Member States to have recourse to the institutions, procedures and mechanisms of the Treaty for the purposes of taking among themselves and applying as far as they are concerned the acts and decisions required for giving effect to the abovementioned Agreement.

2. The United Kingdom of Great Britain and Northern Ireland shall not take part in the deliberations and the adoption by the Council of Commission proposals made on the basis of this Protocol and the abovementioned Agreement.

By way of derogation from Article 148(2) of the Treaty, acts of the Council which are made pursuant to this Protocol and which must be adopted by a qualified majority shall be deemed to be so adopted if they have received at least 44 votes in favour.

The unanimity of the members of the Council, with the exception of the United Kingdom of Great Britain and Northern Ireland, shall be necessary for acts of the Council which must be adopted unanimously and for those amending the Commission proposal.

Acts adopted by the Council and any financial consequences other than administrative costs entailed for the institutions shall not be applicable to the United Kingdom of Great Britain and Northern Ireland.

AGREEMENT ON SOCIAL POLICY CONCLUDED BETWEEN THE MEMBER STATES OF THE EUROPEAN COMMUNITY WITH THE EXCEPTION OF THE UNITED KINGDOM OF GREAT BRITAIN AND NORTHERN IRELAND

The undersigned 11 HIGH CONTRACTING PARTIES, that is to say the Kingdom of Belgium, the Kingdom of Denmark, the Federal Republic of Germany, the Hellenic Republic, the Kingdom of Spain, the French Republic, Ireland, the Italian Republic, the Grand Duchy of Luxembourg, the Kingdom of the Netherlands and the Portuguese Republic (hereinafter referred to as 'the Member States'),

WISHING to implement the 1989 Social Charter on the basis of the '*acquis communautaire*,'

CONSIDERING the Protocol on social policy,

HAVE AGREED as follows:

Article 1

The Community and the Member States shall have as their objectives the promotion of employment, improved living and working conditions, proper social protection, dialogue between management and labour, the development of human resources with a view to lasting high employment and the combating of exclusion. To this end the Community and the Member States shall implement measures which take account of the diverse forms of national practices, in particular in the field of contractual relations, and the need to maintain the competitiveness of the Community economy.

Article 2

1. With a view to achieving the objectives of Article 1, the Community shall support and complement the activities of the Member States in the following fields:

— improvement in particular of the working environment to protect workers' health and safety;
— working conditions;
— the information and consultation of workers;
— equality between men and women with regard to labour market opportunities and treatment at work;
— the integration of persons excluded from the labour market, without prejudice to Article 127 of the Treaty establishing the European Community (hereinafter referred to as 'the Treaty').

2. To this end, the Council may adopt, by means of directives, minimum requirements for gradual implementation, having regard to the conditions and technical rules obtaining in each of the Member States.

Such directives shall avoid imposing administrative, financial and legal constraints in a way which would hold back the creation and development of small and medium-sized undertakings.

The Council shall act in accordance with the procedure referred to in Article 189c of the Treaty after consulting the Economic and Social Committee.

3. However, the Council shall act unanimously on a proposal from the Commission, after consulting the European Parliament and the Economic and Social Committee, in the following areas:
— social security and social protection of workers;
— protection of workers where their employment contract is terminated;
— representation and collective defence of the interests of workers and employers, including co-determination, subject to paragraph 6;
— conditions of employment for third-country nationals legally residing in Community territory;
— financial contributions for promotion of employment and job-creation, without prejudice to the provisions relating to the Social Fund.

4. A Member State may entrust management and labour, at their joint request, with the implementation of directives adopted pursuant to paragraphs 2 and 3.

In this case, it shall ensure that, no later than the date on which a directive must be transposed in accordance with Article 189, management and labour have introduced the necessary measures by agreement, the Member State concerned being required to take any necessary measure enabling it at any time to be in a position to guarantee the results imposed by that directive.

5. The provisions adopted pursuant to this Article shall not prevent any Member State from maintaining or introducing more stringent preventive measures compatible with the Treaty.

6. The provisions of this Article shall not apply to pay, the right of association, the right to strike or the right to impose lock-outs.

Article 3

1. The Commission shall have the task of promoting the consultation of management and labour at Community level and shall take any relevant measure to facilitate their dialogue by ensuring balanced support for the parties.

2. To this end, before submitting proposals in the social policy field, the Commission shall consult management and labour on the possible direction of Community action.

3. If, after such consultation, the Commission considers Community action advisable, it shall consult management and labour on the content of the envisaged proposal. Management and labour shall forward to the Commission an opinion, or, where appropriate, a recommendation.

4. On the occasion of such consultation, management and labour may inform the Commission of their wish to initiate the process provided for in

Article 4. The duration of the procedure shall not exceed nine months, unless the management and labour concerned and the Commission decide jointly to extend it.

Article 4

1. Should management and labour so desire, the dialogue between them at Community level may lead to contractual relations including agreements.

2. Agreements concluded at Community level shall be implemented either in accordance with the procedures and practices specific to management and labour and the Member States or, in matters covered by Article 2, at the joint request of the signatory parties, by a Council decision on a proposal form from the Commission.

The Council shall act by qualified majority, except where the agreement in question contains one or more provisions relating to one of the areas referred to in Article 2(3), in which case it shall act unanimously.

Article 5

With a view to achieving the objectives of Article 1 and without prejudice to the other provisions of the Treaty, the Commission shall encourage co-operation between the Member States and facilitate the co-ordination of their action in all social policy fields under this Agreement.

Article 6

1. Each Member State shall ensure that the principle of equal pay for male and female workers for equal work is applied.

2. For the purpose of this Article, 'pay' means the ordinary basic or minimum wage or salary and any other considerations, whether in cash or in kind, which the worker receives directly or indirectly, in respect of his employment, from his employer.

Equal pay without discrimination based on sex means:
  (a) that pay for the same work at piece rates shall be calculated on the basis of the same unit of measurement;
  (b) that pay for work at time rates shall be the same for the same job.

3. This Article shall not prevent any Member State from maintaining or adopting measures providing for specific advantages in order to make it easier for women to pursue a vocational activity or to prevent or compensate for disadvantages in their professional careers.

Article 7

The Commission shall draw up a report each year on progress in achieving the objectives of Article 1, including the demographic situation in the Community. It shall forward the report to the European Parliament, the Council and the Economic and Social Committee.

The European Parliament may invite the Commission to draw up reports on particular problems concerning the social situation.

DECLARATIONS

1. Declaration on Article 2(2)

The 11 High Contracting Parties note that in the discussions on Article 2(2) of the Agreement it was agreed that the Community does not intend, in laying down minimum requirements for the protection of the safety and health of employees, to discriminate in a manner justified by the circumstances against employees in small and medium-sized undertakings.

2. Declaration on Article 4(2)

The 11 High Contracting Parties declare that the first of the arrangements for application of the agreements between management and labour Community-wide—referred to in Article 4(2)—will consist in developing, by collective bargaining according to the rules of each Member State, the content of the agreements, and that consequently this arrangement implies no obligation on the Member States to apply the agreements directly or to work out rules for their transposition, nor any obligation to amend national legislation in force to facilitate their implementation.

PROTOCOL ON ECONOMIC AND SOCIAL COHESION

(*Annexed to E.C. Treaty*)

THE HIGH CONTRACTING PARTIES,

RECALLING that the Union has set itself the objective of promoting economic and social progress, *inter alia*, through the strengthening of economic and social cohesion;

RECALLING that Article 2 of this Treaty includes the task of promoting economic and social cohesion and solidarity between Member States and that the strengthening of economic and social cohesion figures among the activities of the Community listed in Article 3;

RECALLING that the provisions of Part Three, Title XIV, on economic and social cohesion as a whole provide the legal basis for consolidating and further developing the Community's action in the field of economic and social cohesion, including the creation of a new fund;

RECALLING that the provisions of Part Three, Title XII on trans-European networks and Title XVI on environment envisage a Cohesion Fund to be set up before 31 December 1993;

STATING their belief that progress towards Economic and Monetary Union will contribute to the economic growth of all Member States;

NOTING that the Community's Structural Funds are being doubled in real terms between 1987 and 1993, implying large transfers, especially as a proportion of GDP of the less prosperous Member States;

NOTING that the European Investment Bank is lending large and increasing amounts for the benefit of the poorer regions;

NOTING the desire for greater flexibility in the arrangements for allocations from the Structural Funds;

NOTING the desire for modulation of the levels of Community participation in programmes and projects in certain countries;

NOTING the proposal to take greater account of the relative prosperity of Member States in the system of own resources,

REAFFIRM that the promotion of economic and social cohesion is vital to the full development and enduring success of the Community, and underline the importance of the inclusion of economic and social cohesion in Articles 2 and 3 of this Treaty;

REAFFIRM their conviction that the Structural Funds should continue to play a considerable part in the achievement of Community objectives in the field of cohesion;

REAFFIRM their conviction that the European Investment Bank should continue to devote the majority of its resources to the promotion of economic and social cohesion, and declare their willingness to review the capital needs of the European Investment Bank as soon as this is necessary for that purpose;

REAFFIRM the need for a thorough evaluation of the operation and effectiveness of the Structural Funds in 1992, and the need to review, on that occasion, the appropriate size of these Funds in the light of the tasks of the Community in the area of economic and social cohesion;

AGREE that the Cohesion Fund to be set up before 31 December 1993 will provide Community financial contributions to projects in the fields of environment and trans-European networks in Member States with a per capita GNP of less than 90 per cent. of the Community average which have a programme leading to the fulfilment of the conditions of economic convergence as set out in Article 104c;

DECLARE their intention of allowing a greater margin of flexibility in allocating financing from the Structural Funds to specific needs not covered under the present Structural Funds regulations;

DECLARE their willingness to modulate the levels of Community participation in the context of programmes and projects of the Structural Funds, with a view to avoiding excessive increases in budgetary expenditure in the less prosperous Member States;

RECOGNISE the need to monitor regularly the progress made towards achieving economic and social cohesion and state their willingness to study all necessary measures in this respect;

DECLARE their intention of taking greater account of the contributive capacity of individual Member States in the system of own resources, and of examining means of correcting, for the less prosperous Member States, regressive elements existing in the present own resources system.

PROTOCOL ON THE ECONOMIC AND SOCIAL COMMITTEE AND THE COMMITTEE OF THE REGIONS

(*Annexed to E.C. Treaty*)

The Economic and Social Committee and the Committee of the Regions shall have a common organisational structure.

PROTOCOL ANNEXED TO THE TREATY ON EUROPEAN UNION AND TO THE TREATIES ESTABLISHING THE EUROPEAN COMMUNITIES

Nothing in the Treaty on European Union, or in the Treaties establishing the European Communites, or in the Treaties or Acts modifying or supplementing those Treaties, shall affect the application in Ireland of Article 40.3.3. of the Constitution of Ireland.

GENERAL NOTE
This Protocol is discussed briefly in the Introduction and General Note.

DECLARATIONS

GENERAL NOTE
The declarations are statements of intent by the Member States of the European Union but they are not an integral part of the E.C. Treaty or of the TEU. The declarations are not enforceable in the E.C.J.

DECLARATION ON CIVIL PROTECTION, ENERGY AND TOURISM

The Conference declares that the question of introducing into the Treaty establishing the European Community Titles relating to the spheres referred to in Article 3(t) of that Treaty will be examined, in accordance with the procedure laid down in Article N(2) of the Treaty on European Union, on the basis of a report which the Commission will submit to the Council by 1996 at the latest.

The Commission declares that Community action in those spheres will be pursued on the basis of the present provisions of the Treaties establishing the European Communities.

DECLARATION ON NATIONALITY OF A MEMBER STATE

The Conference declares that, wherever in the Treaty establishing the European Community reference is made to nationals of the Member States, the question whether an individual possesses the nationality of a Member State shall be settled solely by reference to the national law of the Member State concerned. Member States may declare, for information, who are to be considered their nationals for Community purposes by way of a declaration lodged with the Presidency and may amend any such declaration when necessary.

DECLARATION ON PART THREE, TITLES III AND VI, OF THE TREATY ESTABLISHING THE EUROPEAN COMMUNITY

The Conference affirms that, for the purposes of applying the provisions set out in Part Three, Title III, Chapter 4 on capital and payments, and Title VI on economic and monetary policy, of this Treaty, the usual practice, according to which the Council meets in the composition of Economic and Finance Ministers, shall be continued, without prejudice to Article 109j(2) and (4) and Article 109k(2).

DECLARATION ON PART THREE, TITLE VI, OF THE TREATY ESTABLISHING THE EUROPEAN COMMUNITY

The Conference affirms that the President of the European Council shall invite the Economic and Finance Ministers to participate in European Council meetings when the European Council is discussing matters relating to Economic and Monetary Union.

DECLARATION ON MONETARY CO-OPERATION WITH NON-COMMUNITY COUNTRIES

The Conference affirms that the Community shall aim to contribute to stable international monetary relations.

To this end the Community shall be prepared to co-operate with other European countries and with those non-European countries with which the Community has close economic ties.

DECLARATION ON MONETARY RELATIONS WITH THE REPUBLIC OF SAN MARINO, THE VATICAN CITY AND THE PRINCIPALITY OF MONACO

The Conference agrees that the existing monetary relations between Italy and San Marino and the Vatican City and between France and Monaco remain unaffected by the Treaty establishing the European Community until the introduction of the ECU as the single currency of the Community.

The Community undertakes to facilitate such renegotiations of existing arrangements as might become necessary as a result of the introduction of the ECU as a single currency.

DECLARATION ON ARTICLE 73D OF THE TREATY ESTABLISHING THE EUROPEAN COMMUNITY

The Conference affirms that the right of Member States to apply the relevant provisions of their tax law as referred to in Article 73d(1)(a) of this Treaty will apply only with respect to the relevant provisions which exist at the end of 1993.

DECLARATION ON ARTICLE 109 OF THE TREATY ESTABLISHING THE EUROPEAN COMMUNITY

The Conference emphasises that use of the term 'formal agreements' in Article 109(1) is not intended to create a new category of international agreement within the meaning of Community law.

DECLARATION ON PART THREE, TITLE XVI, OF THE TREATY
ESTABLISHING THE EUROPEAN COMMUNITY

The Conference considers that, in view of the increasing importance of nature conservation at national, Community and international level, the Community should, in exercising its powers under the provisions of Part Three, Title XVI, take account of the specific requirements of this area.

DECLARATION ON ARTICLES 109, 130R AND 130Y OF THE TREATY
ESTABLISHING THE EUROPEAN COMMUNITY

The Conference considers that the provisions of Article 109(5), Article 130r(4), second subparagraph, and Article 130y do not affect the principles resulting from the judgment handed down by the Court of Justice in the AETR case.

DECLARATION ON THE DIRECTIVE OF 24 NOVEMBER 1988 (EMISSIONS)

The Conference declares that changes in Community legislation cannot undermine the derogations granted to Spain and Portugal until 31 December 1999 under the Council Directive of 24 November 1988 on the limitation of emissions of certain pollutants into the air from large combustion plants.

DECLARATION ON THE EUROPEAN DEVELOPMENT FUND

The Conference agrees that the European Development Fund will continue to be financed by national contributions in accordance with the current provisions.

DECLARATION ON THE ROLE OF NATIONAL PARLIAMENTS IN THE
EUROPEAN UNION

The Conference considers that it is important to encourage greater involvement of national Parliaments in the activities of the European Union.

To this end, the exchange of information between national Parliaments and the European Parliament should be stepped up. In this context, the governments of the Member States will ensure, *inter alia*, that national Parliaments receive Commission proposals for legislation in good time for information or possible examination.

Similarly, the Conference considers that it is important for contacts between the national Parliaments and the European Parliament to be stepped up, in particular through the granting of appropriate reciprocal facilities and regular meetings between members of Parliament interested in the same issues.

DECLARATION ON THE CONFERENCE OF THE PARLIAMENTS

The Conference invites the European Parliament and the national Parliaments to meet as necessary as a Conference of the Parliaments (or 'Assises').

The Conference of the Parliaments will be consulted on the main features of the European Union, without prejudice to the powers of the European Parliament and the rights of the national Parliaments. The President of the European Council and the President of the Commission will report to each session of the Conference of the Parliaments on the state of the Union.

DECLARATION ON THE NUMBER OF MEMBERS OF THE COMMISSION AND
OF THE EUROPEAN PARLIAMENT

The Conference agrees that the Member States will examine the questions relating to the number of members of the Commission and the number of members of the European Parliament no later than at the end of 1992, with a view to reaching an agreement which will permit the establishment of the necessary legal basis for fixing the number of members of the European Parliament in good time for the 1994 elections. The decisions will be taken in the light, *inter alia*, of the need to establish the overall size of the European Parliament in an enlarged Community.

DECLARATION ON THE HIERARCHY OF COMMUNITY ACTS

The Conference agrees that the Intergovernmental Conference to be convened in 1996 will examine to what extent it might be possible to review the classification of Community acts with a view to establishing an appropriate hierarchy between the different categories of act.

DECLARATION ON THE RIGHT OF ACCESS TO INFORMATION

The Conference considers that transparency of the decision-making process strengthens the democratic nature of the institutions and the public's confidence in the administration. The Conference accordingly recommends that the Commission submit to the Council no later than 1993 a report on measures designed to improve public access to the information available to the institutions.

DECLARATION ON ESTIMATED COSTS UNDER COMMISSION PROPOSALS

The Conference notes that the Commission undertakes, by basing itself where appropriate on any consultations it considers necessary and by strengthening its system for evaluating Community legislation, to take account in its legislative proposals of costs and benefits to the Member States' public authorities and all the parties concerned.

DECLARATION ON THE IMPLEMENTATION OF COMMUNITY LAW

1. The Conference stresses that it is central to the coherence and unity of the process of European construction that each Member State should fully and accurately transpose into national law the Community directives addressed to it within the deadlines laid down therein. Moreover, the conference, while recognising that it must be for each Member State to determine how the provision of Community law can best be enforced in the light of its own particular institutions, legal system and other circumstances, but in any event in compliance with Article 189 of the Treaty establishing the European Community, considers it essential for the proper functioning of the Community that the measures taken by the different Member States should result in Community law being applied with the same effectiveness and rigour as in the application of their national law.

2. The Conference calls on the Commission to ensure, in exercising its powers under Article 155 of this Treaty, that Member States fulfil their obligations. It asks the Commission to publish periodically a full report for the Member States and the European Parliament.

DECLARATION ON ASSESSMENT OF THE ENVIRONMENTAL IMPACT OF COMMUNITY MEASURES

The Conference notes that the Commission undertakes in its proposals, and that the Member States undertake in implementing those proposals, to take full account of their environmental impact and of the principle of sustainable growth.

DECLARATION ON THE COURT OF AUDITORS

The Conference emphasises the special importance it attaches to the task assigned to the Court of Auditors by Articles 188a, 188b and 206 of the Treaty establishing the European Community.

It requests the other Community institutions to consider, together with the Court of Auditors, all appropriate ways of enhancing the effectiveness of its work.

DECLARATION ON THE ECONOMIC AND SOCIAL COMMITTEE

The Conference agrees that the Economic and Social Committee will enjoy the same independence with regard to its budget and staff management as the Court of Auditors has enjoyed hitherto.

DECLARATION ON CO-OPERATION WITH CHARITABLE ASSOCIATIONS

The Conference stresses the importance, in pursuing the objectives of Article 117 of the Treaty establishing the European Community, of co-operation between the latter and charitable associations and foundations as institutions responsible for social welfare establishments and services.

DECLARATION ON THE PROTECTION OF ANIMALS

The Conference calls upon the European Parliament, the Council and the Commission, as well as the Member States, when drafting and implementing Community legislation on the common agricultural policy, transport, the internal market and research, to pay full regard to the welfare requirements of animals.

DECLARATION ON THE REPRESENTATION OF THE INTERESTS OF THE OVERSEAS COUNTRIES AND TERRITORIES REFERRED TO IN ARTICLE 227(3) AND (5)(A) AND (B) OF THE TREATY ESTABLISHING THE EUROPEAN COMMUNITY

The Conference, noting that in exceptional circumstances divergences may arise between the interests of the Union and those of the overseas countries and territories referred to in Article 227(3) and (5)(a) and (b), agrees that the Council will seek to reach a solution which affords with the position of the Union. However, in the event that this proves impossible, the Conference agrees that the Member State concerned may act separately in the interests of the said overseas countries and territories, without this affecting the Community's interests. The Member State concerned will give notice to the Council and the Commission where such a divergence of interests is likely to occur and, when separate action proves unavoidable, make it clear that it is acting in the interests of an overseas territory mentioned above.

This declaration also applies to Macao and East Timor.

DECLARATION ON THE OUTERMOST REGIONS OF THE COMMUNITY

The Conference acknowledges that the outermost regions of the Community (the French overseas departments, Azores and Madeira and Canary Islands) suffer from major structural backwardness compounded by several phenomena (remoteness, island status, small size, difficult topography and climate, economic dependence on a few products), the permanence and combination of which severely restrain their economic and social development.

It considers that, while the provisions of the Treaty establishing the European Community and secondary legislation apply automatically to the outermost regions, it is nonetheless possible to adopt specific measures to assist them inasmuch and as long as there is an objective need to take such measures with a view to the economic and social development of those regions. Such measures should have as their aim both the completion of the internal market and the recognition of the regional reality to enable the outermost regions to achieve the average economic and social level of the Community.

Declaration on Voting in the Field of the Common Foreign and Security Policy

The Conference agrees that, with regard to Council decisions requiring unanimity, Member States will, to the extent possible, avoid preventing a unanimous decision where a qualified majority exists in favour of that decision.

Declaration on Practical Arrangements in the Field of the Common Foreign and Security Policy

The Conference agrees that the division of work between the Political Committee and the Permanent Representatives Committee will be examined at a later stage, as will the practical arrangements for merging the Political Co-operation Secretariat with the General Secretariat at the Council and for co-operation between the latter and the Commission.

Declaration on the Use of Languages in the Field of the Common Foreign and Security Policy

The Conference agrees that the use of languages shall be in accordance with the rules of the European Communities.

For COREU communications, the current practice of European Political Co-operation will serve as a guide for the time being.

All common foreign and security policy texts which are submitted to or adopted at meetings of the European Council and of the Council as well as all texts which are to be published are immediately and simultaneously translated into all the official Community languages.

Declarations on Western European Union

of Belgium, Germany, Spain, France, Italy, Luxembourg, the Netherlands, Portugal and the United Kingdom of Great Britain and Northern Ireland, which are members of the Western European Union and also members of the European Union on

DECLARATION I

The Role of the Western European Union and its Relations with the European Union and with the Atlantic Alliance

Introduction

1. WEU Member States agree on the need to develop a genuine European security and defence identity and a greater European responsibility on defence matters. This identity will be pursued through a gradual process involving successive phases. WEU will form an integral part of the process of the development of the European Union and will enhance its contribution to solidarity within the Atlantic Alliance.

WEU Member States agree to strengthen the role of WEU, in the longer term perspective of a common defence policy within the European Union which might in time lead to a common defence, compatible with that of the Atlantic Alliance.

2. WEU will be developed as the defence component of the European Union and as the means to strengthen the European pillar of the Atlantic Alliance. To this end, it will formulate common European defence policy and carry forward its concrete implementation through the further development of its own operational role.

WEU Member States take note of Article J.4 relating to the common foreign and security policy of the Treaty of European Union which reads as follows:

[*see above*]

A. *WEU's relations with European Union*

3. The objective is to build up WEU in stages as the defence component of the European Union. To this end, WEU is prepared, at the request of the European Union, to elaborate and implement decisions and actions of the Union which have defence implications.

To this end, WEU will take the following measures to develop a close working relationship with the Union:

— as appropriate, synchronisation of the dates and venues of meetings and harmonisation of working methods;
— establishment of close co-operation between the Council and Secretariat-General of WEU on the one hand, and the Council of the Union and General Secretariat of the Council on the other;
— consideration of the harmonisation of the sequence and duration of the respective Presidencies;
— arranging for appropriate modalities so as to ensure that the Commission of the European Communities is regularly informed and, as appropriate, consulted on WEU activities in accordance with the role of the Commission in the common foreign and security policy as defined in the Treaty on European Union;
— encouragement of closer co-operation between the Parliamentary Assembly of WEU and the European Parliament.

The WEU Council shall, in agreement with the competent bodies of the European Union, adopt the necessary practical arrangements.

B. *WEU's relations with the Atlantic Alliance*

4. The objective is to develop WEU as a means to strengthen the European pillar of the Atlantic Alliance. Accordingly WEU is prepared to develop further the close working links between WEU and the Alliance and to strengthen the role, responsibilities and contributions of WEU Member States in the Alliance. This will be undertaken on the basis of the necessary transparency and complementarity between the emerging European security and defence identity and the Alliance. WEU will act in conformity with the positions adopted in the Atlantic Alliance.

— WEU Member States will intensify the co-ordination on Alliance issues which represent an important common interest with the aim of introducing joint positions agreed in WEU into the process of consultation in the Alliance which will remain the essential forum for consultation among its members and the venue for agreement on policies bearing on the security and defence commitments of Allies under the North Atlantic Treaty.
— Where necessary, dates and venues of meetings will be synchronised and working methods harmonised.
— Close co-operation will be established between the Secretariats-General of WEU and NATO.

C. *Operational role of WEU*

5. WEU's operational role will be strengthened by examining and defining appropriate missions, structures and means, covering in particular:
— WEU planning cell;
— closer military co-operation complementary to the Alliance in particular in the fields of logistics, transport, training and strategic surveillance;
— meetings of WEU Chiefs of Defence Staff;
— military units answerable to WEU.
Other proposals will be examined further, including:
— enhanced co-operation in the field of armaments with the aim of creating a European armaments agency;
— development of the WEU Institute into a European Security and Defence Academy. Arrangements aimed at giving WEU a stronger operational role will be fully compatible with the military dispositions necessary to ensure the collective defence of all Allies.

D. *Other measures*

6. As a consequence of the measures set out above, and in order to facilitate the strengthening of WEU's role, the seat of the WEU Council and Secretariat will be transferred to Brussels.

7. Representation on the WEU Council must be such that the Council is able to exercise its functions continuously in accordance with Article VIII of the modified Brussels Treaty. Member-States may draw on a double-hatting formula, to be worked out, consisting of their representatives to the Alliance and to the European Union.

8. WEU notes that, in accordance with the provisions of Article J.4(6) concerning the common foreign and security policy of the Treaty on European Union, the Union will decide to review the provisions of this Article with a view to furthering the objective to be set by it in accordance with the procedure defined. The WEU will re-examine the present provisions in 1996. This re-examination will take account of the progress and experience acquired and will extend to relations between WEU and the Atlantic Alliance.

DECLARATION II

The Member States of WEU welcome the development of the European security and defence identity. They are determined, taking into account the role of WEU as the defence component of the European Union and as the means to strengthen the European pillar of the Atlantic Alliance, to put the relationship between WEU and the other European States on a new basis for the sake of stability and security in Europe. In this spirit, they propose the following.

States which are members of the European Union are invited to accede to WEU on conditions to be agreed in accordance with Article XI of the modified Brussels Treaty, or to become observers if they so wish. Simultaneously, other European Member States of NATO are invited to become associate members of WEU in a way which will give them the possibility of participating fully in the activities of WEU.

The Member States of WEU assume that treaties and agreements corresponding with the above proposals will be concluded before 31 December 1992.

DECLARATION ON ASYLUM

1. The Conference agrees that, in the context of the proceedings provided for in Articles K.1 and K.3 of the provisions on co-operation in the fields of

justice and home affairs, the Council will consider as a matter of priority questions concerning Member States' asylum policies, with the aim of adopting, by the beginning of 1993, common action to harmonise aspects of them, in the light of the work programme and timetable contained in the report on asylum drawn up at the request of the European Council meeting in Luxembourg on 28 and 29 June 1991.

2. In this connection, the Council will also consider, by the end of 1993, on the basis of a report, the possibility of applying Article K.9 to such matters.

DECLARATION ON POLICE CO-OPERATION

The Conference confirms the agreement of the Member States on the objectives underlying the German delegation's proposals at the European Council meeting in Luxembourg on 28 and 29 June 1991.

For the present, the Member States agree to examine as a matter of priority the drafts submitted to them, on the basis of the work programme and timetable agreed upon in the report drawn up at the request of the Luxembourg European Council, and they are willing to envisage the adoption of practical measures in areas such as those suggested by the German delegation, relating to the following functions in the exchange of information and experience:

— support for national criminal investigation and security authorities, in particular in the co-ordination of investigations and search operations;
— creation of data bases;
— central analysis and assessment of information in order to take stock of the situation and identify investigative approaches;
— collection and analysis of national prevention programmes for forwarding to Member States and for drawing up Europe-wide prevention strategies;
— measures relating to further training, research, forensic matters and criminal records departments.

Member States agree to consider on the basis of a report, during 1994 at the latest, whether the scope of such co-operation should be extended.

DECLARATION ON DISPUTES BETWEEN THE ECB AND THE EMI AND THEIR SERVANTS

The Conference considers it proper that the Court of First Instance should hear this class of action in accordance with Article 168a of the Treaty establishing the European Community. The Conference therefore invites the institutions to adapt the relevant rules accordingly.

APPENDIX 2

EUROPEAN COMMUNITIES ACT 1972
(as amended by the Treaty on European Union)

(1972 c. 68)

An Act to make provision in connection with the enlargement of the European Communities to include the United Kingdom, together with (for certain purposes) the Channel Islands, the Isle of Man and Gibraltar.
[17th October 1972]

PARLIAMENTARY DEBATES
Hansard, H.C. Vol. 829, col. 1199; Vol. 831, cols. 264, 443, 629; Vol. 832, cols. 259, 555, 1041, 1251, 1385, 1457, 1575; Vol. 833, cols. 303, 437, 550, 669; Vol. 835, cols. 229, 381, 531, 641, 1290, 1408, 1548, 1689; Vol. 836, cols. 206, 395, 531; Vol. 837, cols. 1441, 1579; Vol. 838, cols. 714, 837, 1271, 1397, 1510, 1639; Vol. 839, cols. 239, 375, 479, 619, 735, 851, 1195, 1327, 1442, 1579; Vol. 840, cols. 243, 383, 556, 697, 1862; H.L. Vol. 333, cols. 1223, 1358, 1380; Vol. 334, cols. 460, 466, 547, 589, 751, 789, 858, 903, 949, 982, 1045, 1218, 1278, 1369, 1417; Vol. 335, cols. 202, 329, 1134.

PART I

GENERAL PROVISIONS

Short title and interpretation

1.—(1) This Act may be cited as the European Communities Act 1972.
(2) In this Act [...]—
"the Communities" means the European Economic Community, the European Coal and Steel Community and the European Atomic Energy Community;
"the Treaties" or "the Community Treaties" means, subject to subsection (3) below, the pre-accession treaties, that is to say, those described in Part I of Schedule 1 to this Act, taken with—

(a) the treaty relating to the accession of the United Kingdom to the European Economic Community and to the European Atomic Energy Community, signed at Brussels on the 22nd January 1972; and

(b) the decision, of the same date, of the Council of the European Communities relating to the accession of the United Kingdom to the European Coal and Steel Community;

(c) the treaty relating to the accession of the Hellenic Republic to the European Economic Community and to the European Atomic Energy Community, signed at Athens on 28th May 1979; and

(d) the decision, of 24th May 1979, of the Council relating to the accession of the Hellenic Republic to the European Coal and Steel Community;] [and

(e) the decisions, of 7th May 1985 and of 24th June 1988, of the Council on the Communities' system of own resources; and

(f) the undertaking by the Representatives of the Governments of the Member States, as confirmed at their meeting within the Council on 24th June 1988 in Luxembourg, to make payments to finance the Communities' general budget for the financial year 1988;] [and

(g) the treaty relating to the accession of the Kingdom of Spain and the Portuguese Republic to the European Economic Community and to the European Atomic Energy Community, signed at Lisbon and Madrid on 12th June 1985; and

(h) the decision, of 11th June 1985, of the Council relating to the accession of the Kingdom of Spain and the Portuguese Republic to the European Coal and Steel Community;] [and

(j) the following provisions of the Single European Act signed at Luxembourg and The Hague on 17th and 28th February 1986, namely Title II (amendment of the treaties establishing the Communities) and, so far as they relate to any of the Communities or any Community institution, the preamble and Titles I (common provisions) and IV (general and final provisions);]

(k) Titles II, III and IV of the Treaty on European Union signed at Maastricht on 7th February 1992, together with the other provisions of the Treaty so far as they relate to those Titles, and the Protocols adopted at Maastricht on that date and annexed to the Treaty establishing the European Community with the exception of the Protocol on Social Policy on page 117 of Cm. 1934.]

[and

(m) the Agreement on the European Economic Area signed at Oporto on 2nd May 1992 together with the Protocol adjusting that Agreement signed at Brussels on 17th March 1993.]

and any other treaty entered into by any of the Communities, with or without any of the Member States, or entered into, as a treaty ancillary to any of the Treaties, by the United Kingdom;

and any expression defined in Schedule 1 to this Act has the meaning there given to it.

(3) If Her Majesty by Order in Council declares that a treaty specified in the Order is to be regarded as one of the Community Treaties as herein defined, the Order shall be conclusive that it is to be so regarded; but a treaty entered into by the United Kingdom after the 22nd January 1972, other than a pre-accession treaty to which the United Kingdom accedes on terms settled on or before that date, shall not be so regarded unless it is so specified, nor be so specified unless a draft of the Order in Council has been approved by resolution of each House of Parliament.

(4) For purposes of subsections (2) and (3) above, "treaty" includes any international agreement, and any protocol or annex to a treaty or international agreement.

GENERAL NOTE
  The words omitted from subs. (2) were repealed by the Interpretation Act 1978, Sched. 3.
  Paragraphs (c) and (d) were added by the European Communities (Greek Accession) Act 1979, s.1.
  Paragraphs (e) and (f) were added by the European Communities (Finance) Act 1988.
  Paragraphs (g) and (h) were added by the European Communities (Spanish and Portuguese Accession) Act 1985, s.1.
  Paragraph (j) was added by the European Communities (Amendment) Act 1986, s.1.
  Paragraph (k) was added by the European Communities (Amendment) Act 1993, s.1.
  Paragraph (m) was added by the European Economic Area Act 1993, s.1.

General implementation of Treaties

2.—(1) All such rights, powers, liabilities, obligations and restrictions from time to time created or arising by or under the Treaties, and all such remedies and procedures from time to time provided for by or under the Treaties, as in accordance with the Treaties are without further enactment to be given legal effect or used in the United Kingdom shall be recognised and available in law, and be enforced, allowed and followed accordingly; and the expression "enforceable Community right" and similar expressions shall be read as referring to one to which this subsection applies.

(2) Subject to Schedule 2 to this Act, at any time after its passing Her Majesty may by Order in Council, and any designated Minister or department may by regulations, make provision—

(a) for the purpose of implementing any Community obligation of the United Kingdom, or enabling any such obligation to be implemented, or of enabling any rights enjoyed or to be enjoyed by the United Kingdom under or by virtue of the Treaties to be exercised; or

(b) for the purpose of dealing with matters arising out of or related to any such obligation or rights or the coming into force, or the operation from time to time, of subsection (1) above;

and in the exercise of any statutory power or duty, including any power to give directions or to legislate by means of orders, rules, regulations or other subordinate instrument, the person entrusted with the power or duty may have regard to the objects of the Communities and to any such obligation or rights as aforesaid.

In this subsection "designated Minister or department" means such Minister of the Crown or government department as may from time to time be designated by Order in Council in relation to any matter or for any purpose, but subject to such restrictions or conditions (if any) as may be specified by the Order in Council.

(3) There shall be charged on and issued out of the Consolidated Fund or, if so determined by the Treasury, the National Loans Fund the amounts required to meet any Community obligation to make payments to any of the Communities or Member States, or any Community obligation in respect of contributions to the capital or reserves of the European Investment Bank or in respect of loans to the Bank, or to redeem any notes or obligations issued or created in respect of any such Community obligation; and, except as otherwise provided by or under any enactment,—

(a) any other expenses incurred under or by virtue of the Treaties or this Act by any Minister of the Crown or government department may be paid out of moneys provided by Parliament; and

(b) any sums received under or by virtue of the Treaties or this Act by any Minister of the Crown or government department, save for such sums

as may be required for disbursements permitted by any other enactment, shall be paid into the Consolidated Fund or, if so determined by
the Treasury, the National Loans Fund.

(4) The provision that may be made under subsection (2) above includes,
subject to Schedule 2 to this Act, any such provision (of any such extent) as
might be made by Act of Parliament, and any enactment passed or to be
passed, other than one contained in this Part of this Act, shall be construed
and have effect subject to the foregoing provisions of this section; but, except
as may be provided by any Act passed after this Act, Schedule 2 shall have
effect in connection with the powers conferred by this and the following sections of this Act to make Orders in Council and regulations.

(5) [. . .] and the references in that subsection to a Minister of the Crown or
government department and to a statutory power or duty shall include a Minister or department of the Government of Northern Ireland and a power or
duty arising under or by virtue of an Act of the Parliament of Northern
Ireland.

(6) A law passed by the legislature of any of the Channel Islands or of the
Isle of Man, or a colonial law (within the meaning of the Colonial Laws Validity Act 1865) passed or made for Gibraltar, if expressed to be passed or
made in the implementation of the Treaties and of the obligations of the
United Kingdom thereunder, shall not be void or inoperative by reason of
any inconsistency with or repugnancy to an Act of Parliament, passed or to
be passed, that extends to the Island or Gibraltar or any provision having the
force and effect of an Act there (but not including this section), nor by reason
of its having some operation outside the Island or Gibraltar; and any such
Act or provision that extends to the Island or Gibraltar shall be construed
and have effect subject to the provisions of any such law.

GENERAL NOTE
   The words omitted in subs. (5) were repealed by the Northern Ireland Constitution Act 1973,
s.41 and Sched. 6, Pt. I.

Decisions on, and proof of, Treaties and Community instruments etc.

3.—(1) For the purposes of all legal proceedings any question as to the
meaning or effect of any of the Treaties, or as to the validity, meaning or
effect of any Community instrument, shall be treated as a question of law
(and, if not referred to the European Court, be for determination as such in
accordance with the principles laid down by and any relevant decision of the
European Court [or any court attached thereto]).

(2) Judicial notice shall be taken of the Treaties, of the Official Journal of
the Communities and of any decision of, or expression of opinion by, the
European Court [or any court attached thereto] on any such question as
aforesaid; and the Official Journal shall be admissible as evidence of any
instrument or other act thereby communicated of any of the Communities or
of any Community institution.

(3) Evidence of any instrument issued by a Community institution, including any judgment or order of the European Court [or any court attached
thereto], or of any document in the custody of a Community institution, or
any entry in or extract from such a document, may be given in any legal proceedings by production of a copy certified as a true copy by an official of that
institution; and any document purporting to be such a copy shall be received
in evidence without proof of the official position or handwriting of the person
signing the certificate.

(4) Evidence of any Community instrument may also be given in any legal
proceedings—
   (a) by production of a copy purporting to be printed by the Queen's
      Printer;

(b) where the instrument is in the custody of a government department (including a department of the Government of Northern Ireland), by production of a copy certified on behalf of the department to be a true copy by an officer of the department generally or specially authorised so to do;

and any document purporting to be such a copy as is mentioned in paragraph (b) above of an instrument in the custody of a department shall be received in evidence without proof of the official position or handwriting of the person signing the certificate, or of his authority to do so, or of the document being in the custody of the department.

(5) In any legal proceedings in Scotland evidence of any matter given in a manner authorised by this section shall be sufficient evidence of it.

GENERAL NOTE
The words in square brackets in subs. (1) were substituted and added by the European Communities (Amendment) Act 1986, s.2.
The words in square brackets in subss. (2) and (3) were added by the European Communities (Amendment) Act 1986, s.2.

PART II

AMENDMENT OF LAW

General provision for repeal and amendment

4.—(1) The enactments mentioned in Schedule 3 to this Act (being enactments that are superseded or to be superseded by reason of Community obligations and of the provision made by this Act in relation thereto or are not compatible with Community obligations) are hereby repealed, to the extent specified in column 3 of the Schedule, with effect from the entry date or other date mentioned in the Schedule; and in the enactments mentioned in Schedule 4 to this Act there shall, subject to any transitional provision there included, be made the amendments provided for by that Schedule.

(2) Where in any Part of Schedule 3 to this Act it is provided that repeals made by that Part are to take effect from a date appointed by order, the orders shall be made by statutory instrument, and an order may appoint different dates for the repeal of different provisions to take effect, or for the repeal of the same provision to take effect for different purposes; and an order appointing a date for a repeal to take effect may include transitional and other supplementary provisions arising out of that repeal, including provisions adapting the operation of other enactments included for repeal but not yet repealed by that Schedule, and may amend or revoke any such provisions included in a previous order.

(3) Where any of the following sections of this Act, or any paragraph of Schedule 4 to this Act, affects or is construed as one with an Act or Part of an Act similar in purpose to provisions having effect only in Northern Ireland, then—

(a) unless otherwise provided by Act of the Parliament of Northern Ireland, the Governor of Northern Ireland may by Order in Council make provision corresponding to any made by the section or paragraph, and amend or revoke any provision so made; and
(b) [....].

(4) Where Schedule 3 or 4 to this Act provides for the repeal or amendment of an enactment that extends or is capable of being extended to any of the Channel Islands or the Isle of Man, the repeal or amendment shall in like manner extend or be capable of being extended thereto.

GENERAL NOTE
Paragraph (b) of subs. (3) was repealed by s.41 of and Sched. 6, Pt. I to the Northern Ireland Constitution Act 1973.

Customs duties

5.—(1) Subject to subsection (2) below, on and after the relevant date there shall be charged, levied, collected and paid on goods imported into the United Kingdom such Community customs duty, if any, as is for the time being applicable in accordance with the Treaties or, if the goods are not within the common customs tariff of the Economic Community and the duties chargeable are not otherwise fixed by any directly applicable Community provision, such duty of customs, if any, as the Treasury, on the recommendation of the Secretary of State, may by order specify.

For this purpose "the relevant date", in relation to any goods, is the date on and after which the duties of customs that may be charged thereon are no longer affected under the Treaties by any temporary provision made on or with reference to the accession of the United Kingdom to the Communities.

(2) Where as regards goods imported into the United Kingdom provision may, in accordance with the Treaties, be made in derogation of the common customs tariff or of the exclusion of customs duties as between Member States, the Treasury may by order make such provision as to the customs duties chargeable on the goods, or as to exempting the goods from any customs duty, as the Treasury may on the recommendation of the Secretary of State determine.

(3) Schedule 2 to this Act shall also have effect in connection with the powers to make orders conferred by subsections (1) and (2) above.]

(4) [...]
(5) [...]
(6) [...]
(6A) [...]
(7) [...]
(8) [...]
(9) [...]

GENERAL NOTE

Subsection (3) was replaced by the Customs and Excise Duties (General Reliefs) Act 1979, Sched. 2, para. 3.

Subsection (4) was repealed by the Customs and Excise Management Act 1979, Sched. 6, Pt. I.

Subsection (5) was repealed by the Customs and Excise Duties (General Reliefs) Act 1979, Sched. 3, Pt. I.

Subsection (6) was repealed by the Customs and Excise Duties (General Reliefs) Act 1979, Sched. 3, Pt. I.

Subsection (6A) which was added by the Finance Act 1978, s.6(8), was repealed by the Customs and Excise Duties (General Reliefs) Act 1979, Sched. 3, Pt. I.

Subsection (7) was repealed by the Customs and Excise Management Act 1979, Sched. 6, Pt. I.

Subsection (8) was repealed by the Customs and Excise Management Act 1979, Sched. 6, Pt. I.

Subsection (9) was repealed by the Customs and Excise Management Act 1979, Sched. 6, Pt. I.

The common agricultural policy

6.—(1) There shall be a Board in charge of a government department, which shall be appointed by and responsible to the Ministers, and shall be by the name of the Intervention Board for Agricultural Produce a body corporate (but not subject as a statutory corporation to restrictions on its corporate capacity); and the Board (in addition to any other functions that may be entrusted to it) shall be charged, subject to the direction and control of the Ministers, with such functions as they may from time to time determine in connection with the carrying out of the obligations of the United Kingdom under the common agricultural policy of the Economic Community.

(2) Her Majesty may by Order in Council make further provision as to the constitution and membership of the Board, and the remuneration (including

pensions) of members of the Board or any committee thereof, and for regulating or facilitating the discharge of the Board's functions, including provision for the Board to arrange for its functions to be performed by other
bodies on its behalf and any such provision as was made by Schedule 1 to the
Ministers of the Crown Act 1964 in relation to a Minister to whom that
Schedule applied; and the Ministers—

(a) may, after consultation with any body created by a statutory provision
and concerned with agriculture or agricultural produce, by regulations
modify or add to the constitution or powers of the body so as to enable
it to act for the Board, or by written directions given to the body
require it to discontinue or modify any activity appearing to the Ministers to be prejudicial to the proper discharge of the Board's functions;
and

(b) may by regulations provide for the charging of fees in connection with
the discharge of any functions of the Board.

(3) Sections 5 and 7 of the Agriculture Act 1957 (which make provision for
the support of arrangements under section 1 of that Act for providing
guaranteed prices or assured markets) shall apply in relation to any Community arrangements for or related to the regulation of the market for any
agricultural produce as if references, in whatever terms, to payments made
by virtue of section 1 were references to payments made by virtue of the
Community arrangements by or on behalf of the Board and as if in section
5(1)(d) the reference to the Minister included the Board.

(4) Agricultural levies of the Economic Community, so far as they are
charged on goods exported from the United Kingdom or shipped as stores,
shall be paid to and recoverable by the Board; and the power of the Ministers
to make orders under section 5 of the Agriculture Act 1957, as extended by
this section, shall include power to make such provision supplementary to
any directly applicable Community provision as the Ministers consider
necessary for securing the payment of any agricultural levies so charged,
including provision for the making of declarations or the giving of other
information in respect of goods exported, shipped as stores, warehoused or
otherwise dealt with.

(5) Except as otherwise provided by or under any enactment, agricultural
levies of the Economic Community, so far as they are charged on goods
imported into the United Kingdom, shall be levied, collected and paid, and
the proceeds shall be dealt with, as if they were Community customs duties,
and in relation to those levies the following enactments shall apply as they
would apply in relation to Community customs duties, that is to say:—

(a) [The Customs and Excise Management Act 1979 (as for the time being
amended by any later Act) and any other statutory provisions for the
time being in force relating generally to customs or excise duties on
imported goods; and]

(b) [sections 1, 3, 4, 5, 6 (including Schedule 1), 7, 8, 9, 12, 13, 15, 17 and 18
of the Customs and Excise Duties (General Reliefs) Act 1979 but so
that—

(i) any references in sections 1, 3 and 4 to the Secretary of State
shall include the Ministers; and

(ii) the reference in section 15 to an application for an authorisation under regulations made under section 2 of that Act shall be
read as a reference to an application for an authorisation under
regulations made under section 2(2) of this Act;]

and if, in connection with any such Community arrangements as aforesaid,
the Commissioners of Customs and Excise are charged with the performance, on behalf of the Board or otherwise, of any duties in relation to the
payment of refunds or allowances on goods exported or to be exported from
the United Kingdom, then in relation to any such refund or allowance [sec-
tion 133 (except subsection (3) and the reference to that subsection in subsec-

tion (2)) and section 159 of the Customs and Excise Management Act 1979 shall apply as they apply in relation to a drawback of excise duties.]

(6) The enactments applied by subsection (5)(a) above shall apply subject to such exceptions and modifications, if any, as the Commissioners of Customs and Excise may by regulations prescribe, and shall be taken to include section 10 of the Finance Act 1901 (which relates to changes in customs import duties in their effect on contracts), but shall not include [section 126 of the Customs and Excise Management Act 1979.]

(7) Where it appears to the Ministers, having regard to any such Community arrangements as aforesaid (and any obligations of the United Kingdom in relation thereto), that section 1 of the Agriculture Act 1957 should cease to apply to produce of any description mentioned in Schedule 1 to that Act, they may by order made by statutory instrument, which shall be subject to annulment in pursuance of a resolution of either House of Parliament, provide that as from such date as may be prescribed by the order (but subject to such savings and transitional provisions as may be so prescribed) the Act shall have effect as if produce of that description were omitted from Schedule 1.

(8) Expressions used in this section shall be construed as if contained in Part I of the Agriculture Act 1957; and in this section "agricultural levy" shall include any tax not being a customs duty, but of equivalent effect, that may be chargeable in accordance with any such Community arrangements as aforesaid, and "statutory provision" includes any provision having effect by virtue of any enactment and, in subsection (2), any enactment of the Parliament of Northern Ireland or provision having effect by virtue of such an enactment.

GENERAL NOTE

Subsection (5), para. (a) was substituted by the Customs and Excise Management Act 1979, Sched. 4. Paragraph (b) was substituted by the Customs and Excise Duties (General Reliefs) Act 1979, s.19(1) and Sched. 2, para. 4. The words in square brackets in the last part of the subsection were substituted by the Customs and Excise Management Act 1979, Sched. 4.

In subs. (6) the words in square brackets were substituted by the Customs and Excise Management Act 1979, Sched. 4.

Sugar

7.—(1)(2) [*Repealed by the Agriculture (Miscellaneous Provisions) Act 1976, Sched. 4, Pt. I.*]

(3)(4) [*Repealed by the Food Act 1984, s.134 and Sched. 11.*]

Cinematograph films

8.—[*Repealed by the Films Act 1985, s.7 and Sched. 2.*]

Companies

9.—(1) [*Repealed by the Companies Consolidation (Consequential Provisions) Act 1985, s.29 and Sched. 1.*]

Restrictive trade practices

10.—[*Repealed by the Restrictive Trade Practices Act 1976, Sched. 6.*]

Community offences

11.—(1) A person who, in sworn evidence before the European Court [or any Court attached thereto], makes any statement which he knows to be false or does not believe to be true shall, whether he is a British subject or not, be guilty of an offence and may be proceeded against and punished—

    (a) in England and Wales as for an offence against section 1(1) of the Perjury Act 1911; or

    (b) in Scotland as for an offence against section 1 of the False Oaths (Scotland) Act 1933; or

   (c) in Northern Ireland as for an offence against [Article 3(1) of the Perjury (Northern Ireland) Order 1979].

Where a report is made as to any such offence under the authority of the
European Court [or any Court attached thereto], then a bill of indictment for
the offence may, [...] in Northern Ireland, be preferred as in a case where a
prosecution is ordered under [...] [Article 13 of the Perjury (Northern Ireland) Order 1979] but the report shall not be given in evidence on a person's
trial for the offence.

   (2) Where a person (whether a British subject or not) owing either—

   (a) to his duties as a member of any Euratom institution or committee, or
as an officer or servant of Euratom; or

   (b) to his dealings in any capacity (official or unofficial) with any Euratom
institution or installation or with any Euratom joint enterprise;

has occasion to acquire, or obtain cognisance of, any classified information,
he shall be guilty of a misdemeanour if, knowing or having reason to believe
that it is classified information, he communicates it to any unauthorised person or makes any public disclosure of it, whether in the United Kingdom or
elsewhere and whether before or after the termination of those duties or
dealings; and for this purpose "classified information" means any facts, information, knowledge, documents or objects that are subject to the security
rules of a Member State or of any Euratom institution.

This subsection shall be construed, and the Official Secrets Acts 1911 to
1939 shall have effect, as if this subsection were contained in the Official
Secrets Act 1911, but so that in that Act sections 10 and 11, except section
10(4), shall not apply.

   (3) This section shall not come into force until the entry date.

GENERAL NOTE
   In subs. (1) the words "or any court attached thereto" were added by the European Communities (Amendment) Act 1986, s.2(b).
   In subs. (1)(c) the words in square brackets were substituted by the Perjury (Northern Ireland) Order 1979 (S.I. 1979 No. 1714), Sched. 1. The words omitted were repealed by the Prosecution of Offences Act 1985, Sched. 2.

Furnishing of information to Communities

   12. Estimates, returns and information that may under section 9 of the
Statistics of Trade Act 1947 or section [3 of the Agricultural Statistics Act
1979] be disclosed to a government department or Minister in charge of a
government department may, in like manner, be disclosed in pursuance of a
Community obligation to a Community institution.

GENERAL NOTE
   The words in square brackets were substituted by the Agricultural Statistics Act 1979, Sched.
1, para. 4.

SCHEDULES

Section 1   SCHEDULE 1

DEFINITIONS RELATING TO COMMUNITIES

PART I

THE PRE-ACCESSION TREATIES

   1. The "E.C.S.C. Treaty", that is to say, the Treaty establishing the European Coal and Steel
Community, signed at Paris on the 18th April 1951.
   2. The "E.E.C. Treaty", that is to say, the Treaty establishing the European Economic Community, signed at Rome on the 25th March 1957.

3. The "Euratom Treaty", that is to say, the Treaty establishing the European Atomic Energy Community, signed at Rome on the 25th March 1957.

4. The Convention on certain Institutions common to the European Communities, signed at Rome on the 25th March 1957.

5. The Treaty establishing a single Council and a single Commission of the European Communities, signed at Brussels on the 8th April 1965.

6. The Treaty amending certain Budgetary Provisions of the Treaties establishing the European Communities and of the Treaty establishing a single Council and a single Commission of the European Communities, signed at Luxembourg on the 22nd April 1970.

7. Any treaty entered into before the 22nd January 1972 by any of the Communities (with or without any of the Member States) or, as a treaty ancillary to any treaty included in this Part of this Schedule, by the Member States (with or without any other country).

PART II

OTHER DEFINITIONS

"Economic Community", "Coal and Steel Community" and "Euratom" mean respectively the European Economic Community, the European Coal and Steel Community and the European Atomic Energy Community.

"Community customs duty" means, in relation to any goods, such duty of customs as may from time to time be fixed for those goods by directly applicable Community provision as the duty chargeable on importation into Member States.

"Community institution" means any institution of any of the Communities or common to the Communities; and any reference to an institution of a particular Community shall include one common to the Communities when it acts for that Community, and similarly with references to a committee, officer or servant of a particular Community.

"Community instrument" means any instrument issued by a Community institution.

"Community obligation" means any obligation created or arising by or under the Treaties, whether an enforceable Community obligation or not.

"Enforceable Community right" and similar expressions shall be construed in accordance with section 2(1) of this Act.

"Entry date" means the date on which the United Kingdom becomes a member of the Communities.

"European Court" means the Court of Justice of the European Communities.

"Member", in the expression "Member State", refers to membership of the Communities.

Section 2   SCHEDULE 2

PROVISIONS AS TO SUBORDINATE LEGISLATION

1.—(1) The powers conferred by section 2(2) of this Act to make provision for the purposes mentioned in section 2(2)(a) and (b) shall not include power—

(a) to make any provision imposing or increasing taxation; or

(b) to make any provision taking effect from a date earlier than that of the making of the instrument containing the provision; or

(c) to confer any power to legislate by means of orders, rules, regulations or other subordinate instrument, other than rules of procedure for any court or tribunal; or

(d) to create any new criminal offence punishable with imprisonment for more than two years or punishable on summary conviction with imprisonment for more than three months or with a fine of more than £400 (if not calculated on a daily basis) or with a fine of more than [£100 a day].

(2) Sub-paragraph 1(c) above shall not be taken to preclude the modification of a power to legislate conferred otherwise than under section 2(2), or the extension of any such power to purposes of the like nature as those for which it was conferred; and a power to give directions as to matters of administration is not to be regarded as a power to legislate within the meaning of sub-paragraph (1)(c).

2.—(1) Subject to paragraph 3 below, where a provision contained in any section of this Act confers power to make regulations (otherwise than by modification or extension of an existing power), the power shall be exercisable by statutory instrument.

(2) Any statutory instrument containing an Order in Council or regulations made in the exercise of a power so conferred, if made without a draft having been approved by resolution of each House of Parliament, shall be subject to annulment in pursuance of a resolution of either House.

3. Nothing in paragraph 2 above shall apply to any Order in Council made by the Governor of Northern Ireland or to any regulations made by a Minister or department of the Government of

Northern Ireland; but where a provision contained in any section of this Act confers power to make such an Order in Council or regulations, then any Order in Council or regulations made in the exercise of that power, if made without a draft having been approved by resolution of each House of the Parliament of Northern Ireland, shall be subject to negative resolution within the meaning of section 41(6) of the Interpretation Act (Northern Ireland) 1954 as if the Order or regulations were a statutory instrument within the meaning of that Act.

[4.—(1) The power to make orders under section 5(1) or (2) of this Act shall be exercisable in accordance with the following provisions of this paragraph.

(2) The power to make such orders shall be exercisable by statutory instrument and includes power to amend or revoke any such order made in the exercise of that power.

(3) Any statutory instrument containing any such order shall be subject to annulment in pursuance of a resolution of the House of Commons except in a case falling within sub-paragraph (4) below.

(4) Subject to sub-paragraph (6) below, where an order imposes or increases any customs duty, or restrict, any relief from customs duty under the said section 5, the statutory instrument containing the order shall be laid before the House of Commons after being made and, unless the order is approved by that House before the end of the period of 28 days beginning with the day on which it was made, it shall cease to have effect at the end of that period, but without prejudice to anything previously done under the order or to the making of a new order.

In reckoning the said period of 28 days no account shall be taken of any time during which Parliament is dissolved or prorogued or during which the House of Commons is adjourned for more than 4 days.

(5) Where an order has the effect of altering the rate of duty on any goods in such a way that the new rate is not directly comparable with the old, it shall not be treated for the purposes of sub-paragraph (4) above as increasing the duty on those goods if it declares the opinion of the Treasury to be that, in the circumstances existing at the date of the order, the alteration is not calculated to raise the general level of duty on the goods.

(6) Sub-paragraph (4) above does not apply in the case of an instrument containing an order which states that it does not impose or increase any customs duty or restrict any relief from customs duty otherwise than in pursuance of a Community obligation.

5. As soon as may be after the end of each financial year the Secretary of State shall lay before each House of Parliament a report on the exercise during that year of the powers conferred by section 5(1) and (2) of this Act with respect to the imposition of customs duties and the allowance of exemptions and reliefs from duties so imposed (including the power to amend or revoke orders imposing customs duties or providing for any exemption or relief from duties so imposed).]

GENERAL NOTE

In para. 1(1)(d) the words in square brackets were substituted by the Criminal Law Act 1977, s.32. See also amendments made by the Criminal Justice Act 1982.

Paras. 4 and 5 were added by the Customs and Excise Duties (General Reliefs) Act 1979, Sched. 2, para. 5.

Section 4   SCHEDULE 3

REPEALS

PART I

CUSTOMS TARIFF

Chapter	Short title	Extent of repeal
6 & 7 Eliz. 2. c. 6.	The Import Duties Act 1958.	The whole Act, except— section 4; Part II, including Schedules 3 to 5; in section 12(4) the words "fish, whales or other natural produce of the sea, or goods produced or manufactured therefrom at sea, if brought direct to the United Kingdom, are", and paragraphs (a) and (b); and sections 13, 15 and 16(1) and (2). In Part II, section 5(2), (3), (5) and (6), section 7(1)(c) with the preceding "and", section 9(4) and section 9(5) from "and" onwards.

Chapter	Short title	Extent of repeal
8 & 9 Eliz. 2. c. 19.	The European Free Trade Association Act 1960.	In Schedule 4, paragraph 1. The whole Act.
1965 c. 65.	The Finance Act 1965.	Section 2, except subsection (5).
1966 c. 18.	The Finance Act 1966.	In section 1, in subsection (1) the words between "1958" and "chargeable", and subsection (6). Section 9.
[...]		
1971 c. 68.	The Finance Act 1971.	Section 1(1) to (3).

The repeals in this Part of this Schedule shall take effect from such date as the Secretary of State may by order appoint.

GENERAL NOTE
The words omitted were repealed by the Finance Act 1978, s.6 and Sched. 13, Pt. I.

PART II

SUGAR

Chapter	Short title	Extent of repeal
4 & 5 Eliz. 2. c. 48.	The Sugar Act 1956.	In section 3, subsection (1) from "including" onwards and subsection (2)(b). Section 4(2) and (3). Section 5, except as regards advances made before this repeal takes effect. Sections 7 to 17. Section 18(3) and (4). Sections 19 and 20. Sections 21 and 22, except as regards advances made and guarantees given before this repeal takes effect. Section 23, but without prejudice to the modification made by subsection (2) in the articles of association of the British Sugar Corporation. Sections 24 to 32. In section 33, in subsection (1) the words "regulations or", in subsection (2) the words from the beginning to "subsection", subsection (3) and subsection (5). In section 34, the words "or the Commissioners". In section 35, in subsection (2) all the definitions except those of "the Corporation", "financial year of the Sugar Board", "functions", "the Government", "home-grown beet" and "pension", in subsection (3) the words "or of the Corporation" and subsections (4) to (7). Section 36(2). In Schedule 3, paragraphs 2, 3 and 4. Schedule 4.
5 & 6 Eliz. 2. c. 57.	The Agriculture Act 1957.	Section 4. In section 36(2) the words "and to sugar beet".

Chapter	Short title	Extent of repeal
10 & 11 Eliz. 2. c. 23.	The South Africa Act 1962.	In Schedule 2, paragraph 5.
10 & 11 Eliz. 2. c. 44.	The Finance Act 1962.	In section 3(6) the words from "the Sugar Act 1956" onwards. Part II of Schedule 5.
1963 c. 11.	The Agriculture (Miscellaneous Provisions) Act 1963.	Section 25.
1964 c. 49.	The Finance Act 1964.	Section 22.
1966 c. 18.	The Finance Act 1966.	Section 52.
1968 c. 13.	The National Loans Act 1968.	In Schedule 1, the entry for the Sugar Act 1956, except as regards advances made before this repeal takes effect.
1968 c. 44.	The Finance Act 1968.	Section 58.

The repeals in this Part of this Schedule shall take effect from such date as the Minister of Agriculture, Fisheries and Food and the Secretary of State acting jointly may by order appoint.

PART III

SEEDS

Chapter	Short title	Extent of repeal
1964 c. 14.	The Plant Varieties and Seeds Act 1964.	Section 5(3). Sections 20 to 23A. Section 25(8)(b) and the word "and" preceding it. Section 32. In section 34(2) the words from "or in the Index" to "into force", and the words "or fact". Schedule 5.
1968 c. 29.	The Trade Descriptions Act 1968.	Section 2(4)(a).
1968 c. 34.	The Agriculture (Miscellaneous Provisions) Act 1968.	Schedule 7, except amendments of section 1 of or Schedule 1 or 2 to the Plant Varieties and Seeds Act 1964.

The repeals in this Part of this Schedule shall take effect from such date as the Minister of Agriculture, Fisheries and Food and the Secretary of State acting jointly may by order appoint.

PART IV

MISCELLANEOUS

Chapter	Short title	Extent of repeal
9 & 10 Geo. 6. c. 59.	The Coal Industry Nationalisation Act 1946.	In section 4, in its application to the Industrial Coal Consumers' Council, subsections (1) to (8); and in its application to the Domestic Coal Consumers' Council, in subsection (2) the words "to represent the Board and", in subsection (3) (as applied by subsection (4)) the words from "and where" in paragraph (a) onwards and subsection (5). Section 4(9), (10) and (11).

Chapter	Short title	Extent of repeal
10 & 11 Geo. 6. c. 48.	The Agriculture Act 1947.	Section 2(2).
15 & 16 Geo. 6. and 1 Eliz. 2. c. 44.	The Customs and Excise Act 1952.	Schedule 6, except for cases in which the value of goods falls to be determined as at a time before the entry date.
1 & 2 Eliz. 2. c. 15.	The Iron and Steel Act 1953.	Section 29.
5 & 6 Eliz. 2. c. 57.	The Agriculture Act 1957.	Section 2(6)(b), with the preceding "or". Section 3. Section 8(1), and in section 8(2) the words "and subsection (1) of section 3". In section 11 the words "and 'special review'" and the words "or special review".
10 & 11 Eliz. 2. c. 22.	The Coal Consumers' Councils (Northern Irish Interests) Act 1962.	Section 1(1) and (2), in so far as they apply to the Industrial Coal Consumers' Council.
1963 c. 11.	The Agriculture (Miscellaneous Provisions) Act 1963.	Section 9(8).
1967 c. 17.	The Iron and Steel Act 1967.	Sections 8, 15 and 30. Section 48(2)(b). In Schedule 3, the entries relating to section 6 of the Iron and Steel Act 1949. In Schedule 4, section 6 of the Iron and Steel Act 1949 as there set out.
1967 c. 22.	The Agriculture Act 1967.	Section 61(7). Section 64(6). Section 65(5).
1968 c. 48.	The International Organisations Act 1968.	Section 3. In section 4, the words "other than the Commission of the European Communities".
1970 c. 24.	The Finance Act 1970.	In Schedule 2, paragraph 5(1) from "Where, by virtue" onwards, and paragraph 5(2) (b) and (c), except for cases in which the value of goods falls to be determined as at a time before the entry date.
1970 c. 40.	The Agriculture Act 1970.	Section 106(5).

Section 4   SCHEDULE 4

ENACTMENTS AMENDED

A: *Customs Duties*

A(i): *Import Duty Reliefs etc.*

1.—[*Repealed by the Customs and Excise Duties (General Reliefs) Act 1979, Sched. 3.*]

A(ii): *Customs and Excise Act 1952*

2.—[*Repealed by the Finance (No. 2) Act 1975, s.75 and Sched. 14, Pt. 1; the Finance Act 1976, Sched. 15, Pt. 1; the Finance Act 1978, Sched. 13, Pt. 1; the Customs and Excise Management Act 1979, Sched. 6.*]

B: *Food*

3.—[*Repealed by the Food Act 1984, s.134 and Sched. 11.*]

C: *Grading etc. of Horticultural Produce*

4.—(1) Part III of the Agriculture and Horticulture Act 1964 (grading and transport of fresh horticultural produce) shall be amended as follows:—
   (a) in section 11 (power to prescribe grades) there shall be added at the end as a new subsection (3)—
        "(3) Regulations under subsection (1) above shall not apply to produce of any description for the time being subject to Community grading rules; but in relation to any such produce the Ministers may by regulations—
            (a) make additional provision as to the form of any label required for the purpose of those rules or as to the inclusion in any such label of additional particulars (not affecting the grading of the produce);
            (b) provide for the application, subject to any modifications specified in the regulations, of all or any of the following provisions of this Part of this Act as if the produce were regulated produce and as if the standards of quality established by those rules were prescribed grades.";
   (b) at the end of section 22(3) (which provides against the grading etc. of produce by agricultural marketing boards otherwise than in conformity with regulations under section 11(1) or 21 or, in Northern Ireland, any corresponding provisions for the time being in force there) there shall be added—
        "This subsection shall apply in relation to Community grading rules as it applies in relation to regulations under section 11(1) or 21 of this Act or, as regards Northern Ireland, under any corresponding provisions.";
   (c) in section 24 (interpretation of Part III) there shall be inserted after the definition of "authorised officer" the following definition:—
        "Community grading rules" means any directly applicable Community provisions establishing standards of quality for fresh horticultural produce.
(2) In section 2(4) of the Trade Descriptions Act 1968 (which provides that certain statutory descriptions and markings are to be deemed not to be trade descriptions) after the words "the Agriculture and Horticulture Act 1964" there shall be inserted the words "or any Community grading rules within the meaning of Part III of that Act".

D: *Seeds and other Propagating Material*

5.—(1) In the Plant Varieties and Seeds Act 1964 there shall be made the amendments provided for by sub-paragraphs (2) to (5) below.
(2) In section 16(1)(c) (preventing spread of plant disease by the sale of seeds) for the words "the sale" there shall be substituted the word "means", and after section 16(1) there shall be inserted as subsection (1A):—
        "(1A) Seeds regulations may further make provision for regulating the marketing, or the importation or exportation, of seeds or any related activities (whether by reference to officially published lists of permitted varieties or otherwise), and may in that connection include provision—
            (a) for the registration or licensing of persons engaged in the seeds industry or related activities;
            (b) for ensuring that seeds on any official list remain true to variety;
            (c) for the keeping and inspection of records and the giving of information;
            (d) for conferring rights of appeal to the Tribunal;
            (e) for excluding, extending or modifying, in relation to or in connection with any provision of the regulations, the operation of any provision made by the following sections of this Part of this Act or of Part IV of this Act, and for the charging of fees";
and the provisions relating to offences connected with seeds regulations shall be amended as follows:—
   (a) in section 16, for the words from "which concerns" in subsection (7)(b) to the end of subsection (8) there shall be substituted the words "he shall be liable on summary conviction to a fine not exceeding £400"; and
   (b) in section 18(2) for the words from "for an offence" in paragraph (b) to the end of paragraph (c) there shall be substituted the words "for any other offence"; and
   (c) in section 25(7) for paragraphs (a) and (b) there shall be substituted the words "to a fine not exceeding one hundred pounds".
(3) At the end of section 16 there shall be added a subsection (8)—
        "(8) The Ministers acting jointly may make seeds regulations for the whole of Great Britain".

(4) In section 29 (which extends Part II to seed potatoes) after the words "seed potatoes", in both places, there shall be inserted the words "to any other vegetative propagating material and to silvicultural planting material" and at the end of that section there shall be added as subsections (2) and (3)—

"(2) The Forestry Commissioners may establish and maintain an official seed testing station for silvicultural propagating and planting material, and seeds regulations may confer on those Commissioners any functions the regulations may confer on a Minister, and the Commissioners may charge or authorise the charging of fees for services given at any such station or in connection with any such functions; and accordingly—

(a) references in this Part of this Act to an authorised officer shall include an officer of those Commissioners; and

(b) in section 25 above the references in subsections (3), (4) and (6) to a person duly authorised by the Minister shall include a person duly authorised by the Commissioners.

Any expenses incurred or fees received by the Commissioners by virtue of this subsection shall be paid out of or into the Forestry Fund.

(3) In relation to matters concerning silvicultural propagating or planting material or concerning the Forestry Commissioners, 'the Minister' shall in this Part of this Act mean, in relation to Wales and Monmouthshire, the Secretary of State, and the reference in section 16(8) to the Ministers shall be construed accordingly."

Accordingly in section 30(1) in the definition of "official testing station" there shall be omitted the words "by the Minister or Ministers", and in section 38(1) in the definition of "the Minister" after the word "means" there shall be inserted the words "(subject to section 29(3))".

(5) In section 10(1) for the name "Plant Variety Rights Tribunal" there shall be substituted the name "Plant Varieties and Seeds Tribunal", and in paragraph 5(1) of Schedule 4 there shall be added at the end of paragraph (b) (which sets up, to furnish members of the Tribunal, a panel of persons with specialised knowledge) the words "or of the seeds industry".

(6) [*Repealed by the House of Commons Disqualification Act 1975, Sched. 3 and the Northern Ireland Assembly Disqualification Act 1975, Sched. 3, Pt. I.*]

E: *Fertilisers and Feeding Stuffs*

6. After section 74 of the Agriculture Act 1970 there shall be inserted as a new section 74A—

"74A.—(1) Regulations under this Part of this Act, with a view to controlling in the public interest the composition or content of fertilisers and of material intended for the feeding of animals, may make provision—

(a) prohibiting or restricting, by reference to its composition or content, the importation into and exportation from the United Kingdom, the sale or possession with a view to sale, or the use, of any prescribed material;

(b) regulating the marking, labelling and packaging of prescribed material and the marks to be applied to any container or vehicle in which any prescribed material is enclosed or conveyed.

(2) Regulations made under subsection (1) above with respect to any material may include provision excluding or modifying the operation in relation to that material of any other provision of this Part of this Act; but, subject to any provision so made, references in this Part of this Act to feeding stuffs shall apply to all material which is intended for the feeding of animals and with respect to which regulations are for the time being in force under that subsection.

(3) Any person who contravenes any prohibition or restriction imposed by regulations under subsection (1) above, or fails to comply with any other provision of the regulations, shall be liable on summary conviction to a fine not exceeding £400 or, on a second or subsequent conviction, to a fine not exceeding £400 or to imprisonment for a term not exceeding three months, or to both.

(4) With a view to implementing or supplementing any Community instrument relating to fertilisers or to material intended for the feeding of animals, regulations may provide for the application, in relation to any material specified in the regulations, of all or any of the provisions of this Part of this Act, subject to any modifications which may be so specified."

F: *Animal Health*

7.—[*Repealed by the Animal Health Act 1981, s.96 and Sched. 6.*]

G: *Plant Health*

8.—(1) In the Plant Health Act 1967 there shall be made, with effect from the entry date, the amendments provided for by the following sub-paragraphs.

(2) In section 1(1) (by which the Act has effect for the control in Great Britain of plant pests and diseases) the words "in Great Britain" shall be omitted; and—

(a) in section 2(1) and section 3(1) (orders for control of pests) after the words "thinks expedient" there shall be inserted the words "or called for by any Community obligation";

(b) at the end of section 3(1), after the words "preventing the spread of pests in Great Britain", there shall be added the words "or the conveyance of pests by articles exported from Great Britain";

(c) in section 3(5) (which extends the time limit for summary prosecutions of certain offences) there shall be omitted the words "where the offence is one in connection with the movement, sale, consignment or planting of potatoes".

(3) In section 3(2)(a) (which provides for the removal or destruction of infected crops etc.) there shall be inserted after the word "removal" the word "treatment" and after the words "any seed, plant or part thereof" the words "or any container, wrapping or other article", and in section 3(2)(b) (which provides for entry on land for those and other purposes) there shall be inserted after the word "removal" the word "treatment" and after the word "land" the words "or elsewhere"; and the words "or elsewhere" shall also be inserted after the word "land" in section 4(1)(b) (which also relates to entry).

(4) At the end of section 6(1) there shall be added the words "or, in the case of an order prohibiting or regulating the landing in or exportation from Great Britain of any articles, shall be subject to annulment in pursuance of a resolution of either House of Parliament".

H: *Road Vehicles (Driving under Age, and Drivers' Hours)*

9.—(1) [*Repealed by the Road Traffic (Drivers' Ages and Hours of Work) Act 1976, Sched. 3, Pt. I.*]

(2) In Part VI of the Transport Act 1968, in section 103(1), after the definition of "employer" there shall be inserted the words " 'the international rules' means any directly applicable Community provision relating to the driving of road vehicles on international journeys"; and—

(a) after section 96(11) there shall be inserted as subsection (11A)—

"(11A) Where, in the case of a driver or member of the crew of a motor vehicle, there is in Great Britain a contravention of any requirement of the international rules as to periods of driving, or distance driven, or periods on or off duty, then the offender and any other person (being the offender's employer or a person to whose orders the offender was subject) who caused or permitted the contravention shall be liable on summary conviction to a fine not exceeding £200";

and in section 98(4) (failure to comply with regulations as to keeping of records etc.) after the words "regulations made under this section" there shall be inserted the words "or any requirement as to books or records of the international rules", in section 98(5) after the words "of regulations under this section" there shall be inserted the words "or of the international rules", and in section 99(5) (falsification of records) after the words "regulations under section 98 thereof" there shall be inserted the words "or the international rules";

(b) in section 99(1) (power of enforcement officer to inspect records and other documents) there shall be inserted after paragraph (c)—

"(d) any corresponding book, register or document required by the international rules or which the officer may reasonably require to inspect for the purpose of ascertaining whether the requirements of the international rules have been complied with"; and in section 99(3) after the words "subsection (1)(a)" there shall be inserted "or (d)";

(c) in section 98(2) (power to make provision supplementary and incidental to the provision made under section 98(1) as to the keeping of books and records) there shall be inserted after the words "supplementary and incidental provisions" the words "including provisions supplementary and incidental to the requirements of the international rules as to books and records", and after the words "for the purpose of the regulations" in paragraph (a) the words "or of the international rules".

(3) At the end of section 95(1) of the Transport Act 1968 there shall be added the words—

"but the Secretary of State may by regulations make such provision supplemental or incidental to, or by way of adaptation of, this Part of this Act as is in his opinion called for to take account, in relation to journeys and work to which the international rules apply, of the operation of those rules and to ensure compatibility of operation between section 96(1) to (9) as they apply to other journeys and work and the international rules; and regulations made under this subsection—

(a) may in particular make exceptions from the operation of section 96(1) to (6), and include provision as to the circumstances in which a period of driving or duty to which the international rules apply is to be included or excluded in reckoning any period for purposes of section 96(1) to (6); and

(b) may contain such transitional and supplementary provisions as the Secretary of State thinks necessary or expedient;

and a reference to the international rules shall be deemed to be included in any reference to this Part of this Act in sections 35(2)(b), 62(4)(b) and 64(2)(c) of this Act and in paragraph 2(5) of Schedule 9 thereto."

(4) In Schedule 2 to the Road Traffic (Foreign Vehicles) Act 1972, in the entry relating to sections 96 to 98 of the Transport Act 1968 and regulations and orders thereunder, there shall be added at the end of the words in the first column the words "and the international rules within the meaning of Part VI of that Act."

GENERAL NOTE

Subparagraph (4) was amended by the Wages Councils Act 1979, Sched. 7 and the Employment Act 1980, Sched. 2.

I: *Road Transport* (*International Passenger Services*)

10. [*Repealed by the Transport Act 1980, Sched. 9, Pt. 1.*]

INDEX

References are to page numbers